ABOUT EUROPE

Cultural Memory
in
the
Present

Mieke Bal and Hent de Vries, Editors

ABOUT EUROPE

Philosophical Hypotheses

Denis Guénoun

Translated by Christine Irizarry

STANFORD UNIVERSITY PRESS
STANFORD, CALIFORNIA

Stanford University Press
Stanford, California

English translation and Preface ©2013 by the Board of Trustees of the Leland Stanford Junior University. All rights reserved.

About Europe: Philosophical Hypotheses was originally published in French under the title *Hypothèses sur l'Europe: Un essai de philosophie.* ©2000 Éditions Circé. All rights reserved. Translated and published by arrangement with Éditions Circé.

This book has been published with the assistance of the French Ministry of Culture—National Center for the Book.

Ouvrage publié avec le concours du Ministère français chargé de la culture—Centre National du Livre.

This book has been published with the assistance of the research group "Littérature française XIXe–XXIe siècles" at Paris-Sorbonne University and the Atelier de Recherches Théoriques et Poétiques (Artépo).

Ouvrage publié avec l'aide de l'équipe "Littérature française XIXe–XXIe siècles" de l'Université Paris-Sorbonne et l'Atelier de Recherches Théoriques et Poétiques (Artépo).

This work, published as part of a program of aid for publication, received support from CulturesFrance and the French Ministry of Foreign Affairs.

Cet ouvrage a bénéficié du soutien des Programmes d'aide à la publication de CulturesFrance/Ministère français des affaires étrangères et européennes.

No part of this book may be reproduced or transmitted in any form or by any means, electronic or mechanical, including photocopying and recording, or in any information storage or retrieval system without the prior written permission of Stanford University Press.

Printed in the United States of America on acid-free, archival-quality paper

Library of Congress Cataloging-in-Publication Data

Guénoun, Denis, 1946- author.
  [Hypothèses sur l'Europe. English]
  About Europe : philosophical hypotheses / Denis Guénoun ; translated by Christine Irizarry.
      pages cm.--(Cultural memory in the present)
  "Originally published in French under the title Hypothèses sur l'Europe: Un essai de philosophie."
  ISBN 978-0-8047-7385-0 (cloth : alk. paper)--
ISBN 978-0-8047-7386-7 (pbk. : alk. paper)
  1. Europe--History--Philosophy. I. Irizarry, Christine, translator. II. Title. III. Series: Cultural memory in the present.
  D16.8G81813 2013
  940.01--dc23   2012045372

Typeset by Bruce Lundquist in 11/13.5 Adobe Garamond

For Paola, my Princess Europe

Contents

	Preface	xi
	Translator's Acknowledgments	xv
	Abbreviations	xvii
1.	On Beginning	1

PART I. EUROPE CROSSWAYS

2.	On the Figure	7
3.	Other Names	24
4.	The Holy Roman Empire	32
5.	Straits	36
6.	On Transport	40
7.	What Is an Island?	43
8.	On Thinking	48
9.	Orient	51

PART II. ON NATIONAL REVOLUTION

10.	France-Germany	57
11.	On the Kingdom	62
12.	Religions	69
13.	Surrection	75
14.	Nation	81

15. On Germany	92
16. Looping Back	104
17. A Hypothesis for the Twentieth Century?	114

PART III. TRANSPORTS OF ORIGIN

18. Loads	121
19. On Beingness	123
20. Places	138
21. Exodus	147
22. Absent from the World	159
23. Black Stone	176

PART IV. NO RETURNS

24. Capital	190
25. Images	195
26. Value	204
27. Becoming	216
28. On Experience	222
29. . . .	231

| *Notes* | 237 |
| *Works Cited* | 307 |

Preface

What makes Europe into a *question* for our world, present and future—and not just a historical or cultural given—comes from a deep ambivalence that marks the European phenomenon as much in terms of the facts as in thought.

Indeed, if we search for what sets the culture of Europe apart, what belongs to it properly speaking and what might constitute its patrimony or its core identity, we uncover assets that are undeniably precious, and whose constitution has required endless patience and energy; yet they are difficult to grasp in and of themselves: a certain general idea of what is human, a vision of being as a whole, a concern for what is broadest and for what is most common—in a word, a penchant for the universal. How strange that, in the end, Europe may not have produced anything for itself beyond this milieu in which it is itself dissolving; that its singularity may consist in denying that it is singular and in affirming or giving rise only to that which it shares with everyone else. Since its dawn, Europe may have only worked toward this excess that resorbs it. Better still, the deep value of European culture may lie precisely in the fact that Europe has been—and may still be—the place that constructed the unreasonable dream of a humanity open to all, and of a radically way of being in common.

This is not to say that Europe might have the prerogative of broadminded views and generosity. First, one would have to be thoroughly acquainted with India, China, ancient America, or immemorial Africa and their thinking to know whether this demon doesn't stir them as well. But above all, the desire animating Europe, to expand and share, has combined with another—contradictory—tendency throughout its history: the inclination to take up this quest, to recognize it as its own, and thereby to endow its natives with an otherwise established identity, that of privileged possessors of the universal and superior specialists of the general. More than one colonial undertaking was legitimized in the name of a brutally despotic universalism. Moreover, it is exactly when the champions of commonality manifest this unexpected particularism that the figure of Europe appears. For there to be a universal, there is no need for the idea of Europe, or the word, or its conception. Other attempts at universality that preceded and influenced the idea of Europe had done without it: the ideas of empire or Christendom were not meant to be specifically European; it was Europe, after the fact, that laid claim to them and annexed them to its heritage. Neither Stoic thought nor the words of Jesus Christ are linked to the continent. When Europe comes on the scene—not when the word is born but when the idea imposes itself—it is at the intersection of these two opposing exigencies: the desire for universality and the concern for its repatriation. This is the hypothesis underpinning this book: Europe was born of this (mis)alliance. Understanding the tension between the ongoing idea of universality—the sole contents of European culture—and Europe's withdrawal into a continental identity is the goal of the following pages.

Today, the question raised by this ambivalence is no longer specifically European. This is because, first of all, examining this ambivalence requires a fairly deep re-elaboration of the concept of the universal—as attempted in this book. It is very important to say today—and everywhere, no doubt—that the universal is not the same as the uniform, or the global. The universal is a process of transformation of human thoughts and practices, and it works to unify and assemble them. On this score, the universal is neither a stable state nor a distant horizon; it is an onward movement, a stride, a transformation. That is why it is always both extensive and intensive: spreading its movement over a broader and greater expanse and affecting each of its agents in their singular depth. The universal is less the becoming homogeneous of the world than its becoming shared, and simultaneously, for each of the world's inhabitants, becoming a human citizen. The universal is not worldwide globalization—which, as we can see, multiplies inequalities, hierarchies, barriers, and injustices. The universal is an ethical process of conjunction and intersection.

Conversely, what is at stake in repatriating things toward the figure of the continental is surely not the recognition of singular histories, legacies, homelands, or affinities. On the contrary: the withdrawal into the representation of Europe as a continent crushes all this through an imaginary investment in an *identity*—that is to say, the worship of sameness and of that which is like oneself, the appropriation of history and commonality by way of the self of a supposed European subject.

In this double sense, the ambiguity that works its way through the history and thinking of Europe turns into our question, a question for everyone, for the planetary citizens of today and tomorrow. It is the question of the relation between the desire to share and the urge to appropriate, between a calling and a return—between our momentum and our image.

Translator's Acknowledgments

Thank you to Emily-Jane Cohen, for her trust and patience; Sarah Crane Newman, Emma S. Harper, and Mariana Raykov, for their hard work and dedication; Norris Pope, for his trust; Alice Froment-Meurice Irizarry, for her patience and proofreading skills; Mila Reichhold, for providing housing free of charge and occasional subsidies; Erika Abrams, for help with Patočka; Pascal Massie, for help with Aristotle; Jean-Luc Nancy, for help with Hegel; Lisa Cerrato, for help with Plato references; Jennifer Cazenave, for help with references and very insightful comments; Heath Warren, Alyssa Spencer, Lori Romersa, Barry Nelson, Jürgen Seidel, for giving me "day jobs"; and Denis Guénoun, for writing an exciting book and for his trust.

Christine Irizarry

Abbreviations

GENERAL ABBREVIATIONS

Cz.   Czech
Fr.   French
Gk.   Greek
Gm.   German
It.   Italian

TITLE ABBREVIATIONS

Ak.   The "Akademie Edition" of Immanuel Kant's works
HE   Patočka, *Heretical Essays*
HW   Heidegger, *Holzwege*
Idee Kant, "Idee zu einer allgemeinen Geschichte in weltbürgerlicher Absicht"
Idée Kant, *Idée d'une histoire universelle au point de vue cosmopolitique*
MM   Freud, *Moses and Monotheism*
PE   Patočka, *Plato and Europe*
UH   Kant, "Universal History" (i.e., "The Natural Principle of the Political Order")

ABOUT EUROPE

1. On Beginning

We may imagine the beginning as the origin—as the absolute point of departure. The beginning is an axiom: it *goes without saying, on its own*; nothing precedes it; it is set in the act that posits it. It finds the principle that makes it go in itself. It is immobile, the prime mover. Or else, for example, the biblical incipit that designates the pure initial start (the opening without preliminaries, the header: "In the beginning . . . "), the initiator without a cause (the one who begins: "God"), the first gesture ("created"— exactly this, to begin). Three times in the beginning, the beginning itself, alone, reiterated in its solitude.

But this beginning can only be grasped or put into words in a fictional discourse—a legend, fable, or parable. Thinking that intends to be theoretical never claims to reach this point of origin properly on its own (though it may dream of doing so). Scientific, philosophical, or literary beginnings spring from work, expelled after a period of gestation or a process. It takes long labor to beget the thought of the big bang. The axiom is built. The beginning finishes off: this is the second pre-hypothesis—and it is Hegel's, for whom the beginning is the result. The science (of logic) presupposes the whole movement of phenomenology (of the spirit). The first gesture of science takes up again the last act of knowledge. The beginning is (at) the end.

Third prototype: the beginning in the middle. This is Gilles Deleuze's supposition, and his manner. Reading him, one always has the impression of starting en route or getting there after the beginning. He recommends this formally: do not give thought to things at their origin, where they are not yet formed, but in the heart of their development, where their being asserts and shows itself. At its origin, the thing is still caught within that which precedes it; we should come aboard the process in the middle, as onto a moving train.[1] To think in motion, in becoming—inasmuch as becoming moves along, which is to say, not in its (supposed) initial impulsion, but in the drive of its mobility. The beginning is median, as it were, yet not as a simple mean-time or inter-mediary—less than being. Or perhaps yes, precisely—it is there, within the mediation, movement, process, and nonimmediate that one has to think.[2] Nonlogical mediation—it could be the middle of the world, the driven middle, of the world on the move.

Here, of course, we prefer to take this path, the one cutting across [*traverse*]. But to start elsewhere than at the beginning does not mean beginning just anywhere. Such an inception presupposes that *processes* exist, that one latches onto them, and that one sets out to think in their midst. The wish here is to think (within and about) development, (within and about) becoming. Becoming is a matter of thought. To think about becoming means thinking, quite simply. That which wants to be thought is nothing but that which is becoming. To think means to acknowledge as thought that which is becoming. That is why the thought of becoming has to be produced on the move, on the way. One has to think as it comes to be—as it comes. But "as it comes" is not just "in any way whatsoever." One has to come aboard what is coming and not miss it by a misstep. This implies, first, that one should not think within the residence of dead zones, or not only or mainly there. One has to think starting from living zones. Dead zones are provenances reduced to the state of origins. Secondly, do not become immobilized in imaginary zones. And this is the most difficult; one should rather think in zones of effectiveness. This is a question of the real, of the true—the most difficult question, which one certainly should not bypass or flee. What is coming—where we must climb aboard while it is moving—is truth.

*

Why Europe, then, to start with? So as to probe something. Europe is neither an origin nor an end. Europe is neither a foundation nor a grounding, nor a goal or a completion, but rather a median or intermediary object. A middle (in-between place [*mi-lieu*]). As a matter for thought, Europe is in progress, on the way—for moving across. I was not born there, as a matter of fact; I came to it, and took it along the way. Or rather Europe took me and carried me away. I was born in Africa, as were my father and my mother, my grandparents and their fathers and mothers, their grandparents, and so on, for all we know or may guess, for a long time, a very long time. Stemming, perhaps, from groups and families that had been crisscrossing the Mediterranean for centuries, many of them in Arab countries, some in the Iberian Peninsula, but coming from Arab countries, and returning after being expelled, crossing the Mediterranean or traveling along its shores, like Aeneas, like Paul, Jews like the latter, coming from Palestine long ago, they said, but living in Arab countries for centuries; coming from Arabized Jews or Judaized Berbers, or from departing Sephardic Jews, or others who left no traces. Every genealogy is an exclusion of thousands or hundreds of thousands of ancestors. I made the calculation. Let us imagine that my name is X. I can find and confirm the filiation of one of my ancestors named X—during the fifteenth century, for example. Let us call my generation $g1$. My parents are $g2$: there were two of them. Of my grandparents, $g3$, there were four. Of my great-grandparents, $g4$, eight. Let us assume there are three or four generations in each century.[3] Since the fifteenth century, this amounts to six centuries—twenty-one generations. How many ancestors did I have at the $g21$ level? My calculation yields 1,048,576, with the same ranking. In the fifteenth century, at a putative moment of history, I have (arithmetically speaking) one million, forty-eight thousand, five hundred, and seventy-six ancestors. And therefore, when I say that I stem from X, who during that time had the same name as I do, I am eliminating one million, forty-eight thousand, five hundred, and seventy-five members from my ancestry, and additionally all those from the subsequent generational layers (situated between the two moments in time, during these six centuries). Of course, I cannot claim to know where they all lived—all those, the ones before them and after them—even supposing a high rate of endogamy that would reduce their numbers. One would have to be unbearably obsessed to take for granted that they were all Jewish, or all from Oran, or all speakers of Arabic. But it is quite likely that a good number of them hung around the Mediterranean, between one monotheism and another, various ports and trading posts, certainly more numerous in the south, returned to the south after more than one mass expulsion. What were they speaking? Mostly Arabic, and a little Spanish, and for prayers a mixture based on Hebrew, which they barely understood. I was born in North Africa, by the sea, toward the middle of the twentieth century. The legendary memory of parents, grandparents, great-grandparents, and beyond them said this: we have been here *forever*.

Now, Europe took me away in the following circumstances. All Algerian Jews became naturalized French citizens by a decree issued in Tours

(France) in 1871.⁴ Within four generations, my family changed languages, thinking, and lifestyle—and finally their continent. My great-grandfather Rabbi Chalom Djian, who lived in Oran and died in 1929, spoke only Arabic, dressed like an Arab, and ate sitting on the floor. My grandmother was a pious and observant village schoolteacher, but with a sense of humor. My father was a middle-school teacher and a member of the Communist Party, with Enlightenment ideas. Then I came. I have never known a word of Arabic. The French language is my native land. I think as an atheist, there's no going back. At the end of the Algerian war, we came to France, as did a million others.⁵ Like them, we were "repatriated." This is the paradox: we were "repatriated" to a fatherland from which we had never come, since my ancestors—so much at least is established—had been living in Algeria long before its conquest by the French. Europe took us and carried us away on the run—and we were happy. My father, who had supported its war of independence and had paid the price for it, no longer saw Algeria as his home, our future. He was hopelessly in love with France and with Europe the beautiful: Spain, England, Italy—and Germany; the Prado, the jovial, uncompromising Churchill, Michelangelo, Beethoven, and Marx. Worshipping France as the land of the rule of law and of equality, he joyfully let himself be torn away from his ancestral shores and never returned. He is buried in Marseille.

This is not perhaps the provenance of an authentic European. Maybe. And yet the hypothesis that came to light little by little in the course of this work might be that, unexpectedly (in a transferential, nonfounding mode), such a history dovetails with, or reiterates, Europe's primordial constitution—that Europe is not a patrimony of native people but of passengers, which it carries on board or on its deck; that every European is passing through, traversing it; and that Europe is not thinkable outside of this: crossed, which is to say, both covered or crisscrossed with roads, and as *a crossing* [*traversée*]—Europe as a passage. And therefore, Europe the provisional, to be crossed, overstepped, freed from itself. Intermediary Europe, Europe-process. Mid-way [*mi-lieu*].

On this (non-originary, noncompleted, an-archic) score, Europe may be a good object-of-thought—that is to say, a good vehicle—with which to begin. Let us see this as the initiatory and preliminary hypothesis—let's say, hypothesis zero (*ho*).

PART I　　EUROPE CROSSWAYS

2. On the Figure

Here is the first hypothesis:

"Europe" is one of the names of the return to self of the universal, which is to say, of the universal as a figure. (h1)

This proposition concerns what we should understand—hear or read—in the name of Europe. Before we assess it, let us note that it posits, almost in passing, an equivalence between "return to self of the universal" and "universal as a figure." The proposition thus assumes that the figure is equivalent to a turnaround. Now, this equivalence potentially contains another one, and it is useful to shed some light on this.

What is a "return"? The French *Le Robert* dictionary classifies the senses of this word [*retour*, in French] in two sets of meanings. On the one hand, there are the physical or dynamic senses, which convey the general idea of a "backward movement, a displacement toward the point of departure or a change of direction"; on the other, the "abstract" senses, related to the "idea of repetition, regression, or exchange." Let us follow the latter path, where the first sense is "return to" [*retour à*]. "Returning," here, is first of all "returning to."

What is "return to"? "To return, actively or passively (to one's habitual or previous state, to past activities). To return to normal [*retour au calme*]. To return to the source. 'Returning to nature, that is, abolishing society.'"[6] In this abstract sense, which I shall adopt provisionally, the return (as "return to") strongly implies a return to self. To return (*to* normal, *to* the source) is to return to what one was or was supposed to be, as one was—formerly. We cannot claim (at least not in a radical sense) that we are "returning to" (to a past time; to a place, for what took place there; to a past state of things) without wanting to *find ourselves again* in the position, situation, or posture that we used to occupy. The "return to" a past requires a return to a self (past, fugitive, vanished self). Now, to continue this series, "returning to" (self) implies returning in the sense of "turning back" or "reverting to" [*retour sur*]: to come back (now) to what one was (before) is first of all reversing something one is today, as when we say "reversing a judgment," that is, recanting or disclaiming it. *Retour sur soi-même*, turning around or reverting to oneself, according to the *Littré* dictionary, means a serious self-examination of one's behavior.[7] Thus, returning to oneself in this sense first of all means turning or reverting to oneself, questioning oneself, observing, evaluating, and judging what one is today; and then coming to—as in waking up, thereby abolishing the state in which one was: sleep, intoxication, error.

I am thus positing that "return"—any return—as "return to" is necessarily a return to self, and thus in the first place a reversion to self. Every return turns around—be it a consideration, a reflection, or a self-judgment—and there is no return that does not revert back toward itself. Reverting to self is the essence of returning, in its generality. When we say that the figure is equivalent to the return to self, we are saying that it is equivalent to the return itself, as return. By holding on to both ends of this chain of equivalences, we come to the production of a second hypothesis, which we should extract for the sake of clarification, although the first one contains it:

The figure is the return. (h2)

First, we shall deal with the hypothesis about Europe (*h1*). The second hypothesis—its general scope—remains suspended for now.

*

By saying that Europe is a term naming the return to self of the universal, we imply something else about the universal; we presuppose the thought of some previous or preliminary thing in addition to this return. "Returning" comes afterward: there would thus have to be something universal "before" this return, "before" the figure—before Europe. In a first approach, the universal would be "first" (before the figure) the movement of an expansion, a widening and an enlargement, and this is the movement that a return would (possibly or necessarily?) follow.

Let me lay this out graphically. Such a sketch is also a figure—this is something for which I shall have to try to account (as well as for a certain usage, here, of philosophy with its practices and figurations).[8] My drawing is in the shape of a loop:

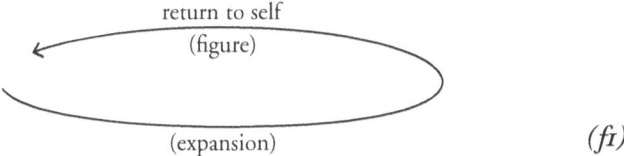

(f1)

A remark about this sketch: since the universal is first the movement of an expansion (shown by the lower part of the curved line), the reversion to self should aim at this movement and this line. But the return (the upper part of the line) misses its aim: it does not come back to the movement as movement, or to the expansion as a widening or process. The return comes back to the origin of the movement; it *refers* the movement to its origin. Now, in the movement, the origin goes missing. The return then produces the image of a point of departure, as a point and as a departure—a cutoff and a parting. That is where the arrow projects itself: toward the supposed origin of the movement, which—in the movement—is lacking. The return points to the beginning: it construes the movement as the aftermath of its departure, and constitutes its beginning as a point—an originating, abstract, and immobile locus; a fixed motor.[9]

How is this schematization relevant for Europe? It is an invitation to think of Europe in a double fashion: within the movement of the universal (as the moment, course, and tracing of this movement), as well as (indissociably) in the retreat of this drive—its closure and sealing. This leads us to say that through this initial expansion, which holds and underlies it, Europe is always conveyed as the project of a world, and this globalizing drive toward worldhood is unassailably and inextricably linked to its very idea and its first becoming.[10] Constitutionally ("always-already," "originating there," so to speak, but inasmuch as its origin fails it), Europe comes forth, producing worldhood [*mondialité*]. With its return, it wants to represent this universality that carries it (it wants to be its representative), and with this gesture, it gives shape to the universal—and misses it. This is what we shall call Europe's continent-form, its *continence*.[11] Europe's continentality (its shape, its outline on the surface of the earth) is its return to itself, its backlash and failing. Having taken on this shape, Europe reconsiders the worldly globalizing movement that carries it, and rethinks (reproduces) it *from its originating point*, now pointed, inscribed at the heart of its continentality—starting at the point of departure. If, starting with the figure, we revisit this world-producing movement, we may understand it (being carried out) as a continental extension and expansion, and further perhaps as the clearing of land, *mission civilisatrice* [civilizing mission], and colonization.[12]

*

How is one to understand this before/after relation, as I have just developed it? There are two overlapping but distinct ways of doing so, tracing the first on an ideal plane and the second on a concrete one.

On the plane of idealities, my hypothesis amounts to considering that the movement of the universal (as becoming or process) *logically* comes *prior* to the position of the figure of Europe; it precedes and conditions it. The figure of Europe emerges by virtue of the fact that the movement of this expansion turns around and comes back to itself; it is identified and named (or baptized).

This logical priority of the universal as an expansion that one could term "pure" clearly appears in Kant's essay "Idee zu einer allgemeinen Geschichte in weltbürgerlicher Absicht" ("Idea for a Universal History with a Cosmopolitan Aim"). As a matter of fact, neither the name "Europe" nor the adjective "European" appears at any time in this short work, which is worth analyzing. In its ninth thesis, close to the ending, after lengthy considerations about the universal in and for itself, Kant writes: "It seems, at first sight, a strange and even an absurd proposal to suggest the composition of a *History* according to the idea of how the course of the world must proceed, if it is to be conformable to certain rational laws. *It may well appear that only a Romance* [Gm., *Roman* (i.e., a novel)] *could be produced from such a point of view.*"[13] Kant extracts a "guiding thread" [*Leitfaden*] from this story (*Idee*, pp. 408 and 409), in spite of this reservation:

> Thus, suppose we start from the history of *Greece*, as that by which all the older or contemporaneous History has been preserved, or at least accredited to us. Then, if we study its influence upon the formation and malformation of the political institutions of the Roman people, which swallowed up the Greek States, and if we further follow the influence of the Roman Empire upon the Barbarians who destroyed it in turn, and continue this investigation down to our own day, conjoining with it episodically the political history of other peoples according as the knowledge of them has gradually reached us through [*durch*] these more

enlightened nations, we shall discover a regular movement [Gm., *Gang*] of progress through the civil constitution of our part of the world [Gm., *Staatsverfassung in unserem Welttheile*] (which is probably destined to give laws to all other parts of the world).[14]

This history has a beginning. The first scene of the story (or novel) can be situated in a determined time and place, ancient Greece. Does this make it an origin or a point of departure? It is not so simple; Kant does not situate any primordial event—any unprecedented taking-place—in Greece that might bring *itself* about, self-evidently there without anteriority or exteriority. Greek originality is not contained in one pure event, but in a *transmission*: "suppose we start from the history of *Greece, as that by which all the older or contemporaneous History has been preserved, or at least accredited to us*" (emphasis added). There is some history before that, or elsewhere. But it is thanks to Greece that we know it; it is Greece that tells it. Greece transmits, preserves (*aufbehalten*), and attests (*beglaubigt*). The origin is transfer, and such is *the very originality of the origin*, that which makes it a beginning: elsewhere things take place but are not transmitted; here, one preserves, gives, and transmits—all of history (the whole story) begins. The Greeks are historical because they are historians. Kant repeats this in a note on the same page:

It is only a learned Public [*gelehrtes Publikum*] which has had an uninterrupted existence from its beginning up to our time, that can authenticate Ancient History. Beyond it, all is *terra incognita*; and the History of the peoples who lived out of its range, can only be begun from the date at which they entered within it. In the case of the Jewish People this happened in the time of the Ptolemies, through the Greek Translation of the Bible, without which little faith would have been given to their *isolated* accounts of themselves. From that date (taken as a beginning when it has been determined [*wenn dieser Anfang vorerst gehörig ausgemittelt worden*]), their records may then be traced upwards [(*man kann) aufwärts ihren Erzählungen nachgehen* (i.e., one may retrace their stories—Trans.)]. And so it is with all other peoples. The first page of Thucydides (says Hume) is the one beginning of all true History.[15]

Thanks to the "learned Public," which controls the chain of transmission that enables ancient histories to reach us, every kind of knowledge is available, and this chain starts in Greece. It is, for example—but what an example!—only thanks to its translation into Greek during Roman times that the Bible enters our history. Translation makes for a well-established (*ausgemittelt*) beginning (*Anfang*). It lays out and establishes the beginning *in the middle* (*ausgemittelt*). To translate is to transmit; the beginning is (in) the change of space and languages. This is where universality (the universality of universal history) starts up. Then comes Rome, which absorbs the Greek state and gives instruction to the barbarians who bring about its destruction—followed by us. Other peoples are known only through (*durch*) the consecution of these educated nations forming a chain. All this is imparted and will keep imparting itself to the totality of the world, through the movement of an expansion and a progressive extension. In these passages, as in the rest of Kant's essay, the word "Europe" does not appear.

From the quoted sentence "we shall discover a regular movement of progress through the civil constitution of our part of the world (which is probably destined to give laws to all other parts of the world)," we might plausibly assume that Kant had Europe in mind when he wrote these lines. He uses the term *Welttheil*, "part of the world," however, and nothing in this implies *continence* or the continentality of Europe. Moreover, there are words available in German to designate this: *Kontinent, Festland, Erdteil*. All these words are related to the *earth*: its firmness (Fest-*land*), division (*Erd*-teil), or containment, precisely, retaining and containing it in its continentality (*Kontinent*). Kant speaks of a "part of the world"—the earth is not the world: the world—at least in its concept—includes extraterrestrial realities:

> The part that has to be played by man is, therefore, a very artificial one. We do not know how it may be with the inhabitants of other planets or what are the conditions of their nature; but, if *we* execute well the commission of Nature, we may certainly flatter ourselves to the extent of claiming a not insignificant rank *among our neighbours in the edifice of the world* [Gm., *Weltgebäude*]. It may perhaps be the case that in those other planets every individual completely attains his destination in this life. With us it is otherwise; only the species can hope for this.[16]

We are not necessarily alone in the world; other planets may bear other inhabitants. But be that as it may, we earthlings will not be in a bad place in this edifice if we do our share and accomplish our role in this universal history—in the fulfillment of its idea.

In its simple flow, this text only says one thing: since the first Greek transmission, which inaugurated the chain of stories and inheritances, the universal has been expanding and extending to the totality of the world. The term designating this movement of expansion is "history." *It so happens* that we find ourselves in a phase when this growth has reached this part of the world, which is ours under current circumstances (and charged with a mission). From here, there will be an expansion throughout the whole world, bearer of a worldwide, cosmopolitan citizenry, which a priori does not exclude the inhabitants of other planets. This process (*Gang*: step, gait, movement, flow of this course) merely traverses our space. Nothing in this calls for the concept of Europe, as such, though we should account for the fact that *today* Greece is said to be a part of this continent, and that the extension might thus cover something that *perhaps* (since Kant does not say this) resembles what *we* call Europe. But the determination of the universal as a continuous expansion, from the Greek movement to the interplanetary union of the world, in no way presupposes any reference to the continent of Europe (to its figure or name).[17] It is in this first sense that one may say that the universal "precedes" Europe conceptually; Europe is not its prerequisite.

*

We may also describe as a concrete process what we just laid out as an ideal development—it is a matter of chronology. From this point of view, the assertion that the universal, as expansion, "precedes" Europe is tantamount simply to saying that this was set in motion before there was a Europe, and that Europe only constituted itself in the reactive jolt (the turnaround or retreat) of previous stirrings.

This brings us to challenge two formulations having to do with birth. The first posits that the movement of expansion of the universal was *born in Europe*—by virtue of the fact that this movement was born in Greece, and that Greece is in Europe. Against this double supposition, which amiably presents itself as self-evident, it requires once more to be asserted that Europe, like all things on this earth, has to be thought of in terms of constitution, process, and development—of history. Any eternity, even recently formed, is a mirage—a fetish. It is not thanks to a matter-of-fact distribution of land (of continents) on the surface of the planet that there is a "Europe" or even "some" Europe, nor is Europe the innocent name of one among several dispositions that are fortuitously continental. Europe has not always been there; it was produced as a historical determination, a category, and a form. And even if one can locate some of its premises in the space of ancient Greece, its constitution essentially comes afterward. It is around the end of the putative Middle Ages, not earlier, that it becomes organized under the aspect that we now know.[18] With regard to the set of meanings that necessarily comes to mind as soon as we utter this name, and for the sake of historical exactitude, we should not hesitate to posit that ancient Greece was not part of our Europe, since what I am designating as Europe was fundamentally unknown in the lives of ancient Greeks. And therefore, even if it was "born," even in Greece (which is debatable), the universal was not—at all—born in this Europe.

This chronological reminder nonetheless brings us face to face with the need to ask what the ancient Greeks were saying when they handled this term, since they evidently had a use for it: "Europe" is a Greek word, transmitted to us along with so many others (e.g., the words "museum" and "metronome," though the ancient Greeks obviously knew neither museums nor metronomes as we understand them).[19] No doubt, *what we call Europe* somehow relates to what the Greeks designated in this way, and this is obvious, as in any heritage or etymology. And surely, we have to question this relation: when our "Europe" came to configure itself (and got its name), it was obviously neither indifferent nor fortuitous that this name reappeared; and by way of it a certain "load"—Greek ammunition—was transported all the way to us.

The Greek word *Europē* has two meanings: it designates a mythological character, and a certain relation between places. In the latter case, which I shall tackle first, there are two phases in its use: "It seems to have designated first the continent in relation to the Peloponnese and the islands; and second, a part of the world in relation to Asia Minor and Libya."[20] Now, an attentive examination of the uses of this term in the latter sense leads one to a remarkable finding. In a long series of these uses,[21] the word "Europe" appears within a syntagma that designates the passage from Asia to Europe, or the return from Europe to Asia, in the immediate vicinity of terms that designate a crossing, traveling across the sea or the span of the *pontus* (the straits—the Hellespont, the Bosporus—or the Euxine [Black] Sea),[22] or journeying from shore to shore. Here are a few examples among dozens of occurrences:

So Darius crossed over into Europe . . .

. . . towards the western darkness there is no passage; turn back the ship's sails again to the mainland of Europe. . . .

Will not the whole barbarian army cross from Europe over the Hellespont?

... when on that earlier day Zeus' famous son Heracles encircled with destruction the city of Troy, you came back to Europe with your share in this high renown.

The Persians, who conquered the Medes, did, indeed, finally become masters of almost all Asia; but when they attacked the nations of Europe also . . .[23]

This link clearly appears in Herodotus, for whom the usage of the term is almost always associated with the idea of crossing, of the *pontus*, of passing from shore to shore. As one reads these pages one after the other, one comes away with the impression that the word "Europe," in a way, does not exactly designate *a place* but rather the relation between places, a passage or journey: from one shore to the other of the Black Sea—*pontus*—separating and linking Asia—which is to say, the Persian Empire—to the Greek Hellenic space.[24] Let us consider this hypothesis for a moment. It would hold that "Europe" is not the name of a space viewed in itself, in its autonomy or its self-referentiality, but that it points toward two land areas,[25] *two* spaces, facing each other, to the exact point of their separation, their limit, and the passage at this point. There would be a Europe only as facing Asia and set before it—and secondarily, as if through the reproduction of the same relationship, facing "Libya," that is, Africa. The distribution of these three parts of the world would only occur at the very determined site where they separate and distinguish themselves, face one another, allowing back-and-forth passages that generally involve warfare.

Let us note that within the scope of this hypothesis, the three parts of the world cannot be "seen"—that is, designated as such or named—except from a vantage point situated *between* them, which is to say, *from the sea* or the span of the *pontus*. This partitioning is a partitioning of sea- and border-crossers [*passeurs*]: sailors—or warriors who have to cross the sea. The tripartite "continental" division of the world is formed from a maritime and military starting point of spans and passages: from this site in the eastern Mediterranean where one can simultaneously "see" the shores of Greece, Asia Minor, and Egypt.[26] In order to understand these Greek names, one would have to stop thinking of continentality from a terrestrial perspective, as the relation to itself of a territory that is secondarily limited by water. In one's mind, one would have to situate oneself in a median, intermediary, and maritime space, a threshold of crossings and bridges, from where one would see the land, the shores, and their relationship (their face-to face).[27] From this outlook, each land area would only show one shore—opening onto a boundless geodesy—on the other side, without any border, at least any known one.[28] One might thus construe the tricontinentality of the world as a threefold terrestrial border, starting from the passageway, the channel or pass (as in Pas-de-Calais, Strait of Dover). Such would be the thinking—starting from water, the median, and the passage—decipherable in the Greek names for the continents.[29] But the usage of the term is even more determined. In nearly every case, we notice that the word is used in a context that evokes the passage from Asia to Europe, and not the other way around. The corpus of Herodotus's uses of the word—by far the most extensive one—thus comprises eighteen instances linked to the passage from Asia to Europe, and only four associated with the passage in the other direction.[30] Now, the latter are characterized as *returns*, and this points to the precedence of the outward journey, while the other use seems secondary in relation to it. It plainly seems that Europe designates *the thing toward which one travels, the area where one lands when coming from the shores of Asia*. And the study of the myth of Europē unexpectedly reinforces this interpretation, as does Herodotus's own astonishing geographical commentary.

*

It is indeed time to ask ourselves who "Europe" is. Here is a summary of the legend.

Once upon a time in Tyre there was a princess named Europe. Once, at night, while she lay on her bed in the palace of King Agenor, her father, she had a dream: two areas of land, which looked like two women, were quarreling about her, the land of "Asia" and the "farther shore." The first wanted to protect and watch her, while the second, because of Zeus, wanted to take her away across the sea. The puzzled princess woke up and resumed her activities and games. She went to pick some flowers near the sea, with other princesses who were her friends. And there a magnificent gentle bull appeared and persuaded her to climb onto his back, and she did so after some hesitation. The bull then stood up and ran toward the sea. While crossing the water, he revealed that he was Zeus, and that he had taken this animal form to abduct her because of his great love for her. Europe thus went to Crete, mated with the bull, and became the mother of "glorious sons."[31]

These lines summarize a text by the second-century B.C.E. Alexandrian poet Moschus, a kind of "small epic"[32] in a sensual almost courtly genre, a "pretty fairy tale drawn from mythology,"[33] which offers the most complete account that we have, it seems, of Europē's destiny.[34] What does this fable tell us? That Europē was born at Tyre: in Phoenicia, on the eastern shore of the Mediterranean. Herodotus found this astonishing: Europē is *Asian*.[35] Her story begins while the girl, still a virginal "maid unwed," is asleep, says Moschus (Moschus, p. 189). This tale is going to draw her out of her sleep and out of her virginity. She is dreaming: this story or history (of Europe) comes out of an Asian dream. The dream is filled with "strife" between two land areas, "both in the shape of women" (p. 189) but whose names in the text are remarkable: "Asia, and *the farther shore [antiperēn]*" (p. 189; emphasis added). Here again we have the two areas facing one another [*qui s'af-frontent*]. But the land facing Asia *has no name*—not yet. Moschus is specific: of these two women, "one had the guise of a stranger, the other of a lady of that land, and closer still she clung about her maiden, and kept saying how 'she was her mother, and herself had nursed Europa'" (p. 189). The conflict opposes *a stranger* (*xeinēs*) to a native, who calls to mind the mother of Europē, representing her Asian filiation, her sheltering native land. In this dream, it is the stranger who literally *pulls it off*: "that other with mighty hands, and forcefully, kept haling [i.e., pulling along] the maiden" (p. 189). Europē did dream of an abduction, away from her native land, toward a foreign and unknown destination. But though it may have been "forceful," this abduction did not violate her: Europe was pulled away and did not resist. Better yet, we learn that upon waking, the girl leapt forth "in terror, with beating heart," but then "raised her timorous voice": "'Ah, and who was the alien woman that I beheld in my sleep? *How strange a longing for her seized my heart* . . . blessed gods, I pray you, prosper the fulfilment of the dream'" (p. 190; emphasis added). The dream is thus the realization of a desire.[36] To be snatched away from her native land is Europē's desire, something she longingly and passionately covets. Her desire comes as a surprise and frightens her—but it carries her away.

Let us read on. When she wakes up, the princess seeks out her friends. They go to pick flowers, each carrying a basket, and

> Europa herself bore a basket of gold, a marvel well worth gazing on, a choice work of Hephaestus. He gave it to Libya, for a bridal-gift, when she approached the bed of the Shaker of the Earth, and Libya gave it to beautiful Telephassa, who was of her own blood; and to Europa, still an unwedded maid, her mother, Telephassa, gave the splendid gift. (pp. 190–91)

Europe is therefore a descendant of Libya: her mother was of her own blood. Europe, born in Asia, shares the blood of Africa;[37] as for Libya, she has got together with Hephaestus—the Shaker of the Earth. The present (the flower basket) stems from this union (when she entered "the bed").

Then the abduction occurs. Zeus appears suddenly, in the shape of a bull. An extraordinary power of seduction emanates from him, literally. This is not a bull that "feeds in the stall,"[38] and his "coming terrified not the maidens, nay, within them all wakened desire to draw nigh the lovely bull, and to touch him, and his heavenly fragrance was scattered afar, exceeding even the sweet perfume of the meadows" (p. 193). This bestial apparition is *erotic*: indeed, *eros* is the *desire* to touch, which has overtaken the young women. In fact, the bull has stopped near Europē and "kept licking her neck, and cast his spell over the maiden" (p. 193)—which, like the seduction by smell, is the way of an animal. Then he quietly invited her to climb (onto his broad back). Inviting her friends to do the same, she smiled and "sat down on the back of the bull"; and that is when he "leaped up immediately . . . and swiftly he sped to the deep [the sea]" (p. 193).

Then comes an amazing passage across the sea. The bull skips across the water without wetting its hooves. All around, fish are dancing. Zeus is riding the waves like a dolphin. The Nereids arise and splash out of the salt water, and, "riding on the backs of sea-beasts," form a procession trailing the couple. The "Shaker of the World," Hephaestus, appears and guides "his brother on the salt sea path." Tritons gather all around, "these hoarse trumpeters of the deep, blowing from their long conches a bridal melody" (p. 194). Europē is sitting on the bull, clasping the animal's great horn with one hand. With the other, she gently lifts her garment to keep it out of the water. Her "deep robe" turns into a sail, "swelled out by the wind," speeding up the journey (p. 194).

Then, when she sees herself "now far off from her own country" [*gaiēs apo patridos*]—"neither sea-beat headland nor steep hill could now be seen, but above, the air, and beneath, the limitless deep" (p. 194)—she speaks to the animal and asks about the meaning of her adventure.

> Whither bearest thou me, bull-god? What art thou? how dost thou fare on thy feet through the path of the sea-beasts, nor fearest the sea? . . . Lo, neither do dolphins of the brine fare on land, nor bulls on the deep, but dreadless dost thou rush o'er land and sea alike . . . alas for me that have left my father's house, and following this bull, on a strange sea-faring I go. (pp. 194–95)

The bull reveals that he is Zeus and that he has abducted her out of love [*pothos*], and that he will make her his wife and the mother of "glorious sons." So he spoke, and all he said "was fulfilled." And this is how the tale ends.[39]

Europe was thus *abducted*—from Asia, her paternal house, the country of her birth. She was carried away, over the sea, toward an unknown destination, doubtless taken by force, but consenting to it and even yearning for this abduction, which is as forceful as desire itself. And (this is what is striking to Herodotus) she is taken in a completely obscure direction, toward a *nameless* land. It will be Europe, of course, but there is no patronymic name; it is the land across the way, a foreign country. Europe's abduction takes her toward an anonymous strangeness, and, if Europe refers to something for the Greeks, this is it first of all: it is not the land across the way and its proper name, but the movement of tearing away, and carrying away, from the paternal land, from Asia as the land (being-land of the land), toward this strange nameless place. This is what Europe is: being torn away from Asia. Capture, rapture—forceful yet delicious, worrisome and desirable—*abduction itself*: toward the west, necessarily, because this movement is the one that carries and drives the sun, which also goes up and takes off [*se lève, s'enlève*].[40]

Herodotus writes, in book 4 of *The Histories*:

> No one knows for certain whether or not there is sea either to the east or to the north of Europe; it is known, however, that lengthwise it is equal to the other two continents together. I have no idea why the earth—which is, after all, single—has three separate names (each of which is the name of a woman) . . . nor can I find out the names of those who decided upon these boundaries or how the continents got their names. Most Greek authorities claim that Libya is named after a woman called Libya who was a native of that continent, and that Asia is named after the wife of Prometheus. However, the Lydians lay claim to the name too; they say that Asia is not named after Prometheus' Asia, but after Asies the son of Cotys and grandson of Manes, who also gave his name to the tribe at Sardis called Asias. As for Europe, not only does no one know whether it is surrounded by water, but the origin of its name is also uncertain (as is the identity of the man who named it), unless we say that it is named after Europa from Tyre, *and that before her time the continent was after all as nameless as the other continents were*. But it is clear that *Europa came from Asia and never visited the land mass which the Greeks now call Europe*; her travels were limited to going from Phoenicia to Crete, and from there to Lycia. Anyway, that is enough about all this; we intend to use the standard names of the continents.[41]

Strange text, rather dense lesson—filled with amazement that someone gave three distinct names to this "single" land mass. And there is lucidity in this amazement: for this partition is not thinkable when one starts from the land, the being-land of the land, endowed with a proper name—landed property. Naming divides it—into the tripartite division of the unity of the soil. Only the movement of a *departure* can explain it: one has to start away from the land and leave it in order to see it in three *parts*. Herodotus examines these three mysterious names. There is nothing unsettling about the first one: Libya is a native woman; Africa is African. Hegel will later write: "Africa proper, as far as History goes back, has remained—for all purposes of connection with the rest of the World—shut up; it is the Gold-land compressed within itself."[42] Africa (seen from Greece, that is, or from philosophy) is the name of self-identity, of the terrestrial properly speaking. As for Asia, things are more dubious: she may be Prometheus's wife—though she would not be Asian, but rather Greek, in a way. Herodotus makes a correction: Lydians (people of Asia Minor) say that the name comes from them. That is better—unfortunately, it is the name of a man, Asies or Asias. "Asia" points to an identity that is already uncertain and unsettled. Herodotus prefers to believe that these two land areas bear the names of beings born there: genealogical names, autochthonous names, names of one's native land (*gaiēs apo patridos*), true patronymics. As for Europe, on the other hand, one slips into namelessness or absurdity. One either knows nothing of that name and its provenance, or else—which in a way amounts to the same thing—the name derives from the Tyrian Europē. Now, this woman was first of all born in Tyre—*therefore, at the time of the birth, the land of Europe had no name*; second, Tyre is in Asia, *therefore Europe is an Asian woman*, and the name of Europe does not come from Europe properly speaking, as name-of-a-land-area; and third, *Europe never came to Europe* (to the "continent"), going only as far as Crete.

Europe is not the proper name of a land mass but the name of the abduction, of being torn away from a native land and of the crossing toward an unknown country in the west.[43] A last remark is necessary. Herodotus's final observation is rather astonishing: Europe "never visited the land mass which the Greeks now call Europe; *her travels were limited to going from Phoenicia to Crete*." Strictly speaking, Crete is not in Europe. What is Europe, then? What is this land? We find again here the primary meaning in Greek, which has remained in the shadows until now. Europē, according to Pierre Chantraine's etymology, "seems to have designated first the continent in relation to the Peloponnese and the islands."[44] Europe is neither the islands *nor the Peloponnese*: it is neither the islands nor the peninsula. Europe would be the continent in its depth—in its very continence. Europe would not be designating the maritime sea-related element, as maritime. Europe for sure is not the Mediterranean, then—it is precisely the opposite way—and the term includes neither the islands nor the peninsulas, inasmuch as the former and even the latter are in the grip of the sea element, held by it, and carried along by this moving medium. Let us hold on to this: in due time (during the constitution of our "Europe") this determination will be decisive.

The two Homeric uses of the word, said to be its first attested mentions, point in this direction:

There the lord Phoibos Apollon / resolved to make a lovely temple and spoke these words: / "Here I intend to build a beautiful temple / to be an oracle for men who shall always / bring to this place unblemished hecatombs; / *and as many as dwell on fertile Peloponnesos / and on Europe and throughout the sea-girt islands /* will consult it . . . "[45]

"Europe" names neither the islands nor the Peloponnese. This clearly confirms that *even in this first Greek sense, Greece—as Greece—is not strictly speaking in Europe.*[46] Greece, to be sure, is also the islands, and certainly the Peloponnese: otherwise, Argos, Sparta, Corinth, Patras, Epidaurus would not be Greek—nor would Mycenae, Naxos, Chios, or Lesbos. And since Europe is not a part of Greece, it designates the continental access that Greece faces, this land as land, more landlike than the islands or the peninsula, land properly speaking, fundamentally landlike, without any maritime outline or boundary, *which one enters and into which one pushes forth when one comes from Asia by sea*. Europe is the continence that one reaches—opposed to the one from which one comes. Europe would then be the name of this *new land* where one comes ashore, and into which one penetrates. What this will have required is an initial land mass—paternal and sleepy—and being torn away from this home; traveling, being carried away across the waters; stopping at islands, land held and borne by the sea; and then, *passing into Europe*, reaching the continent across the way, penetrating into the boundless depth of its land. Europe is the terrestrial horizon of this journey, the new land to be crossed and conquered, the backcountry awaiting to the west, a backcountry of border-crossers, sailors, and warriors: not one's place of origin—like the sun's—where one awoke and arose. No, it is the backcountry into which one enters, penetrates, and sinks, and that one will discover. *Europe is the passage to Europe*—the second homeland.[47]

*

The second formulation to challenge, the one about the origin or birth, is close to the first, but subtler and more powerful. It appears in a text by Edmund Husserl, the justifiably famous "Vienna Lecture," which one is bound to come across frequently in this context:

> Spiritual Europe has a birthplace. By this I mean not a geographical birthplace, in one land, though this is also true, but rather a spiritual birthplace in a nation or in individual men and human groups of this nation. It is the ancient Greek nation in the seventh and sixth centuries B.C. Here there arises a *new sort of attitude* [emphasis added] of individuals toward their surrounding world. And its consequence is the breakthrough of a completely new sort of spiritual structure, rapidly growing into a systematically self-enclosed cultural form; the Greeks called it *philosophy*."[48]

We may start by subscribing to some of these statements. (1) In ancient Greece, there was a sort of "event" that can be construed as the historic constitution of something *new* ("new sort of attitude," "new sort of spiritual structure"). (2) This constitution has to be characterized as "arising" or developing, "growing," forming; that is, as a process and as history. (3) We can in fact define this event as a "birth," *provided that one thinks of birth as a process and not an origin*. Birth has a story or history: process, development, transfer, opening, *as well as* production of something new—the coming, formation, and constitution of a singularity. (4) Lastly, let us agree (cheerfully) that what was born there is linked to what the "Greeks called . . . philosophy." Husserl goes on to suggest a determination for it, which we should reread. But it is precisely what the *Greeks called philosophy* that we must consider (as formation and history), and not *Philosophy* as an essence or something eternal, even if—and we shall soon tire of repeating this at every opportunity—what we are practicing under this name is a discourse that evidently has some kind of relationship with what happened in Greece.

On the other hand, two other assertions should be challenged, namely, (5) that the Greeks, first of all, as agents and carriers of this event (or coming or birth) should be thought of as a *nation*: ". . . in a nation or in individual men and human groups of this nation"; and it will later become understandable why the use of the word "nation," in the sense that *we* (modern Europeans) give it today, in the sense that we irrevocably cannot help *but* give it—why this word or concept is unsuited to designate the Greeks, and even less the Greeks as those bringing forth the universal, unless it is used as an anachronism that paralyzes thought by linking the object of thought with its reverse side and its retreat; and why this *naming error* ties in with an error of assignation regarding what is *born*. (6) Finally, and especially, this other thesis, the focus of the disagreement—that what is *born* in Greece at that moment *should be Europe*. Indeed, Husserl does not assert—as in the statement discussed earlier—that the universal was born in Europe because it was born in Greece. Rather, he says something subtler and more difficult to refute: the universal was born in Greece *as Europe*. What came forth in Greece, then, is Europe (Europe spiritually speaking, or philosophy)—as a development, a breakthrough, and the teleological history of the universal. Now, for two main reasons, this thesis needs to be challenged. First, we must try to show that what emerged in Greece (even supposing it to be close to what the concept of the universal addresses) cannot be thought as Europe. What is produced is the first locatable transfer, the first transmission, the first (inherited) narrative of the development (or process, or expansion) of what philosophy at a specific moment will call the universal. The trace found (again) in Greece and reread as its history is the trace of a moment in time during the formation of the universal as a movement, extension, broadening, and crossing of boundaries. This is not Europe: in Greek thought, there is nothing associating the name of Europe with *this*—neither as theory nor as politics nor as art. What remains, of course, is the little princess, who also oversteps boundaries; and mythologically, no doubt, she is available as a figure freeing up any provenance and belonging. But she is still a drowsy silhouette, sleeping and waiting. The Greeks never called on her to shape their production of universality, of free thought; and still less on the continent to circumscribe it and ascribe a topography to its origin. The Greek opening, which is certainly self-conscious, lays claim to belonging as *citizens*, and to *Hellenic* life, and this is not posited as European. Europe is neither the city nor Greece. *Neither the city-state nor Greece is European.* Europe will be produced much later, in the turnaround of this movement, in its identification, naming, and figure. So that if Europe is not thinkable outside of this expansion of the universal—if it is in a sense nothing else—it can nevertheless not be identified with it either, because between this expansion and its return to itself (between the Greek "event" and the formation of Europe), many far-reaching events have occurred, and time and history have been at work. And ascribing the birth of Europe to the Greek moment reduces this work and flattens this history onto its opening, reconfigured as an origin.

The second compelling reason for challenging this assertion (that the birthplace of Europe was Greece) is that, for reasons organically linked to the preceding ones, it is urgent to (re)think a nonteleological history: to (re)affirm that the concept of history is not necessarily held to the development of a finality at work, a finality that transcends history, a horizon that orients it and gives it meaning. It has become commonplace to dismiss history for its supposed teleology. I shall posit the opposite, namely, that teleology, and the archeology that of course mirrors it, crush and flatten history, and dissolve it in negating its *thinking*. Consequently, only a flattening of the entire history of this world, and of this continent, which is one of its phases, can thus arise from the (teleological) idea that Europe was born in Greece as the rise of the universal,[49] and reducing us to a choice between shameless Europeolatry and resentful Europeophobia. It is necessary to disengage history from its supposed end as well as from its mythical origin. The task is to think *against* the end of history, and to give thought to *history against* the end of history—to think history against its ending.[50] One should think of Europe as a moment, or era. As a crossing. Traversing and getting across it—to get out of it.

3. Other Names

Something further about the first hypothesis (*h1*): in it, "Europe" is designated as "one of the names of the return to self of the universal," and this assumes that there are other names. Let us examine two of these, which historically precede the formation of our object, Europe; they take shape as outlines upon which the figure of Europe will trace itself, but without exactly superimposing itself.

The first of these names, "empire," is also a name of the universal as a figure, but the return that it indicates is carried out within a specific regime: the regime of sovereignty. Rigorously, empire is the name of universal sovereignty.[51] The uni*vers*al is not the whole; it is a movement, a *vers*ion or extension turned *toward* [*vers*] something. When it turns around, this movement leaves aside some zones that its development potentially touched. As it comes back to itself, universality produces a remainder. The first figure can thus be completed:

(*f2*)

The remainder that the empire produces has a name: barbarism. It is a word from before the empire—in the precise Roman sense that is going to concern us. Every name partakes of an anteriority—an etymon, metaphor, or borrowing. Every naming is a renaming. Thus barbarism, which stood for a mode of exteriority from before the empire, comes to designate *what remains*, when the empire—the project of universal sovereignty—turns around and is given its figure.

The second name is that of the church. This one too is a term designating the universal as a figure. Within what regime? The "sacred"? Here, the category of the "sacred" is irrelevant. The sacred involves other relations, which we shall examine later on. To determine the universal returning within the church, it is more useful to appeal to its Greek meaning. For the Greeks, *ecclesia* is simply "assembly," a word that is strictly and exactly *political*: *ecclesia* is the assembly of the people, that which constitutes and governs the polis as such. About the church, then, we shall say that it is the return to itself of the universal *within the regime of the assembly*. In the mode of the return, of the figure, the church designates the form or the project of a universal assembly. This returned universal also produces a remainder. What remains outside of the church? Pagans. The pagan is first of all a *paganus*, or peasant. Paganism involves the countryside, because the church is an assembly in a town or city—a polis.

These two terms call for yet another remark. The empire has a seat, which is Rome; and the church has its seat in Rome as well. Between these two figures, a community of the place-name, seat, and base takes shape. What is this place? It is the Roman world, that is to say, *Romanity as world*. But it is also the Mediterranean, the sea between land masses. Finally, it is the Occident, the west, where the sun goes down. We shall have to come back to all these characteristics—and ask ourselves, Why is Rome the place of the joined institutions of the empire and the church, the locus of their conjunction, the unity of their site, without any fusion or confusion between them—all this, in spite of permanent temptations, in spite of the indefinite historical reiteration (in the history of the empire, the church, and then Europe) of the endless caesaro-papist dream, the major fantasy of all European despots? The emperor won't be bishop, nor caesar the pope. What is the reason for this singular articulation, the simultaneous positioning of a same space *and* a separation, a separation inscribed in their topical community, like an internal cut without any scars? What kind of a wound is it; of what and of whom?

*

Let us examine this cut, which disconnects the empire and the church, and separates the assembly from sovereignty. How does this rift come about? In any case, the separation occurs after the Greek "event" (the first transfer). During the classical period, the Greek city is unaware of this divergence: it does not distinguish between sovereignty and assembly—the assembly, and only the assembly, is sovereign.[52] Stating this, of course, requires an anachronism. Our idea of sovereignty has no rigorous equivalent in Greek thought—for reasons that precisely have to do with what we are attempting to think here; namely, that sovereignty, as a *separate* agency, will only be constituted later on. But there is some authority, power, and supremacy, and it is the assembly that holds them. The assembly constitutes the holder of this power from which all the others derive, an agency we now construe as sovereignty. The citizens, unsubjugated agents of political decisions, partake in this supremacy: they are "sovereign," in this sense, over slaves, women, and foreigners—or colonies. The polis thus carries out this sovereignty—which is why sovereignty should not be thought of as such: nothing distinguishes it from the political itself, which is produced as the assembly. This is what theoreticians of the body politic like Rousseau, who never stopped meditating on citizenship *as* sovereignty, will attempt to spell out—irrevocable sovereignty, inalienable in its essence, of the body politic, that is to say, of the people assembled as a body, of the *city*. Sovereignty, then, is exactly the assembly itself, convening.[53]

Now, the city-state is also the city. Of course, to be quite rigorous, one cannot reduce the Athenian body politic to the city of Athens. "Athenians" were the citizens not only of the polis but of Attica, who all had the same status in that regard.[54] The distinction between the demes of the city and those of the surrounding countryside was, however, already making itself felt. This distinction, which the "constitution of Athens" covers up, haunts its institutions and hampers their functioning; and this disjunction of the city and the city-state, still very latent, is at the root of their later evolution, the dissociation that would separate the assembly and sovereignty.[55]

For the characteristic of the following time period is the growth of this tension between the agency of the city (the city-state as city) and the agency of the citizenry (the city-state as body politic). At first this tension is negated and covered up. Rome is the supposedly common name of that city and the title of its successive expansions (colonization, commerce, annexations, and so on). Rome invented a citizenry that was not restricted to the city, since one could be a Roman from anywhere, from any shore of the Mediterranean. "Rome" was thus both within and outside of the city walls. But one difference hangs over this: the new city-state, the scattered body politic of citizens in all parts of the world, *cannot form an assembly*. There is no *assembly of the republic*—despite all of Rousseau's historical and logical contortions to demonstrate the opposite.[56] Only the city-as-town forms an assembly. Now, the republic is no longer the city: it extends to its colonies. What we could say is that the concept of republic consists precisely in the fiction that the city and the colonies are equal in the city-state. The republic is the space known for the unity of the colonies and the central power, the imaginary unique locus of politics freed from the polis as urbanity or *urbs*.[57] The republic is centralist in its essence: it postulates the imaginary unity of the center and the outlying areas, of the metropolitan center and its colonies; it is a city-country [*cité-pays*], the dream of absorbing the whole country (its landscapes, its farmers, its countryside)[58] in the fictitious space of the city-state: of the city and political urbanity.[59] However, should colonization go on and spread out, then it will bring forth a world—or rather, *the* world. Encircled by colonies, the Mediterranean is the Mediterranean *world*, the Roman *world*—the world itself: it is within this movement, little by little, that the world as *mundus* is framed, precisely, and it is no longer the Greek *cosmos*. The substitution of the *world* for the *country*, the constitution of the world as world, exactly designates the point (or the process) at which the republic breaks up and gives way to the empire.[60] The empire, of necessity, is empire of the world or empire over the world: *imperium mundi*.⁶¹ We can find the precise and rigorous formulation of this link retrospectively in Corneille, whose Augustus says:

This empire absolute on land and sea,
This *sov'reignty over the universe* [i.e., over the whole world—Trans.]
This boundless greatness, this illustrious rank
Which by such toil and blood was earned for me . . . ⁶²

This is a rigorous concept of empire: *sovereign* power, exercised over the world, the *whole world*, over land and waterways, shores and sea. It took a flawless clairvoyance to attribute these words to Augustus, who instituted the Empire, the *imperator* whose "reign" or "century" brought the Republic to an end. Corneille knows this passage: in the final part of the play, Livia announces to Augustus that "Rome with a joy both keen and deep consigns / Unto thy hands *the empire of the world*."⁶³

Rome consigns its sovereignty into the hands of the emperor. With this transfer, the distinction is established between Rome the city and Rome the empire, the city and the world, city-space and citizen-space—between *urbi* and *orbi*.

Let us provisionally formulate this new hypothesis:

The world is: what the empire subjugates. (h3)

*

Now, *there is no assembly* of the empire (of the world). Imperial "politics" is "politics" of the world, or world "politics"; and thus, polis without assembly, without *ecclesia*, and without body (politic). The world (or that which is subjected to imperial domination, and sovereignty), as we shall see, may be presented or represented but certainly not convened in a session. *There is no assembly of the world*. If (provisionally, and foreshadowing a later development) we allow ourselves to guess at, suspect, or scent the radical position of coming-to-be-in-common in the assembly,⁶⁴ if we agree to this (to let a useful consequence of this appear), if the assembly reveals itself in this way (as *coming-to-be-in-common*), and if the world, for its part, cannot be assembled, it follows that:

There is no being (in) common of the world—only its (re)presentation. (h4)

There is an empire of the world, a government, a sovereignty of the world, and even politics (without assembly) of the world; but there is no being-assembled. As Rome makes itself into its empire, this is what is lastingly expelled from politics and sovereignty, and thus from the world: the assembly itself, the *ecclesia*, thanks to which the Greeks brought about their being-in-common. Another *ecclesia* gathers, then, convening as strangers in the world, heterogeneous in relation to the world, and transcendent. It establishes itself as *assembly of the people of God*, because his "kingdom is not of this world." With the empire (of the world) established upon (or as) the impossibility of assembling, it constitutes this gathering as the alterity that escapes and transcends it. This foreignness, with the common-being that it brings, moves outside of the realm that the empire governs, that is, outside of the world. And so the assembly of the people of God, the new *ecclesia*, is born. The new church of the people of God—called Christian—is the church of that time, the *age or epoch of the world*. It constitutes itself before the world as that which doubles it and goes beyond it. It duplicates the world, borders it, is coupled to it, never blending, never a part of it. Present to the (secular) world or withdrawn from it (by its rule), the church covers it, and overlaps with it in its duality and difference. The name of this paradoxical extension over the entire face of the world, the attribute of this relaunched rewinding universality is *Catholic*. The Roman Catholic Church: the universal turned back toward itself, given figure—as assembly.

Sovereignty (of the world) and assembly (of the people) are thus formed as rival and separate regimes. But either one can exist only in their coupling, produced by the division of a single body. Each one—like the tiny beings in Plato's allegory—dreams of returning to oneness and repairing origins. Church and empire are twinned but inverse productions: sovereignty without assembly, assembly without power. Church and empire will not leave each other alone; they will not stop being rivals and trying to annex each other, with each pope wanting to be sovereign and each emperor dreaming of being pope. The theologico-political: this is the theoretical name of this mimetic and interminable ambiguity, the name of that which governs our history, at least as history of this world, and it is the name of a double formation, which conditions the future possibility of Europe, and where its figure will come to rest. The theologico-political is the space within Romanity where the—mimetic and unhappy—rivalry between church and empire is played out. Rome is the name of their site (of their seat) and of their (common) place. Rome is the (proper) name of a (common) locus: the theologico-political.[65]

*

Two *eras or time periods* appear on either side of Romanity, and Rome provides the passage between them. The first and older one is the *age or epoch of the assembly*. It does not encompass all that precedes Rome, but only the phase that I shall conveniently term "Hellenic,"[66] determined as a political era; that is, the era of the city-state as polis, able to form an assembly, which we should call *ecclesial*, reviving in this word all its pre-Christian semantics, which Christian ecclesiality inherits and yet conceals and masks. The second and modern era is the *age or epoch of the world*, the imperial era of the world, the time of the world as an area of submission to the empire. Our fourth hypothesis (*h4*) proposes to think of it as the *age or epoch of (re)presentation*: because the world, unable to assemble, can only be (re)presented. (Re)presentation is what happens when the assembly disperses. (Re)presentation is certainly political, as Rousseau complained. But it is also, accordingly, (re)presentation of the world. The world is (re)presented because it is not gathered. That which assembles is the polis. That of which there is an assembly is the polis. Confluence toward the *ecclesia*[67] is coming-to-be-common; it is the gathering of the political, its bodification [*faire-corps*].[68] This gathering is the space of an *us*: citizens, Athenians. There is no *presentation of the world* in this, but rather a *cosmos*, the arrangement of celestial spaces in or under which the assembly sits; and in front, no one—no world [*aucun monde*]. Just us—and the cosmos above and all around. The world is what happens when assembling has become impossible because of its extension and colonial expansion. This, and only this, should be (re)presented.

To clarify this hypothesis, let us show one of its consequences. Each of these eras has produced its own "art," though, to be rigorous, we should amend this statement from the start: while both have indeed produced the kinds of effects that we call "arts," only the second and modern era has produced them *as arts*.

The age of the assembly produced the theater, or more exactly tragedy and comedy—which we, and not ancient Greeks, call theater. *Theater* to them (at least during the classical era, the time of theater and assembling) is the name of a part of the space of their dramatic festivities: the part of the "public," the bleachers where the viewers gather, the gathering setup, and the viewing place. We moderns are the ones who call the art of representation "theater"; the Greeks spoke of tragedy and comedy. They were festivals during which competitions, contests, and games took place, competitions for tragedy and comedy, contests and games like those in gymnastics, music, or poetry. What is the contest and what is at play in tragedies and comedies? It is the genealogy of power (on stage), and the seal and the voice of the common (in the chorus). Theater is the political *put into play* (put on as play?)—it is theater ecclesial in its principle, produced as the (re)production of the assembly.[69] Theater puts into play the coming-to-be-common. At the theater, the world—told and commented—is not (re)presented.

The age of the world produces the image, for the world is that for which there can only be (re)presentation. The world is under the authority of the empire; it has constituted itself as world by excluding from its scope the possibility of assembling and thus of coming-to-be-common. The world, powerless to gather, can only be convened before a gaze—frontally, as spectacle. The world presents itself as spectacle of the world. The world is that of which there is an image: *imago mundi*. It is within this framework that we should think of the progressive constitution of painting, for example, as a factory of images: during post-Roman times, as frontal presentation of the world to the gaze, on a flat surface standing before us. This is a major event: at a given moment in history, one set out to present the world in images, as a spectacle, *as that which presents itself—there, in front—to the gaze*. Such a showing is quite different from cartography, for example, which describes the world in itineraries and paths that have been traveled or will be,[70] or from the painting of objects merely presented in themselves and primed (colors, drawing of the surfaces), or composing "scenes" or episodes from life. In a specific determined time period, this strange idea asserted itself—that the world presents itself as a spectacle and can be shaped on a flat surface set before one's eyes. This idea is far from obvious, despite the irreversibly familiar way in which we deal with it now: this idea demands first of all that one should change over to the thought that the world is *in front*. Strange hypothesis: the more obvious way is to assume it to be *around* oneself—in the front, the back, and on the sides. One had to come up with the idea of the *world right there in front* [*monde là-devant*]: as a spectacle offered to perceiving eyes, the only organs that are really frontal, whereas the ears open up a lateral world; the senses of smell and touch, a surrounding world; and taste, an interiorized world that has been absorbed, savored, or sucked. This idea arises in great part *with* a certain constitution of painting, or the constitution of a certain kind of painting, that is to say, with the production of the world as image, as a spectacle that is shown. *It is a strange idea*, if only for this reason: in order for the world to present itself right there in front, in order for it to be what I am seeing there before me, for the world to be in front of me and I before it, face to face, I have to be outside of it; this presupposes the world outside of me. The world of which there is an image or spectacle is outside of myself and faces me; and soon enough such is the idea of *mundus*. Of the *cosmos* we are a part, or a center: it includes and surrounds us. The cosmos can globally enclose an "us" that questions it, an assembly—and thus, a theater. One had to exit the cosmos for the world to be presented to me, frontally, as image and spectacle. This is what I call the invention of painting here.

It is an idea foreign to theater, because the theater is not from that time. The idea of painting, which is to say, the idea of the image, necessarily comes after Romanity and is written into its legacy. If the only world is the world subjugated to the empire, and if the only image is of the world, then the image is imperial, or post-imperial, in its very possibility. The imperial sway of the world is putting on shows of the world that it subjugates. The world must be imaged, imagined, presented as a spectacle, as soon as one is no longer dealing with this *we* involved in politics, and that the assembly—as *coming-to-be-common*—constitutes. Politics is always the affair or coming-here of a *we*. Politics is us, irrevocably so.[71] By contrast the world is what presents itself—there—as a spectacle. The world is the system of images of the world, whereas politics is us. That is why theater suits the era (or eras) of the assembly. *As for images, they circulate during empires.*[72]

4. The Holy Roman Empire

We are now equipped with three figures (of the universal). Two are bound together: church and empire. The third, Europe, follows them. Unsurprisingly, they have a few attributes in common. An unavoidable question then arises: how did we move from the former to the latter? The question remains, even supposing that the church and the empire are contemporaneous and in accord (the name of this articulation being Rome). How are we to understand the way in which Europe follows (imperial and ecclesial) Rome, if it is true that Europe is in fact the inheritor of Rome, while not strictly and plainly Roman?[73] My fifth hypothesis intends to answer this question:

Europe configures itself facing Islam. (h5)

Let us look closely at this hypothesis. It points to the movement of *self*-figuration of Europe (the act of shaping *itself*), carried out in "facing" or being face-to-face with [*face à*] Islam. What does "facing" mean? It refers to the face. In French, *face* is *visage*. Being "face-to-face" means being "vis-à-vis."[74] *Facing* is the face-to-*face*, the con-frontation of two beings facing each other, one facing the other, the other facing oneself. The con-frontation is played out in the *vis*ual (vis-à-vis), the vision of the face of the other, as visible, or as visage. The face-to-face is set up through the gaze toward the other and the gaze of the other. At play in the face-to-face is the movement of the specular constitution of identity, its becoming-visible: its double formation in the image of the other before oneself, and in the image of oneself as an other. The face-to-face begets and captures the image of oneself *as* this other—image-identity, in other words, and portrait.[75] To say that Europe configures itself facing Islam is to say that the movement constituting Europe as a figure (as return to itself, self-image, and identity) is carried out vis-à-vis the otherness of Islam, and that the relationship Europe-Islam (and back again, Europe-Islam-Europe), the specular formation of mirrored images, is the primordial relation of identity, constituting Europeanism;[76] and that Europe thus takes Islam to be its most essential other. Europe's identity forms vis-à-vis Islam, facing it. This hypothesis calls for three immediate remarks.[77]

First, it amounts to saying that Europe is not a patch of land confronting various exteriorities (Asia, America, and so on), of which Islam is simply one. What I propose is to think that Europe comes about in the way it does (which is to say, as this figure we call Europe; *this* conformation of the return to self of the universal) in the confrontation with a determined and specific otherness, namely, Islam's.

Second, this posits that Europe's relation with Islam is not a secondary exteriority affecting a Europe that is already formed, but rather calls on

Europe's memory (a repressed memory or anamnesis) of its *own* identity constitution as a return—positing, then, that this repression is a kind of primary repressed memory, as it were.

Third, to assert in this sense that Islam is Europe's other is neither to consign Islam to an essential exteriority in relation to European history nor to exclude it from the definition of Europe as an alien outsider. On the contrary, it is to inscribe the relation with Islam into the heart and deepest place of the movement of identification of Europe as such. Repressing Islam, for Europe, is repressing the gesture that forms it: it is repressing that which, from its birth onward, establishes Europe as the failure of its projected universality, the interruption and reversal of its process (of the universal as expansion, bringing on Europe)—repressing that which *constitutes* it as a return and a retreat: its *very being itself.*

What, then, does this fifth hypothesis propose? It deals with the following analysis. The breakdown of the politico-theological complex of the empire-church in Rome should be understood as unfolding throughout three sequences of events, three fractures, one opening in the north, the second in the south, and the third in the east.[78] Indeed, in the dislocation of Romanity, there is no rift in the west—not yet, it is too early. Romanity has no west at its border—its world is the Occident, the absolute west. These three fractures are distinct, and each breaks the Roman world following a singular process. Let us try to describe their fracturing.

Invasions in the north—but the future of this fracture will not be to delimit Europe; it will not trace its outline. The fracture of these invasions will draw a line along an *internal* rift, within what will become established as Europe (at a later date). The invasions do not cut Europe off from its outside, but bequeath to it a tension that will split it internally (later on, after it is constituted). These invasions are not what shapes Europe's difference, and they do not lead to the criterion that will distinguish Europe from the *rest of the world*. They spark an *internal difference* in Europe, which will be visible at its core after it is formed.

This division opposes Germans and Romans. It will be at work for a long time—and it still is. It is the north-south fault line *within* Europe. In the process of constitution that I am trying to relate, Germans and Romans will be Europeans—soon. This line is not a borderline between Europe and an exterior north. Europe has no external north at all—besides the North Pole, "end of the world." The only north Europe knows is internal—namely, Germanity, so-called *northern peoples*, mythologies, cultures and languages, which will be part of the European inheritance and inscribed in its figure, as an interior difference. The north is not what separates Europe from its other. And let us recall that during the time period of which we are speaking—the age of invasions, the "High Middle Ages"—there was no formed Europe, but only the world, engaged in the—still blurry—process of taking apart its Roman constitution.

How does this complex assemblage fit together? the apparent destruction of Romanity by these invasions, and yet the production of Germanity as an inside of Europe? The reason for this is fairly clear. The waves of "barbarians" are attacking something as a whole, namely the empire-church—the theologico-political complex. But their fight produces two very differentiated effects: claiming victory over the empire, they subject themselves to the church. They convert to Christianity and adopt the religion of the defeated ones. The invaders (the "Germanic tribes") will thus carry on a rather complex relationship with the Roman legacy. They will be both insiders and outsiders: outside of the empire, and inside the church—and this is going to inflate the theologico-political difference in the history of later centuries, keeping it in place and bringing it to the fore. These new dealings will be a component of Europe—and this is why, in my view, it is inaccurate to define Europe, consistently, as Roman. Europe will be made from a singular assemblage, from the inside and the outside of Rome, with the presence in its midst of Germanic people, politically[79] non-Roman and ecclesiastically Roman—a fault line later re-produced within Europe, as a political borderline (with the German question and its various diffractions) *and* a religious one (with the Reformation and its consequences). But this double tracing, which Europe inherited from the invasions, will pass *into* Europe, splitting it at its core.

Now, it is interesting to note that during this time (in the heart of the "Middle Ages") a fiction arises, which will be very active: it is a general synthesis of the elements gathered in this space. This synthesis would aim, at first, at the unification of the theologico-political—that is, the reunion of the church and the empire, the empire turned ecclesial: the Holy Roman Empire. It also would like to be a reunion of the north and the south, of the invaders and those invaded, a synthesis of Romanity and Germanity. This fiction will thus bear the name of these elements: the Holy Roman Empire of the German Nation. *But this synthesis will be a failure.* There will never be an effective reunion of those four components; this name will always bespeak a pretension of the entity thus named, much more than it will describe its reality. The synthesis will never happen as such—only as a politico-religious fiction. It is Europe, precisely, that will take shape in its place. Now, while Europe may well be a Romano-Germanic composition (the Roman-German difference being an internal one), *it will never be a Holy Roman Empire*. There will not be any European Holy Roman Empire, despite this insistent fiction, and attempts to create one by Charles V, Napoleon, and even, in a sense, the Third Reich.[80] Why will the double figure of the Holy Roman Empire remain powerless to generate Europe as Europe and to configure it? It is because Europe designates the return to itself of the universal in accordance with another modality, another regime, different from those that these names convey. Europe gives figure to (turns around) the universal neither as empire nor as church—neither as sovereignty nor as assembly.

In other words, Europe is neither a kingdom nor a people.

5. Straits

Let us examine the second fracture dislocating Romanity, or the Roman world—the world as Roman. It is the fault line that opens up in the south [*midi*]. Islam arrives in the Roman space from the south, in a way that one could describe as exactly symmetrical to the arrival of the invaders—the "barbarians"—in the north. And yet the two events have a profoundly different impact. In what way? Insofar as Islam, when it penetrates the Roman world, does not become caught up in it, neither in its political nor in its religious mode. Islam functions *as* a complete theologico-political exteriority. Like the northern ones, the southern invaders fight against the authority of the empire, and subdue it wherever they are victorious. But they do not convert. They register in the space of this world *as* the irruption of a total heterogeneity, which revokes the theologico-political system and all its constitutive duality. Islam is the impervious stranger in its opposition to Rome.

(Does this mean, in truth, that for Rome Islam is a pure, essential exteriority? *Precisely not*. The relationship—religious and political—that it strikes up with the Roman world is deeply complex. It is even precisely because its exteriority is much less "essential" that its lack of submission will be stiffer. The "Germanic tribes" pouring into the Roman territory know almost nothing about this world. The Muslims know a great deal—*and have even constituted themselves as such*, in certain ways, *by refusing and revoking this*.[81] That is why their struggle will be more global—in a political and religious sense—while the "Germanic tribes" undergo Christianization. Muslim exteriority vis-à-vis Rome is radical because it is based on their originary kinship. Between them, there is no heterogeneous essence, but rather a radical conflict—something altogether different.)

Islam is this outside-of-Rome that irrupts within its space and shatters it. The Germans had also previously smashed the empire. But by converting to Christianity, they redrew an internal split at the core of Romanity, doubling and accentuating the theologico-political difference. Islam shows its religious as well as its political difference: its inscription in the Roman world thus traces a purely spatial or geographical limit. Islam's intrusion shatters the unity of the Roman space by opening a breach that separates the north and the south, henceforth set against each other as the north and the south of the sea. Something in the essence of Romanity is here torn up for good. For the Roman world, the sea was the common place—a locus of unity and exchange. After this rift, the sea becomes the border—a limit and an obstacle. Islam pushes the Roman space onto the shore and onto *land*. Henceforth the sea is going to be the in-between of worlds, the hollowed-out place in the world [*creux-de-monde*], that delimits these two facing land masses. The inscription of Europe happens precisely in this process. *Europe is exactly this: Romanity (the church and the empire) pushed back toward the land*, the (Roman) world re-territorialized. And since I am positing that the figure is the return, it is necessary to note, perhaps surprisingly, that Europe—the return to itself of the universal—is a return toward the land and to the land, through the very gesture that inscribes its difference and traces its figure. This return is a production of origin: the land, as land, was not there at the beginning. Nothing at the beginning was defined as land. Though there was some land, there was also water—ports: anchorages and voyages. The return to the land is the movement of (re)territorialization; it constitutes the land as the supposed origin toward which one must come back. The return to the land is supposed to be (is substantivized or subjectivized as) the primordial, original land, land of the fathers, of origins and ancestors—the fatherland. The return to the (supposed) land is a configuration of a territory, a production of fatherland. It is what happens here to the universal, and what happens to it *as* Europe: facing the irruption and invasion of Islam as politico-religious outsider, it represses and pulls back (returns) in its self-directed movement (toward its selfsame self, self *as* same, the return of its movement toward itself as identification)—through the production and configuration of its (supposedly) initial land.

Europe is the land-related figure of a fatherland of the universal. (h6)

This territorial (re)figuration produces two kinds of related but distinct effects. First, an effect of *continentality*. What is configured in this process is exactly Europe as a continent, keeping to its land masses, and limited to their boundaries: continentality, here, means containment. The Europe that is de-termined is Romanity turned continental, Romanity contained. And this is what makes for the extreme symbolic power of the tightest maritime boundaries of this separation by water, points eminently suited to representing the vis-à-vis or face-to-face relationship of Europe and Islam: the straits, or narrows, of Gibraltar and the Bosporus.[82] And that is why, ultimately, after much uncertainty, the border (of Europe—the idea as well as its territorial form) stabilized there, rather than in Granada or Smyrna.

Secondly, there is an effect of originarity, or *fatherland effect*. The fatherland is not the land insofar as it is surrounded by water or a borderline; it is the ancestral land. The origin is what one supposes to be the beginning of genealogy, the point of the first ancestor. But there has never been a first ancestor: all of them had fathers. Which one, then, makes up the first one, the original ancestor, the ancestor at the origin? It is the one *buried there*, and he is revered. The founding (of a fatherland) is the burial or terrestrial in-terment of the origin. And this is the very gesture—the radical root-gesture—of any *founding*: the lowering into the ground, the foundation—that is, into the soil or land—of that which will constitute the origin.[83]

Now, these two effects will not lead to the same things, even though both sets of consequences are obviously related. Europe's continentality, in particular, could have been an obstacle to its worldwide vocation, as it re-launched (in its colonizing ways) the values of universality, if Europe had not also been able to boast of its status as the land of the origin and the place of foundation—the fatherland—of the universal. This is where all the rhetorical statements about spiritual Europe, which is not and yet also is continental Europe, will be able suitably enough to take root. Let us recall Husserl's ambivalence about this, shifting his ground at the same time or before many others.[84] Europe is thus the figure of a return to the land, as a retreat to continentality, but also a return to the origin, that is, a production of origin, the origin of the universal, the foundation, the initial takeoff of the idea of universality.

It becomes understandable why the Greek name "Europē" was applied to this entity when it was configured toward the end of the "Middle Ages."[85] (1) If "Europē" designates a depth of land into which one plunges, a land without boundaries—rather than terrestrial masses surrounded by water, or islands, or peninsulas, or land presenting itself to someone entering it who is coming in from the sea—this name could resonate with a (re)territorialization, the process by which Rome is pushed away from the sea and onto its shores. (2) If Europe designates the land one enters and into which one sinks in a movement precisely coming from Asia across the straits—if Europe's name, then, comes from Asia Minor, that is, the southeast—from this region and in the direction of this axis, this name had been especially available to feature the retreat of Romanity, since Islam's forward push was carried out at that time, in great part precisely there, and in this direction.

But one can doubtless also ask oneself what strange relationship associates Europe as the fatherland (of the universal)—this figure of the land of origins and the ancestral soil—with the myth of Princess Europē abducted from Asia. Indeed, there is a problem: for the European imaginary, Europe is Europe, and that is all. We have thus seen that Herodotus expressed surprise at the myth that makes Europē not a real European. But at another level, one can say that the myth reveals something conveyed *beneath* the idea of fatherland: namely, that the first ancestor, the ancestor who was buried, is the *first one buried* here—and therefore he came from elsewhere. We can find traces of this *foreign provenance* in many originating figures (e.g., Abraham, Quetzalcoatl, Aeneas), perhaps in all of them. If the founding ancestor always comes from elsewhere to become a founder, and to be buried there as the origin, what outlives him, then, is the complex and doubtless infinite play of comings and goings. We can see this movement with Europē's basket. When she goes to play with her friends, she is holding a basket of gold, the work of Hephaestus, that had been given to her collateral ancestor Libya, and this basket is embellished with a drawing that the poet describes at length.[86] Io is the figure on the basket—another woman whom Zeus abducted. But Io's abduction turns Europē's around in two ways. First, Zeus is not the bull: it is Io who is the heifer. Second, the sea voyage, which the ornamental motif on the basket depicts in detail, takes place in the opposite direction: from Greece (Argos) to the banks of the Nile—where Io becomes a woman (again). Now, this tale supposedly predates the other one, since it decorates Europē's basket. Europē's abduction, a *mise en abyme*, is given its form (again) as a return: there had been, before that, a woman abducted from Greece toward Africa (or the Nile, seen as the exact boundary between Africa and Asia);[87] she was abducted *as* an animal and later on—over there—transformed into a woman.[88] Afterward, it was the turn of a (the) sleeping woman to be abducted and to come to Crete: to the midpoint [*mi-lieu*] of the sea, the median between continental areas, where the whole story starts. But all these figurations, abductions, and returns pertain to the element of myth: the re-constitution of the beginning as origin. For *us*, the beginning comes later, in the middle of seas, the world, and history—in *the element of transport*.

6. On Transport

We can now better see what the figure of Europe is opposed to, or rather follows, that which precedes it and that it inverts and makes into a figure. What this (territorial) figure follows, that which reverses itself in it and retreats as the (re)territorialization of the universal, is that which precedes and underpins all forms of the universal, the universal prior to or beneath any figure, that is to say, upstream from any return to self: *the universal as transport*. It is the very concept of Romanity, or its "essence," as it were.[89] Rome "invents" the universal—for Romanity is its very movement, as the generalization, expansion, and homogenization of areas—through the practice, the openings, the relationships, and the becoming-world of transportation. That is why the space that is properly Roman—its interior—is the sea: an expanse specifically for transport, a kind of place for "pure" transportation. Water is the moving element, the element of mobility. On water, everything moves, nothing stays in place. What water carries is always floating, drifting, flowing, and moving from place to place: anchors are what fixates things, and being fastened to the land—the land at the *bottom*, grounding the *sea*. Every ground, every foundation is terrestrial, by essence. The maritime element does not found anything; it merely carries: it transports and displaces.[90] The sea, determined as principal space (inside-space, principle-space, or center, which it is for the Roman world), prompts the thought of an original transport, which is to say, a thinking of the origin as transport, or even more so, of a transport of the origin.[91] The supposedly primordial terrestrial or earthy element on the contrary calls for a thought of foundation, or of the grounding origin (the buried origin), the archi-origin: of the fatherland.

That is why the fairly conventional thesis according to which Rome did not invent anything (not mathematics, philosophy, history, or politics, which are Greek; nor monotheism or Christianity, which are Jewish),[92] but transported everything (displacing, extending, generalizing, or constituting it as a world) is true only with the notable exception of the specifically Roman invention of Roman law.[93] It is not the idea of justice, of course, or trials, summoning procedures, judicial rulings, but the idea of rights and the law [*droit*], *jus* (for which there is strictly no Greek word), the judicial as such—because the judicial is *the regulation of transactions and transfers,*[94] of transportation and exchanges, or more exactly of exchanges that are mediated by transportation, or nonimmediate exchanges. Exchanges in an immediate neighborhood, involved only within the space of their proximity, could not care less about the judicial. The judicial touches them only when they are enclosed or in the grasp of a generality that the transitivity of different, separate, and remote spaces produces. The judicial shapes the compatibility and the translatability of spaces: and translation is another designation for transport. It is therefore as the law of transactions and transport that the judicial turns into the reflection of universality. The judicial is the *abs-traction* of the universal. The judicial tractably draws (extracts, abs-tracts) the universal from places, as their transitivity or mutual translatability. *The abstract universal is judicial*, even if the abstraction that is its tool is developed before the empire.[95]

*

It is relevant for the church as well as the empire that Romanity should be the space of transportation.

What is the empire? It is what happens when the republic no longer manages to govern the world. The republic is suitable for one country. The empire is the submission to a single domination and the same commanding structure of the near and the distant. The empire is the regulated unity of remote spaces—the authority of the *imperator*, the general in command of faraway armies, who comes home triumphantly. *Imperare* means to command as a master, but more strictly, to take measures and engage in preparations, or to force to produce, and thus to require a delivery or to requisition: *imperare arma, obsides, frumentum, pecuniam*.[96] *Impero* includes *in* and *paro, parare*. *Parare* means to prepare and to strive to obtain or procure, and thus to obtain with money or buy.[97] The *imperator* is also the supplier or furnisher. The emperor furnishes the world with the unity of its provisions and resources. It homogenizes the space of their transportation and unifies the rule of their transactions.[98]

This is also true of the church, and first (but not only) because Christianity is the imperial religion.[99] The church is constitutively imperial—*long before the emperor's conversion*. The church is necessarily built in the same space as the empire, that is, in the world as the *Roman world*. The church has been cohabiting with this world, one could say, since their simultaneous birth: here, I take very seriously the theological definition of the church as the assembly of disciples, since the event of the Last Supper. Not in order to give credit to its historical reality necessarily (though this is not excluded), but rather to think of its *constitution*.[100] Now, this legendary event takes place during the very formation of the empire. The birth of Christ bisects the dated span of the "reign" of Augustus, who instituted the imperial regime: the *imperium* of Augustus lasts from 23 B.C.E. to 14 C.E. Christ preaches and dies during the time of Tiberius, the "first" emperor in the legal sense. The constitution of the church and the empire are strictly contemporaneous.

But the actions of Paul, who mainly instituted it, mostly mark the native inscription of the church within Romanity, as the space of transport. Paul is a (proud) Roman citizen: he is, exactly in the imperial and universalist sense of the word, as a non-Roman Roman, a Roman from outside Rome or even Italy. He is a Roman of the judicial universal, eyeing the world in this way, and roaming through it accordingly. He is a traveling man of the sea—we know all that the church owes to these ceaseless crossings, from shore to shore: its constitution as universal church. Paul is the man who writes, "there is neither Jew nor Greek," barbarian or Scythian (circumcised or uncircumcised, slave or free, man or woman), and he writes this four times;[101] that is to say, he transcends the "national" (or at least the native), and moves toward the universal. Paul *writes* this in his *letters*. It has been said that the epistolary arts are one of Rome's few literary inventions.[102] Few or not—it matters little here: if this art stamps "literature" with a seal of Romanity, it is obviously because the letter or epistle is the literary genre of transportation, something written at a distance to be read at a distance, to be carried and conveyed all the way to the reader, and that discloses itself as an art (unlike oratory or dramatic arts) through this necessary portage. The fact that Paul's writings are Epistles, which are carried from shore to shore so as to unify the communities that border the sea in the universality of their church, is the seal indelibly marking Paul's actions and thought as pertaining to the Roman world, the network of (maritime) roads, voyages from port to port, and crossings.

7. What Is an Island?

It is time to say a little more about the relation of land and sea. Here, Hegel opens the way:

As the firm-set earth, or the soil, is the basis of family life, so the basis of industry is the sea, the natural element which stimulates intercourse with foreign lands. By the substitution for the tenacious grasp of the soil, and for the limited round of appetites and enjoyments embraced within the civic life, of the fluid element of danger and destruction, the passion for gain is transformed. By means of the sea, the greatest medium of communication, the desire for wealth brings distant lands into *an intercourse, a law-based relationship that introduces the contract.*[103] In this traffic is found one of *the chief means of culture*, and in it, too, trade receives world-historical significance.

Note.—Rivers are not natural boundaries, though people have in modern times tried to make them so. Rather do they, and more especially the sea, bind men together. That Horace (*Carm.* I. 3) is wrong when he says: ". . . deus *abscidit* / Prudens Oceano dissociabili / Terras, . . ."[104] is shown by the general fact that basins of rivers are inhabited by one nation or race. This is proved even more conspicuously by the relations of ancient Greece with Ionia and Magna Graecia, of Brittany with Britain, of Denmark with Norway, of Sweden with Finland and

Lapland, in contrast with the slight intercourse obtaining between the inhabitants of the coast and those of the interior. We have only to compare the position of the nations who have frequented the sea with that of the nations who have avoided it in order to discover what a means of culture and commerce it really is. Observe how the Egyptians and Hindoos have become dull and insensible, and are sunk in the grossest and most shameful superstitions, while all the great aspiring nations press to the sea.[105]

The problematic center of this page is a *thesis about waterways*: oceans and great rivers are not natural boundaries, "though people have in modern times tried to make them so," an allusion to Fichte's statements about such boundaries.[106]

The debate between Hegel and Fichte bears on the function of waterways. For Fichte, aquatic masses separate: they dissociate precisely the things that need to remain separated, that is, "whole political entities" [Gm., *politische Ganze*]. For Hegel, on the contrary, waterways unite. To support this assertion, Hegel adduces three kinds of arguments. First, people or tribes settle in the basins of great rivers, which bring and keep them together, constituting their very principle of unity.[107] This evidently could apply to the Nile or the Ganges, and would call for—at least—a more nuanced view than the violent historico-geographical fantasy in Hegel's text. Secondly, the peoples living along the coasts of the Aegean, the Ionian Sea, the English Channel, the Skagerrak, and the Baltic have numerous and lively relations among one another. The Mediterranean, overall, is a particularly rich and differentiated example of this.[108] Third, there is the rather significant fact that these relations created by the watercourses, established from one shore to the other of rivers and the sea, often connect the inhabitants of the two shores more closely than is the case with peoples of the coast and the interior.[109]

Following Hegel here, we may then ask ourselves, *What is a harbor or port?* The standard idea of a port makes it the outlet of a land area toward its exterior: the means by which a region looks and communicates across the sea, toward other land masses. The port is the result of the land's movement toward the sea, or the river, so as to open up to an exteriority. But by reversing one's look, one may think instead that a port is an establishment founded by people who came from the sea, a beachhead in an unknown area, which needs to be surveyed, a stopping point along a sea route. This happens to be the history of numerous harbors: Marseille in France, for example, was a Phoenician and then a Greek city long before it became a continental city—if it ever did. Marseille is to be understood as a city relating to the sea (just as coordinates are related to an axis), relating to maritime routes much rather (and indeed much earlier) than to the land. A port is a *seaport*—from sea to sea, with a stop.

But it is necessary to point out that it is not just the function of water (water-as-limit, water-as-barrier, or water-as-gatherer) about which Hegel and Fichte differ; it is the conception of that which is separated or joined by water. In other words, the two visions *are not about the same people*. For Fichte, the people are of the land, defined by it, and thus contained around their terrestrial foundation—something Hegel perceptively identifies as *family values* from the outset in the passage quoted above. They are people bound to the stability of their being, people *as being*, fundamental and founded. This is exactly what Fichte calls a "whole political entity," and it is not surprising that this "whole" finds its prescription in nature even before it exists politically: "Certain parts of the *surface of the earth, together with their inhabitants*, are visibly *determined by nature* to form whole political entities."[110] Nature has shaped the destiny of these territories, and their inhabitants, and has compelled them to constitute political entities—political entities of the land, naturally, since their first foundation. If one reads this interpretation with a Hegelian eye, one has to relate the foundation and the family: as noted, the foundation is the burial place of the origin, which is to say, the locus of the ancestor's tomb. The idea of land posits the people in their being as an ancestral genealogy, as ethnicity, and as race.

Conversely, Hegel observes that people gather and scatter around water: therefore, the people are that which spreads, from the water, over the banks or shores. They are people whose center and heart is maritime. The being of the people has to be thought in a marine setting, the medium of transportation; that is their very nature and inmost essence. Strictly, they are *people without grounding [peuple sans fond]*, they have no boundary markers, no boundaries: what can have bounds is a land mass, relating first of all to its heart or center, that is, its grounding—its foundation, its buried origin, the burial place of ancestors who have initiated its history. The sea is (in) another element: "The sea itself is limitless, and it is not conducive to the peaceful and restricted life of cities as the inland regions are."[111] In the debate between Fichte and Hegel, what is at stake is not just a thesis about water, or, with it, diverging positions about the idea of borderlines. What is in question is the essence of the people—as a being grounded in its land, or a wave-borne boundless being without grounding.

To bring out this difference, let us ask, *What is an island?*[112] Two kinds of answers are possible. First, one may think that an island is a land mass in the middle of water, and it is its land (its being-land), outlined by water, that defines and determines its being. In this relationship, as Hegel puts it, "the sea is only the limit, the ceasing of the land."[113]

What about insular people, in this case? They are the people whose being the land begets, from its heart and depths, who reach toward the water, aiming to get out and confront the outside. They are people construed from their inside (their origin, foundation, interiority—their genealogy, the burial of their origin, the fatherland of their ancestors). These people are grounded, tied to their foundation; the political form of this condition, rigorously speaking, is fundamentalism. This relationship can be shown in a figure:

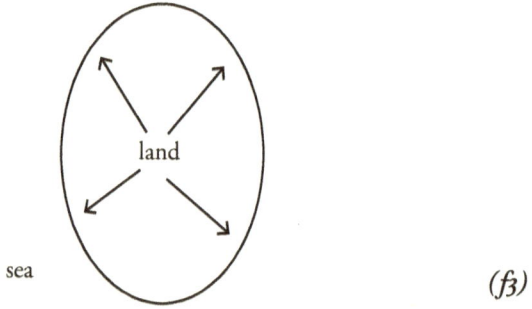

(f3)

But there exists another mode of thinking about insularity, an insularity construed *from the port*. How is a port established? We have suggested that it starts from the sea and its sea routes, as a stop along the way. This is its figure:

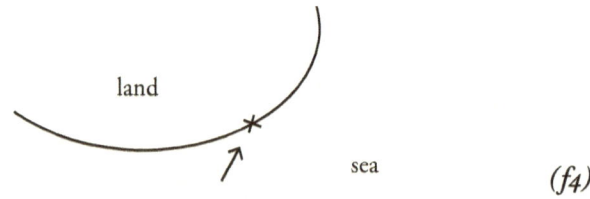

(f4)

After the port is set up, the sea route keeps going, most often along the coast; and in this way one discovers the maritime face of the coastal area. New harbors—each a new stopping place—are established:

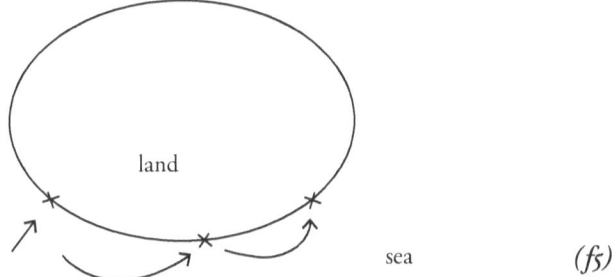

(fs)

An island, then, is nothing but the tracing drawn by a sea route when it returns to one of its ports; it is a land mass encircled by a route, which loops around then closes. In this process, the production of interiority and insularity happens as a result. Interiority (of the inland area) is not a given, from which one might have to exit; it is an outcome, the effect of a meeting: the product of the fact (unexpected for the traveler) that the route, without ever going backward, again finds a port that is already settled. The inside is what the route contains and girds. *Terra firma*, in its insular delimitation, and its enclosure, is a sailor's invention (or discovery). Such is—and we know this story—the whole matter of the *production of America*. The people, then, are the traveling people, who set something up along the way wherever they are stopping. Founding people: instituting harbors, islands, and continents. But foundation occurs when the people want to convert the stopping place into a fatherland: the *Aeneid* is the eminent emblem of this; it is the ever-ambiguous double narrative of Romanity discovering itself as a sea voyage of outlaws and never-returning homeless drifters—but whose epic adventure, precisely, produces some foundation and some origin. Its writing is exemplary in that it uncovers the ambiguity that is constitutive of the desire for a foundation: the desire for an origin, a fatherland, the primariness of the land, and further by the same token the gesture of the production of this origin as the burial of the traveling ancestor, the in-stallation and production of a tomb. One might say the same of westerns as founding film narratives that, by bringing to a halt the journey, the race to conquer, produce the nation. This migratory hypothesis invites us to step away from thinking of the grounding, fundamental, and archaic origin, so as to examine how it was invented and found, as transport and burial of the origin in the discovered land.

8. On Thinking

These pronouncements about transport are just as much hypotheses about thought. A number of formulas that will have seemed peculiar and even inconsequential turns of phrase are, or try to be, *propositions of thought*—pro-positions about thought, about the turns and ways of thinking [*le tour et la manière de la pensée*]. Let us try to pinpoint, and make explicit, a few of these gestures and turns, by taking things up again, as at the outset: about the universal, followed by the return, and then by the figure.

First, *the universal as transport*, a formula that may have come as a surprise. It seems to lack rigor and precision. In the regime of transportation, one would expect to see a description of *the movement of universalization* and universalization as a movement, and one would expect a definition of the universal, if it exists, as the outcome or result of this movement. And if one negates any actual existence of the universal, which is then apprehended as an image, a value, or an ideality, one would rather be inclined to treat these productions as effectuations, or even as imaginary (or axiological, or ideal) compensations of universalization as a real, material, or concrete movement. In a word, movement (transport) would be thought as a production, and the universal as a product. In this sense, "universal" would be the appellation of the transported rather than the transport, the effect of transport conveyed by the transport itself.

Now it is indeed from this setup that we are stepping away. Indeed, it is the universal (and not universalization) that I propose to construe as transport: which is to say, as movement and becoming. It is not the becoming-universal, but the universal *as* becoming, universal-becoming. It is a way of saying that there is nothing to think in the universal except the transport that effectuates it; the universal *is* this very transport and is in no way distinct from what displaces and carries it. The universal *is not even* an image or idea. *There may simply not be any image*—no ideality. Or else the supposed image (supposed-image), in its inmost nature, its constitution, and its being, is something like this: transport—movement, carrying [*portée*].

Secondly, in this same schema and perhaps even more markedly, one may have been astonished by this insistent formulation: the figure is the return. Arguably, it might be more acceptable to consider the figure as the product of the return—its effect or outcome—and the return as a movement of figuration. One might say that the figure is the product of figuration, and it is from this second (inferred) position that the figure precisely negates the movement and presents itself as motionless, as a fixed and static image, as an image of fixity and staticness, an image *as* fixity and staticness in themselves: an effect negating its cause, a production forgotten and negated by its product. And yet, as with the universal, I stubbornly maintain that the figure that turns around the universal is *nothing but* the movement of this return, and that the figure *is* this movement, this very return; and that it would be giving too much credit to its fantasy to imagine that there might exist (even in the imaginary or as imaginary) this presumed fixity to which the figuration leads as to an end. The figure is not the end of the movement of figuration (of the return), the figure *is* this movement; *there is nothing to think in the figure except the movement of return.* There are two ways of putting this. Either there is no imaginary, or the imaginary is this movement. In this sense, the figure still is transport—simply put, it is a returning transport. This was doubtless what could come as a surprise in our first figure (and the others repeating it):

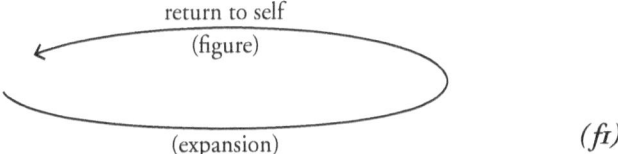

(f1)

The figure has neither beginning nor end; it *is* the movement. The figure is transport without origin or end, which does not mean that it does not produce any stop or port. The figure is always a *traced line figure*, the movement of a point, the production of a graphic, an inscription [*écriture*], or drawing. One must not take the figure at its word when it comes out as fixated, as immediacy and tabular planeness of that which offers itself to the gaze and the blink of an eye. The figure traces itself, builds and draws itself. And even the gaze is a journey and a transfer.

Third, as might be expected, universal transport is also the universal as metaphor—not to reduce it to a "merely" metaphorical value, but to express, as well, that it is exactly insofar as it is metaphorizing that all thinking is transportation, a carrying or conveying of thought. There is, in this, a position of the "originarily" metaphorical character of any proposition of thought, but as transport of the origin: and this does not lead back to any properness, be it ancestral or remote, but on the contrary comes to posit that every gesture of thinking is thinking inasmuch as it transports and therefore metaphorizes. On the condition that one does not miss what such a position implies (or assumes) about metaphoricity itself: because bringing together both values, transport and metaphor, while it is a reminder that transport is also and always metaphorical, also entails that one should hold the metaphor to be an actual, real, and concrete transport—because there is no ideal or image (except through metaphors). *The metaphor is a real transport*, of which there are simply two kinds: onward transport [*transport aller*], or returning transport [*transport-retour*]. Onward-going: in the sense of what goes, how is it going, or life that goes on. As Arthur Rimbaud writes, "It is the sea gone away."[114] Return: figure, transport again, but coming back, turning around, and referring back to itself, to the image of itself, to the self as image; transportation *to* the origin, the foundation, and the presumed genealogy. Yes, *what goes on* is two things, which are different: the universal, and its figure. It is a single movement, but taken, for the former, in its expansion and its spreading—its going onward—and for the latter, in its return—to itself. The universal *as* transport, and the figure *as* return. Which comes down to saying that the movement of the universal—a primary movement, before the figure; a movement from underneath, which carries and transports the entire schema and all (or any) history—exceeds and overflows any universality inasmuch as it is given figure, into any figure whatsoever (sovereignty, assembly, or fatherland), *and in certain respects the very idea itself of the universal, taken here as a beginning along the way*. Europe is one of these—determined—figures of the universal. To understand it and think through it (to discover what there is to think *beneath* its name) is to refer it to its double movement: of going ahead one way, the way life goes; or of returning—the figure of itself, image-itself.

9. Orient

When the Roman world breaks apart, it is through ("Germanic") invasions, from the north, and, from the south, through separation (from Islam). There is nothing in the west—only the sea, without any limit or crossings, a place where the world, together with the sun, drops down, sets, and dies. The Occident, extreme boundary. And to the east?

A third fault line opens there, which bears no resemblance to the two earlier ones—unless it resembles *both*, precisely. It is the one that cuts off the Latin world from the Byzantine world, at the end of the Roman era. This rift shows a singular character. It is construed as a schism between east and west. The empire is dismembered and the church is rent. In each case, a new kind of entity takes shape in Byzantium: it is *oriental*, outside of the Latin world, and yet pretends, outwardly, to re-present its essence. Tradition and legitimacy: Byzantium, the second Rome. The Orient-Occident opposition, which designates the rift, conveys this equivocation: earlier, the Orient was the outside of Rome, which saw itself as the very west itself.[115] The new Orient-Occident division (Byzantium-Rome) carries over to the core of the Roman world (to which Byzantium initially belongs) a previous opposition, which had been external. This fracture is like the reflection and replication within Rome (both church and empire) of the relation between Rome and its outside. The cut is both external *and* internal to Romanity. For a long time, the space forming there (the Byzantine Orient) will remain external *and* internal to its western double—within Europe *and* outside of it.

After the (internal) fault line in the north, and the (external) split at the south, a scission occurs in the east, both external and internal to Europe, and it gives rise to the long-lasting ambiguous form of *eastern Europe*—the Eastern Orthodox Church and Eastern Roman Empire, always laying claim to interiority but excluded. The term "western Europe" is a pleonasm, since Europe is what remains in (or of) the west after the threefold break in the north, the south, and the east—the duplicity of the link with the western alter ego (America) has to do with this doubling (the replication of another self, another selfsame) of the destiny of an absolutely singular Occidentality. As for eastern Europe, it is ambiguous in three ways.

First, there is the absence of a borderline: the borders are clear in the south (the sea and the straits); in the north, the limit is blank (there is nothing to oppose to it). The eastern border is problematic. It is undecidable (is it the Ural Mountains?) and gives rise to infinite variations (is Moscow European?)—and not because there might be any void beyond it, as in the north. Indeed, there are other territories in the east, and other peoples and beliefs.[116] It is Europe's obsessive fear that destruction might come from there: from Asia, the Great Other (barbarians, Yellow Peril, oriental despotism), who may come in at any time, because the limit is neither clear nor closed. Europe, paradoxically, has no continentality in the east—in the sense of boundary markers, continental de-termination, or continence. Europe is the cape of Asia, the cape of the world.[117] Only in the west is it "itself": Europe's identity (its very being, its being-Europe) is its Occident. Hegel writes: "In Asia, the sea is without significance, and the Asiatic nations have in fact shut themselves off from it. . . . In Europe, however, this maritime relationship is of vital importance, and it creates an enduring difference between the two continents. The European state is truly European only in so far as it has links with the sea."[118]

In the west, Europe is de-termined: by its maritime exteriority. And this involves its very identity: a state cannot be European unless it looks to the sea. It is inasmuch as overlooking the sea is not given to them (or that they do not know this given or gift) that the states of Asia are non-European—Asian—and it is inasmuch as they are welded by a continental bond—to Europe. The difference with Europe is this bond. Asia is Asia because it is fastened to Europe in this way, because of its absence of shores.[119] The east of Europe is its non-Europeanism. First ambiguity: Asia is the continuation of the land of Europe, and this continuity sets them at odds.

The second scene of this ambiguity is the relationship with "Eastern Christianity." The Eastern Orthodox Church is the sister of the other one, which is also "Christian"—a branch that grew from the same tree, stemming from the Apostles' meal, the foundation of the church in Rome, and Peter's heirs. But it is Rome's adversary, its rival. Byzantium, the second Rome, assumes that Rome has fallen, and therefore that (Catholic Roman Western) Europe has usurped its destiny and legitimacy. The Eastern "Christians" are brothers of those in the west, but enemies.

So-called communism brought the third ambiguity: *eastern Europe*. This division came on top of the previous one: eastern Europe fit into the space of a certain oriental Christianity—though their borders were not rigorously identical: in the east, there was Catholic Poland, and in the west, Orthodox Greece—though after some uncertain times. But the center was in Moscow, the pole of Orthodox Christianity since the fall of Byzantium: Moscow, the third Rome. Communism, too, was external *and* internal to Europe, internal as the fruit of European history and revolution,[120] and external as the reverse of the Europe that was supposedly democratic, liberal, and bourgeois (western Europe). External *and* internal, as the *cessation* of European revolution, and only soaring with its particular form of bureaucratic totalitarianism in the filiation of this failure, without which communism is incomprehensible.

The east is ambiguous, by essence. The north is inside, the true outside is in the south, and the Orient is a deceitful equivocation. Europe is instituted in the play of this ternary structure: inside north, outside south, undecidable east. Now, it is nothing less than striking that this tripartite division today is *the very shape of the world*, and this may account for the concept of semi-periphery, suggested by Immanuel Wallerstein.[121] Between an internal north (the rich countries of the planet: a north internal to itself, to its idea as the idea of a world construed from the north, from wealth, and thus also from science, technology—or philosophy) and a south supposedly completely other (the global south, always outdone and beside itself, the south of every kind of poverty and distress, pure danger and yet also a fantasy for every kind of youth—demographic youth, youth and future of the world), between these two opposing figures irreducibly facing each other in their powerlessness, unable to utter or produce the world as a whole, the east is the ambiguous figure of that which is neither inside nor outside, neither itself not another, the semi-periphery, which finds its place neither at the center nor at the outer limit. In this sense, the east-west relationship has always been a deceptive front: it was all about the north-south relation.[122] The east was a fiction helping to conceal or contain actual confrontation ("containment" [Fr., *endiguement*], in the sense of continence, *is* an appropriate term).[123] Now that the east is gone, Europe has been facing its real barbarians, the Arabo-Islamic ones, who are now coming (back), all the way to its heart, and showing again the initial exclusion that is the foundation of Europe, its primary repression [*refoulement*]—if Islam makes a comeback in Europe, it is as its (archi-)unconscious. But this scene of the return is no longer only played out in Europe: the south devolves upon all in the world—what is now coming back to the world is the south, as its reverse. Since the east has dissipated, what has come back to the world is its repressed, which stood as the third world but was only the world itself seen from its other side—its founding fracture.

Why then is the world—everyone—haunted by the south? Why does this haunting return [*revenance*][124] devolve not only upon Europe but upon the whole world, the whole empire, imperialism, and imperiality of the world? Is the world an extended Europe, as some colonial-continental dreamers may have believed? No. We must turn the proposition around, put it "back on its feet":[125] "the world" is nothing but—in its imperial(ist) regime—this universal (this transport and metaphorical expansion) of which Europe was the turnaround, the containment, and the continence: the repatriated figure. What comes back again as the south of the world is the *cessation* of the universal that makes up *Europe-itself*. The failure (the reverse) of which Europe is the figure. The revenant, the repressed, of *Europe-identity*. What comes back again is the rest.

PART II   ON NATIONAL REVOLUTION

10. France-Germany

Expansion *and* withdrawal, onward transport *versus* returning transport, metaphoricity-figurality: these couples—linked but strained, with the first term always carrying the other one, and the second turning the first one around—point to the ambivalence inscribed in the native constitution of Europe, structuring its concept. One should not take this primordial equivocation as a logical contradiction, or a dialectic of the essence: it is not a matter simply of saying that Europe is both one thing and its opposite, because of a duality at the origin or an a priori division. It is about a historic and actual process: Europe is a movement that opens up and turns around, and takes the name "Europe" precisely at the point where its opening converts into a turnaround.

Let's assume that this ambiguity works its way into all European productions and leaves its mark there. Europe's inventions—all of them and all at once—will thus be outgoing *and* withdrawn, going *and* coming, metaphorical *and* figural, not because this would apply to everything in this earthly world (on the contrary, we would like to think that this is not the case for everything—all history, all politics), and not because some original sin might hold us captive of duality (and thus not under the rule of a general dialectics), but because the reversion that structures Europe and defines it (Europe being the name of a point of return—as in a quilting- or cross-stitch) shifts over to everything that Europe brings forth—at least to anything Europe produces that is *European*, to all the *European* implementations of Europe. After all, Europe can also give rise to something that escapes it and that does not hold to its concept.

Worldly *and* continental: all that Europe does and makes is this *and* that. Let us try to show this with two European inventions, the revolution and the nation. It is in the light of this double turn—expansive and figural—that we shall interpret each one, in their constitution, their reach, as well as the programmed power of their connection.

*

Romanity, which Islam has pushed back, recedes toward the north, and, shored up in the northwest, it leans on the ocean. This northwestern posture will mark European matters for a long time. In the south and the east, the retreat leaves two territories, Africa and Asia, in enemy hands. But the two borderlines are drawn differently.

The meridional borderline is clear-cut in the end. After Islam's rush to the north, which carried it into Gaul and ensured several centuries of its presence in the Iberian Peninsula, the lengthy Christian reconquest pushed this other hypothesis about the world back toward the south, until the fall of Granada. In 1492, "European" territory in this region was entirely de-Islamized.[1] This did not entail a coupling ipso facto of Christianity and the continent. The process of de-Islamization went on for several decades and overflowed its bounds; soon the Spaniards were taking Oran. In the mind of the reconquerors, this eviction of Islam had to continue at least to the Holy Land. However, the boundary stabilized at the straits in the course of the modern era: Christianity in the north, Islam in the south, with the sea as the frontier between them. Crossing it later on—by way of colonization—would not affect the definition of Europe: moving across would be construed as the expansion of a protective hegemony. Europe-*itself* stops at Gibraltar.

At the Bosporus, the boundary markers are less clear. At the beginning of the fifteenth century, while Christianity is holding up in Constantinople, there are many Turkish settlements to be found in Thrace, and when the Eastern Roman Empire collapses, it is on the western bank, seemingly in Europe, that Islam casts anchor—and it is still there. Indeed, the reflux of Romanity toward the northwest, which carries the Ottomans to the gates of Vienna, will soon be contained and held back, and the border between the two spaces stabilized around the strait, but only *around* it: the border will not coincide with it. Here, the continental limit of Europe remains a topographical idea. Using Gibraltar as a model, one may think of Europe stretching to the Bosporus, with Asia beyond it—but it will never be this way. The Bosporus is in Asia, or Islam is in Europe—a double indetermination, which was never decided and is a testimony that the native bond between Asia and Europe, *at this point* (that is, at the exact spot of its birth), has not been cut. The debate is still going on.²

Actual border or *geo-graphic idea*: at each strait, the boundary markers of Europe thus have a different implication, and here the usage of the Greek term shows its resources. The word "Europē," let us recall, offered a duplicity that enabled it to designate the idea of fatherland as well as of continent. Homer's Europe is the inside, the depth of the earth; and this makes this term available for a patriarchal or patronymic meaning— the land of the first ancestors, of the origin, and thus of the deeply buried foundation. Herodotus's Europe, on the other hand, is the other side of the strait, the shore beyond the *pontus*: and this exactly fits the later designation of the land bordered by water. Why then ultimately choose this Greek term, and this ambiguity—rather, for example, than a final fixation on the Latin word "Occident"? In the complexity of this process (of Europe's conformation as such), we can locate two clues. First, Rome generalizes and universalizes Greece's contribution—not only Greece's, in fact, but it does not matter at this point now. Rome constitutes itself with this "secondarity" [*secondarité*], Rémi Brague asserts.³ Therefore, the Roman reference that the name "Occident" conveys is not very suitable for searching for the foundation and origin of Europe (just as Rome's maritime specificity is unsuitable for any terrestrial imaginary). But above all—secondly—what is falling and needs to give up its place during the collapse of Byzantium because of the Turko-Muslim push *is Romanity itself*, in its last double avatar, the Eastern Roman Empire and the Eastern Orthodox Church. The Roman model is unsuited to designate the new entity arising from this catastrophe, since it is precisely all of Rome that fails and pulls away. As often is the case, one has recourse to the ancient to designate what is new—a gesture of re-naissances, revolutions, and *risorgimenti* [resurgences]: one accounts for novelty (of that which appears and crops up) as the reappearance or resurrection of a past that was buried and comes to light again.⁴ The final disappearance of the Roman Empire frees up a space that becomes available for a new entity: the latter comes forth progressively, invoking an archaic identity. And this is exactly what produces the figure *as a return*—all the more so since this word, Europe, which precisely designates the continent in its alterity, its face-to-face encounter with the enemy on the other shore, lends itself well to the new context in this confrontation: under this name, Europe will not mind reproducing the initial breakup between Greece and Asia, or Hellenes and barbarians, and reenacting the Persian Wars. "Europe" is the land of retreat toward the origin, facing the rush from Asia, which steps across the Black Sea *pontus*. But there is the irony or specular duplicity of the face-to-face encounter, which made the word "Europe" initially, in Greek, designate *Europe seen from Asia*, come from Asia—an Asian desire. Europe, forever offered to the greedy desire of an invader coming across the strait—as if the use of the word carried away the unconscious reversion of its primary repression [*refoulement*]: Europe wishing to be the fatherland of ancestors but *truly* only being the name of the retreat in front of the desire of others—though they brought about her birth.

In this ideo-geo-graphical inscription, Europe thus draws its figure, in the ambiguity of double markings, a continentality bordered by water, *and* a deep land of origins. During the fifteenth century, the shape of Europe is traced and con-formed, becoming clear-cut. The process had begun earlier with the dismantling of the Roman world, and especially with the opening of the fault line in the south, which put the inheritance of Rome face to face with Islam.[5] It keeps going through the eighteenth century, which expounds the European idea, and the nineteenth century, which gives it its colonial expansion,. And it continues today. But it is approximately during the fifteenth century that this process comes into view and *asserts itself*: the middle of the process is there, neither the origin nor the ending, but rather the median zone of its becoming autonomous and assertive—the middle of the movement, the movement along the way running its course, the very zone where one must take things and think them through.[6] By the end of the fifteenth century, Europe had sketched its idea between the two straits, from the Bosporus (indistinct, never clear-cut, never coinciding with the continent-shape) to Gibraltar (sharp, incisive, marked out). Each strait etches an essential feature of this continental figuration, in its own way, as a geographic ideality, on land and on water—Gibraltar, its sharpness; the Bosporus, its uncertainty.

*

Now, just a few decades later, less than fifty years after 1500, and thus in the immediate aftermath of the conformation-stabilization of its figure, Europe breaks down internally. A long crack, slit, or fault line tears it up from the east to the west, like one of those perfectly configured but cracked porcelains or bronzes pulled from the mold. *As if its figure were untenable from birth*, and only showed its external contours under the internal condition of a blowup. This breaking disconnects two pieces that are equally important, two politico-religious entities positioned on either side of a stable and lasting fracture line that separates a Protestant north from a Catholic south. One should mention—to follow the metaphor—that the mold had some air bubbles: the split happened at the time of the perforation of the world toward America. Europe had hardly been drawn up when it spilled outward and broke up inside—on the outside, through the western breach, the fall of the Atlantic wall against which it was leaning; on the inside, through the schizoid split of the Reformation.[7]

For a long time, the Reformation differentiates a Protestant northern Europe from a Catholic southern Europe. The split, which has to do with the state as much as with the church, is set in the course of the sixteenth century, and then will be stable, with Catholic Spain and Italy on the one hand, and Reformed England and the United Provinces on the other—a settled matter henceforth. As many have noted, this fault line approximately redraws the previous dividing line between Germanity and Romanity: this idea is both indisputable and in need of reexamination. But first of all, let us simply look how it is traced out. The dividing line of the Reformation, which shares out the states to the north and to the south, runs across the middle of two entities, France and Germany. For each one the question arises during the sixteenth century: will they fall into the Reformed or the Catholic camp? Their destination is not played out in advance; they lean both ways: Charles V wants to curtail Lutheran dissidence and bring back Germany to the bosom of the Roman Church, or at least to Catholicity;[8] Coligny tilts the French monarchy toward the Calvinist pole—and it is the dread of this shift that sets off the St. Bartholomew's Day massacre.

Thus, the dividing line that disconnects a Protestant north from a Catholic south runs across the midsections of France and Germany. In both cases, this division will be *treated*—but in accordance with two very dissimilar modes, two heterogeneous processes, which will give rise to two different results. During the course of this century and later on, France and Germany will invent two original syntheses, two new historical productions, to solve the religious conflict, which is to say, the fracture between the north and the south (of Europe), that is, the European partition.

Europe is broken, and the split goes *through* France and *through* Germany, and this is where the ways of treating the fracture will be invented: the attempt will be made to re-think, and re-produce, the unity of Europe, first *as* French unity *and* German unity. This is the seventh hypothesis:

> ***French unity and German unity are two ways of treating the politico-religious division of Europe: two hypotheses of European union. (h7)***

Let us examine each one.

11. On the Kingdom

France and Germany were, then, divided by the Reformation. Understanding such a statement evidently presupposes the clarification of some of the notions used here: *Reformation*, of course; the tracing of its division (we shall come back to this); but especially the question (at least in a first phase), What are the entities that the Reformation is tearing apart? Or, what is Germany, and what is France? We are not (not only . . .) aiming at a metaphysical and speculative determination of the essence of these two "nations," but rather at this simple question, *What exactly is the thing that finds itself torn up in this way?* What is the reality and actuality of these two outfits whose politico-linguistic specificity one can vaguely sense? Or further, What are we talking about, exactly, when we are thus discussing "France" and "Germany"?

As far as Germany is concerned, let us leave the matter suspended for the moment. To say that we shall have to come back to it is understating it: the question of the "definition of Germany" reaches far into the analysis of the political constitution of Europe and of the European constitution of politics. Let us be patient. But, *What is France?* This matter seems simpler, at least from this angle. Indeed, what is divided by the Reformation, the entity in which the Reformation produces an effect of schism and splitting, seems easy "empirically" to determine: it is the kingdom of France, France as a monarchy. In the middle of the sixteenth century, this formation displays an observable and attested existence, and the mode of its division is war. The *division of the kingdom* by *religious war* is therefore what is taking place. Kingdom, religion: in order to define "France," these are twin notions that we shall have to question.

*

What is a kingdom? Let us propose a double nature for it: (1) a kingdom is a fragment of an empire; (2) a kingdom is a project for the reconstitution of the (theologico-political) unity of the theologico-political.

First of all, the fragment of an empire. When Romanity falls apart [*se décompose*], the two elements com-posing it are not falling together; it is the empire that collapses. The church holds up: it keeps going, taking in the newcomers. The invaders subject themselves to the church, pledge their allegiance, and are baptized. The fall of Rome is the fall of the Roman Empire. How does the empire fall down? It breaks apart, becomes dismantled and dislocated. It turns into fragmented kingdoms, which share out its space. *The Roman world breaks up into places.* It is the same breakup: the empire blows up into kingdoms, just *as* the world falls apart into places. They are dis-located, which is to say, dismembered in accordance with the topo-graphy and topo-nymy that made up the imperial space.[9] This is what (post-imperial) royalty is, first of all: the regime of sovereignty re-de-termined and reconfigured upon a *soil*—neither a continent bordered by water, nor the deep land of ancestors (though they may of course also be buried there), but a circumscribed soil, with the *royal domain* [*domaine royal*] at its core. Royalty is set up as a *unity of place*, or the unity of place. This is one of its etymological values:

In order to understand the formation of *rex* and the verb *regere* we must start with this notion. . . . *Regere fines* means literally "trace out the limits by straight lines." This is the operation carried out by the high priest before a temple or a town is built and it consists in the delimitation on a given terrain of a sacred plot of ground. . . . The tracing of these limits is carried out by the person invested with the highest powers, the *rex*.[10]

As is the domain, royalty is the *tracing* of sovereignty in space and in accordance with the limits of the place, of a soil circumscribed on its surface.[11] Whoever marks these boundaries is king. The formula that the French jurists made up about the king of France, "emperor within his realm" [*empereur en son royaume*] most explicitly conveys that this local fragmentation is indeed that of the empire.[12]

Then comes the reunification project. Quite a few mirages have surely entered the retrospective vision of the Greek polis as a unity. But it remains true that it knew nothing about the partitioning that we are discussing here—the theologico-political difference (of the theologico-political). This is not due to any homogeneous essence but simply to the fact that this division, a historical one, had not occurred yet. It is precisely Romanity that makes it happen: a new separation, of church and empire, follows the mode of existence of the polis (and the divisions that were its own). The *politeia* splits up into (imperial) sovereignty and (ecclesial) assembly. It is this scission—and the solidarity between the two complexes that it distinguishes and com-poses (the world and the commons)—that organizes and defines Romanity in its completion, and Romanity will ultimately turn this into its legacy. What are these two complexes? The world is strictly that which falls under the sway of the empire; and the commons, or common, is that which assembles itself, that which comes to the assembly, which is to say, the people. (Imperial) world and people (of God—because there is no assembly of the world): this is what Rome com-poses, what Rome (progressively) establishes and organizes as a composition, both a conjunction and a disjunction, an adjoining heterogeneity. Post-imperial kingship, which emerges after the breakup and supersedes Romanity after it is brought down, is a hypothesis reuniting these two agencies into a single regime. The kingdom comes to the fore as a new model for the unity of the ecclesio-imperial setup.[13] But this reunion is dissymmetric. The kingdom is a fragment, an imperial splinter. And thus, the reunification that the church and the empire project into it is produced in an *imperial mode*. The kingdom is a projected reunification of sovereignty and assembly, but in the *regime of sovereignty*. Or, to put it into these questionable terms: while the kingdom is a synthesis of the theologico-political, it is a *political* synthesis of it.[14] It is the desired unity of the common and the world, but in a piece or domain of the world—in a space of sovereignty.

This is what the privileged agency in this reunification expresses, since it is the church that holds on to its extension on the surface of the world, while the empire breaks up into kingdoms and the world into places. The church asserts this: through the articulation and progressive predominance of the theme of its *Catholicity*. Where then can the attempt at (theologico-political) reunification be carried out? Where can the local aspect of the land and the Catholicity of the church become one? At a determined point, where both regimes meet: in the person, the individuality, and the body (proper) of the king. The king is emperor, it has been said, but he is also an apostle. The signs of this double qualification are numerous.[15] Among the more eloquent ones, there is the consecrated coronation [*le sacre*], of course, which transfers onto the person of the sovereign the ecclesial as well as the royal authority—royal because it is ecclesial. The king is *sacred*. The space of the (theologico-political) reunification is the body of the king, that is to say, the royal singularity, personality, individuality, inscribed in his physical uniqueness, which is marked by his power to cure sufferers of scrofula by his touch, the power of his body to heal a body. Why the body of the king and not his soul? Because the body signs and designates the uniqueness and the singularity of persons, within their circumscribed physical extension.[16] What is consecrated is the individualism of the royal person, the unique and precise point where two essences meet; the site and de-termined agency of the theologico-political union. *The body is what is sacred*: the consecration (the sacrament of the consecration) is the condensation of the assembly in the person.[17]

But in reconstituting the unity of the theologico-political in the royal person, kingship seals the setup that was introduced earlier: in his body, the king unites sovereignty with ecclesiality, but he does so as the sovereign. The kingdom does intend to *subject* ecclesiality to the regime of sovereignty—to dominate and reign over it. If the kingdom is the dis-located legacy of the empire, and if the church is the agency of the assembly and of coming-to-a-common-being, one has to say that *the kingdom is the project to reunite the theologico-political by the subjection of the common to sovereignty*. "Subjection" is the determined appellation of this submission. The king's *subject* is the commonality of what is submissive in relation to him—what is submissive *inasmuch as it is common*.

In this way, the reunion necessarily goes unfulfilled—forever projected. For the kingdom, indeed, as a piece, fragment, or splinter of the empire, is of the world—this world. The church, as a branch of the common, is transcendent and exterior to it. The kingdom project is to retrieve the common and repatriate it to the world. Now, the world is that for which there is no common being. The world is the space of sovereignty, united or dislocated. If the king wants commonality for the kingdom, as the kingdom, he is clashing with the world, which is resisting this. If he subjects the church, it is as the mark or figure of the common expelled from the world. The figure of the common can be traced out in the world: as the trace of a lack, an absence, or the border of a hole. The ecclesio-imperial union, which only the king carries, is indefinitely wished for and desired.

Facing this resistance, the king then pretends to communicate his essence, the unity produced in his body, to the whole kingdom: as a piece of the world, the kingdom escapes and resists this projection. Between the king and the kingdom, *intermediate*, projected, and suspended *bodies* are constituted: the nobility, which partakes of sovereignty (being the same by birth or by nature, able to elect the king from its midst), and the clergy, which partakes of ecclesiality (communicating with the king thanks to their dual sacred corporeity).[18] Royalty aims at a reunification of the political unity that the separation of the church and the empire broke up, and this (desired and unfulfilled) reunion projects itself from the king's body toward the kingdom, as intermediate bodies. This is how the kingdom acquires its projected and eerie structure: *the body of the king is its head* (its chief, its capital organ). The soil (domain) is its base, its support, and its locus, finding its expression in the idea of *territory*.[19] Unity of command (archi-unity, mon-archy) and unity of place and competence—both capital and local. And *between* them—below the chief, above the soil—are the intermediate bodies, the makeup of the kingdom. But what is missing from this structure, which is unitary (on top) and dual (in the middle), is the absent third; it is there only as a surplus or an excrescence of being. The third is the hole, the void left by that which was excluded from the kingdom—the excluded and absent from the world, that is to say, commonality. The kingdom has no knowledge of the people, since the agency of the people, of the common—ecclesiality—is outside of the world (of which the kingdom is a part), or else deposited onto it, at a single (sacred) point where it meets it, in the person of the sovereign, who captures all the ecclesiality of this piece of the world, within which all the commonality of the kingdom is inscribed, caught, and captive. The kingdom does not know any people, only subjects—residual figures of the absent and subjected common.

*

As Aristotle puts it, enough said about this—in this case, the imaginary. In actuality, we can give a name to this strange formation uniting sovereignty and assembly *as sovereignty*, and commonality with the world *in the subjection of the world*. This problematic or paradoxical unity of the kingdom is carried out as the *state*.[20] The kingdom joins the (subjected) church together with the heritage of the (broken) empire in the unity of the state. It is *as a state* that it claims to reunite the church and the splinter of empire, and it is as a state that it subjects the common to sovereignty, and it is as a state finally that it takes over and supersedes something that collapsing Romanity had carried. What is it? I propose that the kingdom, as the state, supersedes the beaten empire, as a moment (of the movement) of the universal.[21] It is from the empire (and, by way of it, from the movement of the universal) that the kingdom gets a push or impulsion, which it transforms *locally*. To keep going, the expansion, held within the boundaries of the land, changes and undergoes a metamorphosis. What no longer grows throughout the extension of the world condenses and is densified in the fabric of society. The dismantling of the empire does not stop the process of expansion of the universal, but an "intensive expansion" follows its extensive one. The countless authoritative functions that were subsumed in the empire become homogeneous and organized in a unified whole.[22] Henceforth, compressed within territorial boundaries, these functions cross-react and metaphorize one another. The state is the local *condensation* and the densification dynamic of the (dis-located) empire.

(In this one should call attention to the very use of the concept of state, and *never deal with the state as an essence*—or with anything else, no doubt, but especially not with the state. Properly speaking, there is no [being, essence, or state of the] state, but only, and always, there is statization. More than anything else, the state requires that we think of it as a process, as becoming-state, as the movement and generating of state formations. With the local condensation of the process of the universal, the transformation of the *extension* of the empire into an *intensification* of the regime of sovereignty, the French state, in each phase of its history, is the *state of its statization*. We are here describing one of its phases, the state of the kingdom, the [procedural] unification of the church and a splinter of empire in the heritage and the mode of imperiality.)

But what about the church, the church in its autonomy, in the way it is constituted since the Roman separation? What happens to it here? For it is *the kingdom*, the agency of sovereignty, heir of the empire, that spells out this project of a unity, as a state project—a process of statization. The uncertain fate of the church is the outcome of this very imbalance. The kingdom wants a state church.[23] Now the church is incessantly summoned and urged by the state to join it. Temptation besets the church, either to respond and lose its specificity and the unity of its body; or to refuse and let go of the world for which it answers and that it transcends. The church had been a double of the empire throughout the extent of its expansion; when the empire breaks up and condenses into the state, its double or alter ego—which, being the "empire of the world," made its transcendent surge as the people of God necessary—now becomes detached. The church is then caught in an endless duality, a true double bind of its inclination to be: either it keeps the universality of its surface, and loses its double, which is its security; or it tightens into a local, territorial, and royal church, and loses the status of its universality. It either unseals itself from the theologico-political bond (which constitutes it, from birth), or it negates its being-Catholic.

That is why the kingdom keeps a dual element in its constitution. The church is not plainly within the state—even if the state wants it, and incorporates it on some accounts. The church is also the universal, worldwide, and Catholic floating object of the state's desire, an object that is not circumscribed, compressed, or entirely caught within state borders. The church floats both inside and outside of the body of the state, like a migrant soul. Yet the division or ancient theologico-political difference intended to vanish in the unity of the state persists as a duality or organic duplicity. The state, the heir of the empire, constitutes itself in the regime of sovereignty. Indeed, it is the body of the kingdom, but its *body politic*. This body contains the soul, which is subjected and captive—the state is the sovereign subjection of the common. What is left, however, is the other body, which is spiritual, and it punctures the world—the episcopal, territorial, and royal church, which is nonetheless Catholic. The church and the state—they are not separated: their separation will be at issue only in 1905.[24] But church and state are not fused: the church is the double of the political body as spiritual or mystical body—a universal, migrant, and detached body. This is the double envelope, the double physics, and the *double nature* of the kingdom. There is the material body and the spiritual body, the political and the mystical one—secular arm and regular body.[25] This unity is circumscribed at its base, localized on the land; at midlevel, the two bodies graze, haunt, and respond to each other. *Identity is achieved through the head.* Louis XIV would be able to say it: he was, indeed, the identity of the state.[26]

12. Religions

Thus in the case of France, the kingdom is a theologico-political unity (of the theologico-political), restored under a chief, on a ground, and reconstituted as the state. The wars of religion rip this unity apart. Here we see the emergence of religions *as religions*, that is to say, as something that *divides*. Religions are often defined as "that which unites," an idea that is both false and true. The assembly is what unites: it assembles, convenes, makes everyone flock together, brings about their coming-to-be-in-common. In this, there is only *ecclesia* and church, but no religion. For the religious to come up, a division of the church is necessary—a division of the assembly and a war of worship practices [*cultes*]. In order to say (or think), "This is my religion," it is necessary to have another religion across the way. If there is only one religion, there are only stories, behavior, assembling, ritual, faith, beliefs (uncertain words), perhaps something divine (we'll come back to this), but no religion. It is only as a plurality or duality of religions that religion comes about.[27] In ancient Greece—or in Papua New Guinea before globalization, or in pre-Colombian America—there is no religion. But there is in Rome, no doubt, because of the different kind of worship in the space of the world. The word *religion* is Roman. Objection: *religare* means "to bind." But even if one considers this etymology to be exact, one has to explain the "re."[28] To re-tie, perhaps—but to re-tie is not to tie. To re-tie is to tie what was untied, disunited, and separated. Religion unites, but it unites what was previously separated as part of a whole that is dividing; and this is a new hypothesis.

Religions divide, and they re-tie in part(ie)s what has been divided. (h8)

Émile Benveniste pays close attention to this etymological question.[29] Let us recall his conclusions. After presenting the two hypotheses circulating *since Roman times*, one "represented by Cicero, who . . . attaches *religio* to *legere* 'gather, collect,' and the other by Lactantius and Tertullian, who explain *religio* by *ligare* 'to bind,'"[30] he clearly opts for Cicero's.[31] Now, *legere* means to "gather, collect, recognize," Benveniste says. At the end of his analysis, he is thus led to characterize the sense of the word:

From these connexions [*sic*] we can infer that the sense of *religere* was "to re-collect": its meaning was "to take again for a new choice, to reconsider a previous approach." . . . To take up again a choice already made (*retractare* is the word Cicero uses), to revise the decision which results from it, this is the proper sense of *religio*.[32]

Now, in my view, one does not *take up again* this choice, or *revise* the decision, unless one is at a point when a crisis arises involving one set of worship practices, or of narratives and beliefs, confronted with another practice or another set of narratives and prescriptions. It is in this movement of revision that the religious constitutes itself as such. Religion happens as the *difference of religions*. It acknowledges this difference; it is inscribed in the operation of the division, reuniting (or re-tieing, if you will) the *parts* of what has been divided. And so, in a way, every religion is a *religious party*—the effect of the division of the social, political, or mystical body of the city, the empire, or the kingdom, the organization of this being-divided. With its dream of a reunification of the body, it shares in the vocation of every party, that is to say, the desire for unity *from the starting point* of the division and from one of the parts of what is divided.[33]

The formation of a religion occurs as a cut, followed by its (re)formation as a (religious) party: schism, heresy—Exodus, journey to Jerusalem, or Hegira. In the time period with which we are dealing, this gesture is carried out as the Reformation.[34] In France, the division turns into war.

*

But this is not specifically French: a number kingdoms arose from the breakup of the old Roman Empire; the Reformation touched other countries. What singled out France, as opposed to England or Spain?

My hypothesis is as follows:

(1) The French kingdom was not essentially different *in nature*: the kingdoms of England and Spain also aimed at the re-constitution of the theologico-political unity in a united territory with a unique ruler. There too this reunion was projected as a state and internally pursued the movement of the universal, which became an intensive process. There were differences between them, but from place to place, there were *provincial* singularities: Rome's provinces were not identical. The situation in Spain emerged from the bicephalous unification of Castile and Aragon and the expulsion of Islam from the Iberian Peninsula, the basis of the theologico-political power of the *reyes católicos*, Ferdinand V of Aragon and Isabella la

Católica, who unify the kingdom through their marriage in 1469 and complete the Reconquista.[35] Therefore, from one kingdom to the next, there were *local* specificities—emerging from the dislocation—and no essential heterogeneity. Should we renounce trying to understand France's singularity? No. My view is merely that, contrary to popular mythology,[36] it cannot be understood *in this context, because*

(2) By contrast, the situation of France vis-à-vis the Reformation was unique. Again, the schism of reformation produced a division that followed a line roughly separating the continent into a Protestant north and a Catholic south. Here the particularity of each of the three kingdoms stands out: England is Protestant, Spain is Catholic. What about France? The fracture rather clearly underscores the linguistic partitioning (Germanic, Anglo-Saxon north; Latin south), which itself largely overlaps with (but does not wholly match) some of the indecisive stabilizations of the marches of ancient Romanity. The distribution seems clear-cut on either side of the line: the entire northern part of the continent topples into the Protestant camp; the entire south sides with Rome. *It is the limit that is uncertain*: in the median zone, French-speaking (Latin) Switzerland reforms, although southern Germany, which is more northern, remains Catholic. Now, the dividing line runs across France (but not *geographically*: it splits the inside of French society)—and the debate over the Germanic origins of French nobility, no matter how skewed, conveys this.[37] On its entire surface, France is a superposition of Gallo-Romanity and Germanism. The Roman conquest has covered its territory and so have the invasions. Both have left deep marks, in its language and its identity (even in its name). The dividing line between the Roman world and Germanity runs through the kingdom without parceling out any *regions*, and the religious division cannot settle on any *limes* (only on a "social" frontier?).[38] It bursts throughout the territory, disperses the reformed communities in the north and the south without unifying the regions; here and there it touches various strata and poles, shaping zones of dominance that are social as much as local. The specificity of the French situation is the outcome: when the kingdom of France wishes to deal with the religious division, it will find it deeply disseminated throughout its body.

Undeniably, France topples into the Catholic camp. So do other ancient provinces (Italy) and kingdoms (Spain). But in choosing the Catholic camp, France alone has to deal with such a deep internal gash; it alone will apply such violence to it. Before the decision, in the second half of the sixteenth century, France is deeply *split* inside: numerous cities and rural zones are predominantly Protestant. Entire sections of the nobility convert, which is the case neither in Italy nor in Spain. The outcome is so uncertain and the division so deep that around the 1560s the belief seems to prevail in Europe that France, led by its upper nobility, is going to join the Reformed side.[39] It is this indecision and the uncertain character of this partitioning that set off the wars of religion *as wars* (which neither Spain nor England will experience), together with the French particularity of these wars: the massacres and mass liquidations (not brought about by the Dutch war). This is where we must seek the specific and decisive mode of the formation of France's unity. By opting for the Catholic camp, the French monarchy finds itself with the "task" of having to eliminate a great part of its own body, which has chosen the other side. Spain does hang a few heretics, too, eliminating a dissidence limited to some individuals and a few groups. But in France the "task" is quite different. What is involved is the eradication of part of the French fabric: local zones, people disseminated throughout the territory, even in the capital, but also in many other cities, outlining the bloody cartography of the massacres; entire sectors of the nobility. The process of this elimination (which is deep and organic within the social tissue) passes through three principal stages:

(1) The St. Bartholomew's Day massacre and ensuing massacres: mass eliminations, collective slaughter (three thousand dead in Paris, preceding the massacres in Meaux, Orleans, Saumur, Angers, Troyes, Rouen, Lyon, Toulouse, Bordeaux, and so on).

(2) Shortly afterward, the return to an apparent compromise, leading to the coronation of Henry IV. A Protestant converted and enthroned: the semblance of an absorption through the *head*—as if replaying the conversion scene of the invaders. But the problem is divided, which is to say, there is unity at the head and division at the other levels of the state: freedom of worship, the Edict of Nantes.[40]

(3) A few decades later, the state's abjuration of its commitment—the revocation of the irrevocable,[41] followed by a mass exodus, during which *between two and three hundred thousand Protestants* leave France, moving north, to Protestant Europe.[42]

Massacres, conversion, and exodus: the scene of elimination is replayed three times. But who performs it? This is the decisive point, since in France, it is the state. And since the state is nothing but its statization, the argument here is that the French elimination of Protestantism *cannot be dissociated from the very process of statization*, and that for the time period in question, it constitutes its content or modality. And thus for about a century and a half (1550–1700), the kingdom of France in becoming a state (its becoming as a state; its becoming-state) unfolds and constitutes itself in and through the elimination of Protestantism. As has been noted, the kingdom is not a state, formed as such, by essence, at the point of its birth or its constitution. More exactly, its *constitution* is not given at birth, at the moment when the state extracts itself from what came before it and conditioned it. Its constitution has been proceeding—it has been asserting itself, and it needs to be grasped, not at its point of origin, but in the middle, at the heart (or belly) of becoming, in its median part where becoming unfolds. Constitution is (at) the middle. This is particularly true about the state if (as I suggested earlier) the state is a moment of the becoming of the universal; a moment of *intensification* within the boundaries of its place. The state is the local condensation of the empire, and thus of the movement of the universal in the mode of sovereignty—the state is itself a becoming, a process, a drive, transporting authority functions; it is a metaphorization and a multiple cross-contamination of these functions. The state is always a *statization*, a becoming-state. There is no essence of the state whatsoever, unless it is this middle of its process, its drive, its polymetaphorization of itself, its internal multiplication, and the local intensification of its own constitution. The hypothesis might then be as follows: the (dominant) process of the constitution of the French state, during the (decisive) period of Europe's formation, is to be taken as the process of elimination of the Reformation; and this constitutes France's singularity as a state. France was neither the only one among the kingdoms that arose from the breakup of the Roman Empire to be penetrated by the Reformation, of course (so were the northern kingdoms), nor the only one to opt for the Catholic camp (so did the southern kingdoms). However, it was the only one that, as a state, took upon itself the task of ridding its body of the Reformation through massacres, royal conversion, and conversions and mass exodus. Furthermore, this process is indissociably linked with the becoming-state of the French kingdom as such—it interpenetrates it. At its peak (and by no means accidentally) it occurred mostly under Louis XIV, who brings about and asserts the singularity of

France as a state (its "centralism") *and* simultaneously finishes with—apparently, at least—the repression of Protestantism. Apparently—since repression [*refoulement*], as we well know, is never *finished*.

For this repression is carried out by the state *as the state*: in this task, the king defers neither to the church nor to the nobility. Although elements of the church and of the nobility initially decree the massacres, it is because both the dominant religious orders and the Catholic party among the nobility aspire to direct the state. Later on, at the climax, it is the king who signs the Revocation of the Edict of Nantes—he *is* the state. Now, as has been noted, the kingdom of France was constituted in the post-Roman era as an attempt at a theologico-political reunion (of the theologico-political) and shaped itself with this aim through its statization. Thus, the kingdom was not the state as we understand it nowadays; it was not the state as a set of *separate* functions of the social body as a whole, but was itself the whole of society: "Such is the concept of *society*," Benveniste writes. "In Western Indo-European it is designated by a common term. But this seems to be lacking in the other groups. In fact, it is expressed in a different way. It may be recognized under the name of *kingdom*: the limits of society coincide with the extent of a given power, which is the power of the king."[43]

The process of statization involves the kingdom, which is to say, what we nowadays designate with the concept of the social—a globalism larger than the state, which undergoes statization. The repression of the Reformation cannot be dissociated from the process through which the kingdom (society) becomes a state, thinking, representing, and constituting itself as a state. But *it is a repression* [*refoulement*], an eradication or elimination. The process of statization manifests itself as a rejection. Statization is the movement through which, and within which, the kingdom (that is "society") is constituted as a state by rejecting and expelling a part of its body. And *it is through this process that society comes to acknowledge its difference from the state*: until then, "society" had not construed itself as such; it recognized itself in the theologico-political totality of the kingdom. *There was no social body*. It is because the kingdom expels and rejects outside of itself a part of its body so as to constitute itself as the state that some sociality appears, nakedly, as the object of this repression—and therefore as its rest or remainder, since a repression is essentially interminable. The elimination of the Reformation *constitutes the state* as such, as a process of statization at work in the operation of this repression; and, in the same movement, *constitutes society*, as that which is not incorporated in the state thus constituted, that which is rejected from it. It is then that society invents, finds, and sees itself: as society external to the state, remaining outside of the state that is taking shape—against the state. By constituting itself through the elimination of the Reformation, the state pushes society outside of itself, and against itself—a new hypothesis.

> *Specifically, the French state constitutes itself as the repression—by the state—of the Reformation. (h9)*

This is precisely what calls for and organizes the characteristics of its specificity—and particularly its "centralism," which, as we shall see, is misconstrued as "Jacobinism," even if what is ordinarily designated by this very soft concept of Jacobinism is indeed part of a history that is not unconnected with what I wish to point out here. This specificity is what conditions what follows. The conditioning matters: the state's repression of the Reformation may be the matrix of quite a few later enterprises of state totalization, intent on taking hold of life as a whole (body and soul, the whole kingdom) *as the state*, and thus forcing out what they are repressing and expelling, which from now on will be thought as "society."[44] "Society" thus designates this political remainder (the rest of the body politic—assembly and sovereignty—pretending to reunite locally as a kingdom, and to reconstitute itself as a state), or this rest of politics that resists statization (precisely because statization is carried out as an enterprise aiming to repress society and eliminate it from its body). Society will henceforth be construed as a remainder of the polis outside of the political—the rest of the city, the remainder of citizenship, driven away from any participation in the sovereignty of the state. Henceforth, society will be the political that is external to the state, the noncitizen city, the *civis*, civil order (but not of the state) as such—the society of pure civility, civil society.

13. Surrection

The consequences of this analysis lead us to propose an interpretation of the process of the (French) Revolution—of the Revolution, as French.

> *The resurgence of the repressed of the Reformation is carried out as the (French) Revolution. (h10)*

Before any explication of the content of this hypothesis, its form needs to be explained:

(1) It will be noted that the word "resurgence" is used here instead of "return," as in the commonplace expression "return of the repressed" to designate the reappearance of something censored, because I am advancing the notion that resurgence is not a return. If the word "return" semantically conveys a coming back, the return of something that has left or been driven out, a return is always in a way the return of the recurrent [*retour du revenant*], of the same. That which comes back—as noted earlier—comes down to the same, or comes back as the same, as the selfsame, as identity. One may push the equivalence even further: *the same is what returns.* The same is produced as identity in the space of the return—in the space of figuration, in the image. The identical is imaginary—everything about identity is (caught up in) the imaginary of the return. Therefore "resurgence" [in French *resurgissement*] is preferable here.

The French word *resurgissement* is a quasi-neologism, modeled on *surgissement*, from the verb *resurgir*: "to reappear suddenly again." The word evidently conveys something akin to a return: something reappears, "re-surges," and comes back, as it were. But the cognate meanings and connotations make the words derived from the Latin *surgere* preferable here. First, a *surgissement* is a "surrection": an uprising or uplift, and this brings it close to an insurrectionist vocabulary. *Surgir* is

> the gallicization (1808), following an isolated example . . . and borrowing by Old Provençal, of the Latin transitive verb *surgere*, "to set upright," and intransitive, "to arise," in speaking of people or things; in Vulgar Latin, "to resuscitate" and engage in "insurgence." This verb, made up of *sub*, indicating an upward movement, and *regere*, "to direct, to guide" (see *régir* [to rule]), has led by phonetic evolution to *sourdre* [to seep out, well up].[45]

Surgissement thus combines three desirable values: (a) upward movement, rising, raising [*levage*];[46] (b) insurrection, uprising; (c) a hint, in this movement and rise, toward what is *ruled* [*régi*], directed, and guided—constituted as rectitude, rights, and regime. But the word conveys something else, still, which is more surprising. *Surgir* is

> the (1497) alteration of *sourgir* (1424), borrowed from Old Provençal *sorgir*, "to cast anchor" (1377), from the Catalan *surgir* (1250) "appear on the sea". . . . This maritime term [originally] meant "to alight" [at a port], in *surgir au port* (1497), *dans le*

port (1550), and used alone (1564). With a change of prepositions . . . *surgir du port* has meant "to leave the port" (1603).⁴⁷

It may be surmised that this port-related value is rather fitting here; it will later be our focus.⁴⁸ "Resurgence" thus seems ultimately more adequate (than "return"), and less (simply) caught up in the economy of sameness. It conveys something having to do with *emerging*, with something new.⁴⁹ It might be thought that this risks allowing some kind of resurrection to seep in with the resurgence. This is duly noted. For now, let's say, too bad—or so much the better.

(2) A reticence about using the vocabulary of the "return of the repressed" is understandable: it comes from the use, throughout this work, of the term "return," to designate a process of the constitution of the figure, or even a kind of essence of the figure as such. Be that as it may, a possible difference between resurgence and return should not conceal one thing: *that which surges again in the resurgence is figured as a return*. The return is the figure of that which has re-surged—the re-surged inasmuch as it is given figure—which is to say that the return brings down what has re-surged into the narrow economy of sameness. In the sequence with which we are dealing, this figure has a specific name: "revolution." "Revolution" designates the re-surgence *as* a figure, and as a return. *Révolution* is

borrowed (ca. 1190) from Vulgar Latin *revolutio, -onis* (St. Augustine), "return" and "unwinding," "cycle, return (of souls, through metempsychosis)," and in the Middle Ages, "periodical return of a star to its point of departure" (1086). The word comes from classical Latin *revolutum*, supine of *revolvere*, "to roll back, bring back" (see *révolu* [past, finished, completed]).⁵⁰

The Revolution is thus *given figure* as that which brings back what there was at the beginning—at the outset, at the source, at the origin. Insurrection is construed as resurrection—of what had been there, and then died, and is now coming back. The surge of the new is taken for (and taken up in) the coming back of the old: the new, more ancient than the old—primitive, principial (a regime more ancient than the ancien régime)—the primordial provenance, which the old itself has led astray, concealed, and buried, and which it is a matter of bringing back as the truth (to come) of the present; the new, always apprehended (comprehended) as the return (to self) of the origin. What we have to try to think is the particular importance of the fact that the re-surgence (of what had been repressed as the

Reformation) has been thought, named, and given figure as the Revolution (that is to say, within the economy of the return).

(3) What then is the difference that we wish to keep, or bring out, between "return" and "resurgence," a difference that is no longer semantical but effective? What is produced by and within the resurgence that does not fit into the economy of the return, something we necessarily have to check and think in order to *give thought to the coming newness*? What, in the new, is this gap [*écart*] that the idea of return misses? I am proposing, provisionally, that it is *that which (of the repressed) re-surges, spreads, and is diffused*; that which comes (down to the same), is re-presented, or simply trans-figured: a change of form and aspect, but keeping to what it is. What re-surges spills out and is disseminated—like cancer cells, as it were. They come back, but after having multiplied, spread out, and proliferated. Ultimately, this could be repression *proper*—its failure, its arrest (death sentence): namely, that what it represses does not just come back but re-surges, growing and multiplying, like weeds, exterminated people, and life.[51]

*

The repression by the French state of the Reformation has continued and developed the statization process of the kingdom of France, which is to say, the process of the constitution of the state as a state, merging with it during this phase. During this time period—the core of its development (the middle of this process)—the state *was constituted* as the repression of the Reformation. Meanwhile, it expelled from itself a nonstate civil society, order, and politics. Reduced to nothing within the state, this nonstate civil order—one might say, this sociality—comes to perceive itself as a rejected, shoved-out excrescence of the French state, its excluded third party, the Third Estate. Why *third*? Because this "estate," reduced to nothing in the kingdom, is pushed away from its dual nature and double constitution: outside of sovereignty (politics and royalty) *and* outside of the church (outside of the assembly of the people of God), which is to say, clearly, outside of the theologico-political. The nobility partakes of sovereignty and shares something of the king's nature and essence—the sovereign body, the body of the sovereign. The clergy takes upon itself the mystical essence of the church as the transubstantiated body of God—in both forms, bread and wine, ever since the first Eucharist—and confers on the *sacred* sovereign something of its nature. Asymmetrically joined under the regime of sovereignty, the two form the theologico-political essence of the kingdom. *And still there is a remainder: society.* Its name is the *Third* Estate. And what is it, within the kingdom, within the regime of the kingdom? *Nothing.* Third Estate is the name of this "nothing essential" that society is, under the ancien régime (nothing, because the kingdom has repressed it), which, in coming to think of itself, thinks that the kingdom is not everything but *merely* matches the theologico-political double nature of the state. *The kingdom is nothing but the state*, a repressing power: henceforth, this is the knowledge that begins to loom.

Repressed from the state, in a double way, the Reformation resurfaces elsewhere—an elsewhere both external and internal, extensive and intensive.

(1) Extensively, the (French) Reformation surges back in the various places of exile: northern Europe, America—all the spaces where Huguenots have found refuge and where Protestant France is disseminated and diffracted, encountering other places of the Reformation (e.g., in Germany), or producing new ones (e.g., in Switzerland). Its written account soon becomes one of the sequences contributing to capitalism asserting itself.[52] What the Reformation thus finds again is the outside of the state as *world*, and this process will be worldwide.[53]

(2) Intensively, the Reformation also comes back into the circumscription of the kingdom and onto its soil, and it is here that the resurgent element comes *as* a return: as revolution. The Revolution is the repressed of the Reformation, *inasmuch as it comes back* to the place of the repression, that is, onto the soil, within the boundaries, and onto the terrain of the state. What surges back is the repressed of the state, within the boundaries of the kingdom. It is society, exactly: the *social* Revolution, through the necessity of its constitution.

It is in the latter sense that the surge of the repressed is going to be carried out as an in-surrection: the upswing of what was buried at the very site of the burial, the rise and the uprising of the excluded third element at the locus of its repressive expulsion—in (the) place of the state. It is an insurrection against the state, as the state of the kingdom: against sovereignty as well as against ecclesiality, which the state harnessed and enlisted in its bosom and under its head. The repressed surges back, against the state and *therefore* against the church, which is to say, against the double theologico-political nature of the kingdom, which has shut it out. In the constitution (as the state) of the kingdom, a confusion had come about—an asymmetrical reunion of sovereignty with ecclesiality—which went on and intensified during the repression of the Reformation. The revolutionary resurgence will no longer aim to separate the church from the state: both will be caught in the surrection or uplift of the new constitution. But what turns the insurrection into a return (a revolution) is that, in the case of the one and the other, the resurgence will aim to be the figure of a coming back [*re-venir*], a come-back [*re-venance*], of that which it is attacking, under the aspect of its first, and lost, identity, of its recovered and reconstituted archaic ancientness. The insurrection against the sovereign will look *like* a rebuilt sovereignty, and the insurrection against the church *like* a new assembly. The return of the repressed comes back in the place of repression: the Revolution re-constitutes sovereignty and ecclesiality—the state.

Let us put it another way: in a different process (which does not exist; it is offered here as fiction), the resurgence could have *relinquished* the sites and the procedures of the state. This will be the great fiction of anarchism—a society without a state, and a withered-away state. But this fiction itself is caught in the recursive schema of the Revolution. Let us suggest a different fable, not of a destroyed state—a revolutionary procedure—but of a state that has been relinquished, abandoned, and forsaken—an unlived-in house. To destroy the state means to come back to its locus, and rebuild in its place. To relinquish it is to leave and carry oneself elsewhere. Obviously, a question of sites (of space or world) comes up: when one is caught in the boundaries that circumscribe the state (within the borders of the kingdom), one is led or even forced to reoccupy its space, and this drives one to repair and reconstitute the state. So goes the Revolution: constrained and de-termined within the state's self-given borders, it occurs as a counter-statization and the reoccupation of the domain and the soil—destruction and re-constitution of the State; or even further, destruction of the state *as* its re-constitution, the state's destruction of the state, an ultrastatization or hyperstatization, the destruction of the state through a *passage to the absolute*, a dissolution and resolution, the state's absolutization. The Reformation coming back to the locus of its repression, and thus re-producing itself, in an intensified way, as its state absolutization—such is, in my view (I am saddened by this acknowledgment), the singularity of the revolutionary process (even if, through this reinforced statization, something of the movement of the universal *comes across* and carries on).

14. Nation

The kingdom is this body whose head is the body of the king. The person of the sovereign identifies with the state because it is the tightest and most compact agent of the theologico-political reunification, the intersection or cross-stitch of sovereignty meeting the assembly. The head (the body of the king) identifies with the body: he *is* the state. We shall have to look at the peculiar power of this metaphorical condensation. Of course, it is a metaphor (transporting a sense and a thought), but loaded with a practical and concrete effectivity, and charged with reality (effects). Why? Not every metaphor is charged with this load. The metaphor of the collective body is not a random one: it is the social, mystical body politic of the kingdom, the state, and the church, what we may very provisionally term the common figure of their incorporation. This metaphor proceeds from a determined history, which gives it a *physical* force: it touches on the *nature* of the common.[54] Hence the violence of identification. The royal person fixes the metaphor as a literal meaning and condenses all the effectivity of this incorporation. Should this effectivity turn around, it spits out real murder.

Insurrection strikes at the head: the king's body. And in this body, it hits the head: the king's head is the head of this capital body that is the head of the kingdom. The king's head is the head of the head, the archi-head, which channels the return effect of the Revolution, which decapitates—the state as well as the sovereign. The murder strikes at the theologico-political identity of the kingdom, and the singular person, the anointed, crowned head, and the *sovereign and sacred* body of the monarch. *But as a decapitation, the Revolution comes back and acts at the site of capital identification.* Decapitation is the eminent mark of the figural ambiguity of the Revolution, which is to say, of its ambiguity as a figure, of that which finally locks it into the ambiguity (and the ambivalence and equivocality) of the figure. If the king's head rolls, it is because it identifies the junction of the kingdom's two natures, the nodal point of its dual constitution: a radical gesture aiming to beat down the state and excise any theological and political identity from royalty. But decapitation puts this radicality into practice as a return to the capital site of the state, as a reinvestment in its locus and the enthronement of its replacement. The Revolution is given figure as the advent of a new sovereignty—but new inasmuch as it is brought back to its recovered and virginal first essence. Under a regime that is older than the old, originary, and more principial than the prince, its newness dismisses and supersedes an *usurped sovereignty*—which the monarch had captured, stolen, and redirected for his own benefit. And so, the king is essentially criminal; he is a thief who abused the body of the kingdom. It is a matter, then, of making the people into the new king, and *giving it back* its stolen royalty. The Revolution is the *return* of the people to the capital sovereign position, a position freed by the removal of the monstrous usurper head grafted onto the body of the kingdom. The sovereignty of the people is the return of the third element and its enthronement at the site of maximal identification; it is the capitalization or the *recapitation* of the king-people, the crowning of the People's Front.[55]

The people come back to the sovereign emplacement here. The people constitutively are what assembles and is assembled.[56] The sovereign people are thus the schema of a radical theologico-political reunification, of an annulment, of a complete erasure of the rift, of sovereignty and the assembly thoroughly joined, each taken in its essential determination, without any delegation or displacement whatsoever. The sovereign people stand or are posited as the perfect reunion of what had been disjoined—the church and the empire *absolutely* fused. Understandably, such a figure would be endowed with an irresistible power, both revolutionary and millenarian, political and religious—*revolutionary* in this very determined (millenarian, perhaps) sense that it states the radical restoration, at its roots, of what had been lost at the moment of the constitution of the empire: the First City (fictitiously, on this score, both Greek and Roman), the Republic in its primordial essence, indissociably theological and political inasmuch as it reconstitutes the first unity, of which "the theological" and "the political," when separated, are unhappy, dismembered, and disunited avatars. The revolutionary republic claims to be the full and quasi-reversed realization of what the project of the kingdom had been: it is full because the theologico-political unity (the unity of the theologico-political) presents itself as re-constituted in a more radical fashion (the "theological" being called up at its inception, by what opens it and makes it possible—the *people*, the very thing that forms an assembly); and it is reversed because sovereignty is no longer seen as separate, or autonomous in a superior way, as that which subjects the assembly (the church) under its head: the sovereign, now, is the very assembly itself, ecclesiality at its principle, the people. It is sovereignty invested by its other, ecclesiality and popularity. But it is a *quasi*-reversal, since it is only as the sovereign that the people are in command. To the republic the kingdom bequeaths the key to its setup, sovereignty, as the keystone at the architectonic juncture holding up the building. The revolutionary republic wants to grasp again an essence of the political from before the (theologico-political) split, but it regrasps it *in the mode and regime* of sovereignty. This is not the end of one's troubles: what holds everything together is the memory and legacy of the empire.[57]

The Revolution finishes off the kingdom: it elevates the people in lieu of the sovereign, enthroning and crowning them. The Revolution *bestows sovereignty on the assembly*, thus outlining a new figure, of a hyper-sovereign and an archi-assembly, the chiasm of the king-people, a theocracy of upside-down parallels, headless caesarism, millenarianism in the present tense, now and fulfilled. This figure has a name, *nation*, which continues to be in the news. The nation is the (theologico-political, overturned) figure of the overthrown kingdom. In it one can read the end of the (hi)story: the reunion of the dis-membered, repairing the unitary body, *a body simultaneously political and mystical*. One may look there for the closure of the sequence that opened with the breakdown of the polis. Many will go down in this quest and into this mirage—blinded.

Indeed, the fusion is not complete. Some division remains. In its overthrow, the kingdom has transmitted to the nation a part of its heritage: sovereignty, the agency of sovereignty as command, command of everything. And from the start this legacy will weigh heavily upon the national venture, *but not only* as the reproduction of the general schema of domination—which is no small thing. For what is transferred from the kingdom to the nation (through the revolutionary reversal) is what was constituting it as the kingdom, namely, the succession of the empire—and therefore the trace and the caesura of the theologico-political division. But something else comes along with that: the tracing and the conformation of what made it a fragment, splinter, or piece of broken empire. In other words, what the kingdom passes on to the nation is the power separated, of course—sovereign imperiality—*but also* the form, the cutout, and the boundaries of sovereignty, where the revolution is going to find itself captive and contained. The limits of the state—*the borders*.

*

Thus a hypothesis and a question take shape.
Hypothesis:

The nation is revolutionary. (h11)

One should read this statement as a conceptual and historical marker, without any attractive or deceptive coloring. The nation mentioned here is neither generous nor cold, nor pregnant with the future—nothing like that. It only has, in its build, a conformation and a *type* given by the movement of the (French) Revolution, within which it is born. The nation is revolutionary through its genesis and lineage. This determination affects its genealogy as much *as what descends from it*. It is important to bear in mind that it becomes attached to all the later implementations of its figure, which will all carry—all of them, yes, even the worst ones—something from this initial constitution. Let us first look at the ancestry. While the word is in use before the Revolution, I would like to argue that the modern idea of nation that holds sway over us (thus differing from earlier uses of the term) is the concept built by (and for) the revolutionary enterprise to designate the overthrow of the kingdom. Let me try to articulate and support this hypothesis. *Nation* is

borrowed (ca. 1120) . . . from the Latin *natio, -onis*, derived from the supine [Latin verbal noun with the same stem as the passive participle] of *nasci* (to be born): "birth"; then through metonymy and specialization, a "collection of individuals born in the same time at the same place." In the Christian era, the word is used in the plural, *nationes*, to designate pagan populations, in opposition to the "people of God." In the middle ages, *natio* also takes on the meaning of a "division of the University of Paris."

In French . . . the first sense chronologically is that of "pagans" (in opposition to Jews and Christians in the Old Testament [*sic*]). . . . Based on a different meaning in Latin, *nation* refers to a set of human beings characterized in their language and culture by their common origin (1175), in contrast to *race, gent*. In Middle French, following medieval Latin, [the word] is also used for the division of the University of Paris, organized by language (1470) into "English" (including Germans), people from Picardy, Normans, and "French" (including Spaniards and Italians). The term also applies to a colony of merchants residing abroad (ca. 1475). . . . The modern notion of "nation" actually emerges during the eighteenth century: with the Revolution, the nation becomes a political entity identified with the Third Estate (1789, [the revolutionary theorist Abbé] Sieyès), the revolutionary people, and takes on its definition of "legal person constituted by the collection of individuals composing the State" (Decree of July 23, 1789, with the expression *crime de lèse-nation* [as in *lèse-majesté*—Trans.], in which the word *nation* replaces the word *royauté* [royalty]).[58]

The nation, then, was first a "collection of individuals born in the same time at the same place," and thus "a set of human beings characterized in their language and culture by their common origin." Therefore, to be precise, it is a collection of individuals who share a language and a culture *because of the fact that they are born at the same place*, as the etymology of "nation" notes in relating the term to "birth." Why, before and after the revolutionary period, has this term come to designate the people as the subject of the uprising and then forming the state? Why was it chosen to designate the community of human beings bound by the exercise of sovereignty, rather than other available terms—such as *cité* [city], for example? It is because the circumscription *of sovereignty, and therefore of the people*, was thought as that of a place. Where did this thinking of a boundary [*bornage*] originate? From the de-limitation of the kingdom, of royalty as sovereignty upon its soil, and thus ultimately from the *locality* of the state, that is to say, from the breakup of the empire, fragmented into kingdoms as the world is into places. The topos of the nation (as a community and a place of birth) proceeds from this *dis-location*: "nationals" are born in the same fragment of empire, the same piece of its broken world.

The example of the University of Paris, in fact, shows unequivocally that the determination of these "places of birth" does not stem from an "ethnic," "geographical," or even "linguistic" *given*, in the sense in which we might understand it. The list of the students' origins expresses an administrative division, and assigning their places follows the reading code of the administration that provides its definition: the Germans are English, the Spaniards and Italians are French, while the people from Picardy and Normandy make up *nations*, with full rights. The given of the places *is the given of the administration*. It is the eye of administrative rulings that sees the "countries" [*pays*] and cuts them up: nations are corporate divisions. Noticeably, even the discrimination of languages, which we consider more perceptible in our naive view today, can only take place under textbook criteria. The Spaniards and Italians speak "French," but not the people from Picardy. To put it bluntly, our postulate here says that the same goes for the modern political sense of the "national," which is to say, that nations are *prescribed* (as communities of origin and pro-venances) by the land management register that the dis-location of the empire draws up.[59]

The process is then as follows. The empire breaks up into kingdoms, and these cir-cumscribe provenances, births, and origins. The Revolution overthrows the kingdom while inheriting its territories (domain, suzerainty, preserve). And the nation, the figure of the overthrown kingdom bequeathed to the sovereign people, is called upon to determine, circumscribe and ultimately define the people destined to wear the crown and sit on the empty throne. It is from this process that one may gain an understanding of three fundamental postulations through which the nation constitutes and asserts itself.

First, *the nation is the Third [Estate]*. Here we can recognize Abbé Sieyès's decisive statement [in his 1789 pamphlet *Qu'est-ce que le Tiers-État? (What Is the Third Estate?)*] (destined, as we know, to have wide repercussions), in which the dictionary definition cited earlier justifiably sees one of the stages of the concept's history. Indeed, the kingdom possessed an essentially dual constitution, an ecclesio-imperial one, expressed in the dyad of the dominant orders, the nobility and the clergy. With a kind of diagnostic genius, Sieyès said that in this regime, the Third Estate is nothing—nothing because it is the third, precisely, and because everything fits in *two*; the third is excluded. Even where it does have a seat, it is silenced, *spoken for* by powerful lawyers,[60] "An excellent custom which, intended to provide representation for the Third Estate, has positively excluded it from representation until this very day!"[61] The Third Estate is denied any existence, excluded from all participation in the "political order."[62] The "States-General as we know it at present is simply a *clerico-nobili-judicial* assembly." For the nobility has confiscated the representation of the Third Estate, *to which it* relegates nobles it does not care to admit into its ranks.[63] Rejected from the *political order* and standing for nothing, the Third Estate constitutes itself and seems to itself to be the whole *social order*. In this all but dialectical reversal, in this negation of the negation, the space proper of the nation opens up. The nation is this whole that the "political order" of the kingdom has nullified.

> Who is bold enough to maintain that the Third Estate does not contain within itself everything needful to *constitute a complete nation*? . . . If the privileged order were removed, the nation would not be something less, but something more. What then is the Third Estate? All; but an "all" that is fettered and oppressed.[64]

The nation comes into view: *an "all," in chains and oppressed*—an all prevented from being everything, negated as an all, reduced to nothingness by the (theologico-)political order of the kingdom. The nation is the Third Estate, which turns around and remakes itself as everything; "It would be all; but free and flourishing."[65]

And then, *the nation is the common [le commun]*. The orders are outside of it because they are *separated*. The nation does not separate; it abides in the community of its body. The appellation (or concept) of this separation is *privilege*: private law, for private use, removing itself from the common law.

Anybody who holds a legal privilege of any kind deserts the *common* order, stands as an exception to the *common* laws and, consequently, does not belong to the Third Estate. As we have already said, a nation is made *one* by virtue of *common* laws and *common* representation.[66]

Strange tautology: the nobility is set up as an order by the separation that is its privilege. Since the nation is the "all" from which nothing is separated, the nobility is outside of the nation. And the Third Estate, which the noble order excludes and represses, is the all of it all, the whole of what does not separate, the whole of the common.

Is it not obvious that the nobility possesses privileges and exemptions, which it brazenly calls its rights and which stand distinct from the rights of the great body of citizens? Because of these special rights, the nobility does not belong to the common order, nor is it subjected to the common laws. Thus its private rights make it a people apart in the great nation. It is truly *imperium in imperio*.[67]

The rejection of nobility from the body of the nation is thus the rejection of the rejection, the separation from what separates; it is what re-constitutes the "all," "free and flourishing."

Finally, *the nation is what assembles itself*. It is in this very determined gesture, in this precise moment, that one has to locate the constitutive revolutionary act, the singular operation of the Revolution as such. Even though this sequence of events is so well-known, its appeal is such that its prodigious *impact [portée]* makes a permanent impression: the Third [Estate] *constitutes itself into a national assembly*. Excluded from the place of the sessions, finding the door blocked, the assembly *transports itself* to another—fortuitous, random—place and *(re)constitutes itself there*.[68] The Third [Estate] reconstitutes itself as a nation insofar as it forms an assembly and gives its name to it.[69] The *national* character of the assembly is exactly equivalent to its capacity to convene, without anyone impeding its reunion, and without anyone or anything except itself summoning it to meet; and the radicality of this status is played out at every moment, in its adamant refusal to accept a delay, an interruption, or *any separation*. This is *sensu stricto* what the Tennis Court Oath [Serment du Jeu de Paume] comes down to: the Assembly, as the National Assembly, is inseparable in its essence; the nation is present at the place where the assembly holds its reunion—*at least until the constitution*.[70]

But with this third characteristic (and already with the second one, as we shall see), the nation begins to occupy a very singular position in the "theologico-political" setup and its history. Constituted *inasmuch as it becomes assembled* (inasmuch as it brings about *the common, the being of what is common*), the nation strictly fills the place of ecclesiality, if one recalls that the church is nothing but the transferred name of the assembly as such.[71] The historian Jules Michelet will take note of this: "The cardinal and the archbishop return the same evening to Marly, and fall at the feet of the king: 'Religion is ruined' [*C'est fait de la religion*]!"[72] Let us retrospectively recognize their theoretical rigor: convening the assembly discharges the religious, relieves the church. It is noteworthy in this tale that the king ordered the meeting hall to be shut, "in order to prevent the clergy from uniting with the Third Estate." The revolutionaries' position often expresses this equivocation: while they fight the clergy because of the privileges it possesses, they also call on it to merge with the nation of which it is a part. The separation of the clergy is not essential—it is *abusive*, according to Sieyès.[73] The Revolution overturns the old hierarchy: the kingdom subjects ecclesiality to sovereignty. *The assembly becomes sovereign* by way of the Revolution. It is commonality that is coming back; it had been expelled from the world since the time of the Roman Empire. *The commons comes back to the world*: this is the essence of the revolutionary project—and we shall see all that it carries. That is why the Reformation re-surges: it was already forming this project to dissolve the clerical body—merging the separate body in the common body, the church fusing with the assembly, the body of the people fully (re)constituting the priestly body. Everyone baptized, everyone a priest. The Revolution brings back to the world the subjected common, and wants to enthrone it, constitute as sovereign the whole assembly of the people, freed and flourishing, the full body of the reappeared commonbeing. What the Revolution wants is the re-surrection of the common at the (fragmented and dislocated) place of the empire of the world—the crowning and the *consecration* of the people turned into the king.

(I earlier proposed to see the consecration as the condensation of the assembly upon the person. The consecration of the king-people would then be the self-consecration of the assembly. Where is the condensation? In that it is *as a person*, as unified and singular being, as I [*un moi*], that the assembly consecrates its own enthroning.[74] The consecration of the assembly is that of the common as a person [*personnalité*], and *as a body*. This defines the nation.[75] Why?)[76]

*

Questions (naively asked): why was there not only a re-surgence of the Reformation but a return as well? Why did the reverberating, spreading, extended Reformation not re-surge elsewhere? Why did the repressed return to the place of repression, to the position of sovereignty, to the heart of the state?

In the revolutionary process, this reversion does not seem immediate. That which dominates at the beginning rather evokes a *universal without any return*—for one is in fact dealing with the universal. A reminder: the (speculative) narrative in the present work seeks to grasp the constitution of French unity as one (of two) hypotheses about the union of Europe broken by the politico-religious rift. Let us recall that we are dealing with Europe as an ambivalence: the expanding movement of the universal on the one hand, *and* its turnaround toward itself, which is figural, on the other—the return to the soil of a fatherland. On this long road, I have sought to follow the formation and the course of this ambiguity in the de-composition of Romanity, the relative stabilization of European continentality in the late Middle Ages, and its internal fracturing as soon as it has gained this stabilization, as soon as the continent has had its con-formation. Indeed, what was at stake in the statization of France (the constitution of the kingdom), followed by its overthrow and reversal into a nation, was this unity to remake: the regrouping of the universal—fractured, divided, and dualized—but, within the dislocation itself, continuing to drive forward its process, its progression, its course, and its meta-morphic becoming, from one phase to the next, always carrying the equivocation of its expansion, of its onward transport *and* its figural, continental, and European reversion.

Now, at the start of the revolutionary period, when the concept of nation is laid out,[77] the *return* is barely looming, almost absent: the universal prevails, without retreating, *practically without a figure*. In the first acts and declarations, a very radical universalism asserts itself. The Declaration of the Rights of Man and of the Citizen, for which the National Assembly voted on August 26, 1789, and which the king accepted on October 3, promulgating it on November 3, *did not include the word "France," or "Français," in any of its articles*. Only the preamble indicated that "the representatives of the French people, organized as a National Assembly, . . . have determined to set forth in a solemn declaration the natural, unalienable, and sacred rights of man, in order that this declaration, being constantly before all the members of the Social body, shall remind them . . ."[78] The representatives of the French people state these rights and set them forth. But the rights are those of man and of the citizen—*not those of the French*. The active concept in the declaration is "nation" (and the concept of society)—*not France*.[79] No doubt, the nation, society (or man, or the citizen) are figures, too—identifications, returns. But these figures keep to the limit of any figurality, as it were; they are quasi-abstract; and in them the return does not seem to aim at any place except the locus of essence or essentiality—of the idea, as the idea of universality itself. *The nation is all the men*, all citizens, as if the question of its boundaries and its framework were irrelevant. *Not one nation, then*—this nation here, nation among all nations—but, plainly, *the* Nation.

Let us also note the attitude before the king, as a second sign. As a first step, he keeps his royal function alongside the assembly. We may find this inconsequential and transitory, since the coexistence of two depositaries of sovereignty seems so untenable retrospectively. But when they turn out to be incompatible, the first gesture that touches the king *is his deposition*. Strictly speaking, the deposition is the displacement of the king from the locus of sovereignty, the double transference of sovereignty onto the assembly, and of the royal person toward the *common*, ordinary place, that is, the position of the citizen. He who was king becomes a citizen. Deposition is transference; *decapitation will be a return. Deposition is doubtless always the most difficult part*: a great deal of strength and mobility is required to allow that which has been deposed to live, to be, and to be left alone, at the new place where it finds itself, a common and ordinary place, level with everyone. Deposition is nonregressive, whereas decapitation pays homage to the site of sovereignty, re-investing in its space, and making claims on its body. It is irreverence that deposes and dares look the deposed sovereign in the eye, putting itself at his level. All that decapitation knows is murder—regicide, patricide, deicide; it has been said repeatedly—only to stare down at the mutilated body on the ground, with the fascination owed to prominent corpses,[80] the mutilated body *whose spirit will always come back*: since decapitation is a great supplier of revenants, whereas deposition permits the dethroned *to grow old* and die at the same common level. Considering their stature, we can hardly compare Napoleon and Louis XVI, but we can set Louis XVI side by side with Napoleon III. In his exile, Napoleon Bonaparte leaves no specter behind, only a few partisans here and there. Put to death, the Bourbon king does leave a ghost, which continually returns to haunt us.

Why does the Revolution eventually turn to such violence, then, although so tenuously figural and strongly universal in its beginnings? In its declarations, *the nation* soon becomes *the French Nation*: first, to "declare peace"; then to declare war.[81] Deposition becomes decapitation. "Louis must die because the fatherland [*la patrie*] must live," says Robespierre.[82] I am—grudgingly—convinced that the very idea of "revolution" (of a cycle, a complete turn coming back to its first position) might encompass this figural return. But why the revolution, precisely? Why not the deposit, the transfer, or the journey across something? What kind of necessity has made the inheritor of the kingdom capture in the net of its constitution the undertaking that sought to free itself from it? The answer is that the Revolution, the overthrown kingdom, stayed within the bounds of its territory. The borders were its net. In the effectivity of the process, what happened—as a regressive factor, an operator of figurality, a trigger of the return—*was the war*. It is not as if the tendency could not be spotted earlier, but it remained confused, in competition and in conflict with other tendencies of a universalism that was more dynamic, more open, and more resistant to any reversion. The war came from the borders. Armies seeking to put the king back on his throne poked holes in the envelope of the kingdom. It is indubitable that the French Revolution was eventually expansionistic, aggressive, and belligerent. But it is also certain that until September 1792 and the advance of the armies of the First Coalition, this bellicose ambition had been muted. The war brought the return, just as clouds bring a storm. *The figure is played out at the border*. It rises up fully armed, at the exact point where the war powerfully turns the universal around, to its retreat.

Now, the hole-poking armies of September came from Germany.

15. On Germany

During the breakdown of the Roman world, kingdoms turn up in the space of the dissolving empire and the sites of its former provinces. In Gaul, little by little, but rather early on, the form of the kingdom begins to prevail, as *regnum Francorum*. Next door lies the complex Germanic space. It is complex because Germany is early on both external and internal to the Roman Empire.[83] There, the form of the kingdom does not seem to "take" or assert itself, which is to say, first of all, as far as we can observe, it does not succeed in stabilizing and securing a durable regime. And yet for several centuries, an entity in these lands calls itself the Regnum Teutonicum, later translated as the *kingdom of Germany*, and strives to shape itself as that. But whereas in neighboring France, the process of kingdom formation, though progressive and passing through various stages, asserts itself irreversibly, the nearby related undertaking does not lead to the lasting construction and constitution of the Germanic area as a kingdom.

In the context of linguistic facts, Benveniste notes a comparable heterogeneity.

> When we approach this notion of "king" in its lexical expression, we are struck by the fact that the word represented by *rex* appears only at the two extremities of the Indo-European world and is missing in the central part. We find on the one side *rex* in Latin, while Celtic is represented by Irl. *ri* and Gaulish *–rix*; at the other extremity we have Sanskrit *rāj-(an)*. There is nothing in between, not in another Italic language, nor in Germanic, Baltic, Slavic or Greek, or even in Hittite. This correlation is extremely important. . . . This fact is bound up with the very structure of the societies in question. It is not a simple accident of history. . . . The essential fact which explains these survivals that are common to the Indo-Iranian and Italo-Celtic societies is the existence of powerful colleges of priests who were the repositories of sacred traditions which they maintained with a formalist rigour. . . . However we should guard against believing that it was only because of the archaism of society that these facts have been preserved in these cases and not elsewhere. The changes made in the very structure of institutions have brought it about that the specific notion of *rex* was unknown to other peoples. There are certainly both in Greek and in Germanic words which may be translated as "king." But the Greek *basileús* has nothing in common with the *rāj*.[84]

This information has to be handled cautiously, but it seems to allow us to think that a—linguistic and social—structure was available in the Gallo-Roman space that served as a base or recourse in the constitution of royalty as a form, whereas this same (language-related or social) setup may have been absent in the Germanic area.

If royalty does not "take" there, what *is* the type of constitution that forms on the territory of the former Roman territory of Lesser Germania, giving its singular mode of existence to this piece detached from the empire? I suggest that no specific *figure* of this constitution presents itself, or, at least, is retained and used to identify what is coming there, to the land of the Germanic kingdom [*Germanie*], as the *constitution of Germany* [*Allemagne*]. There is no alternative model for royalty, that would be facing it as a possible (other) way of becoming, for a fragment of the former empire. In breaking up, the empire *gives rise* to the formation of kingdoms—or nothing. And since this nothing is evidently impossible, *it is the idea of empire itself* that presents itself to give figure to the (Germanic) fragment of the empire. As an alternative to royalty, only the idea of empire is available to figure what is coming forth in the "Germanic" space during the dislocation of the empire. What then follows the Roman Empire is the new empire (figurally or "imaginarily," as it were). For some time, there will be no royal constitution in Germany, only an imperial constitution. Or to put it another way, for quite some time, Germany will only be able to give figure to its formation and constitution as perpetuating, inheriting, and superseding the crushed Roman Empire. Accordingly, the constitution of Germany will in principle be highly charged with universality, connected with the imperial idea as such, and furthermore the idea of universality in the *extensive* mode (whereas the constitution of France, as we have seen, is associated with statization, that is, *intensive* universality). This calls to mind the commonplace observation that it took a long time for Germany *to become a nation*—there was a *lack of nationality* in Germany.[85] Germany in this phase is not produced specifically as a nation because the nation is the kingdom turned around and Germany is not produced as a kingdom—because after the breakup of the empire, the Germanic area is not a kingdom (a figure that neither "holds" nor "takes" there), and therefore not the nation overthrowing it, but instead the continuation replaying and superseding the empire itself; therefore the German nation will only be produced later on, *in a different way*.

At the very moment one writes the words "imperial constitution of Germany," one should erase the word "Germany" [*Allemagne*], for what is thus constituted is not exactly Germany, to be precise. Or to put it differently, by virtue of this imperial constitution, what is constituted *is and is not Germany*, at the same time. It is simultaneously Germany and what overflows and exceeds it. Conversely, "Germany" (the idea of Germany, as it were) will form itself all at once while referring to this constitution, this imperial undertaking, *and* against it, as a defect inscribed at the heart of this empire, a *lack of Germany* at the heart of the Reich—lack of nation [*défaut de nation*] is the term later used—here, a lack of kingship, in a way. Excess or lack of kingship, imperial excess over a kingdom in default, the *constitution of Germany* will inscribe itself lastingly into the logic of what one may term (following Jacques Derrida) its supplementary deficiency.

Otto I, known as the Great, who became king of the Regnum Teutonicum [*Germanie*] in 936, has retrospectively at times seemed the major player in the institution of Germany [*Allemagne*]. His crowning as emperor took place *in Rome* in 962, after he had earlier assumed the title of king of Italy (in 951). The Germanic empire, of which Otto I is the first titleholder, thus visibly maintains a very ambiguous relation with Germanity, since for all its being German, the empire in fact comprised the kingdom of Germany and the kingdom of Italy. This has two consequences: on the one hand, the empire is anchored in Germany [*Germanie*] and simultaneously spills over its borders. Now, this ambiguity, which can be considered constitutive of any imperial project or imperialism, is irreconcilable with the formation of a kingdom. Germany cannot constitute itself at the same time as a kingdom and an empire—since, by essence, the kingdom is a response to the decomposition of imperiality.[86] Kingdom and empire are incompatible, at least inasmuch as they cannot *be constituted together*. On the other hand, it obviously makes much sense that the area of the spillover is Italy. Italy is not just any site; it includes Rome—and the imperial design on Rome is decisive: the Germanic entity will never dispense with Rome; it will keep involving Rome in its imperial project and claiming to join the ecclesial legacy with the imperial legacy. From the start, the Holy Roman Empire, too, attempts a unitary overhaul of the theologico-political. It also wants to reunite the church and the empire—and reestablish their imperial unity—*like the kingdom*, thus, as we saw earlier. But the kingdom acknowledges the decomposition of Romanity at least insofar as it lodges in a territory, in a place. The kingdom tries unity, as a unity of place. As for the Holy Roman Empire, in a way it does not acknowledge anything: it wants to join church and empire, remake Rome for good—undivided Rome, ecclesio-imperial Rome, entirely redone. Now, Rome was not that synthesis, except at the end, apparently, just before the fall, and doubtless for that reason, to ward off or greet the imminent catastrophe, an end-of-the-world anthem to the purely impossible. One cannot reunite church and empire: they are the names of that which divides and constitutes itself through the division. A world can join them mythically, magically—and then collapse, myth in hand. However, the Holy Roman Empire cannot or will not accept that ecclesio-imperial Rome is finished and cannot be remade.

Further, the impossible imperial undertaking closes off the paths to the constitution of a kingdom—blocks the constitution of Germany [*Allemagne*]. This is a commonplace of historical analysis.

Because of their transalpine politics, the Saxon emperors have often been blamed for compromising the constitution of "a national body of Germany." A less grandiose, more northern, politics would have led the German people to withdraw into themselves, with a strong central power, whereas their Mediterranean chimeras led them to catastrophe. What is there to say to the detractors of the Ottonian rulers? No one in Germany at that time defended the idea of a "national empire."[87]

Let us skip over what seems an inevitable a posteriori reconstitution: the idea of a "German people," the subject of this adventure, that mistook the path to follow. Prior to this history, no such people existed, in Germany or elsewhere, because the effect of this history was precisely to *produce the people* as such.[88] This process and its ambiguity (both royal and imperial, and thus later national and metanational, as we shall see) produced the German people. No nation existed before the sequences described here led to their being constituted. Moreover, the term "national empire" is simultaneously both contradictory and anachronistic: in its own way, this phrase expresses what I have designated as the process of constituting the kingdom; and it is true that German history oscillates between this (royal) constitution and the imperial re-constitution that would mark the *will to have a Reich* in its successive instances. For the time period that is our focus (the end of the Middle Ages, when kingdoms take shape elsewhere), the name "Germany" [*Allemagne*] pinpoints this indecision exactly.

*

The constitution of Germany as a kingdom has failed. The idea of its imperial constitution is essentially untenable: imperial constitution, supposing it is possible, cannot be *Germany's*. The empire is a universalist idea, and this universalism is extensive and geographical; this is what makes the essence of its project. Now, the idea of Germany (like that of France or Spain) is a product of the breakdown of this universality, its fragmentation into places, its dislocation. Lesser Germany is a province of the empire, like Gaul or Iberia. With regard to imperial universalism, any Germanism is essentially provincial; and because of this, it is as if a double self-destructive tendency were undermining the idea of a Germanic empire. On the one hand, as a universalism, the (Germanic) empire will always essentially tend to exceed the Germanic area, seizing other lands, particularly Italian territories and Rome, whose name and idea are associated with imperiality as such and with its native solidarity with the church. The empire will thus always fail at constituting Germany, because its project will always exceed Germanism as such. But on the other hand, since the idea of empire is universalist and plurivocal, endowed with local multiplicity by virtue of its very extension, multiprovincial in its concept, it will lead Germany to fragment and its parts to multiply, producing various localities and new "provinces," its principalities. In other words, as the empire is going through its dislocation, the transfer onto Germany of the schema of the empire embodies a breaking-up and provincial multiplication—fragmentation into hundreds of principalities. In the context of the empire, Germany is thus a double impossibility: externally, because the empire overspills it into Italy and the east; internally, because the empire dismantles it into principalities.

It is to this impossibility of Germany that a new project responds, by undertaking to reshape it, on a new basis, and to re-constitute it where those first (royal and imperial) endeavors failed. This very different attempt bears the name "Reformation." Predating Martin Luther, the formula "Deutschland bedarf einer Reformation" (Germany needs a reformation) was "the slogan, which was rather vague but well suited to express the imprecise desires and worried aspirations of the German Nation."[89] The famous "Open Letter to the Christian Nobility Concerning the Reform of the Christian Estate," which Luther published in 1520 (one of his three "great Reformation writings"), articulates this project with much structured rigor. Its author's Christian project and his German project—they are inseparable; only our retrospective view sees distinct national and religious intentions in it. For Luther, it is one and the same enterprise: the

Reformation is plainly and evenly both Christian and German. The "Open Letter" is addressed to the *Christian* nobility of the *German* nation. The ecclesiastical project is to constitute Germany. A concept answers this project: the concept of the "German nation," which we shall have to question, while avoiding all the assimilations and anticipations that will not fail to crop up. But from the start we can say something that leaves no doubt whatsoever: *the German nation* is precisely the addressee of Luther's call for a Reformation. If Germany is constituted as a nation, it will be by the Reformation and thanks to it. Or to put it another way, the Reformation is a (new) undertaking for the constitution of Germany, and this constitution will be ecclesiastical: the nation is a theological idea.[90]

To know more about this, we need to read this astonishing text a little more closely.[91] It opens with the famous metaphor of the three walls, and is organized around it: "The Romanists, with great adroitness, have built three walls about them, behind which they have hitherto defended themselves in such wise that no one has been able to *reform them*; and this has been the cause of terrible corruption *throughout all Christendom*."[92] Indeed, the project is for a Reformation, in which the stakes are the fate of Christianity as a whole. The first wall is the distinction between the layman's state and the ecclesiastical state. For Luther, this distinction is an "invention" (p. 66), which he sets in opposition to the unique determination of the "Christian estate." "Yet no one should be frightened by it [this distinction]; and for this reason—viz., that all Christians are truly of the 'spiritual [or ecclesiastical (Gm., *geistlich*)—Trans.] estate'" (ibid.). Among Christians there is "no difference at all but that of office" (ibid.); "as Paul says in I Corinthians xii,[93] We are all one body, yet every member has its own work" (ibid.). As a result, through "baptism all of us are consecrated to the priesthood, as St. Peter says in I Peter ii,[94] 'Ye are a royal priesthood, a priestly kingdom'"; and with the Apocalypse, "'Thou hast made us by Thy blood to be priests and kings'" (ibid.).[95] The development of his thesis is threefold. First of all, the distinction (between ecclesiastical and lay states) has no object and is misleading because there is only one state—*but it is the ecclesiastical state*. The primordial unity in question here is that of the church, that is to say, *the assembly's*. There is only one assembly in the midst of which differences are functional ones, just as the sensory or motor functions of the parts of the body are distinct. The unity that the bodily metaphor deals with is *ecclesial* unity, the first founding unity of the assembly of the people. That is why the thesis is known as *universal priesthood*: everyone who is baptized is a priest; the common state is the ecclesiastical state. It is in no way a secularism that is involved, but on the contrary a general and full ecclesiology, without any reservation. The differences do not oppose an inside and an outside of the assembly but internal functions of the assembly itself. That is why royalty and sovereignty will be thought of as functions of the assembly, internal to the Church as the assembly of the people of God.

In a very logical but nonetheless astonishing way in this context, Luther draws a double conclusion:

Therefore when the bishop consecrates it is the same thing as if he, in the place and stead of the whole congregation [Gm., *Versammlung*], all of whom have like power, were to take one out of their number [Gm., *Haufen*] and charge him to use this power for the others; just as though ten brothers, all king's sons and equal heirs, were to choose one of themselves to rule the inheritance for them all,—they would all be kings and equal in power, though one of them would be charged with the duty of ruling.

To make it still clearer. If a little group [Gm., *Häuflein*] of pious Christian laymen were taken captive and set down in a wilderness, and had among them no priest consecrated by a bishop, and if there in the wilderness they were to agree in choosing one of themselves, married or unmarried, and were to charge him with the office of baptising, saying mass, absolving and preaching, such a man would be as truly a priest as though all bishops and popes had consecrated him. That is why in cases of necessity any one can baptise and give absolution, which would be impossible unless we were all priests. . . . It was in the manner aforesaid that Christians in olden days chose from their number [*aus dem Haufen*] bishops and priests. (Luther, "Open Letter," pp. 67–68)

It is a matter, here, of proposing a theory of *consecration*. But to do so, Luther rigorously distributes the two comparisons he has developed. The first concerns royalty: royal children elect one in their group to *exercise* their power. They all remain equal kings but only one of them is *charged* with royalty; he is the depositary of this function but exercises this power in the name of "the whole congregation [*Versammlung*], all of whom have like power." Later on the same will be said about royalty, in appropriate terms: "the temporal power has become a member of the body of Christendom, and is of the 'spiritual estate,' though its work is of a temporal nature" (p. 71). What defines royal authority is its task; it has no specificity as a state. The sacrament (the consecration of the coronation, in this instance) consists merely in choosing a king among the crowd, which is the common body of which the one consecrated remains a member. But (and the second comparison develops this) *the one performing the consecration is a member of it too*; for, instead of kings, the second part of this passage mentions priests—and it is *essentially* the same thing (this being the thesis here). If a company of "laymen" is in the desert, it will elect from its midst one of its members to carry out all the worship and to bestow all the sacraments. And the designated member will *truly be a priest*, "as though all bishops and popes had consecrated him." The sacrament comes from the assembly as such; the one who is consecrating merely speaks and acts in its name. This "would be impossible *unless we were all priests*"—everyone baptized, everyone a priest. The common, unique state is the ecclesiastical state. *In truth, there are no laymen.*

One is thus clearly dealing with a general ecclesiology here. The one body where all functions are organically integrated is the assembly, and within it there are only mandates, and the allocation and distribution of charges. As mentioned earlier, sacraments are the depositing upon the individual of a sign attesting that the assembly temporarily provides itself with the means of exercising an office. But everything, royalty as well as priesthood, originates from the assembly and is grounded in it.

> From all this it follows that there is really no difference between laymen and priests, princes and bishops, "spirituals" and "temporals," as they call them, except that of office and work, but not of "estate"; *for they are all of the same estate*,—true priests, bishops and popes,—though they are not all engaged in the same work. (Luther, "Open Letter," p. 69; emphasis added)

Rigorously, the Reformation proposes a reunification of the theologico-political, but it is a theological unification. We find ourselves in a situation exactly symmetrical with regard to the one described about the kingdom: while the kingdom was a model of the reunion of the sovereign and the assembly, within the regime of sovereignty, the Reformation deals with a reunion, too, but one that unfolds wholly as an ecclesiality; here, the common space of the sovereign and the assembly is—absolutely—the assembly.

That is why these (royal and priestly) functions cannot be the object of any appropriation. There is neither a lay state nor an ecclesiastical state separate from the common state because there is nothing pertaining properly to the layman or the priest. These functions, which are exercised in the singular, are common by essence and only become singular in the modality of their implementation. This office or mandate never negates the common character of the being that expresses itself through it—this is what the sacrament makes plain. "For what is common to all [Gm., *der Gemeinde*], no one dare take upon himself without the will and the command of the community" (p. 68). No essential appropriation, no legitimate property as the property of a state: any function can be revoked, any mandate rescinded. There is no state—except the Christian state, the state of the assembly, the common state. This common state is given figure by the image of the body, which is more than an image:

> This is the teaching of St. Paul in Romans xii[96] and I Corinthians xii, and of St. Peter in I Peter ii,[97] as I have said above, viz., that we are all one body of Christ, the Head, all members one of another. *Christ has not two different bodies, one "temporal," the other "spiritual." He is one Head, and He has one body.* (Luther, "Open Letter," p. 69; emphasis added)

What these pages convey is thus a project to reform Christianity, that is to say, a general reform of the Church, but, since the Church means "all Christians," in the sense that the Reformation affects the social as a whole. Now, at the same time, this project also sets forth a constitution of Germany. Germans should bring on this undertaking because it is Germany that is touched by its urgency. Now, in the text, the passage from one plane to the other, from Christianity to Germany, is never thematized. The text keeps asserting the unity of the two, but their link—the connection leading from one agency to the other—is never the object of a deductive argumentation. It is the Reformation of Christianity, and equally that of Germany, but nowhere is there an account of how and why Germany thus takes on the destiny of Christianity.

Yet the project itself carried the seeds of this question. If it is a question of remaking the church, precisely to re-constitute it as an assembly, one cannot avoid asking who or what is assembling in this way.[98] A first answer is ubiquitous in the text: they are the baptized. The limit, or difference, between Christianity and all of humanity is baptism. But which place does this limit trace out? How is the assembly circumscribed? What is the boundary, the space, and the topos of the gathering? What is the locus of that which assembles itself? The answer is: the space of the empire's authority, namely, the world. The primitive church was constituted as the obverse or other side of the Roman Empire, and this relation reappears here under a new aspect. The empire was universal, and so was the church. Simply, because of the division, since the locus of the assembly ("its kingdom") was not of this world, the topos of this universality was referred back to the figure of a doubled world. When the empire disintegrated, the question of the place of the (assembling) people became a pressing one: with the empire fragmented into kingdoms, what is the circumscription of the church? Is it the world, Catholic universality? Or the Gallican and Anglican countries? The church is the other of the empire—but which imperiality determines how its circumscription sets itself apart? This question became even acuter on German lands: at this time, there was no circumscription of Germany except that of the empire, which was doubly problematic (the empire was uncertain on its own, and it did not effectively outline Germany). Questions with regard to the place of the people who assemble are inscribed and become acuter in the space that this uncertainty lays out.

This ambiguity marks Luther's text. Why does Germany have to take upon itself a Reformation that concerns all of Christianity? Elements of an answer run throughout his "Open Letter"—dispersed and without any apparent connection. It is because of the "distress and oppression which weigh down all the Estates of Christendom, especially of Germany" ("Open Letter," p. 63)—and elsewhere because the empire (which is a function of Christianity) happens to be in the hands of the Germans;[99] or further, because "God has given us a noble youth to be our head and thereby has awakened great hopes of good in many hearts" (ibid.). The young man was Charles V, who as we know had a Burgundian father and a Spanish mother, whose mother tongue was French, and whose Germanity at this time merely consisted in his election to the head of the empire.[100]

That is why the connection between the fate of Christianity and the task of the Germans, while continuously reasserted, is not the object of any specific thematization. The destiny of the church is played out in Germany—this is the way it is. Accordingly, the fate of this general ecclesiology and its rigorous construction, which I have located in Luther's venture, itself becomes an object of questioning; for this project is in fact universalist in its principle and its expression: it concerns all who are baptized, posited as priests in the regime of a universal priesthood that affects the becoming of the Revelation, the general history of salvation. And yet this church to be reformed and re-constituted is in fact the church of Germany, or rather it is all Germans, baptized, assembled as a church, which is to say,

Germany as a church—or, one could say (to bring out the tension that this thesis contains), the paradox of Germany as a kind of universal church. It is not as though Luther would want the abolition of France or Bohemia, but the conceptual setup he puts in place, by way of a strange connection, joins the thematics of the Reformation of the universal church with the project of the Reformation as the constitution of Germany.

This ambiguity expresses itself in Luther's use (typical for the times) of the term "nation." Let us note that this word is latinate: while Luther germanizes an important part of his linguistic usage, especially in his translations, he does not hesitate to romanize the designation of structurally important aspects of his venture, such as the terms reformation and nation. A complete germanization of the language is not on the agenda (yet).[101]

Three additional remarks about the use of the term "nation":

(1) Within a first set of meanings, widespread throughout the text, the "administrative" use of "nation" persists (as in the use, cited earlier, of the "nation of Picardy at the University of Paris" to designate a group of students). In Luther's text, "nation" is extensively used to designate the group of German delegates who form one of the subdivisions of the imperial diet, an administrative category.

At each meeting of the diet from 1486 onward, the grievances of the German nation were written down, collected, and sometimes published under the title *Gravamina germanicae nationis*, or *Beschwerden der deutschen Nation* . . . and Luther doubtless read the last collection emerging from the 1518 deliberations. . . . For some time, editors and publishers have been able to point to direct recollections of the grievances laid out by the diet against the abuses and exactions of Rome in the "Open Letter to the Christian Nobility."[102]

Among numerous examples, we read: "Now, in this matter the German nation, bishops and princes, should consider that they too are Christians, and should protect the people, whom they are set to rule and guard in things temporal and spiritual" ("Open Letter," pp. 85–86). Here, clearly, the nation is not the people (since its duty is to protect the people), but the equivalent of "bishops and princes," bodies that are present or represented at the diet. And further, "by a law of the emperor or of the whole nation, they should either keep the annates [a form of ecclesiastical tribute to the pope][103] at home or else abolish them again" (p. 125). Luther could not urge "the nation" in our current sense of the term to sign a law, so that the word appearing in the title, the "Christian Nobility of the German Nation," is first of all the nobility that is present at the diet and in the institutions of the empire, able to become involved and support a Reformation.

(2) Nevertheless, it is evident that the sense of the word in this text cannot be reduced to this administrative usage; it goes beyond it, for example, when Luther announces that he is "forced . . . to cry aloud that God may inspire some one with His Spirit to lend this suffering nation a helping hand" (p. 63), a phrase that is clearly related to the later one, "the misery and distress of suffering Christendom" (p. 64). The meaning of "nation" therefore goes beyond its corporate usage, toward something more abstract and general, which tends toward the "national" reality of our language today.

(3) Nevertheless, it would be anachronistic and thus erroneous to read the word in the sense that is familiar to us today. We have seen that the word "nation" did not begin to acquire its current meaning in French until the late eighteenth century, and more so during the nineteenth. At no time can the term strictly be taken in this modern sense in Luther's text, and this can be linked, it seems, to the fact that the term "Germany" [*Allemagne*] is never taken as a historical subject either. Quite often we find in the text a call to "Germans," urging them ceaselessly to perform their task vis-à-vis Rome or the empire. One also finds "German lands" suffering from the exactions of the papacy, which have the means to make them stop. "Germany" crops up, in the geographical sense, but never (unless I have overlooked it) Germany-as-subject, Germany-the-nation. Never is "Germany" summoned to face its destiny, its confrontation with Rome, and so on—"Germans" are. For the modern idea of nation is being shaped but is not fully formed yet. This "cultural," "linguistic," and "historical" reality, which is pre-sup-posed by the reality of the state or politics and is distinct from it, as the subject supposed to be behind its actions, the nation that can be denied or unheeded by the state, the nation that nonetheless forms the state's support, the base of the building, is the nation that Luther's text does not name or conceptualize expressly, even if many of its traits are foreshadowed. Luther's "nation" is an intermediate and transitory notion, between an imperial administrative category and modern political subjectivity or subjectity.

The Reformation of Christianity is born as a project to constitute Germany: this is the paradoxical idea toward which this examination has led us. Now, the Reformation fails as far as constituting Germany is concerned. The movement does not fashion any unity of the Germanic world; on the contrary, it leads to the fixation of its division, a religious, then a geographical, spatial, and political division. Henceforth the new (dual) fracture between Catholicism and Protestantism overlays the dispersion of a multitude of principalities, without reducing it in any way. This division will undergo a very different treatment from the one it can expect in France—a state venture to eradicate one of the opposing creeds, evidently impossible in Germany since there is no *German state* sufficiently constituted to pursue it. Charles V the Catholic attempts this, but he exhibits the impotence of the empire as such to play this role—the (already mentioned) reason being that the empire is unable to reproduce the Roman (worldwide, universal) imperial idea, or to give shape to Germany in its difference and place. The Holy Roman Empire is an ambivalent structure, essentially unstable, caught between its (passéist but utopian) imperial dream and the desire for a Germany. It is this ambivalence and this instability that become fixated as the religious division of Germany: each region adopts the religion of its prince (*cujus regio, ejus religio*). Germany splits up following a line roughly running from east to west, separating a north and a south henceforth cohabiting religiously and facing each other—just as Catholicism and Protestantism cohabit and face each other in Europe, too. The division of Germany is the religious division of Europe. The question of German unity will henceforth come up, in many ways, as the question of European unity.

But the paradoxical fate of Germany is that it divides (or splits, or breaks in two) *without ever having been unified*. Something like a desired and projected Germany breaks up before its formation—*or forms itself broken*. The idea of Germany may be contemporary (or, more strictly, solidary) with the tracing of its own breakup. The constitution of Germany is cracked, like a shape emerging from its mold. It appears at least that among different attempts to form a Germany, none succeeds, all their processes being impeded: the kingdom does not "take"; the empire (as a German one) is impossible; the Reformation splits and fractures. At the heart of modernity, to put it in Hegel's terms, Germany *is not a state*.[104]

16. Looping Back

After the failure of the Reformation to constitute Germany, which repeats the previous failures first of royalty, then of the empire, the Germanic space registers at the heart of Europe as the locus of a shortcoming of politics, constitution, or the state.[105] This lack will give rise to an abundant literature, especially from the end of the eighteenth century onward, when it sparks off countless analyses, commentaries, and regrets—a sign that, once again, the shortcoming is turning into a project. After 1800, the issue of the "constitution of Germany" prevails for quite some time as a structurally relevant theme in politics.

Let us look at the testimony provided by a short essay by Christoph Martin Wieland titled "Ueber teutschen Patriotismus" (On German Patriotism), and published—among many other similar texts—in May 1793:

> I have not yet been able to come to a clear and orthodox concept of what one calls a German Patriot . . . In my childhood I was told about many duties, toward God, my neighbor and myself; duties toward parents and teachers; and no doubt in passing a word about duties toward authority, toward His Majesty the Holy Roman Emperor as the highest ruler of the Empire, and especially toward the Honorable Mayor and the Council of the honorable city of N. N., my dear native city [Gm., *Vaterstadt*—Trans.];[106] but the duty to be a *German patriot* was so rarely mentioned that I cannot recall hearing the word German [Gm., *Teutsch* or *Deutsch*—Trans.] mentioned honorably (Germanity [*Teutschheit*—Trans.]) was still a completely unknown word, then), while I can still vividly remember from my school years that the appellation "German Michel" was one of those only slightly less shameful for a young Alemannic [Gm., *Allemannier*—Trans.] to acquire than to wear the dunce's cap.[107]

Here the shortcoming in politics, constitution, and state appears under the aspect of a lack of patriotism or feeling. The sense of duty can apply to the city (a fragmentary entity, a multiplicity of which makes up the empire) and its officials; to the parents and teachers—that which Hegel will call the multiplicity of private rights and duties: "a register of the most varied constitutional rights [Gm., *Staatsrechte* (i.e., rights of the state—Trans.)] acquired in the manner of civil law [Gm., *Privatrecht* (i.e., private law—Trans.)]"[108]—as well as to the (Holy Roman Germanic) Emperor; but not to Germany—and this confirms that the empire is not the equivalent of Germany and that the feeling for one does not carry over to the other: the empire does not constitute Germany as such. Wieland goes on,

> When the great Persian king Xerxes, at the head of an innumerable army, penetrated into the heart of Greece, it consisted in great part of a multitude of free cities, which were barely larger and more powerful . . . than our imperial cities during their happiest time.[109] . . . These small free cities fared quite well in their indepen-

dence.... However, each Greek city or population had to admit at first glance that it alone—each group by itself—could attempt nothing against an enemy terrifying by reason of their numbers. It was only when they were unified that these Greeks, whom Xerxes would have annihilated in isolation, could reasonably hope to oppose a successful resistance. Therefore they united, and every private passion instantly subsided before the feeling of common distress, as well as every remembered insult or fresh grievance, all jealousy and mistrust: suddenly a burning soul arose throughout Hellas. Athenians and Spartans, Euboeans and Corinthians, Thebans and Plateans—all now felt that they simply were Hellenes and were fighting as brothers for the safeguard and freedom of the common fatherland. This is the reality, as everyone knows. (Wieland, "Ueber teutschen Patriotismus," pp. 7–9)

This text fits in with a long series of—earlier and especially later—writings that seek to establish a parallel between modern Germany and ancient Greece.[110] The comparison will have various functions, and one of the first will be to posit Germany in contrast to Rome: Germany's kinship with Greece arises from their common alienation from the Roman world. Greece was smothered by it and Germany can only be born if it breaks away from it, its vocation being to recover a part of what was lost during the collapse (the Romanization) of Hellenism. This will be one of Fichte's themes.[111] But Wieland does not make the argument explicit. The comparison here bears on patriotism as the feeling of belonging to a political community, and on the intensity of this feeling. In comparing Germany and Greece, Wieland means to convey that *patriotism comes from outside*; it is the Persian danger that creates Greek unity. Before this danger, the cities were engaged in "private passions"—jealousy, memories of ancient offenses or recent injuries, various mistrusts—and in a kind of municipal or city patriotism that satisfies them until this external threat springs up: "These small free cities fared quite well in their independence." Hellenic patriotism, Wieland says, and therefore German patriotism, the object of his comparison, does not find its source in itself, in a kind of self-generated love of self [*amour de soi*], arising from its internal necessity. Rather (to play with Rousseau's distinction), it is a self-love [*amour-propre*] to which outer confrontation, obstacles, and danger give birth. And there is proof:

No sooner had the common danger been removed and the Greeks had enjoyed the first fruits of their victories, than each free state sank back into itself. The common spirit that had worked such great miracles stopped blowing; Hellenes again became Athenians, Spartans, Corinthians, Euboeans, Thebans, and so on. Once again each one thought only of himself. . . . In a word, private patriotism devoured . . . the general patriotism. (Wieland, "Ueber teutschen Patriotismus," p. 10)

When the external source of patriotism dries up, it vanishes as (Hellenic or German) "general patriotism" and reverts to "private" municipal patriotisms. But why did each city not lock itself into its local patriotism and the defense of its identity in confronting the external danger? It is obviously—Wieland says—because the enemy is much stronger in number: its size and geopolitical dimensions are much vaster. The process is heavy with consequences: increasing the size of political units because of the war brings changes that will lead to hegemonic alliances, the fall of the city-states, and their replacement, first by the extensive Roman Republic, and then—again by reason of size—by the Roman Empire. For historians it is a familiar observation: the idea of empires comes from the Orient. It is from the confrontation with the Persian "Empire" that the Greco-Roman western world draws the necessity to build an extensive political construct. As if mimetically with regard to its eastern adversary, Greece starts a political process that will become "imperialist." Wieland notes this effect of the war: after the victory over the Persians, "Athens and Sparta again fought for the honor and the advantages of what they modestly designated the 'hegemony' (leadership) of Greece, which in fact was nothing less than an oppressive domination over the members of the confederation" (Wieland, "Ueber teutschen Patriotismus," p. 10). The sequence of events that Wieland suggests is thus the following: imperialism forms mimetically in relation to an outside threat, and national patriotism is constituted there, in this struggle, this confrontation, this face-off. Starting with this analogy, Wieland continues his argument about Germany:

Now, would not this last case be ours, in fact? . . . Not only is there, I think, a lack of almost everything that would inspire the nation with such a patriotic common spirit: but one can also find in our constitution and situation some causes with strong contrary effects, which make the existence of such a spirit almost impossible. . . . There are perhaps—or rather, there are without any doubt—patriots of the Mark, of Saxony, Bavaria, Württemberg, Hamburg, Nuremberg, Frankfurt, and so forth. But German patriots, who love the entire German Reich as their fatherland . . . where are they? Who can show them to us, and name them? (Wieland, "Ueber teutschen Patriotismus," pp. 12–14)[112]

German patriotism does not proceed from any internal necessity or autonomous finality; it comes from outside. From where?

And so, let us not flatter ourselves too much about our supposed patriotism. . . . As in all ancient hunters' sayings, there is much truth in this one, "any place, where we feel well is a fatherland to us" (*patria est ubi bene est*). . . . For example, this is one way (among others) in which I interpret the patriotic stirrings that began to arise—more or less strongly—among many Germanic populations, against the French hordes who had flooded the most beautiful part of our Rhine regions, from the moment when our people apparently started believing—because of the decrees then passed by the nat.[ional] assembly of December 15 and 21, and the actions based on them at the hands of the French army leaders and their hordes—that this disorganization of any civic order [Gm., *bürgerliche Ordnung*—Trans.] truly did not concern the betterment of our condition, but instead only had to do with spreading the fire of revolt and discord, which had already raged in their bellies for four years. . . .

But even here we do not wish to deceive ourselves. One may ascribe this less to our German patriotism than to the incomprehensible nonsense of the Gallic fanatics and factions; less to the attachment of our people to the common fatherland than to the deep revulsion that the abject murder of King Louis XVI . . . roused in the minds of the German people; less to any conviction, impossible for most, concerning the excellence of our common constitution, than a (perhaps unnecessary) fear . . . to see this enraged mob swinging the burning torch of destruction in our particular fatherland—if there has been a display of such a generally noticeable changed expression in the representation of this matter of the French Revolution, superseding (since last year and especially since January 21 of this year) the ambivalent indifference or wavering opinion among a nonnegligible number of our Germans. (Wieland, "Ueber teutschen Patriotismus," pp. 14–17)

Wieland's argument has several stages. (1) The supposed German patriotism relies in fact on the desire to preserve a certain comfort and a certain suitable life, which in the face of danger will turn into the equivalent of "a (perhaps unnecessary) fear to lose the benefits that [our constitution] has allowed us so far to enjoy" (p. 16). There is no positive attachment to Germany as such based on "the conviction that our common constitution is excellent." Therefore, (2) attachment to the fatherland proceeds from the external threat, from the foreign invasion, from fear—fear of the "French hordes," which is to say, the invasion of the revolutionary troops starting in 1792 and 1793. Now, what is frightening in this invasion? It is not the foreign irruption as such, whose rejection would suppose the previous existence of a national sentiment, but instead the imported disorder, the exactions, and the fire of riot. Indeed, we know that the French troops were not at first rejected as foreigners when they entered Germany. The reception of the French in the Rhine region (warm or wait-and-see, depending on each case) does not seem to have been marked by any violent rejection; on the contrary, parts of this population looked so favorably on the (initially anti-authoritarian and anti-hierarchical) politics and liberating intentions of the invaders that attempts at Franco-Rhenish alliances came to light and culminated in a project to attach a part of the Rhenish province to the French Republic—a project conceived and developed by German revolutionary personalities and not by the invaders.[113] The turnaround, as Wieland suggests, takes place in part at least because of the attitude of the occupation forces, which soon give in to the seductions of imperialist behavior: plunder, ransoming of local wealth, the arrogance of the victors, their excessively authoritarian behavior in the name of exporting the principles of the Revolution, and so on. (3) The most troubling point, of course, is the third one: German hostility to the Revolution, says Wieland, finds its discernible trigger in the "the decrees then passed by the nat.[ional] assembly of December 15 and 21," which contained the order that Louis Capet [the king] appear before the revolutionary tribunal, and the educational reform.[114] From the same perspective, Wieland mentions that German public opinion had turned around "especially since January 21 of this year"—since the execution of the king (the king *of France*).

There is no German patriotism or spontaneous patriotic feeling toward Germany as such.[115] German patriotism is born from the French invasion. This invasion provokes a rejection (the birth of patriotic sentiment) because of the *imperialist* attitude of the occupiers, *as well as the accusation and execution of the king*. These observations can give rise to the following hypothesis: after the successive failures of royalty, empire, and the Reformation,

It is the French Revolution that brings about the constitution of Germany. (h12)

*

One may of course find fault with this last hypothesis as highly Francocentric. France has "made" Germany, as it were, and—connecting this hypothesis to the previous one[116]—the (French) Revolution has made the (German) nation. It is thus an aggressive hypothesis concerning German "identity" as such. I would like to challenge this suspicion and recall how this idea fits within the whole schema that I have proposed. Indeed, if Germany's constitution derives from the French Revolution, that Revolution is seen as the resurgence of the Reformation, which arose in Germany precisely *as a project to constitute Germany* as such. What is transferred to France in the second half of the sixteenth century is exactly what has just failed in Germany *as a national project*. The failure of the Reformation to unify the German lands can be dated to the Diet of Augsburg in 1555, which brought about the religious partition of the empire. This was precisely when the wars of religion began in France, in which the stakes were the politico-religious fate of the kingdom. In those years, and the two following centuries, the repression [*refoulement*] of the Reformation becomes indissociable in France from the process of the constitution of the French state—the becoming-a-state of what is termed "centralization," as something specifically French. The (centralist) constitution of the French state merges with the Reformation's (royal, unifying, and centralized) process of repression, providing all the elements of modern French statehood. What the French state takes on is *its own constitution as a state, as the repression of what had failed to constitute Germany*: the Reformation of Christianity. This is the state that the Revolution overthrows—and it is this overthrow that comes back to Germany as an invasion.

What loops back into Germany with the revolutionary armies from France is thus its own repressed failure to constitute itself as Germany. Reversed in this way, the hypothesis may now strongly be suspected of Germanocentrism. But these two "centrisms" (German and French) are equally deceptive. The origin of the process cannot be found in Germany or France—a process can never be understood from its origin, but only in its development. And this involves France and Germany—commonly—in a becoming that is specific to each but nonetheless connected—their becoming-national, or becoming-a-nation. And one cannot think of the "nationalizations" of France or of Germany as autonomous destinies; rather, they are specific formations driven by a momentum that carries both of them ahead. *Europe is obviously the common appellation of this process*, and here we return to what was announced: French unity and German unity are two divergent answers to its politico-religious division. "France" and

"Germany" are two hypotheses of European union. Putting it this way calls for a cautionary word: while France and Germany are two European processes, thinkable in the—European, solidary and contradictory—community of their onward movement, one should not carry over to Europe the status of an autonomous self-instituted subject, self-sufficient and exhibiting its own identity—an originary, founding status denied to every nation here. In this phase, Europe is nothing except the name of the universal as a movement, turning itself around at the point where it has halted and failed. Europe is nothing *but* the figure of the universal, that is to say, its return (to itself, onto itself) from the spot of its stopping and its reversal; and France and Germany are then formed as attempts to respond to the breaking of this figure, the breakup that happens to it, when it is removed from its mold: the wars of religion. France and Germany are attempts (adverse—associated in their adversity) to (re)apportion [*(re)membrer*] the universal on the terrain of Europe, which is broken. Their (national) "identity" is the imaginary designation of what constitutes them as specifications, as stages in the history of this process. France and Germany are moments (branches or phases) of a historic process that has to be understood as worldwide-European.

That is why the historical account of their two "national questions" seems shackled to the wheel of an incessant back-and-forth movement. *In one sense*, the constitution of Germany is problematized and theorized—and probably carried out—from the turn of the nineteenth century onward, in response and relation to the French revolutionary invasion and its Napoleonic continuation.[117] The hostility to this invasion, the reaction against it, builds up decisively at the death of Louis XVI, though he is king *of France*, and his execution might seem to concern what we call domestic politics today. Now, this execution has a determining impact on the political consciousness of what has to be called Europe here.[118] *But in the opposite direction*, this double observation immediately needs to be turned around: for it is the *entry* into France of the counterrevolutionary armies of the (Austro-Prussian) Germanic coalition that provokes the departure of the revolutionary armies from the territory of the kingdom. The avowed motivation of this intervention is to save the king (while he has been neither deposed nor judged—only crippled) and to reinstate him with his prerogatives. And it is this very intervention that acts as a trigger of his dismissal, of the proclamation of the republic, followed by the sentencing and execution of the monarch. And so, in this specular face-off between the French Revolution and European (mostly Germanic) monarchies, effects and causes inextricably mingle, *in both directions*.

(Let us note that this process confirms that the destiny of French royalty is in no way a question of so-called "domestic politics," even if this notion had any imaginable meaning in eighteenth-century Europe. The fate of the kingdom [and the king] of France matters to all: *it involves the destiny of the theologico-political as such*, the universal lineage of the church and the empire. That is why, as many have pointed out, this regicide is a deicide or a patricide. What is called into question, with the king of France, is the intertwining [in the person, singularity, and body of the king] of the theological and the political, the imperial and the ecclesial, which is to say, the structure of all legitimation inherited from Rome, the genealogy and the lineage of the European theologico-political edifice as a whole—all the monarchies, principalities, and empires of Europe, without any exception. And thus, conversely, the king's sentencing and execution point to the—imaginary and identifying—intertwining of every [German, or more generally national] counterrevolution.[119] The death of the king [of France] ties German hostility into an identity. Henceforth, what "Germany" spurns is the deposition and the dismissal of this ancestral legacy, the patrimony of Europe as such—the whole theologico-political constitution of Europeanism. And, in a specular way, this refusal amounts to a self-positioning.)

To go on with this regression, we may recall that the Germans, *in a way*, in asserting their national legitimacy rebelled against French (linguistic or "cultural") domination of Enlightenment Europe, a domination especially carried out in Germany: let us recall that Frederick the Great wrote his books of political theory—aimed at Germans—in French.[120] Whereas, *in the opposite direction*, France rejected, at the price of a violently murderous civil war, the irruption of the *principle of the Reformation*, born in Germany. Meanwhile, *in one way*, Luther himself, in his project to reform Germany, saw in the kingdom of France a model of autonomy with regard to Rome—"national" *avant la lettre*—something that Germany was tragically lacking and that served as an example.[121] And to this one should add, at last, in the *opposite direction*, in a certain royalist (or other) imaginary, the idea of the Germanic origin of the noble parts of France's social body.[122]

France and Germany thus appear twinned, the doubly mingled branches of a unique arborescence, pertaining to the process that is tearing up and reunifying politico-religious Europe. But beyond the identificatory face-off that this confrontation keeps reproducing between the two nations, it is *the constitutive interdependence of the revolutionary and national problematics* that makes it possible to understand the processual dependence thus described. Revolution and nation are the two sides of a single question, the two poles of one process. And this does not lessen their antagonism, but rather explains it, and interprets the violence of their conflict. There is no revolution that does not rise to become a national hypostasis, and there is no nation that does not bank on a revolutionary uprising. Nationalism can appear progressive (such as France's after 1792), or regressive (such as Germany's a little later), and while this in fact changes numerous characteristics in their description, it in no way affects this kinship: nationalism—every nationalism—finds energy and resources in being charged by the process of a revolution. The counterrevolution is nothing without the revolution that brings it. The counterrevolution wants to crush that which it *counters*, but it does so by imitating it and identifying with the truth of its destiny, and that makes the counterrevolution something other than a passéist restoration. Restoration concerns the rich, who have been dispossessed and are coming back. The counterrevolution has a different scope: it wants to fulfill what the revolution has missed and to negate it by completing, superseding, and finishing it. *The counterrevolution is revolutionary*—this is what makes for its seductiveness, its dangers, and its own demonism. It imitates the revolution just as Satan mimics God. And in this imitation something comes across: the limit is not hermetically sealed. The nation is the appellation, in the revolutionary process, of that which returns to itself, is given figure, and closes up, even as an image of the universal—such as the French universalist nation: expansionist, Napoleonic, and colonizing.[123] But the Revolution is the engine of every nationalism, even the most ferociously reactive one: it only reacts in the conflict and specular rivalry with a revolution that spawns it—such as the German particularist nation: since the particular is nothing but the reverse of the universal and carries some of the universalist charge from which it results. There is a pact between the greatness of France and the freedom of the world, Charles de Gaulle claimed,[124] a universalism incarnated in French singularity just as the divine is in the person of Christ. Fichte wrote that the German nation (in the particularity of his time, his place, and his language) marks the rise of a new humanity, a new creation:[125] the particular taking charge of the destiny of the whole. Such are the two faces of this uprising—divine or diabolical, as one prefers: *Janus bifrons*, nation and revolution, a monstrous two-faced god. Wishing or thinking oneself in solidarity with revolutions *henceforth* must not prevent this acknowledgment. Quite to the contrary—*all the same, one day, there will have to be an insurrection that does not turn into its monstrous form*. That is why we have to keep looking at and describing the double, reversible, and retractable constitution of revolutions and nations; it is *after* this that we have to think.

17. A Hypothesis for the Twentieth Century?

In this view, we can only understand revolution and nation in their interrelation, a specular recognition that associates the images of their two figures, but also a structural and processual solidarity that connects their effectivity. After 1800, this connection strengthens and becomes tense.

The initial situation thus looks like this:

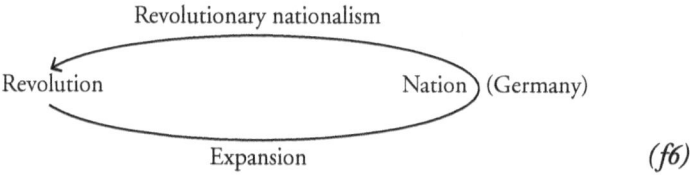

(f6)

The revolution is produced *as* a universalist expansion; it is carried by the expansive movement of the universal. Soon it turns around and comes back to itself as a figure. The point of return is its collision with Germany, where the universal ends up, and a *remainder* appears: the return is specular, *because* it is, in the first place, effective, and effectivity speculates. The Revolution then comes back, toward itself, charged with the national idea. It recognizes itself as revolutionary nationalism. It rejoins itself, re-posits itself as the origin, retraverses and doubles itself; and universalism, which is extensive, is recharged with intensiveness. Doubled revolution, revolution of and within the revolution, total revolution. The name of this intensive and totalizing radicalization is socialism.¹²⁶ Socialism is the appellation of the doubling produced by the turnaround of the revolutionary process, which intensifies and is totalized.

As for the nation, it takes an analogous (effective and specular) turn—but effective because it is specular: speculation works.

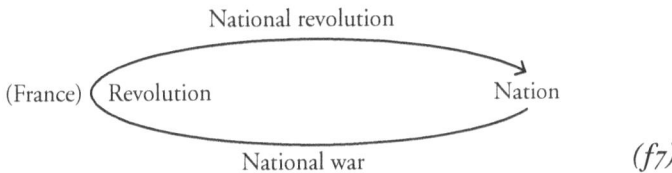

(f7)

The nation exceeds itself, exits from itself to free itself (national war, war of liberation).¹²⁷ It collides with the (French) Revolution. It turns back to itself, charged with the image of the Revolution and with effective revolutionizing processes. It comes back to itself, as a nation recharged with revolution—national revolution. And it finds itself again, retraverses and reconstitutes itself: revolutionized nation, full and total nation, reconfiguring its movement as fundamentalism [*intégrisme*], national-revolutionary totalitarianism—as fascism. Fascism is the appellation of the doubling produced at the core of nationalism by its passage across the revolutionary process.

These two—symmetrical—operations shed some light on national characteristics. Socialism, in this schema, is the product of the doubling of the French Revolution, turning around after the failure of its universalist expansion: the doubled Revolution after being reflected in the mirror of the nation. Socialism is therefore a kind of French production. Let us recall that, in the Marxist vulgate, three sources were said to feed the new revolutionary thinking—three national sources:¹²⁸ political economy (the English theory of capital), (French) socialism, and idealism (philosophical romanticism, which is German). Fascism, on the other hand, is the product of the turnaround of the nation, which retraverses itself after it has been put to the—antagonistic and identity-yielding—test of its conflict with the French Revolution. Fascism did experience its first political victory in Italy and got its name there, but its dominant theoretical apparatus derived from German counterrevolutionary and idealist romanticism.¹²⁹ Significantly, it first sprang up in countries that were formerly subjected to Napoleonic occupation and rejected it.¹³⁰

This circulation, both reversible and symmetrical, had not yet produced its last round. With socialism and fascism facing one another in a specular fashion, the perfect setup was in place for the tragedy of the century, which began to coalesce in 1923 and 1924. In 1918, after the Great War ended, it was anticipated that the socialist doubled revolution would resume its universal expansion. Socialist revolution would be worldwide: and European for that matter, at its outset;[131] and German at first, for that matter.[132] World revolution would start up as a German revolution—and this was what did occur. But in 1923 German revolution drowned in a bloodbath. Socialist revolution then turned around again (the *turn* of this return can be situated between 1924 and 1929). This can be shown in a figure:

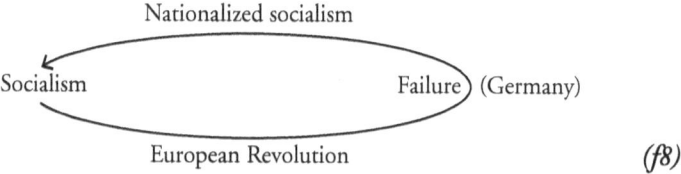

(f8)

After the German failure of the European revolution, socialism withdrew to become *socialism in a single country*. It rejoined itself and doubled up, as if re-traversed by the national—a socialism overintensified and oversocialized by the national appropriation: one may point to this with the empirical designation of Stalinism. Like Salazarism or Gaullism, "Stalinism" delimits a fact, which calls for a concept: *nationalized socialism*.[133]

As for fascism, it spreads out in the space left open by the withdrawal of the revolution: a European counterrevolution, in accordance with the project formed and formulated by Hitler as early as 1924, but that, significantly, does not unfold until 1932, when Stalin's power grab stabilizes. Lenin dies in 1924, but the movement solidifies during ferocious battles between 1928 and 1932.[134] The year 1932 settles Stalin's victory. In the following year, Hitler is brought to power. The plans of German fascism, developing since 1920–24, are implemented against the European counterrevolution, seeking to crush European Bolshevism in hand-to-hand combat so as to retrieve from this struggle *its own identification as socialism*: a counterrevolutionary nationalism turning back on itself, tested by this conflict, as a socialist and complete ultrarevolution; a total, social nationalism, revolutionizing society as a whole; a social nationalism—*national socialism*. It is shown in the next figure:

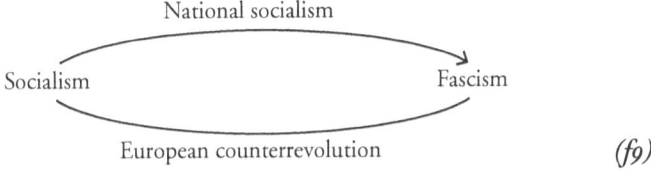

(f9)

The tragedy of the century: national socialism and socialism (which is national) face off and go to war, claiming to leave in the world no other space than the one devastated by their battlefields.

It is worth noting three things about these schemas.

(1) It may be in this relationship of structural solidarity and reversed identification that one should seek an explanation for the frequently noted phenomenon converting one commitment into another: Benito Mussolini, Jacques Doriot, and Marcel Déat cross over from socialism to fascism. It is a widespread phenomenon, which has lately had some new and striking illustrations. It is worth noting that this exchange is only weakly reversible: few avowed fascists have become communists or revolutionary socialists. This dissymmetry has remained unexamined; one might suggest, however, that just as nationalism is an answer, or a figural re-turn of the revolution, fascism is a doubling of figurality facing socialist figurality, something like a return to the return—so that, despite the connection between the two branches of the process, there is no equivalence whatsoever between them, in particular as far as the psychic models required for a commitment are concerned: crossing over to fascism was a passage to more figurality and identification, whereas the passage to communism, in spite of everything, retained a dis-identifying, transporting, and metaphorizing element from its provenance. And the times tended more toward figures than transport.

(2) One can only comprehend Nazism and Stalinism in their mutual relation, one before the other and even, in a certain way, one *within* the other (each rolled up within the other as in its fold). No equivalence here either: Stalinism was the offspring of the failed world revolution, whereas Nazism was its sworn enemy. The first preceded the second: the one more forward going, the other more entwined in returns. Nonetheless, at that stage of their history (when nationalism had vampirized the revolution,

transforming it into this restless corpse, this living dead socialism in a single country), they were welded to one another by the identity-seeking inveiglement that constituted them together and made them devour each other in the embrace of their monstrous coupling. For nationalism, this vampirization was the natural order of things, since the nation had to do with identity in its very principle. For the revolutionaries, who wanted to launch other ventures and believed in this—provisionally to put it this way—it was a real shame.

(3) In any case, this interpretation gives rise to a hypothesis that helps us understand what was such an enigma for so many among them—for so many among us. Why was revolutionary thought so helpless when it came to thinking about the nature of "Stalinism"? The reason is (almost) plain: one would have needed to understand the fundamental dependence of this historic formation upon Nazism, and therefore understand that the whole edifice of the revolution (the edifice of the state, the political and intellectual edifice) rested on this internal and architectonic coupling between the two regimes. This was not about two variants of the common species "totalitarianism," however. Their link had to do with a processual and structural solidarity, being twins; a link of essence and birth that did not let one regime exist without its struggle to the death against the other—a battle for identity, but to death; thus a battle against oneself, made of suicides and scant respite; alliances of tyrannies to give themselves some time to survive and delay the start of their common disaster. Understanding "Stalinism" would have meant understanding how it was essentially joined to Nazism, which meant that Stalinian "transgrowth" of the revolution could *only* be read as the transformation of the revolutionary process under the effect of its struggle against fascism, as *a certain of in-corporation of fascism into the revolution*. And so, revolutionary thinking could not really analyze Nazism either; this would have required that the revolution understand itself and its own national transformation as an incorporation of fascism, and the transgrowth of fascism into Nazism as a reappropriation of identity in a stopped revolution. To be fair, one should mention that certain intuitions of the extreme Left, or of a certain Freudo-Marxism, were not far removed from perceiving this. They paid a price for this—a high price. The secret wasn't worth it.[135]

PART III   TRANSPORTS OF ORIGIN

18. Loads

Europe is a figure. What do I mean by a figure here? I would define it as the turning around on itself of some movement that precedes it and makes it possible. And what is this movement that, in turning around, inscribes the figure? One can call it a "process," as others already have.[1] The figure would then be a process that turns around, the turning around (of itself) of a process.[2] My proposition is a more concrete—more charged[3]—notion: what the figure turns around is transport. Thus the figure itself is transport, but transport turned around, return-transport, made *possible* by this other previous transport—necessarily prior—that the figure presupposes as its momentum and its prerequisite: onward transport, going ahead. There no difference in kind or essence between figure and transport. The figure is wholly transport; there is only a difference in direction or orientation, a *difference of directional sense or way*: onward transport goes ahead one way; the figure comes back the other way. Why pick "transport" over "process"? So as to challenge, as I have done, any *essential* distance between (processual) being and the (figured) image; so as to say, the image is within being, as return to self; so as to deny the *difference of essence* between the real and the ideal—deny that there might be a processual real (in the course of becoming) to which an imaginary regime[4] of fixed idealities might essentially be opposed, posited on another plane of being, on a plane other than being—and so as to do away with the ideality of the ideal. The ideal is thinkable only as effectivity. And since a certain (nonessential) difference does produce ideality, since *there is some ideality, in effect*, this difference has to be thought as a difference between going and coming back, as *a difference of directional ways* [*différence de sens*]. I have said: there is no ideality.[5] I may now more precisely say: no ideality of ideality. Ideality is not ideal, differing in essence, as essence, at the core of the structure of being. Ideality should be thought as practical effectivity, and *as directional sense* [*comme sens*].

But, admittedly, I have another reason:

All transport is transport of something. (h13)

The process proceeds as self-production, as the unfolding of its own becoming, as exposition of the becoming essence of its becoming. If the process is *without a subject*, in the Hegelian sense, it is because ultimately there is no other subject than the process itself, because *the process is the subject*.[6] An unthinkable subject, therefore—like any subject, perhaps,[7] caught in the double bind of the double reference to the sup-position of what is its sup-port—to the sub-jective and sub-stantial previousness that is set under its being—and yet also, contradictorily, to its self-positioning as the ultimate reference, to this being as the very thing itself that is set below, without anything underneath but itself, without any support, or ground.[8] Process, becoming—these are modalities of the substance, the ultimate substance construed as change, as substance of the change. Transport is something else. Obviously, process and transport are on the same side of the conflict, in the same camp—against the fixity of being and its (presumed) immutability. But as thoughts of change they are different: transport is not an autoposition. Becoming and transport are first taken up in the priority of a spacing [*écart*], of a dis-placement. But while becoming tends to become emancipated from the spacing (during the initial determination that made it a type of movement, or a number in the movement, to turn out as *pure* or purified *change*),[9] transport remains pluralized in the articulation of the journey [*parcours*], the support, and the load [*charge*]; it cannot, and will not, free itself from this: this is where it unfolds, and this is its domain. A linking of space and time, no doubt—but also an articulation and a difference between the vehicle and the mobile body,[10] the thought of a mobility that is not "pure": the mobility of a mobile element that is moving because it is conveyed by a vehicle loaded with it—there is no transport without some material, without some transported matter.[11] Transport is material; *the thought of transport is a materialism*. Transport goes ahead, charged. As for the figure, it plays out *as* an empty return—that is, as a figure, the metaphor of an emptied return. The figure is given as empty of matter or load—pure tracing,[12] transcendental line. But there is no full evacuation: coming back, here are the vehicle, the transporter, and even the road—*and especially the remainder, with which the return transport is necessarily cluttered*: tools, waste, and packaging. Plus all that one has also loaded and strapped up for the return, to send it back profitably. Every transport carts something along. Return and figure are charged with a load. Transport abhors a vacuum.

*

As has been noted, the Roman era made transport its rule, generalizing and universalizing it, structuring and constituting its space as a *transportation space*. Rome obviously did not invent transportation, but extended and multiplied it in the extreme, making it a global principle and modality. The Roman world is a world of transportation. One could thus characterize the Roman Empire as sovereignty over the transport of the world, and over the world as the world of transport. It is on the underpinnings of this Roman transportation that the constitution of Europe will come about. Europe is the turning around of a Roman movement. Europe returns (*as if* emptily) to that for which Romanity produced the onward journey [*l'aller*], or the pathway [*l'allée*]: an (emptied) return on Roman pathways [*allées romaines*].[13]

What does Rome transport, then? What loads [*charges*] are thus transported, in its world, from port to port? Everything, of course: supplies, foodstuffs, arms, extracted and manufactured things—everything is loaded and carried; everything is the object of delivery or commerce.[14] *And thus ideas, too, of course*—in the most banal sense of the word. Ideas, too, are carried off and away, charged and loaded, spilling out here and there. Ideas are supplies and materials. Now, among all the ideas with which Rome is charged, universalizing them—which is to say, transferring and decanting them everywhere to the outer limits of the world—two kinds of supplies feed this trafficking particularly, as we know and as is often repeated: Greek and Jewish materials. Above all, Roman transportation is in charge of carrying to the whole world and all the spaces of the world packages of Greek and Jewish ideas. Let me try to say briefly why and how.

19. On Beingness

The culture of the Roman world looks at first glance like the translation and large-scale distribution of a multitude of Greek contributions.[15] Its language feeds on numerous Hellenic roots and turns of phrase. Its mythology and religion, political organization, technological setups, bodies of knowledge, and of course its literary works, exhibit fewer original motifs than they do extensions or transformations of themes and structures directly inherited from Greek cultures. If one steps back from their acquired familiarity, one can only be surprised how much the *Aeneid* or Seneca's plays disclose this dependence and this systematic pattern of borrowing.[16] This brings up a question: what exactly does Rome collect in Greece, so as to translate and distribute it? How are we to think about the kernel or inmost resource of this Hellenicity that the omnipotence of Rome recognizes at the source of its culture? Or further, how are we to name the "essence" of Greece's contribution, propagated by Rome, which will enable European history to unfold?

To this Husserl provides a precise answer: the Greek singularity is to be understood as a "*new sort of attitude* of individuals toward their surrounding world," leading to the "breakthrough of a completely new sort of spiritual structure, rapidly growing into a systematically self-enclosed cultural form; the Greeks called it *philosophy*" ("Vienna Lecture," p. 276).[17] Philosophy is what is new, what the Greeks supply that is original (or originary). *This* is what sparks off the initial shake-up of European history—the shake-up of History, and historicity, as the history of Europe. Husserl knows that his thesis is audacious: "In the breakthrough of philosophy in this sense . . . I see, paradoxical as it may sound, the primal phenomenon [Gm., *Urphänomen*; Fr., *proto-phénomène*] of spiritual Europe" (ibid.).

What is the "systematically self-enclosed cultural form" called "philosophy" to which this "completely new sort of spiritual structure" [Gm., *geistige Gebilde*] leads? The answer, again, is explicit: "Correctly translated, in the original sense, that means nothing other than universal science, science of the universe, of the all-encompassing unity [Gm., *Alleinheit*] of all that is [Gm., *alles Seienden*; Fr., *de tout l'étant*]" (ibid.). Philosophy: universal science, science inasmuch as it is universal, science of beingness. It is this "philosophy, the one science" that later "branches out into many particular sciences" (ibid.). But what else? What makes the jump so radical, so new, in relation to earlier forms of knowledge? Philosophy (science) does not spring up after nothingness. There were formulations in different words before it. What singularity marks this discourse that is the foundation of Greek singularity, and thus of European history, that is, History?[18]

Let us skip through the stages of the argument (ruthlessly reducing Husserl's subtle exposition): science (or philosophy) displays the singularity of the *theoretical attitude* ("Vienna Lecture," p. 282), which is the concern for truth, and the will for truth as truth, that is to say, unconditional or unconditioned truth (pp. 278, 287, and 350),[19] free from any attachment to practical interests—practical needs and conditioning, practical ambitions and intentions in the surrounding world. Science is the concern for the true, unbound from the useful praxis that belongs to the "natural attitude" (p. 282). The theoretical attitude sets off the singularity of a *pure way of looking* [Fr., *regard pur*].

Let us illuminate first of all the remarkable, peculiar character of philosophy, unfolding in ever new special sciences. Let us contrast it with other cultural forms already present in prescientific mankind: artifacts, agriculture, domestic arts, etc. ("Vienna Lecture," p. 277)

The theoretical attitude, though it is again a vocational attitude [Gm., *Berufseinstellung*], is totally unpractical. In the sphere of its own vocational life, then, it is based on a voluntary epochē of all natural praxis. ("Vienna Lecture," p. 282)

Man becomes gripped by the passion of a world-view and world-knowledge that turns away from all practical interests and . . . strives for and achieves nothing but pure *theōria*. In other words, man becomes a nonparticipating spectator, surveyor of the world [Gm., *Überschauer der Welt*; Fr., *un regard* (gaze) *jeté sur le monde*]. ("Vienna Lecture," p. 285)

The theoretical attitude distinguishes itself by this tearing away from the spontaneous facts of natural life that structure one's participation in the surrounding world through praxis—practical interests and behaviors, practical finalities. The natural attitude is spontaneous for humans—everywhere.[20] The Greeks produced its *epochē*, suspension, or rise. The gaze takes off: the spectator's nonparticipating, *disinterested passion* substitutes for the practical interests.[21]

Now, this tearing away from natural interests, thus defined, soon turns out to be a *tearing away from the national*. The theoretical attitude drives one to prefer "truth-in-itself" to "everyday truth" ("Vienna Lecture," p. 286), and thus keeps one from accepting a truth that might be subjected to a local or territorial determination.

Clearly, on the other hand, [philosophy's] tendency to spread is not limited to the home nation. *Unlike all other cultural works,* philosophy is *not a movement of interest which is bound to the soil* [Gm., *Boden*] of the national tradition. Aliens [Gm., *Fremd-Nationale*; Fr., *étrangers*], too, learn to understand it and generally take part in the *immense cultural transformation which radiates out from philosophy*

[Gm., *an der gewaltigen Kulturverwandlung, die von der Philosophie ausstrahlt*; Fr., *à cette mutation culturelle violente qui émane de la philosophie*]. ("Vienna Lecture," p. 286; emphasis added)

It is no accident that the two developments are consecutive in the text: it is *because* the theoretical attitude tears one away from the interests of natural life, from practical needs and behavior, that it tears one away from the national. Philosophy, an immense cultural transformation, breaks with a certain relation to the surrounding world, precisely subjected to the natural, native—and thus, logically, national—attitude.[22]

This double emancipation orients the theoretical toward the infinite. The surrounding world's natural grasp is a grasping of finitude.[23] Science produces expressions [*énoncés*] (idealities), with each one providing access to another one at a higher level, without any limit, thus constituting a program of "infinite tasks."[24] The Greek opening is an *opening to the infinite*. It is the opening of historicity as such ("Vienna Lecture," p. 277), hence of a new type of humanity, which is none other than humanity itself, opened to the infinity of its own essence.[25]

To follow Husserl and Jan Patočka (and to return to the questioning that has driven this reading), let us say that what Rome transports and generalizes, what it spreads to the limits of its world, is thus the theoretical attitude; it is philosophy—all at once the *epochē* of the practices of the surrounding world, the upheaval of the natural attitude, and the transgression of nativism (of the national). In this sense, that which Rome transports and distributes, from the starting point of Greece, is the tearing away, that is, *transport itself*—with a new attitude in thinking about it: this tearing away is no longer a loss, but instead the conquest of an opening without boundaries. Patočka sees in Democritus the inventor of the idea of infinite empty space—empty, that is to say, where a world can come about.[26] We can sense the consequences: if the tearing away no longer (or not only) amounts to a loss, if transport does not only lead one astray—to roam or to err—one may then not be forced to expect or seek the return. If exiting, moving across, and opening are what the Greek moment brings, then *the way (the sense) of life is not the return*. The return is not that which gives a direction and sense—not necessarily. We can make out the sense of a way ahead, of that which goes out, opens, and goes on. Supposing (with Philippe Lacoue-Labarthe)[27] that the Greeks bequeathed to the West the Odyssean form of the directional sense as the sense of return—a constraining and difficult form of life as that which comes back; returning life, coming back to its origins, to the lost fatherland, to one's home, to the wife who was left there and is waiting (and to the dog)—then one has to say, at least, that the Hellenic legacy is double: comprising the return *and* the crossing, the Odyssean lesson *and* the philosophical lesson, epic as well as theoretical materials. Like Patočka, I believe that the epic is common to the cultures of the world (and the return as well), while the theoretical is the peculiar posture that seems *only* to appear *there*.[28] Accordingly, if Rome feeds its world with specifically Greek materials, it is inasmuch as Rome *transports the transport*, rather than the "natural attitude," which preexists—everywhere.

Patočka takes up and inflects the propositions of Husserl's "Vienna Lecture"; among all his important contemporaries, he is no doubt the one who proposes the most elaborate philosophical idea about Europe.[29] Patočka also situates in classical Greece the locus and the moment of a kind of break, or rather an initial *shake-up* [*ébranlement*] from which the history of Europe—and, through it, History—ensues. But he identifies the charge of this break as being precisely the emergence of *care of the soul*—or concern or solicitude for the soul.

The Greeks, the Greek philosophers in whom the Greek spirit is expressed most sharply, expressed human freedom by the term: care of the soul. (PE, p. 13)

In this is the peculiar stamp and distinctiveness of European life, in this is also its continuity, that this possibility arose here. In this sense I will try to show you that Europe as Europe arose from this motif, from the care of the soul. (PE, p. 70)

The care for the soul is thus what gave rise to Europe—this thesis we can hold without exaggeration. (EH, p. 83)

Now, the care of the soul is an essential determination in philosophy, a position of its essence: "*the soul* forms the *center of philosophy, Philosophy is the care of the soul* in its own essence and in its own element" (PE, p. 91). Indeed, this is saying that philosophy—its irruption and production—is the agent of the shake-up of Europe's history—and thus of historicity.[30] What is the soul, then, and why is the care for it capable of triggering this shake-up?

The care of the soul is the opening of history because "the conceptualization of the soul in philosophy from its Greek origins consists in just *what is capable of truth within man*" (PE, p. 27). Now, truth does not emerge with philosophy. Myth—Patočka asserts this forcefully—is already involved with truth: "*myth is true*. Real myth is truthful" (PE, pp. 42–43). "The uncovering of the whole world by Greek philosophy is the continuation of this myth" (PE, p. 49). Where then is the break that came—Patočka keeps asserting—with the emergence of philosophy? Here it is: the care of philosophy no longer bears only on *truth*, but on *that which is capable of truth within man*.[31] Philosophical concern is displaced from the true to the soul and its sake, and thus "invents" the soul, as interiority. The interiority of the soul, the soul by itself, the care of the soul in itself, are productions of philosophy, and of Platonism in particular,[32] through this migration of its care from what is true to being capable of truth. A dis-objectivation of the truth occurs, and a loss of its objective rootedness (one could almost say a loss of its objectal fixation),[33] an uprooting,[34] a taking-apart of the bond [*dés-amarrage*], a takeoff [*démarrage*] of the truth: this is what Patočka calls its *reaching forth* [Fr., *essor*] (HE, p. 38).

This is why philosophy lodges essentially within matters of appearance—not of *that which appears* (of that which appears and offers itself to sight), but of appearance itself inasmuch as it appears, of the manifestedness of the manifestation, of the being of apparition.[35] Paraphrasing an astonishing passage in *Heretical Essays*,[36] one could say that apparition as the essence of the *showingness of what shows itself* is an uncovering of the nakedness of the world. Not of its objectivity (its objectality), its supposed reality in itself, but its baring, its stripping, its nakedness itself. The baring of the world is a forcing, a breaking-in, or a *shake-up of its given visibility*, of its visibility as a sense already-given,[37] a sense organized and built from practical exigencies, myths, and traditions—the very thing, no doubt, that Husserl called natural world. The baring of the world in the essence of its apparition, *in the phenomenality of its phenomenon*, is a shake-up of given sense, or accepted sense.[38] It is a nonacceptance of the previous (mythical, ritual, or practical) sense—or, according to Patočka's strong expression, it is a *sobering* [Fr., *dégrisement*] (PE, p. 134). It occurs in the regime of problematicity,[39] the opening of the soul to the *loss of accepted sense*. Being (that which *is*) is stripped bare. And it follows that philosophy is *indissociably* care of the soul *and* thinking of the phenomenality of the world. The baring shakes up the seeing.

Such life does not seek to escape its contingency, but neither does it yield to it passively; since it has glimpsed the possibility of authentic life, that is, life as a whole, the *world* opens itself to it for the first time—it is no longer merely an involuntary background against which that which concerns us shows itself; rather, it itself can now stand forth, as the whole of that which opens up against the black backdrop of closed night. This whole now speaks to humans *directly*, free of the muting effect of tradition and myth, only by it do they seek to be accepted and held responsible. Nothing of the earlier life of acceptance remains in place; all the pillars of the community, traditions, and myths, are equally shaken, as are all the answers that once preceded questions, the modest yet secure and soothing meaning, though not lost, is transformed. It becomes as enigmatic as all else [Fr., *il devient problématique, aussi énigmatique que tout le reste*]. Humans cease to identify with it, myth ceases to be the word of their lips. In the moment when life renews itself *everything* is cast in a new light. Scales fall from the eyes of those set free, not that they might see something new but that they might see in a new way. It is like a landscape illuminated by lightning, amid which humans stand alone, with no support, relying solely on that which presents itself—and that which presents itself is everything without exception. It is the moment of creative dawning, "the first day of the creation," mysterious and more pressing for enfolding and bearing with it the astonished [Fr., *embrasse celui qui s'étonne, l'implique et l'emporte*]. (HE, pp. 39–40)[40]

Such is the fate of the astonished: dawn embraces them, enfolding them *and carrying them away*. Patočka (when he reads Plato, for example) always links these two motifs. On the one hand, the coming of light, the advent of seeing, which determines apparition and phenomenality as such; the opening and the display of the world to the newness of a gaze, as a *gaze looking into what is*.[41] On the other, carrying away: because the soul works by displacement and moving. Furthermore, the soul is movement, by essence. Further still, it is *the essence of movement*, of all movement, the origin of all setting in motion. What moves the soul and makes it the movement that it is is the care and the concern for itself. *The care of the soul is movement itself.*

The soul that takes care of itself is then in motion from immediate uncertainty to circumscribing, delimiting reflection. And *philosophy is in this motion, and this motion is something actual*. (PE, p. 94; emphasis added)

Cosmology has shown where *the soul stands in the whole of existence*; it is *the origin of movement*, it can only be understood in movement. The movement of the soul in its most proper sense of the word is precisely *care for its very self*. (PE, p. 124; emphasis in the first sentence added)

We have already said that in Plato the soul is the principle of movement, and *movement is fundamentally the movement of the care of the soul*. (PE, p. 126; emphasis added)

The care of the soul is a look into what amounts to movement—setting in motion, principle of motion. It is one and the other, indissociably. It is one because it is the other: a looking-in, into that which is, because of the changing of place, being carried away. It is this duality that the concept of the *shaking or shaken* [Fr., *ébranlement*] answers, and it is central for Patočka (particularly in *Heretical Essays*). The care of the soul, philosophy—they shake things up: they tear one away from given and secure meanings and senses; they shake up traditions and myths; they upset beliefs (shaking beliefs), and unsettle; pull away from immobility; open up motricity; push one along the way, or down the road. Immobility is suitable for suicides—the poet does not speak of "the dead," but of "suicides."[42]

The will to permanence is essentially sacral and ritualistic, having to do with a fundamental characteristic of prehistoric truth, i.e., the cosmic-ontological metaphor.... The point of history is not what can be uprooted or shaken, but rather the openness to the shaking. (HE, pp. 35 and 44)

One thus has a basis for saying that the Greek event is the one that tears away [*l'arrachement*]—from the myth, from the given and accepted meaning of the nearby native environment. Literally, Patočka does not put it this way. But what he says allows one to do so: that historic behavior insofar as it is open, is movement, by essence; a movement itself comprising a plurality of partial movements at the core of which

only *one* of these is oriented to the theme of openness, manifestation, unconcealment, and its transmission. *Others focus on the rooting of humans in the open realm* [Fr., *district*] *of the common world of humans* and on the protection and preservation of that world. (HE, pp. 10–11)[43]

History is this composition of partial histories (or stories), micro-histories, minimal movements, among which *only one* is open and historic (which is to say, oriented toward manifestation and unconcealment, as the text puts it). The others, which are more frequent, numerous, and natural, lead to being rooted and to the support and defense of the realm [Fr., *district*] delimited by the practice common to (prehistoric) men. It is these dominant movements that myth expresses, opposing home and foreignness, saying that the "near world is the world of good," and the outside amounts to a threat, which reaches into the near world by way of the unusual, the *unheimlich*, which does not fall "into these forms of rootedness" (PE, p. 54).[44]

On the contrary—Plato and Aristotle have said it and Patočka repeats it—philosophical thought (and history by way of it) is based on astonishment and wonder, on the surprise and amazement of the dis-covery of the world.⁴⁵ Now, what does this amazement contain? It is the baring of the world's *strangeness*. Philosophy, the opening of history, upsets the security of that which is near, discovering *the world as a foreign land*. Philosophy, history: things found by travelers. About life that is "freely human," Patočka writes, "That, however, means life on the boundary" (HE, p. 39).

*

Here, a decisive articulation takes place, for this invention is found to be (by itself, without intervention) political in nature. In this, Patočka is veering away from Husserl, according to whose "Vienna Lecture" the invention of philosophy has political *consequences*: "The conservatives, content with tradition, and the philosophical circle will struggle against each other, and without doubt the battle will carry over into the sphere of political power. At the very beginning of philosophy, persecution [*conséquence* in the French translation—Trans.] sets in."⁴⁶

For Patočka, the invention of philosophy is an event that is intrinsically political, its political reach being indissociable from its unfolding: "That means that the renewal of life's meaning in the rise of political life *bears within it* the seed of philosophical life as well" (HE, p. 40); "History arises from the shaking of the naive and absolute meaning in the *virtually simultaneous and mutually interdependent* rise of politics and philosophy" (HE, p. 77; emphasis added). How can we understand this solidarity? It has to do with the care of the soul, a constitutive trait of philosophy, which is carried out as a *project of true life*, or life *in truth*. Now, life in truth is probably the other name of justice.⁴⁷ Justice is what relates the soul to itself inasmuch as it is truthful and clear. Philosophy "sees justice and all other ἀρετή as the *internal relation* within man himself, between distinct moments from which man is composed, from which is composed his ψυχή (soul). . . . To establish such precise relations signifies justice" (PE, p. 106). Socrates, who initiates the care of the soul, invents and implements this inner operation. It is on this account that he is put to death, as one of "the just and the truthful" (PE, p. 97).

At this point the singular connection that Patočka makes between politics and philosophy is established. In Plato's *Republic*, following discussion of this inner relationship of man with himself, the construction of the city-state is introduced as a development of the question "What is a just man?" (see PE, pp. 100ff.).[48] The political articulation is unexpected: justice is not posited as a relation to the other or others (as a relationship of complicity, agreement, and innocuousness). On the contrary, this notion is strongly refuted.[49] Justice is a relation of man with himself and with truth, with himself insofar as he is open to the truth, and in another context, the figure of Socrates (and his comportment in the face of death—of injustice) personifies this. Justice does not reside *between* humans but *in* them. This is why the introduction of the political in the *Republic* occurs, surprisingly, by way of a kind of analogy: the city is analogous to man, but larger, and the relationship of justice has to be more evident in it, for reasons of size and measure (PE, pp. 116ff.). The political connection is homogeneous in relation to the connection that is internal to everyone, and can thus be seen as its extension and enlargement. Justice is internal to man; it is nonconventional, or non-"social," as it were, *and this interiority is the opening of the political, because this is what men have in common.* What is common among men is interiority—and not exteriority, which appears to connect them. If politics emerges with philosophy, and care of the soul with it, this is because the just community is *the community of this internal relationship* with oneself that makes up justice. "Because care of the soul is possible, the state is also possible, and the community is also possible" (PE, p. 121). For Plato, the primary political question is therefore education, *paideia*.[50] "You see, then, that the question of the polis and its constitution, its constituting, is again the question of the soul, its character and its examination—care of the soul" (ibid.). The institution of the polis springs up in the very *movement* that gives birth to philosophy, in the movement that is philosophy as *movement of the soul*: the shake-up that makes history and sets history into motion. And this is how Patočka defines the political community: it is the community of those who live this shake-up; the community or "unity of the shaken" (HE, p. 43).

This passage into history,[51] as a political event (the event *of* the political; the coming, invention, and production of the political as such), is featured in Patočka's first two *Heretical Essays*, "Reflections on Prehistory" and "The Beginning of History." Here he leans on Hannah Arendt's analyses of labor so as to articulate work—within the framework of the natural world and the traditional way of life—as a participating element in the "bonding of life to itself" (HE, p. 15). Work is thus construed fundamentally as non- or anti-historical. "If we understand work in this sense, then work proves to be not only a nonhistorical factor but actually one working *against* history, intending to hold it at bay" (HE, p. 16). This reference allows Patočka to produce a new determination of the historical difference—of the emergence of historicity. Indeed, the "world of work" calls for a certain corresponding socialness (a structuring of the community, as it were), the *household*. "The world in which *the bonding of life to itself* takes place on the basis of a concealed freedom is the *world of work*; its protocell and model is the household, *the community of those who work* to assure their sustenance" (HE, p. 15; emphasis added).

This world carries away (by way of metaphorization, extension, or prolonging of its essence—this is not clear, here) a certain structuring of power: "The great empires of the ancient world, the first high civilizations and cultures, were in this sense monumental households" (HE, pp. 15–16). Indeed, the "household" is the schema of a world: it posits at the same time the community relation that work implies, which is bound to it (bound to its own bonding, as bonding of life to itself), as well as the form of the power of "great empires," and thus the form and the boundaries of the world itself: "Thus there is no sharp boundary between the world and the 'great household' of the empire" (HE, p. 36).

Which empires? They are the "high Near Eastern civilizations" (HE, p. 23), the ones producing the narratives of the first annalists "in the Near East, Egypt, ancient China . . . in complex and massive social formations, in grand empires with complicated hierarchies and bureaucracies" (p. 28), "theocracies with divine rulers or rulers in the role of managers of divine households." "For that reason there can be no substantive separation or difference between the empire and the universe. Pharaoh . . . the Emperor of China . . . the great king of Persia" (p. 34). In a word, it is about Asia itself. Granted there could be others: the description and the concept would conceivably apply to the great American Indian households (conceived of as "Indian," on an Asian model, by anthropologists). Now, in the Greek consciousness, Asia is the anteriority from which Greece was born; elsewhere means earlier. Birth tears away and transports. The empire is "essentially no more than a giant household or aggregate of households gathered around the central cell of the royal house" (HE, pp. 28–29), and the invention of the political comes as a break with this, driving the household back into the domestic space. The production of history commenced when, as Arendt pointed out, "the sphere of the house ceased to be the core of the world as such, becoming *simply a private domain* alongside and juxtaposed to which there arose, in Greece and Rome, a different, no less important public sphere" (HE, p. 23; emphasis added). The role of the house in life shrank from imperial to domestic. In the space of the world that this withdrawal frees up, a new sphere opens: the *public* sphere—the political.

*

Let us sum things up. The great (Asian) empires are the organization of accepted life in the [Asian] "high civilizations."[52] This is the organization of "great households," work communities bound to the bonding of life to itself, which constitute a world, as a natural world, a world nearby, familiar or familial, circumscribed within the district of a native space. Employing an inadequate Latinism, one might call it basically domestic, given that the strictly preferable Greek term (*oikonomia*) is anachronistic.[53] The irruption of the politico-philosophical—the production of history—breaks with this world regulated by the *oikos*, domestic rule.

History *switches* "worlds." What follows the "world-of-work" presents itself hesitantly and problematically to the new *gaze into what is*,[54] to the soul inasmuch as it is motivated by care of itself. The soul is that which is "capable of this world" [*capable de ce monde*][55]—here I'd say: able to direct this look upon being (upon that which is). What shows itself, then, and bares and discloses itself, is properly speaking the beingness of beings as apparition or manifestedness, the phenomenality of which sets in motion free life and history,[56] and thus Europe as such. Europe is the opening to the bare phenomenality of what is, to the essence of this phenomenality as the inmost movement of apparition.[57] History (politico-philosophical history, inaugurated in Greece) is a *movement toward beingness*, this very movement that carries us toward what is—to the edge, the limit, the boundary of being—and renders life in truth a *life at the boundary*. The Greek opening opens onto the *transcendence of beingness*, or rather, as the French translation puts it, to *transcendence toward the world* [*transcendance vers le monde*]—to be understood here as *transcendence toward beingness*.[58] Transcendence toward: a welcome phrase, which prevents one from understanding transcendence as the exteriority of a being-that-is-beyond, giving back to the term (in accordance with its etymology) the connotation of movement-toward-something, of reaching out, and of direction: transcendence is *toward beings*—it is an orientation. *Transcendence is not a quality; it is a way, a directional sense.*

The *commonality* of humans is their *aptitude for this*. The political opens by means of this breach, and it is a community of souls, community of humans who are just and true, capable of going for the borderline, "alone, with no support" (HE, p. 40), heading for the transcendence of that which is—within this very reaching, takeoff, transport, transfer—transcendence as transcendence toward that which is or beingness. This is the essence of the polis as the community of men in accordance with justice and truth. The *constitution* of the city-state is transferred to the Roman state, to the empire, and through it to the *sacrum imperium* of Christianity—and further still to the states, all the states whose ancestor it is, to such a degree that we are the heirs of this.[59] Does this not lead to idealizing the Greek city—and hence our states, its inheritors?[60] Was the Greek city truly like this? Is this not the idea of a properly divine city? Of course. But here again, Patočka's parry is unexpected. Who in fact describes the city in this way? It is Plato. And when? When the polis is collapsing under the blows of tyranny and war, thus *after the catastrophe*. What we have inherited, then, is the *shattered*, devastated, and wrecked Greek city.[61] This congruence of thought with the political collapse generates the constitution of metaphysics.[62] In this sense, Patočka describes a movement that evokes (and probably demarcates) the movement of historiality as Heidegger thinks it: it is not purely the Greek opening and its transmitted legacy, tradition, and translation that bring about metaphysics; it is the withdrawal, or retreat, a backlash at the opening, starting with Greece itself, from the very beginning—erasure of the origin, which has reached us as retreat or removal *within* the origin, through the text of metaphysics and its history. But the difference between Patočka and Heidegger is considerable. What produces this retreat and this backlash for Patočka is the catastrophe of the polis—the political catastrophe. And just as the constitution of the polis assertively brought this opening as well as political freedom[63] (to simplify, the *era of democracy*),[64] this catastrophe is the collapse of democracy, and of the city's freedom.

An—actual—difference separates the Greek production of the opening (the "birth of history") and its metaphysical reformulation, reworking, and figuration—that is to say, perhaps, its very *idealization*, its figuration as ideality. Just as, intrinsically, the opening was political (and it was impossible, in the opening of history, to dissociate the political from the philosophical *as a movement of opening* [of freedom]), the catastrophe, likewise, is political by essence, and *so is, consequently, the advent of metaphysics*. Metaphysics comes about as the backwash of the political catastrophe: translating all at once that which, in it, makes up the return (retreat, figure), and that which was born and has opened up, and for a while at least, closes up again (transport, shake-up, tearing away). The sway of the transcendence "of the world" is *twofold*: dis-covery, demythicization, transfer, or effective aptitude *to go for the boundary* of what is,[65] through the shake-up of received senses; *and also, and together*, figuration, idealization, retreat: ideal transcendence, transcendence of beingness as ideality.

What reaches us—transmitted and transferred as the idea of the transcendence of beingness—is *the opening and the collapse* of freedom, as political freedom (of the political). This is the Greek legacy of which Rome takes charge. Opening *and* folding back. Transport *and* figure: the onward move *and* the returning move. The advent *and* the catastrophe. The transport is that which Rome transports—*but going both ways*. Patočka does not put it this way—not exactly.[66] But he makes it possible to say it—at least as a hypothesis:

> **Rome transports and distributes, as the idea of the transcendence of that which is, the Greek invention of the political, and the catastrophe of its collapse. (h14)**

*

This schema leaves some things in the shadows. The idea that Rome transports, extends, and generalizes the Greek contribution does not explain (at least not at first) why this contribution is somewhat immobilized (during the time of this extension): if, as Husserl thinks, the source and the kernel of the supplied Greek material are the invention of the theoretical (science and philosophy), it remains to be explained why the Roman era, which spreads this contribution worldwide, is itself so little "theoretical."[67] As if the theoretical had exhausted itself or become tired in the act of its invention; as if it had achieved its complete form—finished and ended—in the gesture of its production, as if it were in-separable from this initial transport—transportation of the origin, detachment, takeoff; and as if the process of *invention* should only start up again much later, with modernity: merely programming, up to this point, the transfer as its single task; carting the initial theorizing thus constituted all the way to the moderns. One would have to explain this disagreement between transport and production, linking a very intense transfer to a reduced inventiveness, with Rome and the Latins using their talent to bring the theoretical to the moderns, as if cryogenically frozen in the inaugural gesture of the theoretical's invention. One would have to understand how Rome is able to transport so well while inventing so little.

For Rome's relation to Greece is not merely a matter of inheritance, or else it includes all the conflictual ambiguity of filiation—and this makes for the strange equivocation of the imaginary foundation of the empire in the *Aeneid*.[68] Indeed, the narrative is a reprise, an imitation, or a kind of Roman remake of the *Iliad* and the *Odyssey*.[69] This makes it strikingly dependent on the Greek legends, since Rome invents for itself a foundation that repeats—in a time-delayed simulation—the Hellenic foundation, similarly drawing the images of its origins from the inexhaustible Trojan War.[70] But while the *Aeneid* gives Trojan origins to Rome, it is, in the great war of foundation, *on the side of the defeated*. Rome is descended from Troy, which is to say, from those Greece defeated. The greatness of Rome sung by the *Aeneid* is a revenge against Hellenicity. We can see the ambivalence of the gesture, since it is only from the Greeks that we have the tale of the Trojan defeat, and by laying claim to this genealogy, the *Aeneid* invokes a ("historical") non-Greek or anti-Greek ancestry, while calling on a "literary" Greek ancestry to express and to think this—a revenge against Greece, but formulated in the code of Hellenic history, in its own narrative framework; *in a word, a kind of revenge of Greece against itself*. Caught in such a snare, Roman transport remains captive of the equivocation: depending on the Hellenic legacy, and making claims against this dependence—a paralyzing filiation.[71] In any case (if one momentarily suspends any knowledge of what happened later), Rome "alone" did seem incapable of rekindling the productivity of the history of the theoretical. Its extension was its exhaustion. Supposing that this matter were ever to start up again, Rome would need an uplift, coming from elsewhere.

20. Places

In order to formulate a hypothesis with regard to this history, and how it intersects with the one that the biblical narratives relate, let us first draw up a kind of model, a conceptual schema, itself hypothetical, which may be helpful.

Let us first come back to this abrupt suggestion: *the origin is the first ancestor.*[72] Genealogy regresses toward the origin, going backward within the filiation and ancestry all the way to its supposed beginning. Now, this beginning itself is not absolute; it has a precedent, and it happens. In all mythical narratives, the beginning *comes about*—it arrives somewhere or happens to someone. The first ancestor himself is not without an ancestry. He is born and proceeds from a genesis. Why point to him as the first one? Let us propose that *the first ancestor is the one who is buried there.* He too had parents and ancestors: elsewhere. He is the one who came, touched, and set foot on these shores; he died there. It is about him that the decision was made to bury him in this ground, in this place. In this sense, the first ancestor (like the beginning) did *come about.* In his line, he is the first whose tomb is *there.* It is this burial and concealment that *founds* the line and the filiation. This interment in the ground is what the *foundation* as such *fundamentally* contains. It characterizes the foundation as an operation and an act—as a moment in a history:

The foundation is the burial of the origin. (h15)

(This is not to say that this foundation took place in the form of a singular historical event that it would be possible, or impossible, to date. Not that one would have to reject the reality of such an event from the start—but the question of this actuality is not the one that needs to be asked here. My view is that historical developments are not to be related pointedly to a founding event, locatable or not. Histories are complex, multiple, intersecting, hierarchized, and differentiated processes, and the assignation to a single point of foundation cannot account for them. On the contrary, it is the foundation model that I wish to question. I would like to unravel and expose the [imaginary or conceptual] content of this model, which assumes and narrates that lineages issue from a founding origin. This is not to say either that pure fictions—virginal and untouched by effectivity—are being questioned. Nothing prevents us from thinking that a chief led his tribes from Mesopotamia to Palestine and was buried there. But there is no guarantee of this: the question pertains to historical research—scrupulous, if possible. On the other hand, there is much to ask about the setup *constituting the history* and story that organizes the filiations [and thus the socializations] around the figure of Abraham as the *first ancestor*, whereby some societies consider themselves of Abrahamic ancestry. I am suggesting that it is the fact that *Abraham is* [supposed to be] *buried there* that constitutes—subterraneously, as it were—this narrative disposition. And this narration does imply *real* effects: the burial place exists, providing a structure for various behaviors, journeys, and wars.)

The origin: the first ancestor. What grounds it as the origin is that the first ancestor is buried *there*. The founding act that institutes the origin is its rooting, its inscription, and its burrowing *there*, into this land, *there*, at this place. Basically the origin is local. Its locality is what engages the relevance of this foundation—and thus of this origin; its actual, current, and present originarity. This is what sets forth the present character—the *presence*—of this past.[73] If the origin is known to *have been* there, much earlier, in a distant past, *it is because it is there, below ground*. The origin is at the foundation. The presence of the past is the tomb.

*

Now, around the grave site, odd things are taking place—spirits lurking and coming back, ghosts appearing. Sometimes even the gods are present. Certain tombs are altars—and all altars are tombs (at least simulated or reproduced). What happened?

An ancestor died. He was buried there. He was a traveler: he had arrived, coming from elsewhere, far away. He was caught in the migration, in ceaseless movement—a nomad or an exile. Or perhaps he had set forth to answer a call, a vocation, or an uprising. But he went on as everything goes, involved in the endless transitivity, transference, and transports of being. He could have died without stopping the journey, like his father and his forebears. The grave site would then be a stopping point: a locus for memory and meditation. But here, for unknown reasons, the burial amounts to a foundation, the production of an origin. The general and infinite transferring seems to stop—*to stop there*, at this place. Something wants to get away from the uninterrupted transferentiality of the whole, escape its mobility, its liquid and maritime essence, so as to burrow there, in-ter itself, make up an origin and a locus. Physical transportation is cut off; a buried body becomes forever motionless. That is, the tomb will be there; henceforth, the origin is there.[74]

And yet, something escapes from this cutoff and comes across. When the body stops, something of the movement that it carried goes on, like a mobile whose motion exits and moves elsewhere, into another body—by contamination, inertia, contagion of the shock, or transfer of the force. It seems to be the very movement itself that goes on. It cannot stop—as if it were a reality distinct from the mobile, provisionally incarnated in it but ongoing once the mobile stops. When the body stops, the movement changes bodies and shifts to another matter. It passes across and is transmitted. The movement and its passage want another body and another matter, something more mobile than the body, better adapted to transportation and transferentiality. There is a *production of lightness*. For example, the ancestor who had arrived leaves again. The ancestor sets off for the realm of the dead. But he does so in another vehicle; he has changed elements—been meta-phorized, transported elsewhere. Necessarily, then, something has not left; something has remained that could not (re)bound—his first body, his heavy matter, the buried one. He leaves again, but something of him stays behind. The tomb is the locus of these *remains*, which are interred—they are the part of him that does not leave. It is this remainder, this buried residue, that makes up the origin—this *grounding* remainder, in this place. But another narrative is possible: it could happen that nothing remains because he has transported and transferred himself so well into this new matter. He completely passed across into the light matter: he wholly arrived and left again, completely metaphorized, remainderless; one could say *eu*phorized—well transported, wholly gone. The tomb is empty, then; the grave is nothing but the marked site of his passage. The whole body was removed. What is the relation between these two stories?

It is what we have been able to notice, namely, that the ancestor comes back to the place of his death. The ancestor is somehow indebted to the locus, and he cannot set himself free from this. He has to come back and *pay* a visit. What does he thus owe? Why can't he leave without returning? It seems that he owes his lightness—this metaphorization, or euphorization, which shifted him from heaviness toward good transport and a good journey. He owes that which is lifted and lightened in himself, that which detaches and sets itself free. He owes his freedom and his departure—*and he owes this to the locus*; it will be important to find out why. Simple economics then come into play, arithmetically based on the debt, and this lets one understand the connection between the two figures of foundation. Let us put it this way: *the less there remains, the more returns*. The less of himself the ancestor has left at the place, the more coming-back he *owes*—as a revenant—the more return.[75] It is the old fable about revenants: those who keep coming back are those lacking a burial place. *There has to be a place for them*, and a marking. Let us imagine that everything (from the ancestor) stays in the grave: embalmed body, fixed soul—pharaonism, perhaps. The descendants, then, even if they have gone elsewhere, are the ones who come back on pilgrimages, to pay a visit to the ancestor who is there, underneath. But this hypothesis is never assured. Remainders are never complete. There *is* something of the ancestor that has left: his mobility, his transferentiality, his euphoria, *his life*. The life in him—his aptitude for transport, rising, and lightness—has gone; and so it has to come back, *there*, returning all the more forcefully and insistently when it has left a smaller residue, less materiality and heavy corporeality.[76] But let us not forget the question that this arithmetic leaves in the shadows: why does it, the life that left it, have to come back *there*, to this locus?

Two regimes of being [*l'être*] are thus produced: the regime of heavy bodies, transporting and transferring themselves, and, if transportation stops, going underground; and the regime of light bodies, which tear away from the earth thanks to lightness, *producing heaven*, circling around places and above, moving away and regularly coming back. This regularity brings about some rites: rites are the convocation, the provocation, and the regularity of the return (to the locus). Rite is the moment of the return of the ancestor to the place of origin. Two regimes of being: transporting of the bodies, coming-back [*revenance*] of the spirits. By forcing the passages, accelerating the rhythms (and much reducing the differences), one could call them physics and metaphysics—phoria, and metaphoria. I am even somewhat inclined to think, here, that the choice of their *production* narrative, or the orientation and *directional sense* of their connection, could be described as *idealism*, or *materialism*, depending on one's belief or wish that the narrative of their formation, *the sense of their history (their story)*, proceed from the lightness of spirits toward the heaviness of bodies, or from the transfer of bodies toward spirits coming back.

The economy that links this coming-back on the one hand and foundation on the other is an economy of the *production of the divine*. It can be depicted as follows:

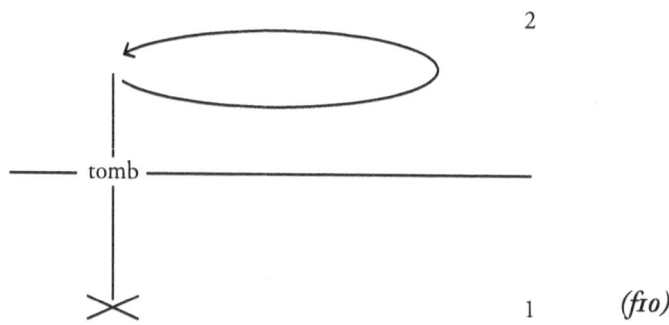

The ancestor's comeback is *divine*—not because the ancestor is the god, necessarily: but the dead ancestor, the first buried ancestor, inasmuch as he comes back and visits the place of origin, is *potentially divine*. Divine is the appellation of this return to the sepulchre. It is in this that the god is not quite the ancestor; for if he comes back, it is because he is not dead, he is not *the dead one*. He is *the coming-back of the dead one*, that which is not quite dead in the dead one, but passes across death—traversing it, puncturing it—so as to come back. The god is not in the grave; the grave is always void of divinity. Divine, in the dead one, is that which does not die. In this sense, and figurally, the gods are immortal by essence—*but as revenants*. They are what traverses death and sets itself free from the heavy body, rises into the element of good transport and good travel. But the gods' lightness is not free; it is constrained by indebtedness. The gods are set free only *inasmuch as they come back*—to the burial place of the ancestor, all the more revenant when the tomb is emptier. Altar: an emptied sepulchre. The divine becomes constituted to the exact degree of the emptying of the grave site, and thus of the insistence of the coming-back, and *thus of the indebtedness toward the locus*. The divine comes back to the locus of origin. Divine is this coming-back, this visitation. "God" is the name of this return of an ancestor: set loose in a different element, another matter, a light and airy return—but a *return to its place*. God: the return (turnaround) of the origin to its "there." Thus: the figure. *The god gives figure to the origin at its place*. All gods come back—*there*—and give figure to this *there* where they come back. All gods are local.

But what is a place? Let us propose that it is the site where the possibility of a marking is positioned—the surroundings that a marking positions and constitutes as its site, as the support of its possibility; that which the inscription or imprinting of a "there" indicates and displays: a stop along a road, a boundary marker, or tracing of a path. As long as one keeps walking, there is no marking: everything sets forth, tears away, takes off; everything is good to take in, eat, and consume. One makes a mark so one can be followed—or come back, or stop. But why mark the stop? Why stop *there*, and not simply stop? Why do dogs circle a spot before lying down there? "There" is not a place—not yet. While turning in circles and lying down, dogs are not marking anything. They pose and point, they dig at the ground and above it. In fact, even words are improper for it: *there* presupposes de-signation; it is already the prototype of markings. And the marking makes the place: the place is a marked posing. "There" is the posing that I mark. Why? The marking wants to be recognized and found again. One marks for those who are following, and for oneself if one is coming back. But why would I come back, *there*? And why does the dog come back?

Let me propose that I come back to approach those who are following. I come (back) to come nearer. What is inscribed is the possible approach—as a place: the locus of connections, of meeting again. Fire, fireplace [*foyer*]: focusing around that which marks the possibility of joining each other—*there*. I am positing (proposing) here that the only locus there is is around the mark of this approach—around this point. One doesn't say, "There used to be some water there, so we are getting together there," but rather: "*Since we are nearing it*, and meeting up, and seeing one another there, this is the watering place [*point d'eau*]." There is water elsewhere, isn't there? The watering place is the point of gathering. Gathering is already saying a little too much; approaching suffices—suffices for the place: one approaches *there*, through *there*.

Or in other words, there is no place except a common place. Places are common places. The place is registered or remarked as a place only inasmuch as it allows and designates a common approach. "For [there] where two or three are gathered together in my name, there am I in the midst of them [Fr., *au milieu de vous*]," Christ says (Matt. 18:20). Note the *there* in this sentence. If you—two or three among you—*there* speak (in my name), well, *there* I am, in the middle [*au mi-lieu*] among you. In a way, the locus is always a focus [*foyer*]: a center, reference point, *mesos*, locus, or way station [*mi-lieu*], around which the approach—the reunion, the *sunagōgē*—takes place. There is no locus that is not a locus of reencounter, proximity, and sharing. Sharing meals, sleep, words. If it is *there*, it is because *there*, in this marked place, I am drawing closer, I am finding you (again). Every locus is at the same time a center and an envelope: a marked place, *around* which one assembles and comes nearer, a gathering point—a place to meet and talk: locus of the limit, of the contour.

(The question arises of whether we can simultaneously say that all places are common, and acknowledge that dogs, bees, and birds such as titmice express something like place recognition. We can bypass the question by reiterating that the place is not just the pose, and reserving the appellation *locus* for the marked pose—*there*—that calls for recognition and approach. We have to be less shy—as we know, animals also leave marks. Let us say it, then: there *are* animal approaches [*rapprochements*]. Within animality something lends itself to recognition; something marks and remarks. There are animal loci. And this means, within animality, too, there are stirrings of a proto-question of the common[77]—a proto-thesis, prototype. Or in another words—to avoid the apparent finalism of the prefix *proto*—a hypotype, or *hypothesis*, of community. The common is not inaugurated—like the inception of a pure origin—with the supposed advent of humans. Or rather, man is not the [pure] origin of man. There is some animal underneath. Transcendence of the human is not to be thought of as an essential difference but as a production—and production demands an antecedence, and materials. Materialism, once again. One again has to think [human] transcendence *within* [animal] immanence, as that which opens it. Transcendence within immanence: the concept of becoming, perhaps. Human commonality takes up, displaces, and transforms something from animal approaches.)

The surprising affinity that brings the *locus* near to the *common*—this is something one may have to track down in the very writings of Aristotle, a research task requiring a more specialized competence. Let me simply suggest that such a study should tackle the homonymy that distributes the question of topoi to "places"—if I may say so—that are far apart, principally in Aristotle's *Physics*, on the one hand, and the *Rhetoric* and the *Topics*, on the other.[78] Let me make two very careful remarks.

(1) The *places* or topoi of rhetoric are *common*; this is obvious: "By specific topics [Gk., *eidē*] I mean the propositions peculiar [Gk., *idias*] to each class of things, by universal [Gk., *topoi, topous*] those common to all alike [Gk., *koinous omoiōs pantōn*]."[79] But why are these common propositions termed *topoi* or *places*, precisely? What is it, in this community of language, that calls for the "metaphor" of locality? The etymology of the term seems unknown, as does the history of the passage from one sense to the other.[80] Without pretending to make up for this lack, it might be suggested that the determination of the *common* and of the *local* may not be unconnected, if the *common place* is this space, this point, where some types of discourse (that are otherwise different) "coincide" or "come down to." The *locus* may be the space, metaphorically, that is *common* to them—or even practically common, as the place where different discourses meet and face off: the place of deliberation, of oratorical confrontation, and thus, as far as rhetoric is concerned, the place of assembly.[81]

(2) Aristotle's *Physics* seems to contradict this way of thinking, since each thing lodges—or transports itself toward—its proper locus, resting there in immobility. Let us first note that this immobility, which is that of the (initial or terminal) place, is only brought up because there is some movement.

> First then we must understand that *place would not have been thought of*, if there had not been a special kind of *motion, namely that with respect to place*. It is chiefly for this reason that we suppose the heaven [Gk., *ouranon*] also to be in place, because it is in constant movement.[82]

Aristotle immediately adds that in this kind of movement one has to distinguish between transport (or "locomotion") [*phora*], and increase/diminution.[83] Now, "'motion' in its most general and primary sense is change of place, which we call locomotion" [or transport—Trans.].[84] Locomotive transport is therefore that which conveys the thing toward its locus: "a body [is] carried to its own place [*pheroito eis ton autou topon*]."[85] The locus, as the place proper, is thus the stop, the end of the transport. Each thing properly speaking is posited there—deposited or in repose— and this seems to exclude any community of the locus. But we may notice that: (a) the (physical) locus is proper to the *thing*, whereas the (rhetorical) locus was common to propositions, elements of discourse. Thus the passage from the common to the proper seems to be a passage from language to bodies;[86] and (b), in the *Physics*, the introduction of the locus proper is made with reference to the common locus, which precedes and conditions it in the argument.

We may distinguish generally between predicating B of A because it (A) is itself, and because it is something else; and particularly between place which is common and in which all bodies are, and the special [i.e., proper—Trans.] place occupied primarily by each. I mean, for instance, that you are now in the heavens because you are in the air and it is in the heavens.[87]

This seems to contradict the just mentioned hypothesis (about the *body proper*) since this passage is about a place common to all. But this mention of the common place is the only one in this text. To the possibly naive reader, it seems to stand there as if to make the place-proper possible, in a way so as to account for the *becoming-proper* of the properness stemming from the common. The "special" locus-proper is that of *propriation*—and this may be what posits it as "physical": "[Each thing] should remain *naturally* in its proper place."[88] Natural: *phusei*. The thing is in *physical* repose in its place, inasmuch as it is proper to it. Repose is the *property*—the *physical* one—of the locus. Or in other words, the *properness* of the locus is physical inasmuch as it is a stopping. This stopping then, in this way, is equivalent to the becoming-proper of the common. The locus, as proper, is the *propriation* (it would be tempting to write "appropriation") of the common (place). But here the *introduction* in the text of the locus proper, as Rémi Brague incites us to read it, becomes quite significant, since the properness of the locus comes up with the designation of "your" place.[89] The place proper is first of all "yours"—an eloquent marking indeed. For one would rather expect the passage from the common to the proper to be a passage to "mine"—as if the becoming-proper were a kind of propriation without appropriation; as if the proper, in any case, in its singularity, kept a *mark* of this commonality from which it issues and which precedes it: a linguistic mark, of invocation, whose astonishingly rare character Brague underscores.[90] While the passage to the *locus proper* as the place of stopped bodies in repose is what marks the singularity of the physical topos in relation to the rhetorical topoi, the very text of this passage conveys the trace of the call—the invocation, the rhetorical approach—of which this passage does sign the stopping, or the end.

*

The gods are local. Places are often (perhaps more than often) holy places, sacred places, loci of the divine, or divine places; thus a plot, something in play, between gods and places, might be surmised.[91] *Lieu* [place or locus], "appeared (ca. 1120) with its general sense of 'determined portion of space'; also in the special sense of *holy place* (ca. 1150), 'temple, church.'"[92] It is worth noting that the two meanings are contemporaneous. Now, if the locus is natively grappling with commonality; if, in a certain way, places are first and foremost common places, places of the common; then something is determinedly at play (or plotted) among gods, places, and community. What?

21. Exodus

Hegel writes:

"What is holy?" Goethe asks once in a distich, and answers: "What links many souls together." In this sense we may say that the holy with the aim of this concord, and as this concord, has been the first content of independent architecture. The readiest example of this is provided by the story of the Tower of Babylonia. In the wide plains of the Euphrates an enormous architectural work was erected; it was built in common, and the aim and content of the work was at the same time the community of those who constructed it.... The ensemble of all the peoples at that period worked at this task and since they all came together to complete an immense work like this, the product of their labour was to be a bond which was to link them together.... In that case, such a building is symbolic at the same time since the bond, which it is, it can only hint at; this is because in its form and shape it is only in an external way that it can express the holy, the absolute unifier of men.[93]

And elsewhere:

For architecture is the first to open the way for the adequate actuality of the god.... Thereby it levels a place for the god, forms his external environment, and builds for him his temple as the place for the inner composure of the spirit and its direction on its absolute objects. It raises an enclosure for the assembly of the congregation, as protection against the threat of storm, against rain, tempest, and wild animals, and it reveals in an artistic way, even if in an external one, the wish to assemble [Fr., *le vouloir-être-ensemble*] ... and the god's temple, the house of his community, stands there ready. Then into this temple, *secondly*, the god enters himself as the lightning-flash of individuality striking and permeating the inert mass.[94]

And further:

> Now when architecture has built its temple and the hand of sculpture has set up within it the statues of the god, this sensuously present god is confronted, *thirdly*, in the wide halls of his house, by the *community*. The community is the spiritual reflection into itself of this sensuous existent [Gm., *Daseyns*], and is animating subjectivity and inwardness. . . . The compact unity in itself which the god has in sculpture disperses into the plurality of the inner lives of individuals. . . . And so only here is God himself truly spirit, spirit in his community.[95]

All these astonishing analyses have to do with architecture. Architecture is the first of five stages in this history-system, this system unfurling as history: the system of particular arts, through which the spiritual moment of art itself follows the path of its progressive dematerialization, the spiritualization and appropriation of itself, which will drive it finally to abandon itself as art for the benefit of religion and philosophy. The succession of the first two phases presents a singularity: if architecture precedes sculpture, it is to build the house of the god before he enters and occupies it. In a more candid—or more totemic—review, one might think that the succession takes place in reverse order: men would first give themselves a god, configure and carve him, and later on concern themselves with housing him (or her), fitting out his (or her) space and habitation. But Hegel imposes the opposite schema. Architecture is the construction of the god's house, but this house is empty. Architecture erects a place insofar as it strips it, tidies and clears away what occupies it, so as to free up an empty space where the god can come; but he will come later, and architecture will then have finished—completed its time, at least, of dominance and hegemony. And this time is long—the time of architecture, the time of this clearing and emptying. It is the whole era of symbolic and Oriental art: a whole time period of the world—Persia, India, Egypt. The mission of architecture evokes that of John the Baptist or Elijah (John the Baptist *is* Elijah, in a way), those who free up paths for the God. Architecture is what does

> *open the way* for the adequate actuality of the god . . . in order to work it free from the jungle of finitude and the monstrosity of chance. Thereby it levels a place for the god, forms his external environment, and builds for him his temple as the place for the inner composure of the spirit and its direction on its absolute objects. It raises an enclosure.[96]

As for John the Baptist, he quotes Isaiah; he is this voice in the desert of which Isaiah spoke, saying, "Prepare Ye the way of the Lord, make straight in the desert a highway for our God. Every valley shall be exalted, and every mountain and hill shall be made low: and the crooked shall be made straight, and the rough places plain."[97] Architecture is thus precursory and announcing something; it makes room, frees and flattens the ground for a God *who has not yet come*.

Now, in the description of this building phase, Hegel's text displays an equivocation. The designation for the temple being built alternates between the house of God (*seines Hauses*) and the house of the community (*das Haus seiner Gemeinde*). The entire argument establishes and reiterates that the house is the community's: it makes room for gatherings, forms an enclosure around assemblies, "reveals in an artistic way, even if in an external one, the wish to assemble" [Gm., *jenes Sichsammelnwollen*; Fr., *le vouloir-être-ensemble*].[98] But the equivalence between house of the community and house of God leads to the question, *What if the divine were simply the common?* What if, in building the house of God, the community made a house for itself, and that is all? A house for the commonality in itself, for that which in itself is the common, being-common—the being-together that makes it being-in-common?

A closer look shows that this is almost exactly what the first text quoted in this chapter says.[99] Goethe wrote that the holy is what links (many) souls together (Gm., *was viele Seelen zusammenbindet*). Hegel interprets this in a very determined way: the holy, he comments, is the "aim of this concord" and *is this concord*.[100] And he doubles the interpretation in invoking the myth of Babel. The builders of the tower erect it together, and the community is at the same time "the aim and content of the work" itself.[101] Building it seems merely to be an opportunity for social contact, but what it aims to erect in truth is the social bond itself, which it externalizes, symbolizes, but also produces and brings to its effectuation. In this sense, "all the peoples at that period worked at this task" and "the product of their labour was to be a bond which was to link them together."[102] This may surprise us: what about the social bond of these "peoples" leading to this construction (or existing "before" it, if you will)? Hegel's answer is clear-cut: these peoples had been gathered by patriarchal and family ties. Now, "the foundation of this social bond does not remain merely a unification on patriarchal lines."[103] What is involved here, then, is the social bond in its very socialness—and not just the simple tie or gathering that makes the family. What is the difference? What is the social bond that the family bond is not? No doubt, it is the common as common, the common of the common, the detached common untied from natural filiations and affiliations, which manifest the bond but at the same time conceal it behind a veil of naturalness. The social bond is commonality in the clear. That is why observing that social bonds differ from patriarchal gatherings is not enough: "on the contrary, the purely family unity [*sic*] *has already been superseded*, and the building, rising into the clouds, makes objective to itself *this earlier and dissolved unity* and the realization of a new and wider one [Fr., *d'une nouvelle et plus vaste société*] . . . such a building is *symbolic* at the same time."[104] The social bond is what comes about when the family disassembles and erases itself. It is the common, released from filiation.

That is why architecture has to clear out space, empty it by removing its natural clutter, and fit out an open and empty space, flat and featureless—*an empty space for commonality*[105]—because the common, inasmuch as it is common, neither is nor wants anything natural, anything preexisting, nothing taking up any room and cluttering it. Nothing steep, no scrubby undergrowth. *The common comes to the desert*, when nature clears things out, or when one has to set it free. The common is (in the) vacuum—un-occupied, un-cluttered by nature, things, or landscapes. Architecture, in erecting the house of the community—the common house—builds an empty house, a house occupied by a vacuum, by this cleared-out space *within and around* which the community gathers (will gather). The community converges and bears down on a void—to gather nothing but itself. What is vacant is this space of inscription where the community will come to (re)mark itself, find itself, and recognize itself. *And this void is (the) divine*: the space where the god will be able to announce himself (herself), and then come. One may object that the god will come to *occupy* this vacuum, fill it, and thus negate it. But this may not be so sure—even in Hegelian terms. For that which will come to manifest itself at the center of the united community is individuality, with its stroke of lightning. Hegel does not say "the individuality of the god," but simply—here—individuality, *der Blitz der Individualität*.[106] And individuality may not be fullness. Or in other—anticipating—words, individuality *in full* may exactly be an idol. But let us wait a little. For now, just this: what architecture does in erecting the common house—so as to leave room for the common—is to empty, declutter, and unoccupy a piece of nature—and thus protect the cleared-out vacant space (with walls and a roof).

Which is to say, architecture designates and manifests this space as a locus—since the locus is doubtless not a thing, or a container, in the sense of a thing that contains. Nor is it, physically, the void that has been contained. Rather, the locus is *containance* [Fr., *contenance*: carrying capacity] *itself*, so to speak; it is the limit of what is enveloping.[107] Containance appears as such by means of vacating, or at least decluttering. Elijah or John the Baptist *frees the way* for the coming god, the place where the god will come. So does architecture: it circumscribes the void, evacuates the spacing in which (within and around which—all at once) the community will be able to gather. *Architecture frees up the place as a common place (place of commonality)*.

This gesture is equivocal, and it does recall the ambivalence of the Temple in Martin Heidegger's political aesthetics.[108] For on the one hand (the deep side, as it were), architecture is anchored in the localization of the place, its locality, its being-*there* (it digs the soil, works on the burial of things and foundations); on the other, it partakes of vacuity, the freedom of the place, its decluttering, its empty and desertlike being. Underneath, it grounds; above, it opens up. Architecture externalizes and manifests—rigorously—the ambiguous logic of the locus: a precise and determined emplacement on land, a point of incision, of reference and marking—but also an empty space, pure containance, immaterial limit, circumscription of the void, locus of common or divine incidence.

"*The community is the spiritual reflection into itself* of this sensuous existent [Gm., *Dasein* or *Daseyn*]. . . . The compact unity in itself which the god has in sculpture disperses into the plurality of the inner lives of individuals. . . . And so only here is God himself truly spirit, spirit in his community, God as this to-and-fro."[109] Powerful formulas: simply, the community is spiritual reflection. And the god's "to-and-fro"—away from things that occupy and clutter, from mountains, scrubby vegetation, steepness, and accidents of the "world"—produces two effects: it sets the place free, as a place—containment, enveloping of a free emplacement—and it sets the god free, as a god, as *spirit*. Spirit is that which, torn away from the world, comes back to it, floats and hovers above it. Such is the god, "truly spirit, spirit in his community" [Gm., *wahrhaft Geist—der Geist seiner*

Gemeinde].¹¹⁰ The structure of a vertical and ternary structure constitutes itself: locus/common/god. The locus is freed, vacated—constituted as locus—making room for the vacuum of the common, within and around which the common assembles and comes about. But this liberation of the locus *frees the god*, as an emanation is freed—a light matter, a gas—freeing him as *genius loci*, which hovers above the place, lingers there, and comes back. Beneath the common, the locus. Above it, the gods. Places and gods are (of the) common. The god (quite simply, the common) is *there*. Or,

The god is the spirit of the (common) place of the common. (*h16*)

The gods are local, the gods are *there*.¹¹¹ The plurality of gods is a multitude of places, gathering points, places of approaches and proximity. Polytheism is polytopical. Gods are linked to places by the ambiguous bond that their nature as spirits designates: all at once anchored *there*, moored to this emplacement and this piece of land, and yet torn away from it. And thus ceaselessly coming back [*revenant*] as light, gaseous—hovering—matter. The gods mark the dependence of commonality with regard to places, its attachment to sites and gathering points, where the common constitutes and recognizes itself. *The gods mark the attachment of the common to the land*—and the ambiguity of this attachment. Each god is like a kite tied to a post stuck in the soil, hovering above it in the wind. The tie, the post—they are the immanence of the divine, its fastening to the earth, its topism. The hovering is its transcendence, its elevation and lightness. Another sketch:

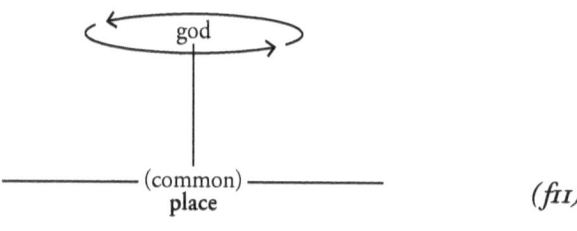

(*f11*)

*

It is from this proposition as a whole that one can try to characterize the Jewish contributions to the history told here. Let us once more recall our question: if "Rome" is the name of the space where materials and supplies are transported and distributed to the outer limits of the world, then, after the Greek material, what is the Jewish material that is disseminated? I contend that exodus is the Jewish contribution—and here is a defining hypothesis for it:

The exodus tears the common away from the place. (h17)

Exodus tells this peculiar—probably original—story: the god tears himself away from the place, sets himself up amid the common, takes charge of its transport, and goes away with it—an invention, it seems; a proposition, a hypothesis for the future, like the Greek contribution: it is said that the gods of nomads do not act this way.[112] Exodus is the god who goes ahead, the god on his way. From a certain angle, this god resembles any other one: he is the spirit of the common, and he hovers above it all. But there is a point where he innovates: he detaches the common from the place, from this emplacement on the earth, and now hovers above the people moving onward—like a pillar of air, like a cloud.[113] He carries on what architecture had started, namely, the liberation of the common, its extraction from the land, its self-positioning. But he pushes ahead: the extraction of the common is a detachment—takeoff—from the place; and the god, among the common, or above it as a spirit, leaves with it, takes off, sets forth, and rises up. The god of the Jews is the god of the common, walking with the common and upon it—set on his way. He is the mobile temple, the tent, the god of walking.

No doubt it matters that it was a slave insurrection that started this uprooting and departure.[114] This produces a double peculiarity, at least in the narration: this god is not just a god of nomads; and he is not a household god that one takes along in exile, as the god of the house, when it is time to flee. He is not a god of the place, or the house, whom one carries along: *he is the god of walking itself*, the god of the community walking away, free from places, relating only to its self-positioning as the community of the common. But beyond this, carrying away the god, setting him on his way, transporting him in this insurrection—all this marks what is new in this rebellion compared to other slave uprisings that did take place, beforehand or elsewhere: the insurgent slaves here decide to *change territories*, to transfer themselves—elsewhere and not in the pharaonic space, a tyrannical or imperial space in the archaic sense of the word. It is said that Egypt is the figure of the world: but the exodus exits this world, but not toward another world, a world beyond the world, outside of the world. It is a lateral exit, by means of a transfer, displacement, reinscription of the common elsewhere, and a reinvention. And it is the walking, on the very land, upon immanence itself, that produces and constitutes an elsewhere distinct from the world (world of empire, of slavery). If the world is under the sway of slavery, then let us exit the world—a proposition that can no doubt be interpreted in a sense of being beyond the world (as a certain—but only a certain—Christian reading will do: let us exit the world toward the hereafter), but can also be understood as, Let us exit the world of the empire, upon immanence itself; let us set out, trace out some paths, produce new spaces—*let us carry ourselves away*.

What comes forth, then, is the common itself, even more released than it was in the temple—the community of the common, more manifest, more carried away, and freer. And where does this renovated common form itself, freed from its matrix, if not in the dwelling place? First of all in the desert: a clear space, locus without locus, archi-decluttered, and empty. A place without landmarks, without prescribed gathering points (without a mountain-locus, river-locus, or tree-locus). Gathering is self-positioned there, without any marking except its own convocation. The desert is like a temple without a place, a temple-world, a temple-land, vacated and available to the common. How does the common form in this emptiness? As utterance, discourse, word or writing, prescription free from any bond to places or things; and this puts the common into words, for itself, as a new inscription, or *attempts to put into words the void that lets the common be itself for itself*. It is the position of unbound commonality, community of the common, outside of any attachment to the locus. The exodus formulates the common as law. And this is how the law is transcendent: given and other. If the law were not given, if it were not coming from heaven, it would be *there*, on earth, at a place. Transcendence of the law is transcendence of the common itself. The common is that which holds up outside of any local, earthly, or visible inscription. The law positions a placeless commonality, without any locus except its very community, without any tie to anything else except to itself. *What the exodus sets free is the transcendence of the common.*

*

The invention of the exodus will produce various effects, transmitted and spread by Rome, and they will be set down in the formation and constitution of Europe.

Transports of Origin 155

(1) First of all, there is what one might term *the opening of the future*—not simply positing that there is a time to come, which seems coextensive with human experience, but thematizing this time as free and not predetermined, and thus *open* to experience and invention. On this topic, Ernst Bloch's analyses seem unchallengeable,[115] for example, about the difference between divination and prophecy (e.g., Greek),[116] divination being the supposed expression of what the future will be, and prophecy functioning as a call, an invocation, and thus a pro-vocation to an action or a responsibility. For that matter, it is probable that the whole prophetizing, messianic, and thus revolutionary dimension that marks European ventures with a very singular seal cannot be thought of without this tearing away that one may term exodic: *tearing away from places* and from servitude, from the place of servitude, and from servitude as the regime of the place; and thus *producing time*, an open, indefinite, and dis-lodged [*dé-logé*] time: emancipating time, time of liberation.[117] Stepping across, set free.

(2) Secondly, there is what one needs to designate as *sublimation*. Indeed, there is a direct link between tearing away from places—exodus—and parting with images. What are images images of? Of gods, they say. Agreed. But they are inasmuch as gods are matched with places, of which they are *the spirit, genius loci, and thus the revenant coming back, and thus the figure*. Not only is the commandment to reject images (and the whole Decalogue) given at the heart of the exodus, and Exodus, but it is immediately joined and matched with the self-positioning of God as the *god of the exodus*, the god of the exit from Egypt:

I am Yahweh, Your God: It is I who brought you out of the land of Egypt, out of the house where you were a slave! You shall have no other gods but me! You shall make no idols, or *any likeness of any thing that is in Heaven above, or that is on the Earth beneath, or that is in the Water under the earth*: You shall not bow down before them, nor worship them: for I, Yahweh, am an exclusive God.[118]

And so, the *dismissal of images* is given in the movement itself of the exodus, relinquishing *elementary* figures, that is to say, ones that are produced in the medium or elements of air, earth, or water. The exit from Egypt (tearing away from the locus, from the world) and liberation are linked, by means of a direct connection, to the repudiation of images. Jean Bottéro holds, regarding the commandments in the Decalogue as a whole, that "especially if one compares them to the axioms—more or less latent or virtual—of other great religions of that era, even the most impressive and venerable ones, from Babylon to Egypt, one perceives *something voluntarily 'spiritual,' profound, and sublime, which forces us to marvel even more* at the genius of Moses."[119]

"Sublime" is the word for it, no doubt. Its theory has been established—by Immanuel Kant—and precisely referred to the commandment about images: "perhaps there is no sublimer passage in the Jewish law than the command, Thou shalt not make to thyself any graven image, nor the likeness of anything."[120] The commandment concerning images truly is *the most sublime*—in the precise sense that this term is given in Kant's third *Critique* (exactly at the heart of the "Analytic of the Sublime"). Kant draws several consequences from this: (a) "This command alone can explain the enthusiasm that the Jewish people . . . felt for their religion . . . or explain the pride which Mahommedanism inspires."[121] The farewell to images sparks this enthusiasm and transport toward the divine. Paradoxical thesis: one likes to believe that images are what excites, seduces, or mobilizes people. This is false, and it is even the other way around. Enthusiasm is a grasping, a penetration by means of imagelessness and figurelessness. Moreover, (b) it is an error to believe that morality, stripped of images, might lose some of its strength. The opposite is true, says Kant: "it would be rather necessary to moderate the impetus of an *unbounded imagination* [Gm., *unbegrenzten Einbildungskraft*], to prevent it from rising to enthusiasm."[122] *Unbegrenzten* here does not mean "unlimited," in the sense that the imagination might have indefinitely spread the field of its competence. On the contrary, the word means that the imagination is projected beyond its limit, as it were, to the external boundary of itself, toward the unimaginable itself, for which it is granted a kind of grasping, which makes it somewhat mad and boundlessly carried away by this excess with regard to itself. Thus, (c) it is rather to calm the ardor of crowds than to fan it that governing bodies authorize or recommend bringing these childish accessories, namely, images, into religion. Images give protection from enthusiasm—and thus, in a sense, from the divine itself.[123] The trace that the exodus left in our history, by way of the dismissal of idols (the figuration of gods and places—celestial, terrestrial, and marine), is thus simply enthusiasm: the peculiar excitement that grips the soul before the void when one *has done away with figures*—an excitement that has written a few pages of our history, as we know, and the matter may not be completely closed, after all.

The use of the term "sublimation" to designate this process may seem somewhat forced. And yet, one needs to link these few lines by Kant with the astonishing pages that Sigmund Freud devotes to the same question in the final parts of *Moses and Monotheism*.[124] In the two chapter sections titled, successively, "The Advance in Intellectuality" and "Renunciation of Instinct [Gm., *Trieb*; Fr., *pulsion*]," Freud establishes his singular conceptual sequence: (1) "In the religion of Moses the Exodus from Egypt served as the proof [for the Jewish people]" (MM, p. 111). But in later times, this exodus was no more than a memory, and it fails to explain the attachment of these people to this God—since the treatment that followed this mark of divine favor was quite bad. In such circumstances, it happens that people depose their gods just as they chase away their kings. But on the contrary, despite their misfortune, the Jewish people have remained unfailingly faithful to their God. Why? "Why [did] the people of Israel, however, [cling] more and more submissively to their God the worse they were treated by him . . . ?" (MM, p. 112). (2) At this point, Freud, as he often does in this book, "jumps" to a neighboring question without clearly indicating the relationship that conditions this consecution. The new question consists in the suggestion "to enquire whether the religion of Moses brought the people nothing else besides an enhancement of their self-esteem owing to their consciousness of having been chosen," and immediately in proposing the answer that "religion also brought the Jews a far grander [Gm., *grossartigere*; Fr., *plus sublime*] conception of God, or, as we might put it more modestly, the conception of a grander [Gm., *grossartigeren*; Fr., *plus sublime*] God" (MM, p. 112). There is no indication yet why this grander sublimity "brings" anything that we might conceive to be satisfying, something comparable or additional to the sentiment of divine election.[125] Let us keep reading. What determines this sublimity? The answer comes soon enough; it is "the prohibition against making an image of God—the compulsion to worship a God whom one cannot see" (MM, pp. 112–13). But how is this prohibition gratifying? (3) Freud then notes that this prohibition "meant that a sensory perception was given second place to what may be called an abstract idea—a triumph of intellectuality [Gm., *Geistigkeit*; Fr., *la vie de l'esprit*] over sensuality [Gm., *Sinnlichkeit*; Fr., *la vie sensorielle*]" (MM, p. 113). The prohibition has a certain relation with the withdrawal of sensuality and the onset of intellectuality as such. Which relation? Again, a "jump": Freud digresses and makes a detour through the attitude of neurotic people and more particularly "the mental phenomenon which we describe as a belief in the 'omnipotence of thoughts'" (MM, p. 113). He posits an analogy between this phenomenon and the historical mutation whereby, during the invention of language, "The new realm of intellectuality was opened up" (MM, p. 113) for humans. Freud thus links this proto-phenomenon of human history with the moment when the "Mosaic prohibition elevated God to a higher degree of intellectuality" (MM, pp. 114–15). And thus, "The dematerialization of God brought a fresh and valuable contribution to [the Jewish people's] secret treasure" (MM, p. 115). We now have more information: the piece added to the treasure [Gm., *Schatz*], the new gratification granted by the sublime commandment is dematerialization—one might say de-sensibilization—and thus the production of intellectuality. *But how is it a gratification?* The only clue comes from the behavior of neurotics. (Neurotic) gratification is the belief in an omnipotence of thinking. The gratification is thus less the advent of the intellect itself than the omnipotence that neurotically attaches itself to it. This is understandable: humanity did not wait for Moses to be intelligent. What Moses brings is not intellectuality but (as a neurotic benefit) the rise of its hegemony. What he asserts is a potency, a power (or possibility), an omnipotence as an omnipossibility. (4) At this point Freud develops the link between the satisfaction of the intellect and the "renunciation of instinct" [Gm., *Triebverzicht*]), which explains that instinctual renunciation[126] (when an external constraint causes this) is a source of displeasure [Gm., *Unlust*]. But when the renunciation of drives results from inner causes that obey the superego, there is another kind of effect: "In addition to the inevitable unpleasurable consequences it also brings the ego a yield of pleasure—a substitutive satisfaction, as it were. The ego feels elevated; it is proud of the instinctual renunciation" (MM, p. 117).

There are two aspects to this process. First, it derives from the superego: it is an obedience. But obedience as such cannot yield pleasure; it is coerced. Where is the pleasure, then? Before the formation of the superego, obeying one's parents was associated with the reward of their love. The same goes for the process of obedience when it is internalized: it brings self-love (MM, pp. 117ff.). How? Through a feeling of dignity and uplifting. Renunciation is uplifting and brings pride. One might think, in the end, that pleasure comes from superego obedience. But the order of Freud's argument is reversed: obeying the superego is a transitory motif, a procedure or a means. What brings pleasure is being loved—being loved by way of not consenting to one's compulsion. There is the satisfaction, the pride, and the uplifting sentiment. Then, gathering part of the sequence in a single statement, Freud writes, "The religion which began with the prohibition against making an image of God develops more and more in the course of centuries into a religion of instinctual renunciations" (MM, p. 118). (5) Laconically he adds, "But ethics is a limitation of instinct [Gm., *Triebeinschränkung*]" (MM, p. 118). This is when the sequence appears as a whole, and it is admittedly striking, articulating *Exodus → sublime God, prohibition of images → withdrawal of sense perception → assertion of intellectuality → renunciation of instinctual drives → ethics*. If I understand this correctly, thanks to "a substitutive satisfaction," the renunciation of instinctual urges brings about Kant's enthusiasm ("the dematerialization of God") as an addition to the people's "treasure." Gratification lies in the absence of images. Freud adds the production of ethics—sublime because it is exodic: the invention of the law.

22. Absent from the World

Let us conflate the results of these two analyses. The Roman world—Romanity as world—thus carries out the generalized diffusion of two contributions, one Greek and the other Jewish, and we may characterize them as follows: the Greek contribution as the idea of the *transcendence of beingness* [*l'étant*] (that which is); the Jewish contribution as the narrative, or law, of the *transcendence of the common*.[127] These two positions, or suppositions, henceforth cohabit in the Roman world, the world as Roman.

The transcendence of, or rather toward beingness is what Patočka meant as transcendence toward the world (HE, p. 49).[128] But in the setup proposed here, as mentioned, the concept of "world" [*monde*] is not suitable to designate precisely what the Greek invention of philosophy has attained or delivered. That toward which philosophy has carried itself, that before which it has constituted itself as pure gaze, or further, that which it has freed or bared, is that which had been the object of practical appropriation, captured by ritual, mythical, or worshipping interest or grasping, which is to say (to keep the anachronism), rather *this* piece of the world inasmuch as it is; and it is there that one has had to clear the position of being [*être*] from any bewitching, spell, or consummation. It is therefore more exact to say that it is beingness that has been the object of this gaze, this liberation, or this baring. The invention of the philosophical comes about as transcendence toward beingness, as a movement of *transporting oneself toward beingness*, by way of the gaze, without capture or appropriation. Rémi Brague opens his book *Aristote et la question du monde* (Aristotle and the Question of the World) by announcing from the start that it is built around a concept (the world) absent as such from Aristotle's works.[129] And he adds, "To say it with Heidegger, it is even . . . *the conspicuously missing element of classical Greek thought.*"[130]

If the Greeks did not know "*the world*" in this sense, is it perhaps because it had not yet eventuated? Greek philosophy thematizes the celestial universe (*ouranos*) or the *cosmos*, "ordered totality of the reality forming the universe,"[131] origin or receptacle for the city—order or constitution of the universe *as* locus or origin of the city[132]—environment, celestial circumscription of the assembly of humans; and further, *oikoumenē*, which is to say, inhabited land—the part of the land that is inhabited, or the land insofar as it is inhabited. None of these concepts corresponds exactly to our idea of world. Our world is a unified idea of all beingness (all that is). We are not suggesting that the Greeks had not thought about "all that is," or that they had not engaged with the question of its totality. What I mean to say is that we are held and involved by *a certain postulation* of the unity of this totality, *as world*. Philosophy, Husserl writes, is the "science of the universe, of the all-encompassing *unity* of all that is."[133] The specific schema or mode of unity of this totality, which allows us to designate it as the world, is not Greek. As "*that which is*" or beingness, no doubt Greek thinking provides it, and probably as totality, too. But as this (worldwide global) *unity* of all that is—unitary model and regime of globality of all that is—the idea comes from elsewhere, and from a later time.[134]

Let us recall the proposition or hypothesis formulated about this topic:[135] the worldly mode appropriate to the unity of all that is *is the mode of imperial unification*. The world is that which the empire subjugates. The unity of the world is thus this totalized unity under a single sovereignty, the *unity of the totality in the mode of submission*. Rome is that which transmutes and transforms the transcendence-toward-beingness into the transcendence of the world. The (philosophical) idea of the (transcendent) unity of the world is produced in and from the era of Romanity. Its formalization as such (and the idea of *universality* resulting from it) may be what is specific in the contribution of Stoicism. The Stoics *process* the Hellenic transcendence-toward-beingness to universalize it into the transcendence of the unified world. The emperor Marcus Aurelius (121–80 C.E.) was a Stoic, and not the least among them.[136] Thus it is Rome that institutes the now radical ambiguity of this agency of the world—since what is *subjected* is also, structurally, the very thing that potentially gives resistance. Submission produces resistance; it subjects only that which resists, insofar as it resists or can resist. That which neither does nor can resist in any way is not to be subjugated, but will only be crushed, absorbed, or ingested. What submission dominates is a resistance. In this way, if the world is *that which is subjected to the empire, it is also that which resists this submission*. (It is another question whether this resistance might allow one to think of an alternative to the empire, or, on the contrary, whether it is too closely bound up with imperial domination to make this possible—a matter of strategic choice: resistance or insubordination.)

*

Now, it so happens that a process of *religious* unification of the common *answers* this imperial unification of the world, as in a dialogue. Why so? Because "Judaism," spread and transmitted to the outer limits of the world, will soon be called upon—by one determination of its developments—to become the *religion* of the Roman world, the religion of Romanity as the world. Christianity is this mutation of the Jewish contribution that makes it suitable to constitute itself as the *religion of the empire*—even if it is not only that. This necessarily leads to the intersection and the encounter of the Jewish contribution with the Greek one, since the very idea of empire is a development or extension of the polis, expanded into a republic and then into the world.[137] The first task in conforming Christianity *as a religion*[138] and a body of doctrines (from Paul to John to Augustine) essentially consisted in the elaboration of this relationship—of Greek philosophy with biblical narratives, and the thinking that arose as a consequence. The framework of this elaboration was the empire as such.[139] In this sense, it is not because it becomes the religion of the emperors that Christianity is the *religion of the empire*. It is so—potentially, beforehand—as the religion *of the age of the empire*, and what this connection contains is precisely constituted by the fact that Christianity represents the juncture of Hebraism and Hellenism, the two main materials supplied to Roman intellectuality, which will ensure their worldwide globalization.[140] A certain worldwide *religious* unification of the common thus answers the imperial unification of the world. The name of this worldwide, para-imperial religious unity will be Catholicity.[141]

Catholicity is an answer to the worldhood of the empire. The "formula" (similar to an algebraic or chemical formula) of Catholicity is "one single people," answering the empire's "one single world." Little by little, a linking formula—key formula, mediating operator—has introduced itself between the two, namely, "one single god," the monotheistic formula. For I am contending here that the invention of the narrative (or the thought) of exodus *is not* monotheism. The exodus *sets the common free from the place*, freeing up the autonomy of a commonality extracted from the locus, of a community of the common, which goes beyond its boundaries and escapes its locality. The god of the exodus is the god who goes out, moves across, and sets free: "I am Yahweh, Your God: It is I who brought you out of the land of Egypt, out of the house where you were a slave." Nothing in this characterization, at this very determined point, is monotheistic.[142] The god of the exodus, as such, shows no solidarity with any *monotheism*. Instead, he rather shares in an *exotheism*, so to speak. Monotheism is something else altogether, since the position of the single god does not necessarily set the common free from the place. On the contrary, monotheism can very well re-posit the locality of the god, but only in positing the formula "one single place"; all that is needed is that all places merge into a single and unique, all-encompassing locus. Now, the unique place that includes and abolishes all places is doubtless that which makes possible the *idea of world*. Unique all-encompassing locus: one single place, because of one single world. The world bears the uniqueness and thus the unity of the locus. *The worldwide global totalization of that-which-is is its local totalization*. The local unity of the world, all-encompassing unity of the place of all places, which dissolves and abolishes them in their difference, *is made possible from the starting point of the project of the empire*. Monotheism is its expression; it is an imperial theism. Exodus was setting one free from the place and inventing a god who steps forth and across, and moves onward,[143] whereas monotheism formalizes a unifying and overlooking god, who is as localized as the ancient gods of rivers, mountains, or the household. The house of the *monotheos*—his mountain, his river—is the world. A question of size. What makes possible (or translates) the passage from *the narratives of exodus* to the *religion of the empire* is the production of monotheism, as the uniqueness and unity of the god answering the unity of the common place (place of the common). Exodus steps across (and sets free); monotheism answers to the empire. They do not carry the same thinking.

Note also:

(1) It is not a question of taking "Judaism" for a religion of freedom and its counterpart "Christianity" for a religion of imperial domination, but rather of questioning the historical process that leads from exodus to Catholicity. It is a complex process: (a) it comprises events *and* narratives, real sequences and meanings. My view here—like Ernst Bloch's, even if it is within a different setup—is that Christianity integrates, transports, and even accentuates certain "exodic" elements—liberating ones, in any case. Conversely, "Judaism," in the way it forms and reforms itself from the Roman constitution of the empire onward, is in no way foreign to its world. The Diaspora, for example, is a structure that is closely dependent on imperial organization: arranged throughout the surface of imperial territories, it can only keep up the system of its connections, the form of its unity, and the force of its cohesion thanks to the means of communication and transportation of the Roman world, as well as its judicial and transactional unity. (b) But also, this process of passing across (from the exodus to the "Roman Catholic" Church), in its median phase, goes through the extreme complexity of the Christic sequence itself. In this, it is important to distinguish the events and texts produced around the Christ of the constitution of the Christian religion. Numerous relations, transports, and filiations are perceptible, between the texts and events on the one hand, and the constitution of the religion on the other. But one cannot mix them up: they are the distinct moments of a becoming. The Gospel narratives and their commentaries relate facts and words linked to Jesus, but they also bear witness to the constitution of a corpus of references for Christianity as a religion. In this complex, the life and the teaching of Jesus are equally distant from the exodus and from Catholicity, as it were. Jesus produces a certain development—a certain transformation—of exodic thinking, and it is important to understand how these elements will be taken up again and reorganized to constitute Christianity, starting with Paul, whose actions and project are clearly linked to the (imperial) evolution of the Roman world.

(2) Freud clearly sets forth the link between monotheism and imperiality in *Moses and Monotheism*. Indeed, Freud considers that it was Moses the Egyptian who transferred monotheism to the Jewish people from the religion of Akhenaten the reformer, after the latter's failed reform of the Egyptian belief system. When Freud asks himself why Akhenaten came to propose this religious reform, at several points he suggests as the only explanation the connection between monotheism and the form of the empire:

> In the glorious Eighteenth Dynasty, under which Egypt first became a world power, a young Pharaoh came to the throne. . . . This king set about forcing a new religion on his Egyptian subjects. . . . The political conditions in Egypt had begun at this time to exercise a lasting influence on the Egyptian religion. As a result of the military exploits of the great conqueror, Tuthmosis III, *Egypt had become a world power.* . . . *This imperialism was reflected in religion as universalism and monotheism.* Since the Pharaoh's responsibilities now embraced not only Egypt but Nubia and Syria as well, deity too was obliged to abandon its national limitation[144] and, just as the Pharaoh was the sole and unrestricted ruler of the world known to the Egyptians, this must also apply to the Egyptians' new deity.[145]

If, for Freud, the exodus was indeed linked to the assertion of monotheism (and its transfer to a population of rebelling slaves), it is because manifestly, for him, worldliness is the only possible way of setting oneself free with regard to the local. A respectable hypothesis: a unique all-encompassing locus may be a necessary stage for any exit away from the place. But such a freeing does not provide a liberation from locality as such, but rather from plurality and multiplicity: it is *poly*theism, then, that is rejected. Monotheism is a monotopism. Exotheism is something else: it is an exotopia, the exit or way out of the locus as such—and thus, in a certain sense, out of the god.[146]

And so, a coherent, linked structure constitutes itself, associating empire and Catholicity; it is a union tied to the unity of a place (the world) and ensured by the unity of a god. But this (horizontal) unity remains split (vertically) by its very duality: the distinction between locus and god, empire and Catholicity, the world and the people, and thus in the end the distinction between the world and the hereafter or otherworldly world. The worldwide global unification of the empire *and* the church is "paid for" by the division *between* empire and church. The price of worldhood is what was earlier (somewhat awkwardly) termed the theologico-political difference. *The price of global worldhood is the duality of worlds.* The structure firmly associates union and division: *local* union of the (imperial) world and the (monotheistic) church, and "ontological" difference, one might venture to say, between beings (of the world) and being (in common).

What one thus notices in this scission or fission is its dual heritage, its double Greco-Judaic provenance—on one hand, the empire, extended city, widening to the dimensions of a world;[147] on the other, the church, extended resumption of the schema of the people, as it asserts itself during the exodus—a Pauline work of substitution, which institutes the *faithful* as one *people*, the continuation and transmutation of what had been the chosen people. One evidently should not consider these two ancestries as disjoined legacies or patrimonies that were dissociated during Roman times—as if the empire were "purely" Greek and the church "purely" Hebraic. There are crossbreedings and chiasmuses in this filiation: the church borrows the "model" and even the name of its assembly from Greek *politics*; and the empire, throughout its constitution, never stops seeking the theological model that may guarantee its worldwide unity. That is why thinking of the "theologico-political" was unsatisfying: the political side of the couple is permeated with theology, as has repeatedly been said ever since it was noted by Carl Schmitt. But the theological pole, for its part, is also thoroughly politicized.

*

It is a commonplace that what we have become accustomed to calling "Christianity" formed at the junction of the Greek and Jewish legacies. What is "Christianity"? It is a religion, in the sense discussed earlier,[148] defined at the same time by a set of institutions and by the corpus of texts (prescriptions and narratives) that circumscribes its limits and strengthens its unity. Christianity is not the supposedly defined contents of the teaching or the life of Christ; it is the whole apparatus that structures it, which is as practical, concrete, and institutional as it is textual, with texts and institutions as mutual guarantees. It is true that Christianity displays the peculiarity (which it shares with other religions, though perhaps not with all of them) that within the body of its texts, it tells the story of its own formation as a religion: this is the singular object of the Acts of the Apostles, and also, in a different mode, of the Epistles, especially Paul's. But this narrative itself was *constituted* as a report about origins—translated, selected, and recognized. The story itself is the outcome of an institutional process.

In this sense, Christianity as a religion is indeed an imperial religion: the establishment of its institutions and its corpus is exactly contemporaneous with the assertion of the imperial regime—taking into account a slight lag of ideologies behind actualities.[149] Above all, the formation of the empire and of this religion are connected by all kinds of threads: by relations of transitivity, metaphorization, reciprocal pledges and guarantees, circulation, commerce, intersecting evictions and their failures, and finally of course by the conversion of emperors and the accession of Christianity to the rank of state religion, which is—literally—the crowning moment of the process, though it only forms its most visible—and quite belated—manifestation, occurring at a point in time when things were beginning to change, if not in nature, at least from one phase to the next.

Christianity thus constitutes the junction between the Greek and "Jewish" sequences.[150] But is it *just* that, in itself? Does all that it contains come down to a com-position of Judaism and Hellenism, and could one deconstruct its whole structure and find nothing but the deposited sediments of these two provenances? Not so. Christianity does tie Judaism and Hellenism together, but with this bond it produces a very singular operation, which takes a new turn with very new effects, making possible the—new—development of the ensuing history. What is this operation and what is new? It seems to me that there are two ways of describing this, linked to two sequences in the story of Christ, at his birth and at his death. The first of these thematics, as we shall see, may be *philosophically* more familiar to us than the second—at least in the sense in which we would understand it here. And yet it is the second one that seems more open. Let us try to spell out this double question.

The idea, in itself, of the *birth* of Christ is not a religious innovation—neither as a human birth, at first inspection at least, nor as a divine filiation: gods usually have sons—heroes, gods, or demigods, of mixed human and divine origin—and these sons are usually born, no matter what their place in the hierarchy of beings might be. In Greek or Roman stories, for example, gods have a birth: they are born as sons of gods or of places, but their coming to life is a common event. This is not to say that there is no mystery or innovative thinking whatsoever in the Christic birth of this god-man: particularly, as soon as there is an attempt to recast the God of the Jews with Greek categories, as being, plenitude of being or absolute being, the possibility of a genesis, a procreation, or a birth is certain to pose a problem for any theorization—as much for the begetting father as for the begotten son. We know to what extent these questions will have generated a deep, slow, and at times tortuous elaboration before finding their theological equilibrium. Nevertheless the "mystery" of the birth of Christ has generally not been thought of from the starting point of this setup but rather as a question of *incarnation*: as a question of the passage of the divine into the human, into human flesh and a body, *which is to say, into the world*. The incarnation is the very radical operation by which God *gives himself* to the world, worldifies himself, so to speak, gives himself over, to reach the status of worldly being. This proposition, which philosophy (Hegel in particular) has commented on at length, is in fact theologically worked out by the Gospel of John, in multiple developments proposed by this text, whose most familiar and famous words are: "For God so loved [ēgapēsen] the world, that he gave his only begotten son, that whosoever believeth in him should not perish, but have everlasting life."[151] This is the content of the incarnation first of all: the delivery of the divine to the world, its intromission or incorporation into worldly beingness.

If one accepts the proposition advanced earlier about the divine,[152] it follows that incarnation is *the common given over to the world*. But in the world the common does not give itself over by keeping its *divine difference*—its incorruptibility, immutability, and divine immortality. It truly gives itself over, without reservation; it *becomes world*, penetrates the beingness of the world. And so, the world is changed by this coming: entranced and suffused with divinity and commonality. The divine that is born, put into the world, is the hypothesis of a putting in common, of a community of the world. In this perspective what the birth and the advent of Christ signify is *the world in common* put to the test: supposing or proposing that the common as such is in the world, or that it *becomes the world*, and thereby is the becoming of the world, the world that has become—starting at the point of this entrance, or trance. The world turned into our common, our being-common or being-in-common—this is the hypothesis of the incarnation. It is a *communism of the world*, a worldwide or worldly communism, which is experienced and incarnated in this incorporation. Any theology (or philosophy) that centers and concentrates on the mystery of incarnation tries to think of the world as that which has become common for us, and as the terrain, the territory, or *locus*, of our community. Incarnation tells the advent of the divine in the world as the delivery of the common to the place—unique and global—and thus to the *local* unity of the totality of beingness. What we have in common is the place of the totality of the world: incarnation requires a communism of the beingness of that which is. A theological appellation pertains to this operation, and it is *salvation* (of the world). According to this view, Christ came to the world *to save it*. Much in the Gospel of John attests to this.[153]

Now, this advent is a failure, and the facts are mentioned from the very beginning: "[The Word] was the true light. . . . He was in the world, and the world was made by him, and the world knew him not" (John 1:9–10). This realization is repeated: "O righteous Father, the world hath not known thee" (John 17:25). The test of the incarnation took the form of a conflict, irredeemably heterogeneous: ". . . but me [the world] hateth, because I testify of it, that the works thereof are evil" (John 7:7). In this perspective (wholly related to his birth), the death of Christ signifies nothing less than the failure of the undertaking to communize (that is, save) the world. This death thus seals the exit of Christ (therefore of the divine, and therefore of the common) from the world, ensuring that the common henceforth is torn from the world in an unmendable way, and that the world as world is decommunized—which is to say, it seals the proclamation of *salvation outside of the world*. "Whither I go, ye cannot come . . . ye are of this world; I am not of this world" (John 8:21–23). The people (the assembly, as the assembly of disciples) becomes the *people outside of the world*: "If the world hate you, ye know that it hated me before it hated you. If ye were of the world, the world would love his own: but because ye are not of the world, but I have chosen you out of the world, therefore the world hateth you" (John 15:18–19). Indeed, he does proclaim, "I have overcome the world" (John 16:33). But this victory is an exit—it occurs as an exit, and therefore sanctions the impossibility of saving the world as such: "And now I am no more in the world, but these are in the world, and I come to thee" (John 17:11).[154] In this sense, the death of Christ is the reverse of the incarnation—its turnaround and retreat: "I came forth from the Father, and am come into the world: again, I leave the world, and go to the Father" (John 16:28). If then the birth of Christ has delivered God into the world and has put him into the world in the process of incarnation, his death (reduced solely to this dimension) takes him away, undelivers and absents him from the world. The death of Christ is the disincarnation of the divine. The world splits. The divine absents itself in it. Henceforth in the world, the common is what is absent. *That is why the tomb is empty*: the divine (the common) is no longer in the world. Nothing of him—not even his body—has been left.

*

And yet. The death of Christ would *hardly be anything* if it were only that. Now, the death of Christ is a tremendous event, and its aftershock has kept reverberating. Why? We do know, perhaps obscurely, that the (hardly challengeable) novelty of Christianity does not stem so much from the birth of Christ (the birth of a god; as we pointed out, all gods are born) as from his death. Yes, an event occurred, and the sudden appearance of something new in the history of religions. God—a god—is dead. This was not an everyday occurrence.[155] Yes, it was tremendous news, and it took a long time for it to be apprehended, or simply formulated, as such—from Hegel to Nietzsche's proclamation.[156] But what does this piece of news say that has not been said elsewhere or earlier? The death of a god is not his (or her) relinquishment, obliteration, or oblivion—since there had in fact already been other relinquished gods; while this one, precisely, because of his death, was not at all forgotten. The Christ who dies does not fade away. What does he do, then? What exactly does the dying Christ do, when he dies? This requires the question of *how* he can die. A god can only die if he (or she) has or is a body. Death is always death of the body. I do not mean to say here that the death of Christ has not affected, for a while at least (three nights? two days?), his whole being, body and soul. But this death, in its completeness, was only possible inasmuch as this being was circumscribed and contained in a body. A soul on its own cannot die: if it dies, it is because it is caught up in the mortality of a body, and that it is held or contained in it. In this sense, the death of Christ does agree with his birth: a physical and corporeal birth. And there the mystery of incarnation does find that which ensures its newness: if incarnation is a new event, a sudden appearance in the history of religions, *it is inasmuch as it makes the death of God possible*. What is new in the birth of Christ is that it opens up the possibility—even the ineluctable character—of his death.

The divine gives itself over to death in the same way in which it was delivered and given to the world, namely, through his or its body. Of the divine itself, something dies, and that is what the divine has delivered to the world. What dies with the death of Christ is the worldliness of the divine, the undertaking to save the world as world, as *this* world. In this the world is *overcome*—one might also say undone: "For whatsoever is born of God overcometh the world: and this is the victory that overcometh the world, even our faith" (1 John 5:4). It is in this sense that the "world passeth away" (1 John 2:17), or, as Paul puts it, the schema or figure "of this world passeth away" (1 Cor. 7:31).[157] Thus, if God dies, it is *through* his body, *as* a body—as this worldly being into which the divine was incarnated. *And yet the grave is empty*: this death, this body was removed from the world, spirited away, withdrawn from the economy of the world that had received and integrated it into the inmost structure of its fabric. Where then did the body of the dead god go? This is the question that will keep haunting the aftermath of this death, as we are going to understand it little by little. This is why the Easter *mystery*, in its strict sense, *strictly is the mystery of the empty tomb*, much before being the mystery of resurrection (which, as such, is not so mysterious after all, but rather a kind of response to the mystery, its elucidation). This is what first becomes apparent to humans: the tomb is empty. *This* is the narrative sequence that pertains to the narrative of Easter. The resurrection, Christ's ascent to heaven, his arrival at the side of the Father—all this will only be *manifested* or told, as such, later on. Easter is the manifestation, the irruption into the phenomenality of the world, or *the epiphany* in its *strict* sense, of this: the grave is empty; the body was removed. Now there is a *hole* in the world; there is a hole in the beingness of the world—a void, an absence. Something of the world was transferred—where to?

Indeed, one may imagine that the body (of the dead god) was transported into pure ideality, that is, into the nonworldliness, nonactuality, or nonreality of images or ideas. And it is undeniable that something like this has occurred at certain times or in certain tendencies of Christianity: an ideal, nonworldly Christ, so fully ushered into the other world that this world is rid of him, as it were, driven toward the autonomy of its purely worldly regime, and thus, if you will, *deprived of its hole*. The hole in the world that is the empty tomb, the black hole of the world, is thus obstructed, plugged, and filled in, as it were; or at least it would pretend or feign to be so, in the garb of semblance or make-believe. The ideality of the divine is an obturation of the mystery; it is the tendency of a Greek absorption of Christianity, the temptation of a purely Greek Christianity,[158] from which the singularity of the Judeo-Hellenic encounter is reduced—and so is the fruit—unheard-of and new—of this encounter, the *death of god incarnate*. This, of course, is not the story of Easter; it is not this trans-position and hypo- or hyperstasis of the divine in the ideal or the imaginary. The story of Easter tells something else.

Something else: the Eucharist. Christ gives his body (his body and his blood: his flesh and his life), and his disciples eat it and drink it. What does this mean? That the body of Christ, the body of the God who dies or is going to die (the meal takes place immediately before the capture, the trial, the execution, and the death; it is carried out with a view toward their imminence), is ingested and absorbed by the disciples.[159] Where is the body of Christ, henceforth? It is in the body of the disciples. *The body is in the body*—this is the first consequence of the Eucharist. That is why he is no longer in the grave: he is absent from it because he has gone into the body of the disciples, leaving no residue. There is nothing left in the grave. *The body is (henceforth) in the body and thus it is no longer in the world*. This transmutation and this transfer indicate that henceforth the body is not the world, the thinking of the body is not the thinking of the world, and that a kind of alternative—a fork branching out, for the divine and thus for the common—makes body and world diverge from one another.[160] The body is another model of beingness than the world: the body requires a way of thinking different from the thinking of the world; *strictly, the body is not worldly*. Or, since the Eucharist, strictly, *it no longer is*. There is a (physical) beingness other than the world. *The world is no longer the totality of beingness*. Here is something new.[161]

Now, this transfer takes place during a meal. The meal is the major figure of the common. Meals eaten in common are the institution of commonality as such—meeting, assembling, and sharing. In its later history, in fact, the celebration (recollection and repetition) of the Eucharistic meal will be conceived of as the foundation or re-foundation of the community. Henceforth, where is the body of the dead god? It is within the common. But what did we say the divine itself was? The common, simply enough. And what does the Eucharist mean, in this sense? The Eucharist means: *the common is within the common*. Henceforth, the common is entirely within the common, only and wholly within it—*and as a body*: the divine is now no longer the sole *spirit of the common*. Since the Eucharist, the divine has been the body of the common, the corporeity, physicalness, physical and corporeal being of the common. It is the (*physical*) *being-in-common*. The theology of the incarnation may have established a communism of the world, in at least one of its construals (the Johannine one?). The theology of the Eucharist establishes a *communism of the common*, or what one could term a *communionism*, since this transfer of the common to the body of the common itself bears the theological name *communion*. Communion is the becoming-common of the common, *as a body*.

Now, as I have been proposing all along, the world can be understood as totalization and imperial unification of beingness. The world is that which the empire subjects—all that it subjects, and thus everything, inasmuch as *everything* is what it subjects. If this is how it is, then the Eucharist means that there is no longer any need to look for commonality within worldliness—within imperiality. There is nothing common in imperiality. There is commonality only of the common, and not of the world. The common is irrevocably (within) itself; it is to be thought of within the autonomous regime of the community, as such, and not as a community of place, or worldly community. *There is no longer any monotheism.* The common (the divine) is no longer to be grasped within the local unity of the world, but in sharing out. The meal is this shared commonality. What the common shares out (sharing itself) is no longer the world but the common itself. The common is within the common, and it is (in) common—nothing else. Christ says to his disciples, Henceforth, as I die and absent myself from the world, *you are the common, that's all*. Nothing other than you. Everything in you, altogether among you.

Among you: this Eucharistic hypothesis agrees with other statements made by Christ. "[Lo] there! for, behold, the kingdom of God is within you" (Luke 17:21). Or, "For where two or three are gathered together [Gk., *sunēgmenoi*] in my name, there am I in the midst of them" (Matt. 18:20), which Luther at one point pushes further by translating: "Where two are gathered as one on earth, there I am in their midst."[162] He does so by omitting "in my name" [Gk., *to emon onoma*], and reinforcing his words toward the sense of a pure theory of the assembly, or a theory of the "pure" assembly:[163] Christ, present at every gathering, at every reunion *as such*—without making the invocation of the name necessary. Among or "in the midst" of you then means that the divine (the common) is there, in the middle of the reunion, *between and among* the ones and the others, standing *in-between*, just as Christ is *among and between* (Gk., *en mesō*: in the middle) the two or three who are gathering. Christ (the divine, the kingdom—the common) is between you, in the *empty* space in-between, which extends between those who are gathered. The common is *in-between*, there, in the cleared emptiness, so that the reunion may be held, *between* the one and the other—not in springs or scrubby vegetation, and not in heaven, but simply in-between and among them.

To this the Eucharist then adds, the common is *within* you.[164] "Within" you means: in the body of each of you. In your body: you have shared it, eaten, and drunk it. And this can henceforth be explained in this way: the *in-between you is within you*. The in-between you is nowhere but in you, in the most singular and shared-out effectivity of your body. One should not even think of the in-between you (this emptiness) as being in the emptiness of the place as place, in this void that is there as a *there*, cleared for the assembly that is gathered in it and around it. The emptiness of the common is nothing of the world—not even this local vacuum of the world that is there. The common is within you, that is to say, in each of you, in the effectivity of singular bodies, where each of you is set and contained. This is the flattest and most prosaic (most atheist) way of putting into words the mystery of the Eucharist, which is doubtless a great incorporated, deposited, and transferred mystery in the singular effectivity of each body: *the in-between you is within you*. And this means: the determined circumscription of your body does not delimit a being shuttered onto itself, since the body contains *within it* this emptiness, this interstice, this relation that is *between him or her and the others*—the common. The in-between you is within you: the singular is open to the common; the singular is (*henceforth*) no longer thinkable in the closed circumscription of a determined beingness. The finite is open. There is something new.

*

The Eucharist thus institutes the *assembly* as the depositary and nonlocal locus of the divine—from now on incarnated—that is to say, of the common and being-in-common. This transfer will rule over the theologico-political question as a whole, which ultimately will ask, "Where is the body of the dead god—the body of the common?" Concurrently or successively, there are three answers one can bring to it.

First, the body of the dead god is constituted as assembly, *ecclesia*, and church. This is the canonical thesis according to which the church is the body of Christ—*corpus christi*. This constitution recurs and reproduces itself at each celebration of the mass, and is at stake in the debate over his real presence: during mass, the church receives and shares the *corporeal* actuality of the divine presence, and not only the effusion of its spirit, or the legendary retransmission of the episode of Jesus's death. But what is the church? What is this assembly constituted in Eucharistic sharing? There are two clashing conceptions of it: the church is all the faithful as a whole—but it is also the separate body of priests, a body that is consecrated (through ordination) and separated, in the flesh—bodily, physically—through the vow of chastity, a separation that the communion under two kinds re-marks. The church then becomes (at least in one sense, which habitual usage has kept up) the separated body of persons dedicated to clerical activities, to the clergy, *which is a body, too*. This is a theologico-political thesis: the existence of the church in its *separation* is at the basis of the institution of the papacy, the authority that doubles, and competes against, the political agency in general and the imperial one more particularly.

In the second hypothesis, the assembly that receives the body of the dead god is simply the assembly, as assembly—a hypothesis that rules Lutheran thinking and the institutional transformations of the Reformation. Like the previous hypothesis, it conceives of the transmission of the body of Christ as a continuation, an uninterrupted chain from the first Eucharistic meal, from one sharing to the next, guaranteeing the real presence of the divine in the assembly. But Lutheran theology holds that the assembly itself (the assembly of the faithful, of the baptized)[165] receives the complete divine body and becomes its depositary, so that any appropriation of *ecclesiality* by anyone—any order or body—is a usurpation.[166] The body of Christ again is the church, here, but as the community of the assembled faithful, without reservation. This assembly has its organization, its sponsors, *its ministers*, who are always revocable: it can in no way be dispossessed of its constitution; it remains the ultimate ecclesial agency, and therefore the locus of the Christic body, which cannot be deported.

There are extreme political consequences for this hypothesis, which in a general way is at the origin of any position of the *body politic*, which is to say, the unity of the political *as a body*. The *corporeality* of this body is only thinkable (on the basis of Paul's indications)[167] as the transfer of the divine body into the assembly, that is, *into the bodies that have received the*

Eucharist and have shared the physical donation of the divine during the paschal meal. In one of its more determined senses, this hypothesis will direct thoughts about the inviolability, unrepresentability, holy and sacred character of the assembly as such. The Reformation is thus at the start of a major revolutionary tendency (Rousseauist, and later council-based, in a very broad sense), which merely pushes its first intuition to its ultimate consequences, and radicalizes it: the divine is the assembly—inviolable, unrepresentable, sacred—because it is the depositary of the dead god. It can only convene continually, never suspending or negating itself. Its convocation is paschal and exodic: exiting, taking one step across, out of the world of servitude.

A third theologico-political hypothesis will still remain available, for quite some time. Indeed, the body of Christ having been transferred to the assembly, and thus to the church, the church in its turn would deposit it into the hands (or the body), so to speak, of the—imperial or royal—sovereign. This, in fact, is the radical and ultimate "mystery" of the sacrament of the consecration: when the divine (the common) has been positioned or deposited onto the physical singularity of the king or the emperor, the latter has become holy and sacred, and he then carries on or in himself something of the corporeality of the dead god. What one can see is that this hypothesis is continually competing against the church's ecclesiality (the body of Christ then finding itself in two places at once, not because it is ubiquitous but because there is a rivalry between two deposits). On account of a radical fidelity to Eucharistic transfer and sharing, the holiness or sacredness of the empire is strictly incompatible with the church's. But we can see that this incompatibility is not *only* a matter of two claims of legacy fighting over their inheritance. It more deeply has to do with the fact that the consecration of the emperor (or of the king who inherits the dislocation of the empire) comes down to *returning* the Eucharistic legacy (the sacredness of the assembly) *to the empire, and thus to the world*. The Eucharist had to do with a commonality or community of the common radically asserting itself as such, in physically sharing or distributing itself among the bodies of assembled individuals, and thus with a new way of grasping the common in themselves, *between and among themselves*. The sacrament of the consecration returns the common to the king, and therefore to a piece or place in the world, an imperial region. The consecration *subjugates* the common— to the kingdom, to the empire and the world. It *subjects* it.

176   *Transports of Origin*

23. Black Stone

This is not enough to make up Europe. The Greek shake-up (the invention of the philosophical), exotheism (Hebraic liberation with regard to places), and transport, and the imperial intersection of these things, come together and characterize Rome—just Rome. Now, Rome does not circumscribe Europe; what Rome carries is worldhood as such, the project of a world as the world. For shifting from Rome to Europe, a retraction or contraction is needed. It is a double retraction, and it is unequal: a retreat to the shore and a territorialization, after facing and losing the south—a complete withdrawal, and an actual break traced out. And facing the east, a westernization, a retreat that is never well outlined and always uncertain—Europe, with an in(de)finite east, becoming western and becoming a cape.

Let us say something about the south.

*

At a seminar in the early 1990s, Jean-Luc Nancy remarked on the fact that in the Kaaba at Mecca, there is a Black Stone: a stone, or object that is full and compact.[168] Whereas in the sanctuaries of other religions designated as "great"—pending a precise inventory—it seems that there are vacancies and voids, or relics (which refer to an absent event or a vanished person), or texts (which call for an interpretation), in short, nothing presenting itself under the aspect of fullness and compactness. A text, a relic, and a fortiori a void, act by *referral*, that is to say, they call for a transfer, a production of meaning by displacement, transition, and distance. The Black Stone at Mecca, on the other hand, Nancy further supposed, offers itself fully, as a compact presence, and it *keeps to itself [se tient en soi]*.[169]

Islam has empty recesses of its own, we might note: in each mosque, the niche of the qibla indicates the direction of Mecca and therefore of prayer.[170] The qibla functions as a sign and a reference; it designates an elsewhere, and one's gaze or thought traverses it to reach beyond it, toward Mecca, which is not there. But the given direction is precisely the Kaaba's and therefore the Black Stone's—which refers only to itself, or rather refers to nothing, keeps to itself, and presents itself fully to the eye, to one's thoughts, and to veneration. *One can only go around* the Kaaba shrine. Walking around the "house" containing the stone seven times is a devotional rite for pilgrims. The stone is central; it is fixed. It organizes and summons up the space around it. *The Black Stone determines an absolute locus.* It is true that, in the Aristotelian sense, the stone is not a place: it is a thing, and its compactness and fullness have to do with thingness. But the stone is set at a place that is absolutely itself: it cannot be moved away or transferred; it has been *there since the beginning of the world.*[171] Consequently, the stone tells two things all at once: compactness of being and absoluteness of the locus. These may just be the two sides of the same position: the compactness of being expresses the absoluteness of the locus as much as the opposite; compactness and absoluteness are mentioned together about the being that nothing separates from its place, the place that does not differentiate itself from the being that is there; nothing can tear apart this being and this locus—being as place, or *being-place.* If this is how it is, then Islam displays a veneration for the absolute place, and an absolute veneration for the place—not for locus in general (or for the idea of place or the figure of place), or for *some* places (which would make it a kind of idol worship), but instead a veneration for *this* very place and no other one, *this place as the absolute locality.* Not a veneration for the *there*, but *veneration-there*. And there, around this place that nothing makes absent or replaces, the totality of the world organizes itself. The world is there; *the world is around the stone.*

The objection will be, of course, that the sanctuary of the Kaaba and its stone are pre-Islamic. Before Islam, this was *one of the divine places* corresponding to one of the gods of the local Arabic polytheism. The question then is to detect why this locus became integrated into the new religious culture and dissociated from others; why it is elevated to the quality of unique locus or archi-locus;[172] why here as elsewhere one goes from a (polytheistic) polytopism to a monotopism—why there is a sole locus from now on, and why this very one *there.*

*

When Muhammad undertook his religious renovation, he started (like many other great religious reformers and possibly *all* of them) by producing a critique of idols, which is to say, of the local gods.[173] What brought on this critique, or called for it, seems to have been what has been termed a "vague monotheism."[174] The break from this polytopic polytheism was no doubt clear-cut but it did not occur all at once, nor without some fluctuation—attested by the "Satanic verses" affair.[175] One thing is plain, however: to launch this critique of idols and local gods, the

Prophet soon began to refer to the existing complex of Judeo-Christian themes and stories. As far as this relationship is concerned, it is pointless here to deal with the respective importance of "influence," "encounters," or "borrowings." The meaningful fact is that the Muhammedan critique of idols was carried out clearly and unequivocally with reference to Judeo-Christian deism.

The Prophet had been in contact with these themes precociously and no doubt profoundly—this comes to light from biographical elements,[176] as well as, and more deeply, from the observation of the "world into which the Arabs came."[177] The "objective" or effective reason, at that time, that led to the criticism and deposition of idols in this region, as well as in others, cannot be discussed here.[178] However, the situation in the Meccan region cannot be abstracted from the history of that time and those places. "Arabia" is neither isolated nor solitary, but geographically and politically circumscribed. Moreover, this region is *all the less* isolated in that the Muhammedan renovation occurred there. The (political and religious) renovation that Muhammad launched sought precisely to inscribe the region of "Arabia" into what was happening at the outer limits of its territory as the *production of a world*. Indeed, Muhammad sought to make the Arabs "come into the world."[179] What Islamism did, first of all, was to *resort to the world* and invoke it *against idolatrous locality*.

What was this world that Muhammad sought to enter? It was, of course, Romanity, the very production of the world, as world. But from Muhammad's perspective, Romanity confronted at least three abrupt limitations:

(1) First, it was *fallen Romanity*—collapsed and obsolete. What the Prophet calls "Rome" is Byzantium:[180] Rome outside of Rome, Rome after the fall. For the Prophet it is a matter of summoning up a world whose mode of appearing from the start has to do with defeat and vanishing. In his eyes, this defeat can be reversed. It is provisional, resulting from an internal defect, a failure. Victory (Rome's victory) will come back—once Romanity and therefore the world have been renovated.[181] What this failure contains is ignorance about the divine as such, though it has been announced, shown, and presented. The gesture of the new revelation will be this re-showing.[182]

(2) The Roman world's second limitation is its territorial boundary, with the other empire facing it in the east, Persia. Now, this limitation undermines its very status of world: the world has no boundaries; the world

is all that is. The geography where Islam is going to insert itself is structured around a fault line in the duality of empires: a partition between the Orient and the West, an essentially impossible scission that is going to mark the inscription of the Islamic project lastingly and deeply; not only because it will reappear quite soon after the Prophet's death, in the schism between Shiite and Sunni (that is, the divide between east and west, the Persian and Mediterranean sides), reproducing within Islam the division that preceded it; but also, more radically, because acknowledging this limit and these eastern bounds will probably prevent the Muhammedan dream from construing itself as being purely assimilated or integrated into Romanity. Remaking Rome (remaking the world) will be at stake, but starting exactly from the point of its oriental limit, that is to say, from the exact point where the east-west difference remains problematic. Islam enters the world through its eastern border—it will thus never be able to credit the world for its pure Occidentality.[183]

(3) Third, and doubling this uncertainty, Rome's Byzantine successor was unstable. Shaken by the Persian war, the (first) invasions from the north, and political uncertainties and theological quarrels, the Byzantine Empire was "debilitated."[184] Byzantium, Emmanuel Berl writes,

> was distinctly anxious and melancholy. It had not been able to sustain itself either in the west or in the east. Heresy and war had led to decline in the Christian Orient barely less than the invasions had in the West. Everything, in truth, was falling to pieces. . . . The restoration of Romania [i.e., the Roman empire] having definitely failed, it seemed that humankind was condemned to shrink back toward a more barbarous and difficult age. For two hundred years the same vicious circle had gone on: *it was impossible either to reestablish or to replace the Roman order.*[185]

These lines serve to characterize the aporia of the "world into which the Arabs came": the Roman order *could neither be abolished nor reestablished*—a kind of double bind, which created a deep ambivalence in Islam.

*

We can thus understand the constitution of Islam as being produced by two contrary motions, which were closely implicated in it and pulled it in opposite directions.

First, Islam aimed to break up with the *locality* that supported it—with religious and political life in Mecca. Islam claims to have set itself free from the idolatrous topism that dominated it, summoning the sponsorship (the truth) of biblical texts or stories. Surah 87, "generally held to be one of the first,"[186] ends with two verses: "Most surely this is in the earlier scriptures, / The scriptures of Ibrahim [Abraham—Trans.] and Musa [Moses—Trans.]."[187] It is not surprising that this will to be free expresses itself through Judaic references. As Muhammad knew, these are common to Judaism and Christianity, and although aware of their differences, he always regarded them as a single body of religion, in which Islam too was meant to participate. Resorting to Judaism here is inseparable from resorting to Romanity,[188] impossible to dissociate from the appeal to Christianity and its Judaic genealogy, which, for Muhammad, is a founding element.[189]

Thus this first Islamic movement simultaneously aims to break with Meccan society and to seek a rapprochement with the Judaic and Christian religions. *It is the movement of the Hegira*: break, separation, and transfer. Transport toward the north. The Hegira and the time at Medina are the time period of projects to connect or join (and why not say to merge) with northern Judeo-Christian Roman space, which Muhammad knows as the north.[190] What these projects encompass exactly is difficult to disentangle. But their existence does not seem challengeable: negotiations with Jewish communities, appeals to convert, Muslim migration to Abyssinia, with messages to the Christian sovereign, envoys sent to other powerful figures in the world,[191] delving more deeply into Abrahamic kinship,[192] and so forth. It is as if Muhammad had hoped for a kind of Muhammedan reunification of "monotheisms," and his admonishing of the world's sovereigns does not seem unlikely. This drive to break up [*pulsion de rupture*] associates Islam with what I have suggested be termed "exotheism" in the Jewish and Christian religions: tearing away from one's soil, transferring outside of the native land: transportation, carrying away, de-parting.[193] Whereas in the initial Greek constitution of the "Occident" this movement was directed toward the west (transfer from Asia, moving across the straits), here I am inclined to read a northwestern direction; and our world, for quite some time, persisted in this: the northwest of the world, north and west together, little by little in this period constituted the place of the strongest polarity proceeding from Rome *and* from its fall—the pole of Europe, then (North) America. But one fact testifies more than anything to the very strong (political, religious, geotopical) meaning of this project and this projection, and it is the Muhammedan prescription, at this point, that *one's prayers be directed toward Jerusalem.*[194] The direction, the "orientation" (an improper term, here), of prayer plays a noticeable part in Muhammad's thought. Prayer reaches toward a defined direction; *prayer has a directional sense.* Here the direction is Judeo-Christianity's primordial teleological focus, the Byzantine and Roman city of Jerusalem, for which Persia was then vying. What Muhammad sets his sights on, in the northwest, is Christianized Romanity; this is then the sense and the range of his thrust.[195]

*

Now, in the middle of the Medina era, Muhammad changed the strategic orientation of his project. The prevailing direction no longer reached toward the Judeo-Romano-Christian north, but reinvested in the south—a new "orientation" that the return to Mecca ultimately manifests. It is true that war with the Meccans had not stopped since the Hegira, showing that, in his projects and thoughts, the Prophet had never relinquished the city. But in this new phase, war intensified, was marked by victories, and above all by intense renewed negotiations, aiming to make the return possible. It is thus not only a question of his return (building up to Muhammad re-entering the city triumphantly as a conqueror),[196] but of a deeper phenomenon, preceding his victory and return: it is a reversal that precedes the return, calls for it, demands it, and ultimately constitutes it in its structure. Re-legitimization of the "sacred" value of the Meccan site: the city, and within it the Kaaba; and within the Kaaba, the stone. The clearest symptom of this is the *reversal of prayer.*

Nay! do you say that Ibrahim and Ismail and Yaqoub [Jacob—Trans.] and the tribes were Jews or Christians? . . . / This is a people that have passed away; they shall have what they earned and you shall have what you earn, and you shall not be called upon to answer for what they did. / The fools among the people will say: What has turned them from their qiblah which they had? Say: The East and the West belong only to Allah; He guides whom He likes to the right path. / And thus We have made you a medium [an intermediary] (just) nation that you may be the bearers of witness to the people and (that) the Apostle may be a bearer of witness to you; and We did not make that which you would have to be the qiblah but that We might distinguish him who follows the Apostle from him who turns back upon his heels . . . / . . . so We shall surely turn you to a qiblah which you shall like; turn then your face towards the Sacred Mosque, and wherever you are, turn your face towards it.[197]

The reversal is thus justified in the following way:

(1) The initial orientation of prayer had the goal of *distinguishing* Muslims with respect to dominant worship cults and marking their difference by detaching them from their practices ("We did not make that which you would have to be the qiblah but that We might distinguish him who follows the Apostle [i.e., the Prophet—Trans.] from him who turns back upon his heels"), and this difference was in common among practitioners of the new religion, Jews, and Christians.

(2) The moment has come to change the direction, and therefore *to turn the prayer toward Mecca*, toward the qibla of the sacred shrine.

(3) This reversal institutes the community as an intermediary nation.[198] What mediation is involved? The context gives an indication: "The East and the West belong only to Allah; He guides whom He likes to the right path. / And thus We have made you a medium (just) nation." The new community introduces a mediation or middle between the East and the West. In the terminology that I am proposing, the median intermediary between East and West *is the south*—between Byzantium and Persia, for example; between Judeo-Christianity and idolatrous cults; between Romanity and its outside: the reversal of prayer constitutes Islam as *the south of the world*. The "orientation" has changed: no longer is there any pretension to (re)join the north or the west (to achieve a kind of merger with Judaism and Christianity—and Romanity). Nor is there any return to a previous state, any retreat or simple restoration (Muhammad enters Mecca as a conqueror and not as a penitent). From now on, *between the Orient and the Occident* something like a renovated south positions itself.[199]

In returning toward Mecca, where does prayer turn? Let us go back to Jean-Luc Nancy's thought, mentioned at the start of this passage, and propose that prayer (re)turns toward something that is the Kaaba, and therefore the Black Stone, and *therefore the locus as locus*, the absolute of place or absolute locality, compactness, homogeneity, self-contained presence of the locus as such, being of the place, being-place in its absoluteness. This is now my hypothesis,

Islam (re)turns toward the place. (h18)[200]

Numerous signs help us to detect that this is not simply a retrogradation: Muhammad, who came back to Mecca, did not settle there but continued to live at Medina. It is the Hegira (departure, tearing away) and not the return that will lend its dating to the constitution of Islam as such—to the opening of an era. Finally, thanks to this extraction followed by this return, the place has gained something that had not been given to it earlier, namely, *its uniqueness*. After the arrival at Mecca, the other sanctuaries are emptied, their idols destroyed. In the Kaaba itself, which contained some, idols are destroyed[201]—the Kaaba loses its local sanctuaries, *all of them except for one, the Black Stone*. What is kept is the presence and the compactness of the *being-of-the-place*. Islam comes back to the place, but to a place uplifted, in its absolute uniqueness, in its monotopism. Why so?

*

It seems that Muhammad had a peculiar relationship with the Kaaba. His family (or clan) was put in charge of guarding the place. His grandfather, Abd al-Muttalib, had lived very near to the building and seems even to have been active, in the building or very near to it (against the wishes of the religious dignitaries? or in spite of them?), as a dowser, making a watering place spring up, called the Zamzam Well, the story of which will be rewritten as a legend, as we shall see. By re-turning toward the Kaaba, Muhammad thus returns toward his ancestry, which is complex: the Prophet's father died shortly before his birth, during his mother's pregnancy. His mother and grandfather would die soon afterward. Notably, according to the legendary account, this father had nearly been sacrificed by his own father (like Isaac, and in a certain sense like Ishmael, by Abraham)—sacrificed, it is said, precisely because of this matter of the well. It was to his family's or to a divine intercession that the future father of the Prophet, still a child, owed his life, and therefore Muhammad too owed his birth only to this intercession.[202] The grandfather making the source of water spring up (or spring up again, as we shall see) in the sanctuary had thus come close to depriving the world of its ultimate truth. But conversely the avoidance of catastrophe meant a consecration of this source.

Now, this matter of water sources had a function, namely, to establish a link, from the personal genealogy of the Prophet all the way back to another archaic and primordial genealogy of Islam as such and Arabism itself. Muhammad brings the ancestry of Arab peoples back to Ishmael,[203] who was the first son of Abraham, born from the union of the patriarch with his servant Hagar when he was already old and deprived of heirs. Arabs are thus directly and eminently of Abrahamic descent, descendants of the elder branch. But Ishmael was rejected by his father: after the latter had a son (Isaac) from his wife Sarah, the eldest who was the son of a servant was cast out to the desert, deprived of migration and transportation to the promised land. This dismissal was a near murder: abandoned, deprived of water, the child is about to die before the eyes of his desperate mother when a divine intervention saves him, making a miraculous well spring up from which he can drink. Its Islamic re-constitution turns this source of water into *the very same one that Muhammad's grandfather rediscovers*; it has in the meantime been covered up and plugged by desert sand.

This genealogical doubling carries multiple meanings.[204] But it perfectly expresses the ambiguity and equivocal character of Islam's position with regard to the other biblical religions: Islam stems from the same (Abrahamic) origin as they do. Ishmael's descendants come from the first line of descent. This gives Islam and Arabism a kinship with Judaism and Christianity, making them their cousins and elders. But Islam is descended from the child *rejected* by Abraham and his relatives; he comes from the despised and excluded branch—his origin is a servant's. We can say that Islam, the elder among the Abrahamic religions, is their repudiated daughter. The Islamic gesture amounts to claiming this double sense—of belonging to the Abrahamic family, and of *superseding* this repudiation, positing at the same time and indissociably its original connection with the Judeo-Christian world and its protest against rejection, exclusion, and a deviation that disinherited it.

This ambiguity is expressed in its relation to spaces. Islam comes from Abraham but not the Abraham who migrated. He is Abraham from before the departure, Abraham in the Arabian desert—the one who, according to legend, built the Kaaba or at least rebuilt it, since it was present from the time of the origin of the world, *like the world itself,* and had been devastated—*as the world had*—by the Flood. Ishmael is the child *deprived of exile*, doubly exiled, as it were—*exiled from exile* and from being chosen, sent back to the initial place. Now, according to Judaism, Abraham torn from his native land is divine transport itself, the ancestor carried away by God. As legend, this functions as a premise of exotheism. With the exodus, (before he does any land) Moses regains the gestures of tearing away and departing that were Abraham's. *In this sense, Islam is an Abrahamism turned around*—re-turned toward the place, the welcoming open locus. Fethi Benslama has beautifully picked up this minute note in Genesis, when God hears Hagar crying, and saves the child from death: "What aileth thee, Hagar? fear not; for God hath heard the voice of the lad *where he is*."²⁰⁵ What God hears is the child *at this place*, for which Benslama uses the wonderful term "place-child" [*l'enfant-lieu*]—we could call it *the child-there* [*l'enfant-là*]. This is the source: the opening of the place, the welcoming generosity of the place, the *gift of the place*. This source is primordial *and* regained, the ancestry is double, as is the spring, as is Muhammad's origin, thus identified and combined, at the same place, the locus itself, *locus of the locus*, the Kaaba.²⁰⁶

It is toward the locus as locus that Islam re-turns the prayer: the place posited in the absoluteness and uniqueness of its being, of its *being-place*. Thus here, in a particularly tense fashion, *the unity of place calls for and founds the unity of god*—answering one another, rigorously. What the Black Stone posits (what *posits itself* there, as black-stone) is the dis-position around it of the *local* totality of beingness, the position of the totality of the world, a whole that is homogeneous, localized, and extended all around. *The world is there*—that is what the stone posits. The stone posits the unity and homogeneity of the world—one could say its transcendental immanence. But answering this unity, necessarily and without reservation, there is the unity of the god involved in its dis-position and guaranteeing it. *Islam is strictly monotheism*—monotheism, without reservation and imperviously:²⁰⁷ answering an absolute monotopism. Islam's cosmic universalism is not one of transport (of transfer, of metaphor) but one of an extended world (around the stone), homogeneously bound to the stone and around it—*literally, in extension*. Not the east and not the west—median locus of the median community, and *in-different* with regard to the theologico-political, since the community, the umma, both transcendent and immanent (political and religious, if these words were not obviously unsuited),²⁰⁸ positions itself within the unity of place as the unity of the totality of the world, around the Kaaba.

*

What I wish to say, at bottom, is that Islam is not external to our history—or it is so in a peculiar way: from the inside. Islam has always wanted and perceived itself to be a moment, time period, or branch of the general economy of revelation—and thus of the general economy of the discovery of the world as world; it has construed itself as an alternative to the northwestern hypothesis, dominant then and now, which is why it has kept its value and its sense as an alternative to the world, or in the world, today. Islam seems external, but it is an exteriority torn away from our becoming, an exteriority that came about and is nonessential. Islam could have become "our" internal affair, in the way that the Germanic affair did so, although issuing from a space at least as foreign to Romanity (and probably more so). But a double obstacle prevented this integration: Islam did not convert, as did the Goth, Norman, and Vandal chiefs. It defined and posited itself as an alternative to Christianity—that which structures its constitution. The hypothesis, which is worth repeating, is that these two formulations are twins: if Islam did not convert, it is because it had invented itself as an alternative at the heart of *our world* and therefore could not convert without vanishing—whereas the Germans, although victors, could be baptized. In other words, Islam did not assimilate into this world, not because it was farther removed from it than the northern invaders, *but on the contrary because it was closer*. The exteriority of Islam marks its proximity. Islam, in *our* history, is the name of this exteriority that sprang up at the internal boundary of our world and swept into it. *An internal exteriority* (to make up this untenable alloy), which has produced the *retraction* of Romanity from which we came forth. This retraction cannot be dissociated from the appearance of Islam—from its rejection of the Judaic-Christian-Byzantine world, as well as from the previous situation, which made this choice a consequence and a symptom: the collapse of Rome, and its impossible relaunching—what Patočka termed *the catastrophe*. A certain constitution of a retracted Romanity is the outcome of this: self-contraction of the empire and the world, withdrawal to its land in the northwest, continentalization. All attempts to go back on this north-Occidental constitution in the face of Islam end up as failures—the Crusades, the French capture of Oran in 1830, Napoleon Bonaparte's dreams. Whereas attempts to re-mark this retraction geographically and give it a continental circumscription all succeed—the Spanish Reconquista, the checking of the Ottoman armies at the sieges of Vienna, the liberation of Greece. It is the figure of our world that is now distributed on either side of this fracture.[209]

The name of this Romanity facing an Islam in retreat, which—in front of it, after it—will now be able to inscribe itself within our spaces and organize their constitution, is Europe.[210]

PART IV   NO RETURNS

It's finally clear: this book is governed by the opposition between the common and the world.[1] There is no community of the world. The world is what the empire subjects; it constitutes itself as such through this submission. Now, the empire comes about because of changes of the "political," which prohibit its assembly; while the common, as politics, comes to the assembly and is that which gathers and thus produces influx and coming. There is no assembly of the empire—that is why the unity of the world comes into play.

The unity of the world is spatial. The empire is an *extension* of the polis—disassembled and extended. Its unity is extensive: offering itself in the mode of *space as generalized topics*, a mega- or tele(o)topism, which integrates all possible loci. Now, this general space excludes the assembly: in order to assemble, one needs a place, and an exit from it. The world is neither an adequate locus nor an exotopia; it is the place of the untenable assembly—place of all places, placeless place in the end, indefinitely encompassing [*englobant*], in-definite. The assembly that answers to the unity of the world is involved in this double constraint: worldly, yet impossible in the world itself. It requires a world outside of the world—counterworld, world-beyond—like the one that the empire subjects, but additionally equipped with the quality of that which, in essence, it lacks: the topical suitability to let one—*everyone*—gather there. This place replicating the world, where everyone can assemble, is heaven. There we shall find everyone, alive and dead, reunited for the last convocation.

This goes against the idea according to which "one" people's accession to historiality goes together with, or commands, the opening of "one" world. If such a population is the agent of the common (and this is worth debating), it does not make up a world—on the contrary: the world is made up, under the empire, as that from which the people are absent, because *the common is not there*.[2] Unless it is there as a figure: as withdrawal of that which fails to turn out and thus returns to its supposed point of origin. This figuration of the common, the mark of its failure and withdrawal, may already be inscribed in the phrase "one people." *One people* may already be commonality running short of its community—retracted before it. As the common, perhaps there never is "one" people, but instead the people, or even just (some) people. "*One* people," then, designates an *appropriation* of the common according to the regime of the figure, of identity, of the "popularity" *of* the people having properly become *this one* people—proper: in a noncommon way. "*One* people" already tells of the turnaround of the common, the retreat of its expansion, and the cessation of its movement. "One people" configures itself where *people*, to paraphrase Deleuze, are what is *missing*,[3] where *the popular* is missing, as in the pleasing French use of *du populaire*, which substantivizes the adjective.[4] In this sense the world (the map of the empire) is thick with this kind of failure—with as many populations (their list is long) as there are figures to count of this withdrawn, run-down, and defunct community. Figures of *extras* [*figurants*]: the only assembly that the world tolerates.

And so the idea of "a" or "one" world has to be suspicious, too. "A world" is a figure of speech. The world is world only in its pretension to be *the* world. The idea of world is natively involved in the project of the universality, totality, and thus oneness of the world.[5] It is only from the vantage point of an age open to the search for other possible world-units (other imperialities)—while an idea of *the* world (of an empire) is in crisis—that "a" world can be observed or designated as such. The *plurality of worlds* points to the open field of this search[6]—unless worldhood as such is on the verge of being undone [*défaite*], and this undoing taken to be a defeat [*défaite*] of thinking, and the withdrawing of any experience, which is a version of nihilism.

The world is without commonality. Now, we are living—so it seems—in *the time of the world*.[7] Of which empire are we the subjects? If our age is that of worldwide globality—achieved or in progress—what imperiality has subjected us? Who is our sovereign ruler?

24. Capital

Hypothesis: the empire that makes up the world today matches what Marxists have called *imperialism*. Imperialism: the empire of capital, having reached a certain phase in its history. Thus it is of capitalism that we are the subjects; it subjects us and structures or constitutes our "relation to" its world.

How to characterize imperialism? In Lenin's analysis, it was supposed to have five distinctive features: the creation of monopolies; the merging of banking and industrial capital; the export of capital; the formation of capitalist associations sharing the world among themselves; the ultimate division of the world among great capitalist powers.[8] Imperialism was thus characterized as a transformation, an internal change within capitalism (the passage to a monopolistic and financial stage) resulting in the extension and the *ultimate completion* of world domination by capital.[9] Now, this tendency toward worldwide globalization is inherent in capitalism from its first historical organizations. It is described in the first pages of the *Manifesto of the Communist Party*,[10] where the following sequence can be tracked: (1) The bourgeoisie, as a class, appears much before the time period of capitalism as a dominant form. It takes shape at the heart of the Middle Ages, and thus within a society that Karl Marx and Friedrich Engels call feudal, in which social relations are organized around the opposition between feudal lords and serfs. (2) The birth of the bourgeoisie is linked to the autonomous constitution of cities.[11] In feudal times, the bourgeoisie was incipient and developing, waiting for the right moment. More recent historical analyses have confirmed or challenged this point of view; in fact, the "bourgeoisie" or proto-capitalist structures have existed since antiquity, tied to commerce and small (or medium) manufacturing production. (3) How, then, can one explain the accelerated development and brutal rise of this class and the production relations that support it, as well as the extension of its importance in numbers and above all in specificity, which led little by little to the general reorganization of collective life, to what is termed *capitalism*, a new mode of societal structuring? The answer is explicit:

The discovery of America, the rounding of the Cape, opened up fresh ground for the rising bourgeoisie. The East-Indian and Chinese markets, the colonisation of America, trade with the colonies, the increase in the means of exchange and in commodities generally, gave to commerce, to navigation, to industry, an impulse never before known, and thereby, to the revolutionary element in the tottering feudal society, a rapid development.

The feudal system of industry, in which industrial production was monopolised by closed guilds, now no longer sufficed for the growing wants of the new markets. The manufacturing system took its place. The guild-masters were pushed on one side by the manufacturing middle class; division of labour between the different corporate guilds vanished in the face of division of labour in each single workshop.

Meantime the markets kept ever growing, the demand ever rising. Even manufacturer [sic] no longer sufficed. Thereupon, steam and machinery revolutionised industrial production. The place of manufacture was taken by the giant, Modern Industry; the place of the industrial middle class by industrial millionaires, the leaders of the whole industrial armies, the modern bourgeois.

Modern industry has established the world market, for which the discovery of America paved the way. This market has given an immense development to commerce.[12]

A very astonishing page—because the two young men who are writing this text [in 1847–48—Trans.] clearly link the triggering of this process to a determined "impulse": the discovery of America, the circumnavigation of Africa, the markets of India and China. Worldwide globalization of activities, planetarization of transportation. What sparks the rise of the bourgeoisie and opens the sequence of its domination *is the discovery of the world*, as world: America, Africa, India, China—nothing is missing. Before that, the world existed; its extension was known (in great part) as well as its rotundity. There were relations with it, and even exchanges. What is in question here is its *discovery*, obviously triggered by the discovery of America, the New World, and thus by the constitution of the world as a world from now on discovered, an open and uncovered world in its completeness and its *globality*; which is to say (let me underscore this), its sphericity, its circulability, the uncovered space of all its *circulations*. The discovery, the *pro-duction of the globalism of the world as world* made bourgeois domination and capitalism possible. Indeed, capitalism is *the time of the world*, the epoch of world globalization.

Contrary to what vulgar Marxism has long suggested, Marx and Engels undeniably see technical change as an effect of this globalization, not as having caused it. With regard to the second and third paragraphs of this text, this sequence strings together the following segments: the opening of new (worldwide) markets brings changes in the trades, the creation of manufacturing, which in turn spark a new division of labor (in the workshops). The initial shock is that of markets opening, which results in the new structure in labor relations. But at this point of the chain a new shock occurs, namely, *the further opening of markets*—a reiterated and reintervening element, which comes knocking at the door again, speeding things up: "the markets kept ever growing, the demand ever rising." It is at this stage, and only at this stage, that the authors bring technical change into play: "*Thereupon, steam and machinery revolutionised industrial production*" (ibid., emphasis added). What is unexpected in this analysis is that technical change appears at the end of the chain of effects. It is true that changes and innovations ("inventions") preceded it for the most part. But their results remained available, as if in reserve and not utilized. There had to be *a demand for technical change*—ordering it, as it were—for these new procedures to be involved in production. The demand—the ordering—is a distortion, between the traditional channels of work and the new tasks. And these tasks in turn have to do with another—upstream—demand, which orders and triggers the movement as a whole. This decisive and repeated demand, which has not ceased to re-order [*re-commander*] this process in various phases of its history, is world globalization, the new worldhood of the world. The technical transformation of capitalism is an effect of the discovery of the world. Of course, one has to conceive of a recursion, a looping return of the process onto itself—and the caused would become causing in its turn. But the core of the *Manifesto*'s thesis remains: it is not technology that has changed the world but the world—epoch-making worldhood—that has changed technology.

What follows in the text insists on this: the age or epoch of capitalism is the age of the world, the world-epoch as such. The bourgeoisie is the global class in the world, the class of worldhood. The process then takes on new features, which *intensify its global wordliness*, as we might say. Indeed,

The need of a constantly expanding market for its products chases the bourgeoisie over the entire surface of the globe. It must nestle everywhere, settle everywhere, establish connexions everywhere.

The bourgeoisie has through its exploitation of the world market given a cosmopolitan character to production and consumption in every country. To the great chagrin of Reactionists, it has drawn from under the feet of industry the national ground on which it stood. All old-established national industries have been . . . dislodged by new industries . . . that no longer work up indigenous raw material, but raw material drawn from the remotest zones; industries whose products are consumed, not only at home, but in every quarter of the globe. In place of the old wants, satisfied by the production of the country, we find new wants, requiring for their satisfaction the products of distant lands and climes . . . we have intercourse in every direction, universal inter-dependence of nations . . . The intellectual creations of individual nations become common property . . . from the numerous national and local literatures, there arises a world literature.

The bourgeoisie . . . draws all, even the most barbarian, nations into civilisation. . . . It compels all nations, on pain of extinction, to adopt the bourgeois mode of production. . . . In one word, *it creates a world* [Fr., *elle modèle le monde*—Trans.] *after its own image.* (*Communist Manifesto*, p. 16; emphasis added)

Something new is happening here. At the beginning of this sequence, the bourgeoisie invades every part of the globe—and if in this sense there is world globalization, it is the worldwide expansion ("nestle everywhere, settle everywhere") of the bourgeoisie itself. But by further spreading and increasing its extension, the bourgeoisie transforms the places where it implants itself. And the effect of its intervention is to give "a cosmopolitan character to production and consumption in every country." And so, what the bourgeoisie triggers when it arrives in these countries is their worldwide globalization, their becoming-cosmopolitan. The bourgeoisie makes national barriers unsustainable, it multiplies the connections between zones, and above all brings forth new types of worldwide activities that are thoroughly global, calling for raw materials, as well as consumers, at the other extremity of the planet. It transforms the zones formerly confined "locally" and "nationally" (nationality, here, in the sense of locality) into zones through which worldwide global currents run. The bourgeoisie globalizes all it touches worldwide; it creates *new needs* (*needs for a world*, "requiring for their satisfaction the products of distant lands and climes"); it expropriates from places their intellectual properties and their literatures. This is how one may understand the last—surprising—sentence, "In one word, *it creates a world* [Fr., *elle modèle le monde*] *after its own image.*" But what is this image after which it models, or fictionalizes [*fictionne*] (as Philippe Lacoue-Labarthe might have put it), the world? No doubt whatsoever: *this image is that of global worldhood*. What capitalism does, then, is *to globalize the world worldwide*, in each of its parts. Henceforth, at each point of the world, *the local is (the) worldly*. We can characterize the process of capitalist world globalization (capitalism *as* globalization):

Capitalism is the becoming-world of the world. (*h19*)

How can we articulate this hypothesis and connect it with this other now familiar one that links the advent of the world to Romanity? We shall simply posit that the constitution of the world proceeds over time: the world did not rise up, in a single gesture, at the advent of Augustus Caesar. The world is the structure of the totality of beingness inasmuch as it is subjected to imperiality. Its submission—its constitution as world—is progressive: first, it is the idea of world (we might say the schema of the world) that forms and imposes itself—a *global* and general idea, which refers the zones of the world to a worldhood that integrates and embraces them. Capitalism makes up the second, much deeper phase, of world globalization: it changes the zones into *world-zones*, or global worldly zones. It weaves worldliness throughout them. Consequently, now, *the world is the world*, at all of its points. Capitalism is the phase of intensification and completion of earlier imperialities—capital, heir to Rome, from which it receives its inheritance and which it carries on, sole empire that really came after the fallen empire. Capitalism, *highest stage of imperialism*. What Lenin terms imperialism is the final phase of this achievement, the ultimate completion of this completion, the end of this ending. But capitalism alone is the becoming of every imperiality.[13]

25. Images

Why? Why this kinship between empire and capitalism? Why does the imperialism of the latter come to supersede the former's imperiality (if the proximity of these two words is not an accident)? What structural affinity of the world is spun between one regime and the other, enabling this transfer of domination conveyed by this lexical pairing?

To answer this question, we need to return to an analysis begun earlier, going back almost to the beginning of this book,[14] when I proposed that the mode *in which the world is grasped is the image*—but not that every experience might be a vision of images or that images might be the mandatory mode of grasping or putting to the test all that experience offers. On the contrary: the image is the very thing that presents itself when the tenor or at least the object of experience is this determined field, *this* constituted mode of the given designated, precisely, as *the world*. In this sense, precisely, the world is that *of which there is imaging*. The world gives or presents itself specifically as *image of the world*, or—almost equivalently for us—representation and spectacle of the world. And since the world (to say it once again) is formed as such through its submission to the regime of imperiality, since there is a world only of the empire, because the empire is itself only insofar as it is *empire of the world*, the result is that the formation and the circulation of images (of the world) take place under the empire and correspond with the type of determined "experience" that the empire constitutes, spreads, and generalizes.[15] The said or supposed "experience" is unlike previous ways of grasping or capturing things; and so, in my view, the preceding epoch of our history (let us say, the time of classical Greece) is not the *age or epoch of the world* but the *age or epoch of the assembly*. The assembly is included in a *cosmos*, it sits on an earth, is convened at a place, but it does not posit any *world*, in the determined sense that I contend this term has acquired since Romanity. That is why the age of the assembly produces the art of theater, the art of the assembly, which re-presents and re-constitutes itself, and puts itself into play; whereas the art of the epoch of the world, in a first stage, is pictorial representation; and later, all that derives from it, carries it forward, and extends it: photography, cinema.[16] To be sure, these two inventions (and two eras) do not fail to establish a few connections: for example, painting, and cinema as well, and even more so, are haunted by theatricality (defunct within them), and they never cease to call upon it or give figure to it.[17] Conversely, after the age of the empire (after having in a certain way disappeared) theater reconstitutes itself, and henceforth the business of the representation of the world (which is *not its* business) is going to hang around it, to such a degree that it exerts an influence and some pressure on what its components are: the [Greek theater's—Trans.] orchestra disappears (then the musical orchestra), the part played by the stage keeps increasing, and especially the (fictive) conception of the stage develops as pure frontality—something that it is not, has never been, and can simply never be[18]—resulting in the frontalization of theatrical architecture. All these symptoms attest to the debate that theater (with a guilty conscience) has not ceased to have with pictorial figurality, or cinema, in which it often seeks to dissolve or extinguish itself.

Nonetheless, beneath these nuances and interactions, we should keep to the hypothesis in all its sharpness:

The time of the world is the time of images. (h20)

Why? Before the empire (let me reiterate), there was no need whatsoever for images. Figurations, figures or figurines, models, and molds do appear—all sorts of objects that show or designate something or someone absent. And play, too: in assemblies, where one can show oneself or others, cast oneself into figures, simulations, or make-believe. Around all that is something like a *cosmos*: an organized whole, a vase, finished or not, but that one can try to conceive, figure, model, or symbolize—or leave alone, far away, because its limits are unknown. None of this makes an image—or an image of the world. For an *image* to form, what is needed is a whole so vast (the empire) that no direct experience of it is possible, *in its unity and its globality*, and yet the necessity of grasping it (required by the empire, the ruling unit directing the empire) imposes the search for a way of taking it in that is unifying, dominating, homogeneous, and circumscribed. And what calls for the constitution of images is thus the consideration of the world as that which cannot assemble (like a city-state) and yet cannot either simply be probed (like a cosmos), because it *does have to* be grasped unitarily and dominated—*inasmuch as it is subjected to the empire*. The image, then, results from the invention of this relation—so strange and unheard-of—in which *the world is summoned there, in front, to be given a flat figure*. Pictorial representation, an incredible idea: not the fact of painting, coloring, or adding pigments to a surface (not even to make figures or figurines appear there), but projecting to *re-present* the whole of beingness as being in front. It matters little if it only shows itself partially: the represented world overflows the representation, on all sides and borders (out of field and off screen, as it were), without making this overflowing affect the status of the representation itself—it could carry on and move onward, but it fixes itself there. This constitution will be progressive: from symbolic frescoes and their self-sufficient self-limitation all the way to perspectival realism and its conventions, and on to the frame in film and its presuppositions and possible movements (e.g., panning shots), the unification and homogenization of the image of the world will not be achieved in one fell swoop at the beginning, but will take time. It remains that the formation of images is a process demanded by the formation of the world (of the empire)—since the whole of beingness needs to be grasped in a single instantaneous take, one capture that will henceforth be determined as gaze, *filmic shot [prise de vue]*, and will therefore define the world as that which presents itself frontally, there before us. The world being too large to be convened at an assembly; the world being nonetheless united by the effectivity of imperial domination—these are the two necessary conditions for it to be re-presented there, in front of us, as image.

*

Since there is significant overlap between them, one is obliged to ask how this hypothesis relates to Martin Heidegger's famous thesis in his essay "Die Zeit des Weltbildes" (The Time of the World Image; in Heidegger, *Holzwege*, cited below as HW).[19] "Where the world becomes image, beingness as a whole is set up as that according to which man adjusts himself, which he accordingly wants to bring [Gm., *vor sich bringen*], have [Gm., *vor sich haben*] and—in a decisive way—set in front of himself [Gm., *vor sich stellen*]," Heidegger writes.[20] The world in this sense is the totality of beingness,[21] and it is a matter of taking or putting it in front of oneself. Now, only the operation of re-presentation makes it possible to refer or transfer the whole of beingness (all that is) in this way. Representation is this gesture exactly.[22] The *vor* [before, in front] in *vorstellen* is continually made again to designate the "before," what-is-in-front-of-oneself, thus placing what is carried, "secured" or "kept" [Fr., *maintenu*; Gm. *ständig*] before oneself in a position that allows orienting, directing, setting up, organizing, or adjusting [Gm., *einrichten*] to take place. That is why the image [*Bild*] is thought as reproduction, copy [*Abbild*], or painting [*Gemälde*], a "painting of beingness as a whole" (HW, p. 89 [82]); the painting is the "image"-itself of this transfer to frontalization.

If painting is thus explicitly designated as, at least, one of the possible paradigms of the constitution of this "world image," the reader might think it is abusive to seek in *Vorstellung*—a "heavy" philosophical concept, which Heidegger extensively elaborated—an echo of the theatrical connotation of the term that one cannot avoid hearing in the French *représentation*. Not so, perhaps: in wanting to establish that "the world becomes image . . . it is one and the same process as the one making man become a subject within beingness" (HW, p. 92 [85]), Heidegger undertakes the analysis of *repraesentatio*. He writes,

Inasmuch as man then puts himself in the picture, he sets himself into the scene [Gm., *setzt er sich selbst in die Szene*], which is to say, into the open surroundings of what is generally and publicly represented [Gm., *in den offenen Umkreis des allgemein und öffentlich Vorgestellten*]. In this way, man sets himself up as the scene in which beingness must henceforth re-present [Gm., *vor-stellen*] and present [Gm., *präsentieren*] itself, that is, be image. (HW, p. 91 [84])

Therefore, there seems to be a great proximity between my suggestions and the analysis to be found in Heidegger's essay: the constitution of the world in accordance with the regime of the image, through the operation of its representation, that is to say, of its frontal or pictorial convoking, following the mode of its frontal positioning. Without reservation we can agree with an assertion such as, "World image [Gm., *Weltbild*],[23] in an essential sense, does not mean an image of the world [Gm., *Bild von der Welt*], but rather the world grasped as image [Gm., *als Bild begriffen*]" (HW, p. 89 [82]).

Am I then saying exactly the same thing as Heidegger? No. The main difference has to do with Heidegger's take on the world that "*becomes* [Gm., *wird*] image" (p. 89 [82] and elsewhere; emphasis added). This is saying that there is some world before this becoming; there is the world before its being grasped as image—both beforehand and elsewhere: "where [Gm., *wo*] the world becomes image" (p. 101 [93]), which indicates that it becomes image *there* and not *necessarily* everywhere.[24] Becoming-image happens to the world, as a "process" (Gm., *Vorgang*) (HW, p. 92 [85]). This was predictable: an entire section of *Sein und Zeit* (*Being and Time*), to which this text explicitly refers,[25] elaborates the concept of a "world" for which the category of image is obviously unsuited. Now, the hypothesis proposed here conceives of the world in the opposite way, as *that of which there is an image*. It is only in the context of what might be called "imageness" [*imagéité*] that the world provides a grip.[26] This is the mode properly speaking of grasping the world; and conversely one may think (even if this point remains to be established) that any image is an image of the world in a certain sense, through the necessity of its constitution. The world is this mode of the totalizing unification of being, which, subjected to imperiality, offers itself as image—spectacle, or representation. To riff on the title of Heidegger's essay, "The Time of the World Image" is, plainly, "The Time of the World."

What are the stakes involved in this difference? A distance, first of all, in historical or chronological appreciation. My interpretation implies that the image of the world, as such, was constituted under the Roman Empire—or is at least made possible from that time onward, even if it took some time to form (as paintings, for example). Not that the contents of this image have remained unchanged—but the relationship in the *representation of the world*—and the spectacularity it summons up—establishes and organizes itself at that time, in my view. The contents of images will vary within this common structure, in the global organization of their pictoriality, which goes from one image to the next and keeps the general form of the *imaged or pictured* [*l'imagé*]. This form, in my view, has proceeded from the empire and is related to it. It runs from the empire all the way to us. It corresponds, if you will, to Hegel's determination of the *romantic* age: the time of Christian representation, which follows Greek classicism and, since Rome, has encompassed all that has been represented after the event or advent of incarnation. One could say (as Heidegger does, but with a different periodization) that *modern* times (Gm., *die Neuzeit*) are the time of the image, if one cares to remember that the word "modern" appears at the very end of Romanity to designate what is *recent*.[27] The time of the image is the time of the modern world (the time of the world insofar as it is modern), but its appearance, in this sense, is connected with imperiality—imperial Romanity. I contend that it was during this time that the image of the world—its representation in the mode of the image (*imago mundi*)—was established and structured.[28]

For Heidegger, on the other hand, the time of the world image is a new age (Gm., *Neuzeit*). Which is to say? It is a time that unfolds "now" (*jetzt*); "it is the world becoming image that marks out the essence of the new age" (HW, p. 90 [83]). The French text translates *Neuzeit* as *les temps modernes* (modern times), and, besides its obvious use, this phrase does seem legitimate from the point of view of the concept ("modern" qualifies the time of newness, time thought in the mode of newness),[29] as much as of periodization, since Heidegger opposes this time period to the Middle Ages (*Mittelalter*) and Hellenicity (*Griechentum*). Opening this entire passage, ensuing here from Heidegger's meditation on the new age (Gm., *Neuzeit*), the problem consists in asking questions about the "world image in modern times [Gm., *nach dem neuzeitlichen Weltbild*]" (HW, p. 88 [81]). At least in its initial formulation, this is a matter of distinguishing that image from those of the Middle Ages and of antiquity (Gm., *das mittelalterliche und das antike Weltbild*) (ibid.). The periodization, then, is as follows: the world image is that of modernity, inasmuch as it differentiates itself from ancient and medieval times. It is even a late modernity, not only posterior to the Middle Ages but (as important developments in the text indicate) closely associated with the Cartesian transformation in metaphysics. As noted, there is a tight entanglement (Gm., *Verschränkung*) between the processes by which "the world becomes image . . . and . . . man [becomes] a subject" (HW, p. 93 [85]), and becoming-subject is achieved within and by way of Descartes's philosophy (HW, p. 98 [91]). This modernity thus does not exactly match what historians call the modern age, which is to say, European history from the end of the fifteenth century, or if it does match it, it is insofar as its essence only fully asserts itself with the development of Cartesian metaphysics (or the Cartesian development of metaphysics).[30] Why this reference point? Heidegger makes no mystery of it: the question about the essence of modernity is tightly linked with the one about the essence of modern science.[31] Ultimately, and indisputably, Heidegger's *Neuzeit*—modern times, the age of the world image—is the age of technology.

Nevertheless let us note one thing in this chronology: the *Neuzeit* seems to be opposed here to antiquity and the Middle Ages. But Heidegger does not in fact speak about antiquity as such, except at the very start of his argument, precisely at the moment when he describes a conception that he is going to refute, according to which the modern image of the world would follow the medieval and ancient [Gm., *antike*] images. As soon as he sets up his problematic (according to which the image of the world *is* modern), it is no longer a question of antiquity but only of the Greeks— "Griechentum" (HW, p. 94 [86]); "Anfang des griechischen Denkens" (p. 105 [97–98]); "zum griechischen Vernehmen" (p. 91 [84]); "die Griechen" (p. 94 [87]); "Der Mensch des griechischen Grundverhältnisses zum Seienden" (p. 105 [97]).[32] The time periods to compare are the modern, the medieval, and the Greek ones. *There is no Roman era* for Heidegger here. Romanity here does not make history. Why not? What differentiates the time of the image from other times or ages of the world is precisely that the (modern) world image demands a *representation of beingness*, casting that which is into images or scenes, and this is foreign to those other times. Other ages have an understanding of that which is that is properly their own: the Middle Ages have *ens creatum* (created being), and the Greeks have beingness as "that which comes out and opens up; that which, as something that is present, overcomes man as someone who is present" (HW, p. 90 [83]).[33] What differentiates the Middle Ages and ancient Greece from the modern age is how they make out and understand being. Rome has no appreciation or understanding [*entente*] of being that is its own. All it does is spread, re-produce, and probably degrade the Greeks' understanding. The Roman age is a non-age.

One can appreciate that the difference with the point of view proposed here is very marked. In my view, it is *precisely* the transformation of the Greek experience into a new mode of grasping beingness, under the effect of the imperial becoming of the city, that generates the constitution of the world as world. Even supposing that this change is a pure degradation, *this degradation would have to be grasped as an experience and the opening of a time, the time of the empire.*[34] Let me repeat it: I understand this grasping (of the world) as a grasping of unified beingness in its totality in the mode or modes of domination. To totalize and unify all that is through domination: this is the program of the empire, which the constitution of the world and its imaged presentation translate. The world is thus the whole of that which is, *ruled* and *dominated*. Perhaps this is not very far removed from Heidegger's contention that "putting together [Gm., *Zusammenstand*; Fr., *le (se) tenir ensemble*] and system pertain to the essence of the image.... Where the world becomes image, the system comes about and dominates [*kommt ... zur Herrschaft*], and *not only in thinking.*"[35] For this is what is at stake: effective domination, not only in thinking. Now, in my view, deleting the Roman epoch from the diagram of the successive "understandings" [*ententes*] of being presents the major drawback of ridding this comprehension of the setup of *imperiality* as a unified and totalizing structure of domination—and of understanding domination only as grounded in the establishment of technology, which is to say, ultimately, of metaphysics.[36] At bottom, for me it is a matter of thinking of the institution of domination as *political*, or rather as an event happening to the political, or the polis: as Patočka would put it, *catastrophe of the political, political catastrophe*. The empire is the catastrophe of the political: this is the hypothesis. The empire (the catastrophe) is what programs domination over all that is. Getting rid of the Roman era is prohibiting oneself from giving thought to this catastrophic institution.

And by the same stroke, this seems to entail missing something with regard to the essence of modernity. Indeed, it is not by accident that modern times, in their decisive phases, have been seen and understood as a *return of Rome*—return of the empire. Here, of course, I first and foremost mean the general structure of the *Renaissance*, which carries out its gesture as a return to Rome, in the various places where it is at work in the fifteenth and sixteenth centuries—a return to the Greeks via Rome.[37] But I am even more thinking of the extraordinary insistence, or persistence, of the imperial schema in all the re-constitution projects of modernity, from Charlemagne and Otto I to Charles V, all the Habsburgs, the czars (caesars), Napoleon, Wilhelm II, all the way *to the idea of imperialism*, and to Hitler and his thousand-year Reich (empire).[38] Finally, I am taking aim at the Reformation, that inverse counterpart to the Renaissance, one of whose founding aims was a return to primitive Christianity (and more particularly to its Pauline origins), and thus, again, to Romanity. In short, to keep silent about Rome in this context is to prohibit oneself from giving thought to modernity, *insofar as it is to Rome that modernity has recourse to determine its project*—while it is within this recourse, which modernity tackles to think and shape itself, that one should examine its technological will. Technics is the *will to dominate*; it transfers the schema of domination onto the relation-to-the-world. Technics is *sovereignty* over nature; and, since Descartes is clearly designated as the point of constitution of its project, one has to read this transfer of the imperial schema in the will to be "masters and possessors of nature."[39] The blind spot marked in the thought process by this deletion of the Roman stage is the (producing and instituting) agency of domination, of which technical mastery is a figure (one among others, though a determining one). What this omission leaves in the shadows is *the political determination of the technical project itself*.

In Heidegger's text itself, we may be able to detect a feature that works as a symptom of this omission. Indeed, the ending of the essay characterizes the effects of the uniformization produced on earth through the extension of technology, having itself emerged from the project that Descartes formulated, to objectify the world and subjectivize man. Heidegger comes to see in this uniformity "the steadiest instrument of complete—that is, technical—domination [Gm., *Herrschaft*; Fr., *empire*] over the earth" (HW, p. 111 [103]). Domination—sway or "empire"? "Empire" in the French translation is forced, the German term being *Herrschaft*, closer to "domination," with the connotation of "rule" or "reign" [Fr., *règne*], "sovereignty," and "power." But this slight exaggeration can be explained, since a little earlier, to designate the field that this uniformization permits us to interrogate, the field of domination, of undivided and limitless sovereignty of technology over the earth (thus, worldwide technical globalization, technological worldhood), Heidegger indicates that subjectivism has reached its culminating point in "the planetary imperialism of man who is organized technologically" (HW, p. 111 [102]). "Im planetarischen

Imperialismus": the (Latin) category of imperialism, imperiality, and empire thus does turn out to be useful for thinking about the domination of technology, and its worldwide planetary (Gm., *planetarischen*) domination, its *production of some world* in the—dominated and mastered—unity of the planet.⁴⁰

26. Value

These thoughts about images arose out of the hypothesis that the Roman Empire and capitalism are in some sense akin to each other, based on the constitution of the world under the empire, on the one hand, and worldwide capitalist globalization, often called imperialism, on the other. As to what effective relation between the empire and capitalism justifies this, I cited my view that the world constituted under the empire presents itself as image, and that "imageness" [*imagéité*] forms the determined mode in which it is grasped. How, then, does this account relate to the question of capitalism? In what way is world production, as it takes place under capitalism, also imparted as an image (as spectacle or re-presentation) to one's experience?

The answer may start appearing to the reader. Capitalism constitutes or re-constitutes the worldhood of the world through the production and circulation of commodities. And commodification is world-making: Marx's insistent expression "world of commodities" [Gm., *Waarenwelt*] has to be understood rigorously.⁴¹ This is why Immanuel Wallerstein legitimately speaks of the "commodification of everything,"⁴² or that Guy Debord writes, "The independence of the commodity has extended to the entire economy over which it rules. Economics transform the world but only transform it into a world of economics."⁴³ The world of capitalism is the world of commodities, of merchandise; it is the world commodified, the world-commodity. Now, *the commodity is an image*.

From its opening, Marx's *Capital* sets forth a thesis that can be summarized as follows. The commodity is first of all a thing. As a thing it has a use. But it only becomes a commodity in the process of exchange, and it is through this process that it acquires a value. Consequently, the traditional distinction between use-value and exchange value, as Marx himself initially expressed it, has to be reframed more rigorously as the difference between use and value. When the thing becomes a commodity, use vanishes in favor of exchange, and that is how value is formed. Value—*qua* value—retains nothing from use, and hence from the thingness of the thing. For value is formed through the exchangeability of commodity-objects, objects that may have a common value, but in no way comprise this common feature in their thingness, or in their use.[44] Use is concrete, specific, and qualitative. Exchange establishes the value as abstract, general, and quantifiable, "as exchange values [commodities] are merely different quantities, and consequently do not contain an atom of use value."[45] Because of this, "The value of commodities is the very opposite of the coarse materiality of their substance, not an atom of matter enters into its composition" (*Capital*, p. 32). Nothing of the thingness is retained in the objectivity of the value—in the merchandise. There is nothing of the thing in the commodity or merchandise. Strictly, *the commodity is not a thing*.[46] If Marx began his exposé by asserting that the commodity is a thing, it was in order gradually to introduce the use-value–exchange value opposition, and then the opposition of use to value, which in fact governs the thing–commodity opposition.[47] From the thing to the commodity, there is a relation: not a relation of identity, or inclusion, or from genus to species, but rather a relation of support, of bearing [*une relation de portage*]. Things are "the material depositories of exchange value" (*Capital*, p. 26) or its bearers; in German, "die stofflichen Träger des Tauschwerths."[48] The thing is a "bearer of value": *Träger von Werth* (or *Werthträger*).[49]

The commodity is not a thing, and yet *it presents itself as a thing*. "The mysteriousness of the commodity-form thus simply consists in this: for human beings, it mirrors [Gm., *zurückspiegelt*] the social characteristics of their own labor as objective characteristics of the products of labor themselves, as the social natural characteristics of these things [Gm., *Dinge*]."[50]

The merchandise or commodity is not a commodity inasmuch as it is exchangeable; it is the (social) process of this exchange that gives it its exchange value, which is to say, its value; which is to say, its reality as a commodity. Thus the features or properties of the commodity as such are social features or properties, expressing the social character of work, of which the commodity is the product, its *abstract* character. Marx sets this forth from the start of his argument: if the commodity can be exchanged for its natural, thinglike properties, it is only because of the social character of the labor put into it—not of the concrete labor, the set of practical, actual, and finalized procedures, but of the *abstract labor*, which is to say, labor socially quantified and therefore measurable. The features of the commodity are thus the social features of abstract labor as a measure—and thus exchangeability—of its value. These are the features that mark its *value-form*, a central concept, which constitutes the essence [*l'être*] of the commodity—its being [*être*] as value, and its being as the form of this value. *The features [traits] of the commodity are the—abs-tract [abs-traits]—social features of labor*. Now, the commodity shows a "mysterious" peculiarity, namely, that these characteristics present themselves as "social natural characteristics" [Gm., *gesellschaftliche Natureigenschaften*]. It has often been said: the commodity's mystery consists in its ability to naturalize its social characteristics, and thus to present its social characteristics as *qualities*—and albeit social, they are the *natural qualities of things*. The commodity integrates the social qualities of work in the model, the idea, or the schema of the thing; it thingifies the social characteristics of work, and presents its own features (characteristic of merchandise, of value) as thinglike features.[51] Things are then endowed with a strange ambiguity: "This is the reason [Gm., *durch dies quid pro quo*] why the products of labour become commodities, social things whose qualities are at the same time perceptible and imperceptible by the senses [Gm., *sinnlich übersinnliche oder gesellschaftliche Dinge*]."[52] Extrasensory sensory things: because the extrasensory (the social or abstract character of the features of the value-form) is integrated in the presentation of the thing as a thing, and thus necessarily as a sensible thing, endowed with material or natural properties. This is the point of view that political economy expresses, and one might say of it that it sticks or adheres to the value-form, that it expresses it as the value itself presents itself, and that it is in this sense *the point of view of the commodities themselves* as commodities: "Now listen how the economist speaks, *expressing the very soul of those commodities* [Gm., *aus der Waarenseele heraus*]: 'Value' (that is, exchange value) 'is a property of things [Gm., *Eigenschaft der Dinge*].'"[53]

Commodities, which are not things, present themselves as things; their famous "fetishism" consists in this: "This I call the Fetishism which attaches itself to the products of labour, so soon as they are produced as commodities" (*Capital*, p. 47). What attaches itself to the products of labor? *The mode of appearing that makes things out of them*, their thinglike appearance. The *fixation*[54] that sticks to commodities, their fetishization, is the apparent thingness of their social characteristics, the integration of their social features in the thingness of the thing. Fetishism is the (tenacious, sticky, necessary) production of appearance that presents commodities in a thinglike mode. In this sense, Étienne Balibar writes, "the commodity . . . eminently is a representation at the same time as an object: it is an object that is always already given in the form of a representation."[55] While the commodity is endowed with a determined objectivity, it is a value-objectivity (Gm., *Werthgegenständlichkeit*). This objectivity differs essentially from the thinglike objectivity of the material properties of the thing, which are joined to its utility. "It is only by being exchanged that the products of labour acquire, as values, one uniform social status, *distinct from their varied forms of existence as objects of utility* [Gm., *Gebrauchsgegenständlichkeit*]."[56] Value-objectivity is not thinglike objectivity. The fetishist mystification[57] consists precisely in making the commodity appear in the thinglike mode of objectivity; this is what Balibar terms "the constitution of objectivity in fetishism,"[58] a kind of fetishistic objectivity or fetish-objectivity, which, riffing on another connotation of these words (object, fetish), one could almost call "objectality," in a quasi-Freudian sense.[59] It is in this sense that there is *representation*: about the commodity (a table, in this case), Marx writes that it is "that common, every-day thing, wood. But, so soon as *it steps forth* [emphasis added; Gm., *auftritt*; Fr., *entre en scène*] as a commodity, it is changed into something transcendent [Gm., *ein sinnlich übersinnliches Ding*, i.e., a sensible suprasensible, or 'perceptible and imperceptible,' thing—Trans.]" (*Capital*, p. 46). It is thus a representation even in this sense.

Representation, objectivization, and simulacrum (of a thing): the commodity is all this. Does this suffice to assert—as has been proclaimed—that the commodity is an image? Not yet. To be sure, a visual analogy does govern the argument: the commodity, as we have seen, "mirrors [*zurückspiegelt*]" the social characteristics of work.[60] Marx goes on: "In the same way the light from an object is perceived by us not as the subjective excitation of our optic nerve, but as the objective form [Gm., *Form*] of something outside the eye itself" (*Capital*, p. 47). The commodity is the form that constitutes itself as representation, as thinglike objectivity, and appears in place of the "excitation" from which it results and that it expresses. The analogy, here, is very organized: the nervous excitation is the social relations of labor. The image that appears is the value-form, the commodity itself. At first reading, one might see nothing but a metaphor in this, a literary image, widespread in philosophy—the comparison of the formation of the form with the optical constitution of the image, nothing more. And yet, upon closer examination, there is more to read. The nervous excitation is social relations. The image is the commodity. But Marx immediately specifies that this metaphor is wobbly: for the luminous excitation is a material phenomenon of which the (optical) image is the result. The commodity as an image does not result from anything material: the commodity-form has "absolutely no connection with . . . physical properties and with the material relations arising therefrom."[61] The commodity is the projection of a purely immaterial reality, the social relations of work—in their *abstract* dimension. Jacques Rancière convincingly argues that, on this score, reality itself (the reality of commodities, of merchandise) is speculative.[62] The reality, the objectivity of the value—the reality of the value as objective reality (Gm., *Werthgegenständlichkeit*)—is the projection or objectivization of an abstract, immaterial, and "speculative" given. As Rancière recommends, one should thus take very seriously the initial statement at the beginning of Marx's chapter on fetishism: "A commodity appears, at first sight, a very trivial thing, and easily understood. Its analysis shows that it is, in reality, a very queer thing, abounding in metaphysical subtleties and theological niceties."[63] It is not only a word: the commodity is theological: it objectifies and incarnates a given that is purely "spiritual"—the abstraction of a determined social relationship. In this sense, it is an image, but with a different meaning of the word: no longer image-reflection, image in the mirror or on the surface of water, mental or cerebral image; but *imago*: fabricated and produced image, statue, portrait or figurine, or painting, or drawing. A *realized* image: the effectuation—real and objective—of an abstract or mental given-in-thought, the objectivization of an idea, projection, or modeling. *A sensible extrasensory thing*, but in a new sense: an object of which the objective existence is that of a form and not of a thing—just as the form-existence of a Van Gogh painting is in a way not its thing-existence. The form-existence is also image-existence (e.g., of a pair of shoes).[64] The commodity *images* the social relation of labor:[65] it is its portrait or cast—and in this sense, indeed, what necessarily adheres to its essence as an image is the fact that it presents the relation as this thing that it is not. But in contrast perhaps to the painting-image, the commodity does not carry an indicator—it does not display the factitious character of its resemblance. It is a fetish that conceals its factitiousness,[66] a trompe-l'œil, a simulacrum, a ghost.

But this is still not enough, it seems, to justify my hypothesis. What is still missing is that in the reflection of the commodity, one imagines that one sees a thing, a "social thing." But what does one see *effectively*? A relation, a social relation. Which is to say? Let us take up again the famous deductive chain that Marx presents at the beginning of *Capital*. (1) First, one sees an appearance: "Exchange value, at first sight, presents itself [Gm., *erscheint*; Fr., *apparaît*] as a quantitative relation, as the proportion in which values in use of one sort are exchanged for those of another sort" (*Capital*, p. 26). This appearance of value (apparent exchange of uses) is thus the appearance of the commodity, the appearance of the relation that each entertains with others, and that is integrated as a property into its quality as a thing, making us take for a relation between things that which will ultimately be determined to be a relation between producers, as we shall see—hence a social relation. This appearance is the "phenomenal form" (the form of appearance or *Erscheinungsform*), which, Marx specifies here, is the form of "something contained in it, yet distinguishable from it." And what is this content? (2) The content cannot be, according to Marx, the exchange of use-values, which in themselves are nothing exchangeable, nothing quantifiable, and which are nothing but concrete, specific, and singular—thinglike—determinations. In order to exchange them, "the exchange values of commodities must be capable of being expressed in terms of something common to them all." (3) Now, it is the case that "[t]his common 'something' cannot be . . . any . . . natural property" of things, nor a feature relevant to their use; but "the exchange of commodities is evidently an act characterised by a total abstraction from use value." Thus, the exchangeable (and therefore value, and therefore the commodity) does not pertain to use *but precisely to its abstraction, to the fact that one abstracts its use*. What does present itself then in fact, in this appearance of the exchange of uses, which in reality is the abstraction of use, in an active sense of "abstraction"—abs-tracting, dragging away from use, outwardly? (4) "If then we leave out of consideration the use value of commodities, they have only one common property left, that of being products of labour." What shows itself under the appearance of commodities is the labor of which it is the product. (5) But this labor can be abstracted from the use-value only on the condition that "we make abstraction at the same time from the material elements and shapes that make the product a use value." One thus has to make abstraction of the product of labor's use and de-thingify it. "Its existence as a material thing is put out of sight." This presupposes, of course, that one abstract the sensible (material, concrete, particular, specific, and qualitative) characteristics of the very labor that generates this product. Therefore one has to abstract labor itself, and constitute and consider it as exchangeable, measurable, and quantifiable labor: no longer as the determined labor "of the joiner, the mason, the spinner," but as "human labour in the abstract."[67] (6) And so, the particular objectivity of commodities begins to appear, which will soon be termed value-objectivity, and which Marx here calls "phantom objectivity" (Gm., *gespentige Gegenständlichkeit*) [translated as "unsubstantial reality" in *Capital*, p. 27—Trans.], consisting in the residue (Gm., *das Residuum*) of "a mere congelation of homogeneous human labour, of labour power expended without regard to the mode of its expenditure."[68] What is showing itself in the form of commodities, that of which it is the form of appearance or phenomenal form, is human labor, and it is undifferentiated, exchangeable, quantifiable: *abstract*. But, then, how can work be quantified (when abstracted from its concrete operations)? (7) It is on the condition of being treated as a *quantity of labor* (Gm., *das Quantum Arbeit*). How is this quantity itself measured? (8) By its translation into duration: "The quantity of labour, however, is measured by its duration, and labour time in its turn finds its standard in weeks, days, and hours"; here we are approaching the end of the process, the limit of the "residue," which one may consider an equivalent of a kind of phenomenological reduction.[69]

What is shown in the commodity—in its appearance (its objectivity) as value—is working time. (9) Now (and this is the heart of the debate), this working time itself cannot be considered to be the *concrete time* of labor or concrete working time. This would come down to assuming that a commodity is all the more valuable when the worker who produces it is slower, Marx objects—and this is false. Thus, the time in question is itself social, itself "abstracted" from the concrete reality of labor, as it were. It is time as the idea of "labour time socially necessary" conceptualizes it. What exactly is this social time? First of all, it is an average—"time needed on an average"—to match the various laboring time periods spent by more or less efficient workers. It is a general average and a social average, counting *globally* for society considered as a whole—a kind of assumed standard, but not only that, since this duration itself varies in relation to the technical equipment available to the worker. A commodity produced with archaic means has *no more value* than one resulting from better productivity.⁷⁰ It is therefore necessary that the "measure" of the worker's technical equipment be integrated into the time of labor. How? Simply, in that this equipment too is construed as "objectivized" or "materialized" labor time.⁷¹ The laborer's tools are commodities and therefore also consist in abstract labor time "congealed" in them. But these tools or machines themselves have been produced with tools or machines that are also materializations of labor time—and so on. Indeed, the labor time necessary for the production of a commodity is labor time that is "socially necessary," and in it, it is *the whole mode of production at a given moment in time* that is expressed, abstracted, and appearing as value. This is the conclusion. Ultimately, what expresses itself is the "total labour power of society, which is embodied in the sum total of the values of all commodities produced by that society": what presents itself and appears in commodities, as well as in "a single commodity," is the *whole* of social relations, *the whole* mode of production—*the globality of the world*, as "world of commodities" (Gm., *Waarenwelt*).⁷² The relations of which the commodity is the element that appears are the world of commodities, the world-commodity, the worldwide globality of the merchant mode of production.

That is why it is legitimate in my view to say that the commodity is an image—not the image of a thing, the reality (or essence proper) of which would thus be masked at the same time as it is mimicked, *but the image of the world of commodities*. Hence, every image is an image of the world.⁷³ This is what Marx indicates when he sees economists "misled" by the "fetishism which attaches itself" [Gm., *anklebt*; i.e., adheres—Trans.] to the world of commodities (*Capital*, pp. 47 and 51). Fetishism adheres to this world; it is stuck to it: idolatry of the thing, as a social thing; thinglike, thingified—and also worshipped—sociality. Balibar puts it this way, "Indeed, the mechanism of fetishism, in this sense, is a constitution of the world."⁷⁴ The commodity and fetishism, stuck to it, constitute the world as *Waarenwelt*,⁷⁵ world of commodities. In this sense, commodity is image—*imago mundi*. It is a strange loop, in truth: since the commodity is the image of the world of commodities and thus image of a world of images, image of the world as a world of images, image of the world-image, image of an image, ad infinitum.⁷⁶

*

The whole hypothesis can thus be confirmed. Yes, there is a relationship between grasping the world as image and its becoming-commodity. The commodification of the world is a development, the phase of a process linked to its imageness—not in the sense that the commodity thus finds a mental origin (in the status of the image), nor that we might suggest its psychological genesis; but on the contrary, since the image is the world's mode of grasping under the empire (the world as *that which the empire subjugates*), in the sense that the commodity can only be understood and come about as a mutation of this first status. This amounts to saying—and here the main hypothesis comes into view—that *capitalism supersedes the empire*. It is a becoming and a transformation of it. To make the connection with our earlier analyses:[77] neither the kingdom, nor the Reformation, nor the Revolution succeed in superseding the knocked-down Roman Empire and taking over after Rome. *Only capitalism succeeds in this*, because it alone, in fact, knows how to take up again and carry on with what the empire had produced as its major work: *the constitution of the world*. Empire and capitalism are the two dominant phases in the process of becoming-world, in the formation of what could be termed the planet, or the cosmos, as the world. The Middle Ages are well named: they are the collection of transitions, intermediary attempts, and discontinued programs between Rome and its relief, that is, the only one superseding it effectively: the process of world domination by capital—the world economy.

(It is worth noting that this allows us to understand the ambiguous connection between Europe and Rome. Europe is not Romanity as such, nor is it its only heir. But since the domination project of capitalism—and its becoming-planetary—has in fact configured itself as a European project, and since it is in "Europe" that it has found its basis and legitimations, it is true in this sense that the European project takes over the Roman heritage, and on this score Europe is the daughter of Rome.[78] But it is so insofar as it is the bearer of the capitalist project of worldwide globalization, a project that visibly carries it away, negating it as Europe, that is, within the closed configuration of its supposed continentality. Europe is the bearer of the becoming-world of the world, which now, in its turn, makes Europe worldly, too. That is why the Roman heritage cannot make up a European *identity*: Europe is its bearer—but gets lost.)

Notwithstanding their differences, this hypothesis is ultimately fairly close to the analysis suggested by Guy Debord in *La société du spectacle* (*The

Society of the Spectacle).⁷⁹ Even if it is not the only term one might apply to turning the world into images, spectacle is a useful concept here.⁸⁰ Here again the idea remains that *the world is something* prior to being turned to image. It is a dangerous idea: it implies that one needs to recover *as the world* that which the image thus paints over, masks, and dresses up. Deadly ambiguity of the revolutionary project: beneath capital, it is a matter of unearthing an innocent world, virginally clean of images and commodities, which the *revolution* henceforth aims to *bring back* to the light of day. The revolution then turns into the reparation of abuse against the world: the abuse of its being turned into image, into a spectacle, which one would have to abolish to recover its actual pure being. This is not far removed from the Heideggerian setup. The image happens to the world as a loss. One has to bring back—to retrieve from oblivion or veiling—beingness, which is caught up in image, in imaged beingness. One has to restore it to its essential or fundamental, nonimaged condition, to what makes beingness be as beingness, *before* any representation, thingifying, or objectivization: that is, to its very being [Gm., *Sein*] itself. The critique of the image, in this sense, brings into play the program of a return to being—and revolution is one name for this program.⁸¹ In any case, as early as 1967, Debord pointed firmly to the relation between commodities and images: "Not only is the relationship with the commodity visible, but it is all one sees: the world one sees is its world."⁸²

Does capitalism then amount to nothing more than imperiality? Is capital nothing but the empire, consolidated, weaving its threads more narrowly, catching the world in a tighter net? No, of course, first of all, because something disappears between Rome and capitalism, namely, a certain form of political imperial rule over the world, a formal unity of political domination, which shuts down with Rome and never comes back—ever—despite all the dreams—and actual undertakings—aiming at remaking it: Holy Roman Empire, Charles V ruler of the Americas, Bonaparte dreaming of the Orient, Hitler's thousand-year Reich; all the way to the complex yet imperial figure of the Father of Nations [i.e., Stalin] whose paternity covered Asia and Europe, hoping for more. None of these undertakings had a worldwide reach or became stable. When there was stabilization (as for the Holy Roman Empire), its worldly reach remained fictitious and incantatory (unlike the Roman *imperium*). When worldwide globality asserted itself, more broadly, the empire (Bonaparte's,

Hitler's) collapsed within a few years. In the end, the only political empire that challenged the effective dominance of capital *and* achieved a worldwide globality of sorts was the authoritarian and imperialist socialism of the USSR. The challenge played out over almost three-quarters of a century—then capitalism raked in all the chips.

But from Rome to capitalism something new appears as well. For the commodity is an image but not just any possible image or any representation (of the world): it is the image of what one owns and what one acquires. Every image turns to image that which is subjected (to the empire): a piece of the subjected world. But the commodity pictures *that which is subjected insofar as it is owned*,[83] an image of the world of which the submission and ruthless exploitation by imperiality is carried out in the mode of acquisition. It is not as if one had to sup-pose a virginally unsubjugated world, preceding any capture. The world is the presentation of the whole of beingness as subjected. But this submission (of the world) involves several regimes. Possession is one of these modes of domination or hegemony. Capital subjugates the world *inasmuch as it owns it*. The commodity is the image of a world that is owned. It turns to image the specific mode of submission that *having* is. All having is not about merchandise: one can have things that one does not "bargain" for [*marchande*]. But the commodity or merchandise exhibits the zone of having—mode of having—that makes it *a determination or effect of submission*. Merchandise-having is a capture and domination of being by and for having, as having. One can say that the world of commodities is the epoch or age of the world in which the world is "being had."

Capitalism is the world's having—world-having. And this leads us to an intentionally hasty assertion. I have argued that *the common* and *the world* are opposed because there is no *being in common*—of the world. We can see now that this deductive reasoning rested on a surreptitious shift. To come to this conclusion, we had to equate *the common* and *being in common*, thinking of the common only in terms of *its being*. It might have been objected that there is some common outside of being (at least at first sight). Indeed, *there is something like a common "having" of the world*. To put it as I did was to assume that the community-of-having is a fictive, illusory, and corrupt commonality. It meant positing that the common demands a community of being and wants common-being. This point obviously needs to be clarified. Henceforth I shall posit that capitalism is the grasping of the world within which any possible community shares the having, and comes about as such; and in which any grasping of what there is—as beingness of the world, as all that is subjected to the sway of capital over the world—is possible only as ownership, acquisition, or "having" of beingness. "Having" is the mode proper of grasping that-which-is under capitalism—its specific imageness. Capitalism is the time (of the image) of the world that determines that which is as that which *one has, or can have*; and that sees being as having, or possible having; and that represents and constitutes beingness in the mode of *having being* [*l'avoir l'étant*].[84] This mode is an epoch or age of the world, which is to say, of the determination of the whole of what there is as that which is subjected to imperial domination. But this epoch has its history and its "time": it is the time of the constitution of all submission into something acquired, of the possession of it all. The time of capital.

(This is what turned into the distress and the misery of so-called "communism," if by this we mean the system organized around the Soviet state. It has been said that the Revolution aims to see the return of the common to the world. In this sense, so-called communism *was* revolutionary—jointed to the project of a commonality returned to the world, or a world returned to the common, a world-in-common. The hitch: there is no being in common of the world. The world in common can only turn out—or at least project itself—as a community of what one has [*communauté des avoirs*], community of ownership, and sharing out the world's "having" [world-having]. So-called communism was a communism of the property of the world: of the common property of the world and its production. But property is a possession that transfigures itself. Even when it touches on being—being-proper—it is the essential metastasis, the essentialization of a possessive, proprietorial grasping. The being that I properly am is my being proper, mine, the being that is proper to me because I possess it in ultimate ownership. It is inasmuch as I own it, properly, that I am it. Property communism was a communism of "having"—while the young people who turned into communists between 1920 and 1970 [just as others joined the Crusades a few centuries earlier] had no wish to share out the world's properties; they did not rally as communists to put any possessions or acquired things in common. *What they wanted was common "being," being in common.* It was their being, or Being, or something of this kind, that they wanted to share—and communicate and commune in this sharing. Their distress and misery was to believe that being in common demanded, as a means or a stage, the community of having, the partitioning of the world among equal owners. The history of so-called communism [our history] was sadly programmed from this conversion of communism into a world project, the project of a world in common—the project to share out possession and its means.)

27. Becoming

Roughly to restate the hypothesis formulated above, there is no common of the world—only its representation, or its possession.[85] At this point, doesn't the revolutionary model—in the regressive Latin sense of *revolutum* that I have characterized—present itself anew? Doesn't it impose itself surreptitiously? Although one may have wanted to turn down the project of this regression and reduction, avoiding the quest for, or requesting of, a pure world that existed before or beneath its capture in images and things acquired, does not the program of this *return to the world*—the same approach—nonetheless lie in wait? Is it not a question, now, of recovering the common, just as it presented itself before the world, in its authentic being—in the polis, for example? Or, further, and consequently, a question of recovering it *underneath*, and buried, because in the world its being would have got lost? One may be concerned to see the program of a *return to the common* insidiously substituted here for that of a return to the world, from which I had wished to distance myself. Am I claiming, beneath the images and values of the world, to release the truth of a buried commonality?

Let us here energetically and carefully reject any project of this sort. In no way is there a common *beneath* the world, at least if this underneath should show itself as a base [*socle*], foundation, or vestige.[86] The common is not underneath, as long as underneath is seen as the deposit of a persistent past. In no way is the common a past. It will not be recovered or exhumed—*the common comes on*. It is what comes on, as the coming—not exactly the future (even if it is that, somewhat—as an effect, at least), but rather *the coming of the future to come*. The common comes: not given, not standing at the point of any origin, or originary, grounding, or essential being. Not even as (at the bottom of) bottomless foundation. It comes about (or this comes about) as a becoming, production, genesis, *change*.

It changes. The common is (*the*) *new*—the becoming of being.[87] By this I want to indicate (factually, as it were) that the common is not given at the beginning of the world, surely, nor at the beginning of humans. Instead, the common is that which happens that is human, that which happens to humans as humanity, somewhat in the sense in which Pierre Teilhard de Chardin and others speak of the process of "hominization." But this concept is not good: it presupposes an essence of man and a process by which humans are tasked to achieve and join this essence. No: the common is that which *turns out* in human becoming as that which (up to this point) has been designated as human, and beyond it (no doubt), one of these days. But *before it, too*: for becoming-common (becoming as becoming-common) did not start with humans. Something is traced out in animality, the becoming-animal of the animal, and its animation; something like life, like the living of life—and therefore before animality already, in a sense. Should one see there a great teleological drive [*pulsion*] carrying the whole creation, communizing it, in a communion from the origin throughout a lengthy process making the common emerge? No: for nothing is given that is external to this becoming and against which one would have to measure it. The common is not that which is achieved *in* becoming by incorporating itself there. The common is the becoming itself—as sense,[88] spacing, and change. The common is the sense and direction of becoming, that which does make becoming into something other than an agitation any which way of the multiple, that for which becoming can be read as the way of sense. Becoming is not senseless. The common is the way of becoming and makes sense of it—exactly and prosaically in the sense in which one can say, "There is becoming" and these words make sense. Common means: there is becoming; there is newness. What is given and gained is possession—and property, its avatar. Properness is given, or gained. What is new is the common—and thus, in human history, that which comes about: not the common happening to history—coming from outside, as some pure event springing out of nothingness—but rather turning out in history as genesis, generating, gestation.[89] The common turns out in history *as history, as the historic itself*, as this (new) fact that there is some history. The common happens to history, as history; it happens to humans as history, that is to say, as change.

The objection will be that there is some very constituted and structured commonality in certain communities ("primitive" ones, for example), and that something new happens to them—the destruction of community, or decommunitarization; and further even that it is this destruction that makes these communities enter history, that by which history happens to them; and that history is thus carried out by means of destruction at least as much as by the production of commonality. This is true if one construes the common in the sense, let's say, of "collective." It is then perfectly absurd to equate the common and the new or the historic: among bees, very visibly, there is some collectivity, or, we hear, among herds of great elephants traveling through the savanna. It is in this sense that the common can give rise to regressive, antihistorical, or imperial formations—and this point of the argument generally brings on the evocation of the vast and heavy communitarianism that seems to have regulated the immobile mechanics of oriental empires, or hordes, or Aztecs, not to mention Stalin, no doubt, with his "oriental" communist despotism enforcing commonality coercibly. Well, my view here is that the fact of thinking of Stalin's power grab and apicultural collections under the same category has to do with fantasy. To be *thought*, these realities require carefully disconnected setups—even if one might thus appear to abuse general ethologies. And my wish will be to leave elephants and bees at the outer limits of this work, even if it means reasserting—purely out of conviction—that becoming-common (common becoming), no more than life, does in fact date from humans; that there is effectively something to think as a *history* of nature, or a natural history; and that on this score, to be sure, one should examine bees and elephants, but also sexedness as such, reproduction through binary fission, the formation of multiplicities, *growth*, extension, expansion, and probably the big bang—using competent skills that are unavailable here.

On the other hand, as far as humans are concerned, the common can come about *as* transport, or *as* figure. Under very different modalities, great imperial ensembles (at the risk once again of mixing up a great variety of historical objects) are precisely *figural constitutions of the common*—constitutions of the common as a figure. This does not just mean making room for a good commonality and a bad one, side by side. The constitution of the Aztec Empire, or the Persian Empire, is a historical event. That they appear at the fringes of what is supposed to be universal history has nothing to do with this.[90] These "empires" were formed and organized and then vanished within the movement of something that has to be thought as history. On this score, while one can easily conceive of the working usefulness of the concept of "prehistoric" societies,[91] there is little to gain in conceding the idea of nonhistorical societies—at least in the case of such "empires."[92] And it seems to me that some commonality does stir up there, working its way and coming forth, not as a god working underground, or an operator under the surface, but as the fact, precisely, that there has been some becoming and some constitution in these societies—some becoming-empire, as it were. These workings of the common (of becoming) are taken up, *or caught* [*se prend*],[93] in figural constitution: mythical, cultic, or ritual constitution. Which is to say, becoming is taken up or caught there, in the form of repetition, return, reiteration of the same. Rites are doubtless exactly that: giving figure to becoming *as* a return. For *the return also is a becoming*,[94] but a becoming carried out *as* a comeback. In these societies, the common (becoming) is given figure as a return (as a coming back), and this figuration is an effectuation. The production of rites, of worship (or, in a more contemporary sense, the production of imperiality, domination, even immobile domination, enslavement to timelessness) is effectively a becoming,[95] and thus a production of commonality. But the common is then produced *as* return, in the mode and constitution proper of the figure, and the figure is at work, enslaves, and dominates *effectively*. As I have said, the figure is transport too, but return-transport. It is this: to come back is to become, but becoming *as* in a backward sense, which produces the figure (the myth, the image) of immobility.

"To come back is to become"; the coming back is becoming: what does this say? It means to say that, strictly speaking, nothing comes back. Nothing comes down—and back—to the same, as the figure of the comeback as a return has figured out. There is no return (to the same): being does not come back. Being is, only insofar as it becomes: if *being* (and not just some *beings*) is, it is becoming. One only comes back to *beingness or that which is*: or, to put it differently, one only comes back in space. The only return there is is spatial: return to the same emplacement, to the same locus. But this return does not make up *being*: *being* is only articulated as apartness between this return and its place, and this distances the place from that which makes its return there—*becoming-space* of space, spacing. This is the temporality of space itself—spacing that spaces out. There is *being*—even spatially—only inasmuch as time affects it. And time does not come back. Time is exactly the appellation of that—of being or concerning being—which does not come back to space, to the same space, to the space of the same or the identical. Nothing, of time, as time, comes back (to the same). Nothing of time turns around, except as a figure. And the figure (of time, of anything) is produced *as* its spatialization. The figure is the spatial, tabular, paged inscription of becoming, becoming *traced out as* returning. Something from time (that which makes the temporality of time) escapes this reversion (any figurable reversion) insofar as it is spatial. Something from time is not drawn in space, and this is the very temporal, temporality as apartness; *différance*, as it were; the *changing* of change; the spoiling; the generating; the verbal involved in every substance; nonbeingness: unfigurable, and not because it is an ineffable essence escaping any concrete or material grasping; but unfigurable, on the contrary, *because it is concrete*, because it is this very motion—graphical, praxical, operative—that carries every figure. Very simply because it is—concretely, materially, practically—*irreversible*.

The coming back becomes: coming back is the becoming that is marked, in space, *as* a return to the locus. That is why coming back is transport, as is the figure—return-transport. But *becoming does not come back*. It is irreversible. Is it simply because it is *within* time, and time, which is irreversible, is the framework and the general form of any advent of being? Should one think of time, willingly or not, as that which has already been there in all eternity, taking in every becoming within its available form as the irreversion of any changes and genesis? Perhaps not. Perhaps time has not been already-there forever. Perhaps it is better to say: time as time has come about, as well—*come about precisely as (the being of) the irreversible*. Perhaps there has not always been time, or becoming. Becoming, perhaps, is (the) new. But *henceforth* nothing will come back any longer. It is irreversible—since the big bang? *Off and gone*.

The common happens to humans as new (as newness). It is not beneath the world, findable, like Troy or Atlantis. If, once again, one seeks a production of commonality—a common genesis, communism in the process of becoming—one will as much as possible avoid seeking it in any of the modalities of the return—and therefore unfortunately not in revolution (regardless of one's affection for it), or at least not in its returning, regressive, and revenant turn. If it is a question of liberating the common of the world (and not making it come back there), it is to an exit from the world and from the worldhood of the world that we are invited—but an exit from the other end: not a return to before-the-world, but an exit *ahead*, onward, where our steps carry us, to achieve a crossing of the world and *traverse it*. Way out—crosswise—from the new side, the new way (of the new). Like birth: labor, genesis, gestation.

The common that is coming does not (newly) share out the world, or its possession, acquisition, or appropriation. The common that is coming emancipates itself from the world and its domination (the domination over the world) as well as from ideologies of its distribution (even generous and egalitarian ones). What now has to be shared is no longer of the order of having. "Having" is no longer the bearer of any sharing, as common, community, communism, or communion. Sharing out the world is merely imperial. It was already true and henceforth it is patently so. The shared-out world can no longer start up the foundation of any community project. The communism that is to come wants to touch being, to be in touch with it—*and pass being*, go beyond it; traverse being, by passing across it. The common that is sought is trans-ontological—or nothing.

*

The common is produced within history, as history, as newness. Productions of newness are to be read with an eye to this—even the production that seems to have come along to remove or dismantle the common, one of the most forceful during these new times insofar as they are new: historical individuality. Individuality—in our thinking and the thinking of many before us—is a historical production: production of newness, common production. It is one of the most active forms involving us with one another: that which we now "have" in common; what we are commonly; what we share. The individual is not an essence—given as essence—co-pertaining to humans since their origin. Individual singularity, in its successive modes (and particularly its position as a subject—the subjective position that is its modern mark) is a determined, historical form sharing out and exposing commonality. It is the circumscription of humanity that humanity, in one of its determined phases, outlines as the agency that raises or deposits its essence and formative condition: the modern mode of producing the human condition, as a common condition. And therefore the point of its supposed formation moves about and is being sought: individuality launched at the onset of adulthood, or by way of christening, or birth, or fetal individuality. *The individual is us*: it is the mode of appearing and presentation of "us," in its inmost constitution. The individual bears the mark of this "we" or "us" in his or her determination as an individual:[96] particularly with regard to his or her sex, a dual or plural mark.[97] Among humans, all individuals are sexed: that is, they partake of the dual or plural condition that incorporates them in the common and inscribes them within common-becoming—and partake of it in the very discrimination of their individuality. But individuality is also marked by a series of common traits, even if it overflows and reworks them: social traits; traits of familiarity, of twinning, fraternity or sorority, of age or class; marks of professional or geographical division. And these common traits only exist insofar as they are individual: they are given in their common form only as individual traits, decipherable as individual marks, in individuals. That is why individuality should not be essentialized. The condition of individuals is not an individual essence; it is a structural and distributive formation, a game (like a throw of dice) that launches a determined constitution *as* a singularity, the ir-reducible singularity of an individual. Individuality nowadays imparts our common condition. It is the most forceful and most recent production of our history, the production of newness, the most certain and most manifestly irreversible production of commonality. The coming of commonality produced in us as history has to be read starting from this production, within it, and within the becoming that now affects and traverses it.[98]

And so, what is now happening to us that is common, starting from the individuality that has devolved upon us and that we are sharing? Or, how is our history now proceeding? What is the historical mode of existence of the common that comes into us and to us—not as a transcendent essence rising from our historical being toward a superiority situated outside of it and above it, nor as a pure incidence dropping onto our lives as the bird of the spirit touching us; but as *the transcendence of our very history-as-history*; as this transcendence that our history is, right with its own becoming, within or right upon its prosaic body? What is the mode of existence of our becoming as common-becoming?

28. On Experience

Inasmuch as it allows us to signal to that which henceforth presents itself as *coming upon us*, I propose that we think of the common's mode of existence—for us, as *our* becoming—in terms of the category (or existential) of transport. However, I do not want to turn this term into a fetish or miraculous word in a system.

I am basing myself here on the sense that *transport* has in classical French, or in Rousseau,[99] where it can be understood as that which carries one outside or to the limit of oneself. Such a transport one would today describe as emotional, of course (joyful, loving, hateful), aesthetic (as one is transported by a musical work)[100] or even ethical, in a certain sense, which carries us all the way *into* the other through commiseration or empathy.[101] Transport, then, can be understood as the mark, sign (or operator) of this: individuals are not entirely contained in themselves; being in-itself [*l'en-soi*] is not the fulfilled form of individuality; the individual is not an essence or a substance whose envelope is closed. Something of the individual passes across to the outside, or to the limit; something moves itself outside, beside, or onto the edge of oneself, and this is a real, effective, operating, and motor movement, which "transport" expresses better than "emotion" (a term too caught up in its intrapsychological and thus "figurative" or figural sense, imbued with excessive, and swooning, interiority). Transport impresses as more jolting, charged, loaded—truck-driving. The objection might be that in Rousseau, as Derrida has shown, this capacity to self-extract relies on the imagination, and therefore involves an imaginary transport, the effect of which is *identification*. It is far from certain that what Rousseau designated as "imagination" fits within the concept we now generally associate with this word.[102] And the classical and psychological use of the word "transport" may be a kind of symptom of what we are here pointing to, signing, or marking with its effectivity, though an effectivity *lowered* onto the imaginary, reduced, or carried over to the imaginary by way of the configurations of the thinking of time. Our time no longer is this time: summoned up here, "transport" no longer designates an avatar of *representation*, whether psychic or aesthetic, unless one considers representation itself an effective and real transport.

Still, to speak of going "beside or outside oneself" is somewhat deceptive. It would seem to indicate that the implication of individuality, taken as an essential closure, proceeds from a movement issuing forth from the center of individuality itself, as a forcible opening provoked by its growth and expansion.[103] With this model, one runs the risk of forgetting that individuality is the outcome of a historical distribution, and that its lines of closure are historically and thus commonly traced out. What goes out, "beside itself," of the individual is thus also the trace showing that the "in-itself" of the individual does not exhaust its constitution, its historical determination, or its common nature, if you will. Individuals are traversed and let themselves be traversed by transports that are henceforth multiple: passionate, aesthetic, as well as ethical, to mention just these.[104] Individuality—closed-in and bordered territoriality—exerts fatigue upon its limits. The spilling of the individual no longer amounts to its sole expression. *Insular containment*, even when inflated, no longer expresses the whole of individual experience—all individuality as experience.

And so it goes for transports of love, of lovers and friends, sexual or metasexual, but always in some fashion—obscurely or plainly—connected to the dual and multiple (multiple *as* dual) transport of sex. Sexed or not, what I am calling love here is the fact of being affected by the *existence* of another—by another *existence*, as much or more than by one's own. I am thus not pointing at exchanges, or intercourse (sexual or not), nor at their possible corresponding gifts and countergifts; but at *affection* as such, which turns the existing of another—inasmuch as the other exists—into an arc constituting one's experience, to a point of irreducibility and irreversibility that is not less than in one's experience of self. It could be said that in hate or in fear (perhaps two modes of the same experience) there is something that fits this definition. Not so. For while it is true that through hate and fear one undergoes the feeling of being affected by an existence other than one's own, it is inasmuch as this other existing is related to one's own, through its effects or particulars. The only hate there is refers to oneself, and in this matter, we have to follow Rousseau—one could say *haine-propre* [hate-proper] just as he uses *amour-propre* to distinguish it from good self-referential love.[105] Love irreversibly experiences the existence of the other, but in a way *referred to the other*, as an irreducible excess of and beyond oneself, as an overtaking and overflowing of oneself—transshipment, transportation. Now, love, we know, is a historical formation. As love, it hardly appears in the Homeric epics and does so very little in ancient tragedies—although envy, desire, sexual appetite, possession, and so on, are frequently and lengthily described. We can read the antecedents of its coming in them, just as we can read them—so differently—in Plato or the Old Testament.[106] But as love, such as has gradually come to the fore in our experience, and from now on constitutes it, it then seemed remote, faint, barely sketched out. In Virgil we can see it soaring, with force and passion. And soon, with courtly tales of love followed by tragedies and novels, it is going to occupy the foreground—the stakes and the stories—of our lives, as the love between lovers, to be sure, because our literature always wants to approach most closely the blind spot of its mystery. And as *love*: because Christ makes it the core of his teaching, because the religion that derives from him slowly but steadily carries its theme to the center of its preaching, because the ethics and morals that have gradually constituted themselves as rectors of our thoughts directly or indirectly have made love the nodal point of their specificity. Western specificity: but from it, the whole of the world *qua* world takes shape, worldly globalization as such—the impact of love in (global) cinema attests to this. It is a specificity of the times, then—a feature of *our time*, irreversibly etched.

Now, love is a mark among others of that which prompts individuals not to keep to the enclosure of their essence. Have they ever? It will be apparent that I don't think so. But something figural or imaginary has made it possible to believe that individuals were "within-themselves."[107] This is no longer the case; and if love bears witness to this fact of the times and shows it, it is because love comes about as new, love tells the newness of our experience and times: the new age (Gm., *Neuzeit*) as the time of love; modernity (no matter how grimacing, monstrous in some of its features, and hateful) as the *epoch of love*. But love does not rescind individuality, nor does any transport. Love neither abolishes nor supersedes individuals by way of growth or fusion. Love is a feature of experience that is radically individual, and it is possible as experience only because individuals are historically constituted, providing the launch pad, as it were, of amorous transport. What love is saying is that which lets individuals take themselves to the limit, exceed themselves, and let themselves be exceeded in the experience of affection by the existence of the other. Love is not *love of the other* in the plain sense of wishing him or her well: it is that, no doubt; but it is also something more, something that goes further—being affected by the other's existence, the other's being, the being of the other as irrevocable. One loves the other above and beyond the good one wishes him or her. What comes to pass, with love, is this: experiencing being, the experience of being, happens to me as the experience of the other-than-me, another experience; the experience of existing can no longer be referred merely to the sole experience of myself. There is some existing outside of myself, beyond myself (something that hate and fear were also able to tell me), and this existing affects me, not in its relation to myself—in the fact that it is referred to the self—but in its referral to an existence insofar as it is other. Only love makes me experience this. In other words, there is something that exists outside of myself, beyond myself, *and I love—that*.[108]

*

There are two possible ways to read this experience of the individual. On the one hand, one can determine it as finitude: individuals experience what exceeds them, what goes beyond them, and thus experience themselves as finite. Individuals experience the existence of an outside-of-themselves as not-proceeding from themselves, not created by themselves, and thus happening to them.[109] But in this sense the other is still, and always, experienced to be other in one's relation to oneself. The other is the alterity of what happens to me. One thus misses the other who happens to me *in his or her relation to his or her own exteriority as such*. Is it then a question of calling upon the facial apparition of the other as other? Perhaps not. A thinking of love, or a thinking that wants to give thought to the effectivity of love, *cannot be satisfied either with a relation to the other, with the alterity of the other*. If others can affect me—in their very existing, as others—and reach me *as experience* in the feeling of their very own alterity, but without being reduced to this alterity called upon to appear before my gaze, or to the frontality of the otherness in the being of others, *it is because something passes from one to the other*. It is neither a substance, nor a current, nor any kind of flow. What I am seeking to say is doubtless difficult to think and can merely appear here as a thought at the limit (of the present book, at least) and as a program. We can attempt to make a sign toward this: from one to the other, *just as* from the other to the one, *something passes and comes to pass*. There is neither just the experience of self-finitude experiencing itself as the experience of an outside, as an excess of oneself, *death of oneself*—relation to the (possibility of) one's death; finitude as being-at-death—nor just finitude as a gaze toward others; nor as a gaze toward the other gaze, as co-apparition of the other and for or toward the other, as *frontal adventitiousness*, as being *face-to-face*. Something crosses over and comes to pass. *Finitude has holes*—porous like skin and yet pure self-limit. Something comes across: something—at least—like procreation, like sexual engendering, coupling and copulation, just to take this one—hardly refutable—example; and more manifestly, the feminine role in procreation: an other, issuing from the depths of oneself (and the other), traversing one's own body and coming into existence. Delimitation, loss, discharges. Life: a possible name (among others), perhaps, for the traversal of one's self—which is never quite simply the life of myself as myself; but always also the life that pokes holes in me and exceeds me, traverses and overflows me. Life pokes holes in finitude. Which is a way of saying (to be bold and shameless about it): if finitude has holes, *so does death*. Death is not an opaque limit. Something traverses it.[110] Something comes to pass there. A thinking of the other is no longer enough (henceforth). There has to be a thought of that which runs and goes from me to the other, from the other to me—something *common*.

This may not be so far removed, after all, from what Ludwig Feuerbach indicated with his concept of *Gattung* [genus]. Let us recall that for him "genus" is the human essence, present as genus (the human genus, the genericness of humans) in each determined individuality. Despite the (philosophical) characteristics of Feuerbach's time, which he cannot escape, it is a mistake too quickly to reduce his thinking to a simple attribution—like that of universals—giving individuals the traits of the genus that they (re)present. It may not only be about the presence in individuals of a trait of the genus, but about the *existence* of individual singularity *as generic*, which is to say (according to what I am trying to set forth) as the common. This genericness affects and runs throughout inmost singularity—what Feuerbach calls "inner life." He writes:

The inner life of man is the life which has relation to his genus, his essence.... Man thinks—that is, he converses *with himself*... man can perform the functions of thought and speech—thought and speech are true functions of the genus—apart from another individual. Man is himself at once I and thou; he can put himself in the place of another, for this reason that to him his genus, his essence, and not merely his individuality, is an object of thought.[111]

One could read this passage (it does lend itself to it) as an appropriating attribution of human essence as a whole to individuality as such, and thus as bringing down or reincorporating the common into the singular—within the limits, the borders, and the finitude of the singular: in a quasi-monadic fashion, as it were. But this is quite the wrong way of reading this. Indeed, that which is attributed to individuals, and is lacking in animals,[112] is a way of overtaking, traversing, and puncturing individuality. Human individuality exceeds and traverses its individual delimitation. That is why this determination of generic individuality is necessarily carried out as a theory of love. This theory is about being carried away:

> Who has not experienced the power of love, or at least heard of it? Which is the stronger—love or the individual man? Is it man that possesses love, or is it not much rather love that possesses man? When love impels a man to suffer death even joyfully for the beloved one, is this death-conquering power his own individual power, or is it not rather the power of love?[113]

Here love is put forward strictly as the force of the common, which overflows and carries away the individual—and the full scope of it appears if we recall that this force, the expression of the generic character, is inscribed *in the individual as such*. That which traverses individuals at the heart of their individuality is that which overflows them. In this light, one should reread the remarkable page Feuerbach devoted to sexual love.[114] The man-woman relationship is construed as fulfillment, as the *truth of the genus*, and this truth is a self-overflowing of individuality,

> for in love, man declares himself unsatisfied in his individuality taken by itself. . . . The individual is defective, imperfect, weak, needy; but love is strong, perfect, contented, free from wants, self sufficing, infinite; because in it the *self-consciousness of the individuality* is the mysterious self-consciousness of the perfection of the genus.[115]

The signs of the times are visible: perfection, self-sufficiency of the genus. But what is also visibly coming forth, *as a theory of love*, is a theory of the overflowing of individuality *by itself*, inasmuch as it carries desires, or feelings, or commonality. This, too, pertains to what we are dealing with here as transport.

Individuality can no longer experience itself in the mode of an insular experience—in accordance with a certain idea of insularity: as that which proceeds from its own inside and reaches outward. This form is figural, as has been shown: an island does *not* come about in this way, and insularity does *not* constitute itself from inside but from its edges, from sailing along its shores. But islands can turn things around and give themselves the image of their setting from the inside of their inmost lands, the borders of which are the shores. No longer are individuals islands, in this sense, or can they be. The contents of their experience can no longer be thought in the mode of a self-projection toward exteriority, nor of the reception and intuition of exteriority as such. My thinking here is that even if the structure of "being-at" [*l'être à*] no longer keeps to (or stays within) the schema of insularity, it no longer accounts for the experience that is forming henceforth either. Obviously, not the experience of "being-at" or "being in (and pertaining to) the world" [*être au monde*]: because if the world is what the empire subjugates, dominates, or (as capital) possesses and represents, being in (pertaining to) the world is being and pertaining to that which is subjugated or represented, that is to say, being leaving itself open to its capture by submission or the image. It may be in this way—as Heidegger strongly analyzes it—that the subject constitutes itself, relying on the production of the world as image, representation, and object. But if this representation is coextensive with the world—the convocation of the whole of beingness or all that is in the structure of the world—we then need to say that being in (pertaining to) the world is dependent on the schema of being-subject, of which it expresses a moment of constitution. Being in (pertaining to) the world is the experience accompanying the constitution of the subject (of the empire). To be in the world is to be subjected. And something from this constitution and this structure persistently remains in the structure of "being-at" [*l'être-à*]. To "be-at" is to be, *from* the starting point of *being*; it is to come to the edge of the world, and take up with the world from the starting point of being-oneself. At the stage closest to its nucleus, it is the schema that will unfold and spread as the constitution of interiority. It is interiority at the extreme edge of its opening, at the limit of itself and its access—right at and upon the world. It is insularity moving toward the beach and acknowledging its access to the sea, or *even finding its origin in it*, and not by sailing around (sailing along the coast is anti-originary)—but rather as the first spark, the inception of a process of flowing back toward its center or inside. "Being-at" does not know the common; it can only think "being-with." Whereas, henceforth, the common is what convokes and traverses us, and this is what one has to try to think—as newness.

The common is not neighboring islands—not an archipelago. There are no individuals thinkable in the autonomy of their essence, with relations between them. Even the ontology of the relation will no longer do. It is a question not of thinking of what links us, but of what is common among us; not of what associates, coordinates, or even exposes me to the other, but of what makes me no longer simply or only myself. When closed, my identity is a withdrawal, a retreat—*henceforth the retreat before the experience of this*. Individuality no longer has to push itself around violently within its essence. Individuals are open. Neither dissolved, nor superseded, nor abolished: open. Something traverses them, swaying their "relationship with others," and their relationship to others sways toward the experience of commonality. What I want is no longer just to relate to the other, or to look toward the other, and it is not the face of others or being face-to-face with them. Henceforth I am seized by that which is common to me and them, him or her: and this brings about, for my being and beyond my being, the commonality with these others—whether or not they resemble me or have black skin or a woman's temperament, a blind gaze, or the chatter of a child. I am seized by the gaze of dogs and the singing of the deaf. This is no longer coming to me only as an experience of the other; it traverses me as transit or transitivity of myself. I am transitive: what dies, even far away—a child without a torso, a woman without eyes—is I: not only I as an image and projected, in a projective identification,[116] but I, now, dying outside of myself because what is dying carries me away and constitutes me. "How could I suffer when I see another suffer," Rousseau writes, "if I do not know what he and I have in common?"[117] Rousseau, of course, deals with transport by means of ideas, the imaginary, or knowledge. Here we are not speaking about knowing—*we are not speaking about suffering*; suffering at a distance is declamatory, imaginary, and compensating. We are dealing with the common seizing us: I am not suffering, I do not empathize; what is suffering or dying is seizing me, and will never again let me go.

In this meta- or tele-phoria of the common that now carries me away, individuality is not an island: it is a port, and doubly so.

The experience relates to ports: coastal sailing, departure on the high seas, landings. Journeys, migrations, and stopovers. Individuality takes shape like a port in this cartography or network with multiple interconnections. And this does not—certainly not—amount to drifting, to wandering the seas without any mooring or place. The port experience is the experience and pleasure of harbors, terra firma, and reencounters—*within* the momentum of travel. It is not a *certain kind* of experience—more port than high seas, more maritime than terrestrial. Rather, experience itself—the [present participle of Latin] *ex-periri*, cognate with peril, pirates, pores, and ports.[118] This is what port means, then: the schema of *exposition* is no longer enough for the common. There has to be *experience*—traversal.[119] The experience of the common is transportive [*transportuaire*].

But in a second sense, along these routes, individuals form as silhouettes, singularities, and gestures. *What* one now has to think of in relation to them is no longer their essence, *it is their port*. Individuality itself: the bearing or *port* of individuals, the look of their gait, their way of lifting their hips or their chin. In this quasi-motionless gesture, who is bearing or supporting whom? It is the common. Carrying and supporting them, raising them, it transports them to the trait of their singularity. But individuality, too, *teleports itself* at a distance from itself, and in this movement, this untranslatable move, it outlines itself as a silhouette, a gait, or a singularity. The port of each body is unique and marks it, making it stand out as a singular body. But that which "ports" the port, where the port transports itself, is the common itself: I transport myself toward the common, to what transits through me and opens me; I report myself to the other (and transport to this other I support in myself), to sit, fetch, stay. It's a peacock displaying its feathers—something that traverses and seizes it, until it jubilantly overflows with such an extraversion and ostentation of colors. But there is a port for horses, and one for peacocks, and *even one for flowers*, one might argue. Indeed: at one end, that which supports this port involves living itself, the historicity of nature; and at the other end, just as much, that which now, historically, is seizing us anew, as newness.

29.

What about Europe? Lately it seems to have been forgotten in these pages. To be sure, the erasure of its name and theme has been intentional—even if all that we have been dealing with in this last part can rightfully be qualified as European: world globalization, world-image, capitalism and its imperialism, communism, revolution, historicity. *All that seems to have come out of Europe.* Let us come back to this for a moment.

Our initial hypothesis was as follows:

"Europe" is one of the names of the return to self of the universal, which is to say, of the universal as a figure. (h1)

This means to say that Europe counts as one of the places that produced the universal and elaborated the idea of universality. But of this work it has not accomplished anything *as a return* (in its returning phase), nor as a figure, then—nor then ultimately as "Europe." In other words, even if it is supposedly "European," this elaboration of the idea of the universal was not the product of a meditation about Europe but about universality. The work, implementation, and operation of Plato, Newton, and Freud (to pick some arbitrary examples) were not carried out as elaborations of the theme, or the schema, of Europe. The question of Europe as such has come to light by way of a return toward its operations and possibly (though rarely) a turnaround of these operations. Let us recall the structuring schema:

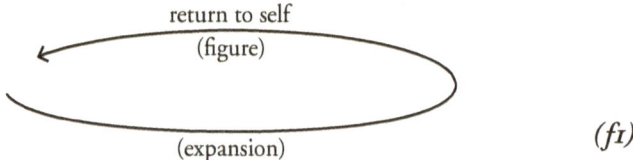

(f1)

The expansion supports the return, which carries it forward, in a certain fashion, and has the same nature. But the return reverses the expansion and sends it back to its supposed starting point. The expansion did turn around at one point, as if hitting a stumbling block, or something exhausting it. And so, *insofar as it turns itself* (*its image, name, and figure*) *around*, Europe is the product of the reversal of the movement of the universal, that is, the product of its stopping and fatigue. While Europe has thus counted as one of the—eminent and singular—places of the production of the universal, it is not as "Europe" that it has worked it out, while thinking of and regarding itself as Europe, and so naming itself. *Europe named itself Europe precisely when this work was stopping*, entering a phase of exhaustion and reversal. And thus—to make my intentions completely clear—I have ceased to speak about Europe so as to take up again in my own way the gesture of European productivity.

This may be exactly what the myth tells us, or rather the legendary, *literary*, and very late variant of it that has reached us. It is not as if the myth had *foreseen* or announced a historical development (the formation of Europe), which came about much later. But the structure of the myth simply made it available to symbolize or allegorize the European feature that is our topic—and this explains, among other things, that Europe rather than another figure was chosen to designate this development. Indeed, being torn from her native land is what happens to Princess Europē and what the myth recounts. This abduction happens to an Asian woman;

Europe is torn away from Asia. The abduction suits her desire—her nocturnal, secret, and amorous hopes. When it is announced, it makes Europe concerned and quivering with excitement. This Asian daughter wants to be abducted: Asia has also begotten this desire for abduction, this hope to leave and be carried away from her native place. Among young women, Europe is the one who has the vision for this project: we know that she can see far and wide.[120] But the land to which her abduction transports her—the land she sees, and foresees in her dream—is the nameless land on the other side. And Europe does want this very thing: to be torn from her soil, her birthplace, toward an unknown and unnamed place in the west. In this way the matter that is more European than any other is the matter of the *production of America*. America is the exhibited becoming of Europe as Europe: the far-off vision of an unknown land in the west, where one wishes to be carried away. Europe is entirely this desire of westernness, this westward run, always westbound, no doubt behind the sun, which it wants to follow or join, and make it impossible for the sun to drop in the sky or set—like Joshua wanting to halt the sun and the moon [Josh. 10:12–13], or Leon Trotsky death as much as the sun. Europe does not want to stop the sun but rather to follow its ride indefinitely and prevent the venture from coming to an end, banish falls and declines, settle indefinitely in the journey itself, take its place in the chariot, sail to the west, endlessly, from one unknown to the next. In this surge—continually relaunched—Europe has produced the world as world. That is why worldhood is European in essence: worldhood is the appellation of the very project of Europe, as self-discovery, discovery of this being-Europe, the new and unknown land that one pursues after being carried off across the sea.[121]

But here it is: the journey turns itself around, through its completion; it finds and joins its point of departure again; and the production of the world is achieved as *globalism*. It is in this return to itself and this turnaround that Europe recognizes itself as Europe: otherwise it was simply the universe—the world of the empire, the Catholicity of the church, the *oikoumenē* of any inhabited or traveled land. And then, as universality, it is superseded by this new empire that it has brought forth: by capitalism and its world; by the worldwide character, becoming-world, and world-image of capital. What is most European, then, is the world as world, that is, *the cessation of Europe*. The universalist project deports itself from Europe as such, and Europeans, putting this into words, will henceforth rely on the idea-of-world, planetarism or cosmopolitics, world citizenship or world revolution, world-city or city-world, the great universal city of men called to appear before itself in complete transcontinentality. In this phase, Europe is no longer necessary for the universal. If it reconfigures itself, *as Europe*, it is necessarily out of fear and by retreating in front of this worldhood that dissolves it within itself, henceforeward out of patriotism, continental nationalism, protectionism of the soil, denying all that it has done and constituted: this worldhood itself, which is nothing but its child—additionally, the name of its operation, in tearing itself away from its birthplace, its nationality always dismissed. Two Europes confront each other, then, and they are doubly impossible: one Europe that is nothing but world globalization itself and only wants Europe as its own abolition; and one Europe that turns around toward itself as a continentality of identities and nationalisms, and for that matter has to deny all that Europe has done, thought, and produced since its inaugural abduction. At this point, there is not much one can do with Europe: if one chooses its universal vocation, it is the world that is involved. As for a national reappropriation, Europe is hardly suitable.

But here it is. Let us imagine that what this book has said is ever so slightly relevant. What it brings out is that *the world, too, is now exhausted*; that it is not the world that is needed; that what has to be done is *to exit the world*—because the world is the name of the domain subjected to imperial domination—nowadays to capital—and the world henceforth and *irreversibly* is the world of commodities, world-commodity, and that *one has to come out of this*, traverse it, set oneself free from this, leave it alone, change histories. But without turning back, without returning to the supposed point of departure: instead, coming out ahead, onward, where our steps lead and where we are looking. An exodic program, as it were: to exit the world of servitude, to come out of servitude-as-the-world, to travel across the desert, to *pass across to the other side*. What offers itself in this crossing—according to Spinoza—is law, its common constitution, the form and possibility of commonality.[122] It is about exiting the world-of-domination to cross over to being-in-common—about letting go of being-in-the-world (being-*there*) so as to be-in-common, one might almost say provocatively. And there is no way of knowing yet whether this program can be thought as "being," or whether letting go of being is involved—a curious *forgetting of being*—for the experience, sharing, and practice of the common. This is something Althusser would call a "change of terrain," for thinking as well as praxis, from thinking to the thinking of praxis—a new experience and practice of thinking.

Supposing it is like this—that it is now the time of untaking, ungrasping, and dispossession of the world, dis*being in* the world—we may have something to do with Europe, anew. For if Europe was one of the places where the universal was elaborated, the program may now be *to follow up on this elaboration in one of its (new) phases*: the elaboration of a universal set free from the world of servitude, from the commodity; not as a program to disenslave or decommodify the world, but as a disenslaving, decommodification, and thus deworldization of common-being. A universal *after the world*: this is the work one may now undertake, in Europe and elsewhere. But while Europe may count as a place where this program is elaborated, it could not be so *as Europe*—so much is clear. It can be, no doubt, thanks to the pursuit and more thorough inquiry into everything, about the universal, elaborated here—as well as elsewhere, but perhaps more so and more irreversibly so. But in no way can it be through the retreat or turnaround toward its own gesture as a European one, in the quest for the contents, the figure, and the identity covered by this name. Moreover, Europe is quite clumsy at this. It can only be in the broadening of its views, opening wide its large eyes—and not in scrutinizing its mirror. Perhaps Europe can help to liberate us from the world (but this "us" is "everyone in the world"). Looking far and wide. For, to be sure, *beyond the horizon of the world, we see nothing now*—letting oneself be carried away by desire, removed from one's native land, to transport oneself toward a beyond-the-horizon so remote that one can neither name it nor see it yet, nor even confirm its existence.

This is what a certain powerlessness on the part of Europe (henceforth) conveys—powerless to be excited by what it contains and by its own essence, powerless in nationalism, powerless to love its own figure. And in this it expresses the best thing it has: its native extraversion, its unnamed, intemperate universion. This is the good fortune we can foretell for Europe: the emptiness of its figure is its positive future.

Notes

Unless otherwise indicated, all translations from French and German are by Christine Irizarry.

ON BEGINNING AND PART I: EUROPE CROSSWAYS

1. See, e.g., Deleuze, *Image-mouvement*, pp. 11–12. On moving trains, see Althusser, *Sur la philosophie*, pp. 64–65; *Écrits philosophiques et politiques*, 1: 581ff.

2. An apt formulation for this might be: the beginning is the passage, which is the Derridean hypothesis, in a sense, and Montaigne's as well. I hope to be able to specify elsewhere what I owe each of them.

3. "[T]here are three generations in a hundred years" (Herodotus, *Histories* 2.142, p. 152).

4. On this topic, see Guénoun, "Un Sémite," p. 23.

5. In honor of my father's memory, I should be more specific: not at the same time as so many others but a year earlier, in 1961, to flee from the fascistic terrorism of the O.A.S. (Secret Army Organization) after an attack aimed at him, who was in favor of Algerian independence, an attack which nearly nailed us—my father, his wife (my mother, *maman*), and me—there, if I may put it this way.

6. Citation from the French historian Hippolyte Taine in the *Petit Robert* (1990), p. 1699.

7. See the *Petit Littré* (1959), p. 1968.

8. For example, see the figures in Bergson, *Matière et mémoire*, p. 115 (picked up by Deleuze in *Image-temps*, p. 65), pp. 159, 169, and 181; Husserl, *On the Phenomenology of the Consciousness of Internal Time*, p. 29; Deleuze and Guattari, *Qu'est-ce que la philosophie?* p. 30; or further, among many other possible examples (Wittgenstein, Lacan), the very unexpected *graphic representation of Dasein* (I thank Paola Marrati for locating it) in Heidegger, *Zollikoner Seminare*, p. 3.

9. Deleuze, rereading Bergson, analyzes the problem of immobile sections of movement in the first chapter of *Image-movement*, pp. 9ff. [See Deleuze, *Movement-Image*, p. 61.]

10. The myth of Japheth attests this expansive constitution of Europe. Noah's three sons (Shem, Ham, and Japheth) provided the substance of a mythological geography during the Middle Ages, since they were said to have received the "three

parts of the world" to share out among themselves. In this distribution, Europe goes to Japheth. The interpretation by medieval commentators sees in this the attribution of *extensio* as such to Europe, based on Gen. 9.27: "God *shall enlarge* Japheth" (Bible [KJV]). Denis de Rougemont writes about this: "The word all these exegetes stress is the one we underlined . . . : *dilatet* in the Vulgate. Japheth (or *Yepheth*, from *phatah*, 'to enlarge, to spread') denotes latitude, width, expansion" (Rougemont, *Idea of Europe*, p. 20).

11. Relating continence and continentality is etymologically evident but semantically bold. Nevertheless, this occurs in some referential texts about Europe. There is the bull who carries off the princess (we shall discuss this later on), which, according to the geographer Mercator, whose Atlas was published in 1595, is "of great continence, but when brought to the other sex is in extreme heat. . . . Such is the nature of Europeans, notably the most Northern ones" (as quoted in Rougemont, *Vingt-huit siècles d'Europe*, p. 21). [The published translation, in *The Idea of Europe*, condenses this passage and omits any reference to "continence": ". . . the bull-god 'does aptly represent the natural disposition of the European'" (pp. 15–16).—Trans.]

12. See Derrida, "D'où vient l'Europe?" in *Penser l'Europe à ses frontières*, p. 22.

13. Kant, "Idee zu einer allgemeinen Geschichte in weltbürgerlicher Absicht" (henceforth cited as *Idee*), p. 407; "The Natural Principle of the Political Order Considered in Connection with the Idea of a Universal Cosmopolitical History" (henceforth cited as UH), no pagination; *Idée d'une histoire universelle au point de vue cosmopolitique* (henceforth cited as *Idée*), p. 25 [emphasis added, except for the terms "History" and "Romance"; further references to this text appear in the body of the text.—Trans.].

14. Kant, UH; *Idee*, pp. 408–409; *Idée*, pp. 25–26. [The words "progress though the political institutions" have been changed to "progress through the civil constitution," the word "Continent" has been changed to "part of the world," and parentheses have been added to conform to the cited German text and the French translation.—Trans.]

15. Kant, UH; *Idee*, p. 408; *Idée*, p. 25n. [Parentheses and the word "one" in the last sentence have been added to conform to the German text.—Trans.]

16. Kant, UH; *Idee*, p. 397n; *Idée*, pp. 17–18n; emphasis added. [The phrase "in the edifice of the world" has been substituted for "in the universe," used in UH.—Trans.]

17. This seems to me Kant's consistent and organized position in this text. Of course there are other texts in which he does mention Europe. Bernard Bourgeois cites some of them in "La philosophie allemande et l'Europe (de Kant à Hegel)," pp. 84–86, noting in his comment that "as reason is established (as the negation of any particularism), it does not owe anything to its European manifestation." And further, "Europeanism is constituted by cosmopolitism and not the other way around"—which coincides, at least in one sense, with what I am trying to articulate here with regard to the priority of the universal as an expansion. On

this score, it is fitting to establish, as Bourgeois does, that "rational Europe is not properly speaking European." It is true that this touches on some astonishing formulations by Kant, who stated [in a handwritten note—Trans.], "I call a nation European only if the constraint it accepts is lawful" ("Europäisch nenne ich eine Nation, wenn sie nur den gesetzmäßigen Zwang annimmt") (Kant, Ak. 15/2, p. 773), which excludes quite strictly any geographical or continental determination, and prefigures further developments, such as Étienne Balibar's remarks about the Europes outside of Europe (see Balibar, "Quelles frontières de l'Europe?" in *Penser l'Europe à ses frontières*, pp. 90–100). In this context, is it suitable for Bourgeois to state, at the outset of his analysis, that "Kant carries out the identification of this continent with rationality"? He does immediately specify, however, that it is a continent that "negates its own particular and natural character, as well as any differentiation in its geographical determination." But does it then even make sense to call it a "continent"? It is somewhat useless and can be hazardous in other analytical contexts, to which I shall come back later, by making Europe (precisely as a continent, that is to say, as a figure, as an *identity*) the subject of world history, exactly inasmuch as Europe would be the only place capable of negating itself—a sort of negative colonialism, in a way. The sentence "Europe is itself, and only as [*n'est elle-même que*] the locus of reason, universality, and self-identity" is unclear: while this "is . . . only as" [*n'est . . . que*] means that thinking of Europe in this way makes it nongeographical, it is Europe as such ("is itself") that is the subject of this thought, and an equivalence between "universality" and "self-identity" is given, which should at least lend itself to a discussion. In any case, this leads Bourgeois (in the quoted sentence: "we shall discover a regular movement of progress through the civil constitution of our part of the world") to translate *Welttheil* with "continent," and thus to posit that "Europe is the continent 'which is probably destined to give laws to all other parts of the world,'" which Kant does not say quite *this way* (he says neither "continent" nor "Europe," precisely).

18. This dating will be discussed later on.

19. "Europe" seems to have been a fairly rare word in Greek antiquity, especially in its geographical meaning. Aside from mentions of Princess Europē, there are two occurrences in the Homeric *Hymns* (*Hymn to Apollo*, ll. 251 and 291), but none in the *Iliad* or the *Odyssey*; none in Hesiod; two in Pindar (*Nemean* 4, l. 70; *Fragments*, l. 70); four in Aeschylus (*Persians*, l. 799; *Prometheus Bound*, l. 736; *Fragments*, ll. 191 and 322); one in Sophocles (*Fragments*, p. 39); frequent uses in Herodotus, but very few in Thucydides.

20. Chantraine, *Dictionnaire étymologique de la langue grecque*, 1: 388.

21. Dionysius of Halicarnassus, *Roman Antiquities* 1.2.2; Pindar, *Nemean* 4, ll. 69–70; Aeschylus: *Persians*, l. 799, *Prometheus Bound*, l. 736; Euripides: *Andromache*, l. 801, *Hecuba*, l. 482, *Ion*, l. 1587, and some mentions in *Fragments*; Herodotus, *Histories* 1.4.103; 2.103; 3.96; 4.89, 143; 5.1, 12; 6.33, 43; 7.8–10, 20, 33, 50, 54, 56, 73, 126, 148, 174, and 185; 9.14.

22. See Herodotus, *Histories* 4.86.

23. "So Darius crossed . . . " (Herodotus, *Histories* 4.89; see also 4.143: "he took ship for Asia, leaving a Persian called Megabazus in command of his troops in Europe"); "towards the western darkness" (Pindar, *Nemean* 4, ll. 69–70); "Will not the whole barbarian army cross . . . " (Aeschylus, *Persians*, l. 799; see also *Prometheus Bound*, ll. 730–36: "This you must leave with stout heart and pass through the channel of Maeotis; and ever after among mankind there shall be great mention of your passing, and it shall be called after you the Bosporus. Then, leaving the soil of Europe, you shall come to the Asian continent"); "when on that earlier day Zeus' famous son Heracles . . . " (Euripides, *Andromache*, l. 801); "The Persians . . . " (Dionysius of Halicarnassus, *Roman Antiquities* 1.2.2).

24. "Asia, for Herodotus, generally means the land of the Persian Empire during the time of Darius, and more particularly the peninsula of Anatolia" (Barguet, in Herodotus, *Œuvres complètes*, p. 1343n1).

25. See Euripides, *Ion*, "the two mainlands, Asia and Europe, on opposite sides" (ll.1586–87). "Continents" translates *ēpeiroin*, for which Liddell and Scott's *Greek-English Lexicon* gives the following definition: *ēpeiros*, "*terra firma, land*, opp. *the sea* . . . later, *a continent*, esp. of Asia" (p. 776, col. 1). Bailly defines it as "Europe or Asia. The two continents (Europe and Asia, Libya being usually associated by the Ancients now with Europe now with Asia)" (*Dictionnaire grec-français*, p. 906). This latter detailed explanation demonstrates that tricontinentality (which Herodotus mentions and questions as such, e.g., *Histories* 2.16 and 4.42, 45, and 198) arises from the face-to-face structure, as a kind of duplication of a face-to-face relation with a set term, and that this head-on op-position, constitutively, is what opposes Europe and Asia, which is to say, as we shall see, Asia and its outside: "he had a dream. He seemed in his dream to see Hystaspes' eldest son with wings growing out of his shoulder-blades; with one wing he cast a shadow over Asia, with the other he overshadowed Europe" (Herodotus, *Histories* 1.209, pp. 91–92).

26. See this remark by Boccaccio, as quoted by Denis de Rougemont: "There is no part of the world that may be said to be common to all nations unless it be the island of Crete. . . . The ancients liked to divide the inhabited world of our upper hemisphere into three parts, which they named Asia, Europe, and Asia. . . . And the island of Crete seems to be situated at the borders of these three continents" (Rougemont, *Idea of Europe*, p. 37).

27. See Euripides, *Ion*, "Their sons in turn, at the appointed time, will settle in the island cities of the Cyclades, and the lands along the shore, which will give strength to my land; they will colonize the plains of the two mainlands, Asia and Europe, on opposite sides" (ll. 1580–87; emphasis added).

28. See Herodotus, *Histories*: "India, for example, is the most easterly part of the inhabited world. . . . Then again, Arabia is the most southerly inhabited land. . . . These are the most remote countries in Asia and Libya. However, I have no

reliable information to pass on about the western margins of Europe, because I at any rate do not accept that there is a river which the natives [barbarians] there call the Eridanus (said to issue into the northern sea . . .) . . . despite my efforts, I have been unable to find anyone who has personally seen a sea on the other side of Europe and can tell me about it" (3.106, 107, and 115, pp. 212–14, 216).

29. This can twice be confirmed—*ad absurdum*: first, we cannot remain insensitive to the fact that the name "Europe," so frequently used by Herodotus, is so rare in Thucydides. Indeed, the question of crossing continents, and their relation to one another, at the very heart of the former's project, is less actively present in the latter's work. This reinforces the impression that, linguistically speaking, the name was not very commonly used, since, by contrast, Thucydides does mention Persia, Xerxes, Darius, and so on, several times. The name Europe is only featured *once* in Aeschylus's *Persians*—where one might expect it more often. Second, in Herodotus both mentions of Europe as a kind of *country*, as a locus posited for itself, rather corroborate one's intuition: the statements, "he also invariably added . . . that Europe was a particularly beautiful place" (Herodotus, *Histories* 7.5), and "Ionians—the ones living in Europe" (7.9) are only *uttered by two Persians*—rather treacherous ones, in fact, since they prod Xerxes to go to war when he "was at first rather reluctant to make war" (7.5, p. 405). Europe's wealth, *as a country* ("a particularly beautiful place, where every kind of cultivated tree grew and the soil was excellent" [7.5, p. 405]), is a fantasy or deception derived from Asians. Furthermore, it is important "not to let those despicable Ionians—the ones living in Europe—get away with making fools of *us*" (7.9, p. 408; emphasis added).

30. For example, "Eventually this expedition of his across the mainland brought him from Asia over into Europe, where he defeated the Scythians" (Herodotus, *Histories* 2.103); "So Darius crossed over into Europe . . ." (4.89); "The Persians crossed the Hellespont by ship and began to march through Europe" (6.43); "You say that you will bridge the Hellespont and march through Europe to Greece" (7.10); "the army the Mysians and Teucrians raised—this was before the Trojan War—with which they crossed the Bosporus, invaded Europe, conquered the whole of Thrace" (7.20); "Meanwhile, his men had been bridging the Hellespont from Asia to Europe" (7.33); "Xerxes poured a libation from a golden cup into the sea and, facing the sun, asked the sun-god to avert any accidents which might stop him from reaching the outer limits of Europe and conquering the whole continent" (7.54); "Over on the European side, Xerxes watched his army" (7.56); "as soon as they learnt that Xerxes was poised to enter Europe, they sent messengers to the Isthmus" (7.172); "Xerxes was on the verge of crossing over into Europe from Asia" (7.174); and so forth. In addition to these, there are the previously quoted instances in Aeschylus, Euripides, Pindar, Dionysius of Halicarnassus (as well as Thucydides).

31. *Histoire de l'Europe*, ed. Carpentier and Lebrun, p. 13.
32. *Grand Larousse encyclopédique*, 7: 7122.

33. Editor and translator Philippe-Ernest Legrand in [Moschus], *Bucoliques grecs*, p. 141.

34. This first developed narrative thus dates from a fairly late period. See Rougemont, *Idea of Europe*, pp. 7ff.

35. Not as far as this text is concerned, of course, but in terms of the legend that is told. [References to Moschus are given parenthetically in the body of the text.—Trans.]

36. The Greek word *pothos* means passionate desire, sensual desire, love (see Liddell and Scott's *Greek-English Lexicon*; Bailly, *Dictionnaire grec-français*, p. 1580).

37. This African ancestry through the mother seems collateral. But the paternal line is direct: Agenor is a son of Libya. See Graves, *Greek Myths*, pp. 194ff.

38. See the description of this astonishing bovine (whose "body was bright chestnut" and whose eyes "ever sent forth lightning of desire") in Moschus, p. 192.

39. "So spake he, and all he spake was fulfilled" (Moschus, p. 196). Robert Graves tells us that Zeus's seduction of Europe occurred at the beginning of May, as "part of the fertility ritual during which Europe's May-garland was carried in procession" (*Greek Myths*, p. 197). The tale of the abduction also appears in a much shorter form in Ovid, *Metamorphoses* 2.836.

40. "*Asia* is, characteristically, the *Orient* quarter of the globe—the region of origination. It is indeed a Western world for America; but as Europe presents on the whole, the centre and end of the old world, and is absolutely the *West*—so Asia is absolutely the *East*.

"In Asia arose the Light of Spirit, and therefore the history of the world" (Hegel, *Philosophy of History* [Sibree], p. 104).

41. Herodotus, *Histories* 4.45, pp. 249–50; emphasis added.

42. Hegel, *Philosophy of History* (Sibree), p. 95.

43. The discovery of America reproduces the gesture that constitutes Europe and its (re)becoming-visible: in this sense, America is Europe re-produced: the abduction, the formative movement of Europe reconstituted, bared and openly displayed. "There lies your way, due west / Then westward ho!" (Shakespeare, *Twelfth Night* 3.1, p. 72).

44. Chantraine, *Dictionnaire étymologique de la langue grecque*, 1: 388.

45. Homer, *Hymns*, pp. 22–23; emphasis added. There are two identical mentions in the *Hymns*, in "To Apollon": ll. 285–92 and, above, ll. 247–52.

46. This statement is reinforced by Aristotle, who writes: "The nations *in cold regions, particularly in Europe*, are full of spirit but are deficient in intelligence and skill. . . . By contrast, those in Asia have intelligent minds and are skilled in the crafts, but they lack spirit. . . . But as far as the race of the Greeks, just as it occupies an intermediate region, so it shares in both conditions" (Aristotle, *Politics* 7.7, p. 12; emphasis added). Greece is thus an intermediate region between (cold) Europe and Asia. Therefore it is not strictly speaking in Europe. Note also Denis de Rougemont's remark that Herodotus's definition of Europe is of "a northern

region not too clearly distinguished from Scythia (which we think of today as the Russian plain). According to him, its axis is the Danube, which he calls the Ister" (Rougemont, *Idea of Europe*, p. 35, on Herodotus, *Histories* 4.48–49).

47. This idea of a *passage to Europe* as constituting Europe itself—its formation and its concept—should, at this point, lead us to ask what *comes across* in this passage, what is transported, abducted, and carried away. We shall come back to this, of course. For now, let us just note that Plato (though an unverified or suspect Plato) says that what comes across, is abducted and carried away, is the law. "Socrates: But whence is it that the best of those ordinances come? Do you know? Companion: From Crete, so they say. Socrates: Then the people there use the most ancient laws in Greece? Companion: Yes. Socrates: Then do you know who were their good kings? Minos and Rhadamanthus, the sons of Zeus and Europa; those laws were theirs" (Plato, *Minos* 318c–d). The children that Zeus has with Europē in Crete, at the end of the journey, are the makers of laws.

48. Edmund Husserl, "The Vienna Lecture: Philosophy and the Crisis of European Humanity," p. 276. The lecture was given in Vienna, on May 7 and 10, 1935. Cited in the text as "Vienna Lecture."

49. "The spiritual *telos* of European humanity, in which the particular telos of particular nations and of individual men is contained, lies in the infinite, is an infinite idea *toward which*, in concealment, *the whole spiritual becoming aims, so to speak*. As soon as it becomes consciously recognized in the development as telos, it necessarily also becomes practical as a goal of the will" (Husserl, "Vienna Lecture," p. 275; emphasis added, except for *telos*).

50. Shortly after drafting these pages, I became acquainted with Jacques Derrida's admirable commentary on Francis Fukuyama's book *The End of History and the Last Man*, specifically: "Permit me to recall very briefly that a certain deconstructive procedure, at least the one in which I thought I had to engage, consisted from the outset in putting into question the onto-theo- but also archeo-teleological concept of history—in Hegel, Marx, or even in the epochal thinking of Heidegger. Not in order to oppose it with an end of history or an anhistoricity, but, on the contrary, in order to show that this onto-theo-archeo-teleology locks up, neutralizes, and finally cancels historicity" (Derrida, *Specters of Marx*, p. 93). I am in total agreement with these words: they validate, after the fact, what the discovery of Derrida brought many of us, and the enthusiasm this generated during the years his thinking emerged. I would only add today that we should read Hegel (and Marx even more, of course) *like this as well*, it seems to me; that is, to spot in them the work of a nonteleological historicity, which also inhabits their concept of history. Which comes down to this: reading Hegel against himself; reading in Hegel the historicity of the process rather than his assigning ends and origins; reading Hegel in movement rather than in his beginning or ending; or, *reading (taking) Hegel right in the middle*. All things considered, this may come close to what Louis Althusser, at a different time, was suggesting with the con-

cept of "process without a subject," in which he saw the "greatest theoretical debt linking Marx to Hegel" ["la dette principale positive de Marx à l'égard de Hegel"] (Althusser, "Marx's Relation to Hegel," p. 183; "Sur le rapport de Marx à Hegel," p. 109).

51. See Barker, "Conception of Europe," in *Legacy of Rome*, ed. Bailey, pp. 45–89.

52. Why favor the democratic model rather than other types of power organization found in Greece? Because, as a clue or marker of the "eventfulness" or the newness of the Greek moment (to remain faithful to Kant's text, quoted earlier), I am using the criterion of *the greatest transfer*, the greatest transmission of history (and stories, and thinking), and of this *public* culture of the "learned public." And we owe Athens the greatest quantum of text transmission, thinking, and *history*. It is in Athens that history begins—with Thucydides, Kant said. It is not an accident that this place, this time, and this point are the ones of the democratic—or *archipolitical*—experience as well.

53. See Guénoun, *L'enlèvement de la politique*.

54. To refer to the political reality of their city-state, Athenians would not have said "Athens" as we do (as in Athens declares war; Athens gives itself a constitution, and so on), but rather "the Athenians."

55. In this regard, it is meaningful that Athens is one of the few Greek political city-states (the only one?) that is not exactly restricted to a city. As a political entity, which is to say, Attica, Athens is already the product of a (small) internal colonization, as it were. Now, more than any of the other cities, it is Athens that brings about the later evolution (as a commercial city, as well as a culture, politics, and way of thinking).

56. See Jean-Jacques Rousseau, *Social Contract*, bk. 3, chaps. 12 ("How the Sovereign Authority Maintains Itself") and 15 ("Deputies or Representatives").

57. I am proposing here that the *public*, the publicness of the public (the publicness of the *thing*—the *res publica*, or what we now term public space), is exactly the supposedly common locus of a nonassembled body politic. The public is the nonassembled common—communication.

58. See Jean-Luc Nancy, introduction to *Penser l'Europe à ses frontières*, pp. 14–16.

59. "In Italy at large the inequality between allies who were really subjects and Roman citizens who acted as sovereigns produced a second and even more menacing cleavage; and though after the Social War a remedy was sought in the grant of Roman citizenship to the allies (88 B.C.), it is obvious that a grant of citizenship which only meant inclusion in a civic assembly that they could not attend was no real bond of union between the Italians and the city of Rome" (Barker, "Conception of Europe," in *Legacy of Rome*, ed. Bailey, p. 56; emphasis added).

60. "[I]t is obvious that a grant of citizenship which only meant inclusion in a civic assembly that they could not attend was no real bond of union between the Italians and the city of Rome, and only proved the inability of the City-State, which, *with the world in its hands*, remained in the sphere of civic ideas, to form

even an Italian State. But it was neither the struggles in Rome nor the cleavage in Italy which in the issue subverted the civic constitution: it was the condition and the problems of the provinces of the Mediterranean littoral" (Barker, "Conception of Europe," in *Legacy of Rome*, ed. Bailey, p. 56; emphasis added).

61. "Thus there is no sharp boundary between the world and the 'great household' of the empire. . . . There is no boundary in principle between the world and the empire" (Patočka, HE, p. 21). "For that reason there can be no substantive separation or difference between the empire and the universe" (p. 34).

62. "Cet empire absolu sur la terre et sur l'onde, / Ce *pouvoir souverain que j'ai sur tout le monde* . . . " (Corneille, *Cinna* 2.1; emphasis added). Trans. in id., *The Cid; Cinna* . . . , p. 138.

63. "Rome, avec une joie et sensible et profonde, / Se démet en vos mains de l'*empire du monde*" (Corneille, *Cinna* 5.3.1765–66; emphasis added). Trans. here from Greenberg, *Canonical States*, p. 126.

64. See my essay "De l'assemblement," in *L'exhibition des mots*.

65. Thus in this sense, this (common) place is the locus of a divergence. It is the (common) place from which the *opposition* of the theological and the political is posited—their opposition, the mimetic rivalry between church and empire. And this gives a slightly different resonance to this double term (the theologico-political), compared to what one often hears, especially in the wake of Carl Schmitt. Indeed, this compound often designates a kind of unique reality or homogeneous medium that is both theological and political, be it at the cost of the difference, between the first and the second part of the compound, of a *secularization*.

If the political were a "secularized theological," then the political would always be theological. And this brings the permanent risk of a kind of dissolution of the specificity or autonomy of the political in relation to the "religious." But such is not the setup suggested here. The locus (Rome) that joins the theological and the political is the space of their rivalry, their competition, their war, and their hatred. Clearly, this war remains incomprehensible if one fails to determine the common space where it takes place, its battlefield: the space of their common provenance, of their kinship, and of their multiple connections. But it is a war, in fact—symbolic, or military—in which politics and "religion," precisely, never cease to posit, display, and reassert their adversity and difference. Decisively, the theologico-political is the *locus of the theologico-political difference*. Or to put it another way, the mark that associates its terms does divide them; the connecting mark that hyphenates them is the very mark of their disunion.

66. Though it does not uniformly concern all of Greece and involves spaces other than Greece, including parts of Rome itself, in time and in space.

67. Toward the Agora, followed by the Pnyx, then the Odeon—successive places in Athens where the *ecclesia* was convened: first the common space of the marketplace, the political, and theater; then the separate space of the political; and finally the unique place of the political and theater together.

68. See Guénoun, *L'enlèvement de la politique*.

69. See Guénoun, *L'exhibition des mots*.

70. On this differentiation, see Dommange, "Sommes-nous capables d'un monde?"

71. See Nancy, *L'oubli de la philosophie*, p. 102; "The Forgetting of Philosophy," in id., *Gravity of Thought*.

72. This question will come up again in pt. IV.

73. Although this book owes a great deal of its original theoretical impetus to Brague, *Europe, la voie romaine* (trans. as *Eccentric Culture*), which analyzes the many links binding Europe to the Roman heritage, I must object to it that Europe is not strictly Roman. Brague shirks two major problems in ascribing Europe solely to Romanity: (1) Rome has heirs other than Europe, or heirs who are not strictly European (in a certain sense, Islam, but also the Eastern Orthodox Church and the Byzantine Empire); (2) Europe, *as Europe*, also has a non-Roman ancestry (Germanity). Europe, then, is at least the *overlapping* of these heterogeneous layers, and one needs to understand by which process this overlapping comes to produce a sharply drawn figure, instead of a shapeless confusion. On this overlap, see Balibar, "Quelles frontières de l'Europe?" in *Penser l'Europe à ses frontières*, p. 94.

74. See the entry for *face à* in the *Petit Robert* (1990 ed.), p. 746.

75. Obviously, the reference here is to Lacan, "Le stade du miroir comme formateur de la fonction du Je," in id., *Écrits*, pp. 93–100; "The Mirror Stage as Formative of the *I* Function as Revealed in Psychoanalytic Experience," in *Écrits: A Selection*, pp. 3–9. See also political commentary on this issue in Dommange, "Le miroir identitaire."

76. And in this way, the movement of figuration is a process of identification. Indeed, if the figure is to be conceived of as a return (that is, as return to *self*, reversal toward one*self*), what it carries out is a return to it*self*, a return identifying oneself as one's selfsame self. This is the fate of the return to the origin, as it were (of the return as producing the origin, as redoing the beginning as the origin): *it comes back to the same*, and posits the origin as the very identity toward which it is coming back—only to fail to recognize itself and to miss itself, in good specular logic.

77. From a factual point of view, one could bolster this hypothesis in various ways. Let us note three of them. First, a somewhat trivial reminder: it seems that the first attested mention of the inhabitants of various European countries (in the modern sense of the word), named "Europenses," occurs in the Mozarabic Chronicle of 754 (once attributed to Isidore, bishop of Beja), which narrates the victory against the Arabs at Poitiers (see Rougemont, *Idea of Europe*, p. 44). Second, more significantly, as various commentators have noted (and often downplayed), most of the plans or projects to unify the states of present-day Europe (often considered forerunners of the idea of a European union) have been projects that their authors have justified as necessary to unite against the Saracen or Turk-

ish enemy. That is true of the first two supposedly "European" schemes: Pierre Dubois's treatise *De recuperatione terrae sancte* (1306), which aimed to organize "Christian society" or the "Christian republic" (since it is still explicitly a question of Christendom, and not Europe) as a kind of federation, for and by "reconquering the Holy Land" (see Rougemont, *Idea of Europe*, pp. 61ff. [and also Pierre Dubois, *Recovery of the Holy Land*—Trans.]; and also Bernard Voyenne, *Histoire de l'idée européenne*, pp. 53–58; and *Traité d'alliance & confédération entre le Roi Louis XI. Georges Roi de Boheme et la Seigneurie de Venise, pour résister au Turc* [1463; *sic;* the title of the treatise, as Rougemont points out, is the one found in the table of contents of volume 2 of the 1747 edition of the *Mémoires* of Philippe de Commynes, which reprints the treatise with corrections, starting on p. 424—Trans.], a project by George or Jiříz Poděbrad, king of Bohemia, inspired by Antoine Marini, a Frenchman). Not to mention, obviously, what will later function as a retrospective ideology in the foundation, or fundraising, of the Crusades. Furthermore, it is remarkable that the "eclipse" of the European idea during several centuries in the Middle Ages, underscored by Rougemont (who firmly believes in "twenty-eight centuries" of Europe [*Idea of Europe*, p. ix]), falls *between* two periods in which the dangers of Islam seem much more active on the continent (and thus during a long period of a kind of latency): between the eighth century, after forays into the south, and the fifteenth century, during the threat in the east—or to put it another way, between the after-Poitiers and the after-Constantinople. Between these two periods, "several centuries of 'European' silence" occurred, and they may well correspond with a provisional and relative stabilization of the relationship between Islam and Christianity (Rougemont, *Idea of Europe*, pp. 49ff.).

78. This proposition is structurally based on Brague, *La voie romaine*, pp. 15–18, but the latter asserts that the east-west schism is what constitutes Europe (p. 13).

79. A more nuanced approach is needed here. We shall come back to this later on.

80. This *fiction* has a complicated but distinct relationship with that described in Lacoue-Labarthe, *La fiction du politique* (trans. as *Heidegger, Art and Politics*).

81. See pt. III of this book, which discusses this topic.

82. The word "straits" = *détroits* in French.—Trans.

83. "Hesiod died at Ascra. Later, when the town was destroyed by the Thespians, the inhabitants who survived the ravage found refuge in Orchomenus. An oracle then gave the order also to collect Hesiod's ashes. They were placed in a tomb at the center of the agora, next to the tomb of Minyas, their eponymous hero, and this means that Hesiod, like Minyas, was honored as a founder of the town. This fact was noted by Aristotle in *Constitution of Orchomenus*" (Mazon, preface, in Hesiod, *Théogonie*, p. ix).

84. See Husserl: "Spiritual Europe has a birthplace. By this I mean not a geographical birthplace, in one land, though this is also true, but rather a spiritual birthplace in a nation" ("Vienna Lecture," p. 276).

85. Dating Europe's constitution as such from the end of the Middle Ages this way clashes with the widely held conviction that Europe was born during the Middle Ages, or at least experienced its first prosperous period as Europe then. This belief ignores the rare but unquestionable appearances of the terms "Europe" and "Europeans" as early as the seventh century, however: see, e.g., what is called Carolingian Europe, "Europa vel regnum Caroli," in the East Frankish chronicles known as the Annals of Fulda (end of the ninth century). In this regard, let us note the following: (1) The constitution of Europe that I am describing is a *process*: while this movement seems to lead to a set configuration after the symmetrical fall of Constantinople, on the one hand, and Granada, on the other, this does not mean that the idea of Europe springs out of nothingness, fully armed, around 1450. It is the fruit of a long elaboration, spread over several centuries, making this concept available, little by little (alongside those of Christianity, the Occident, and the empire), to designate an ongoing process. The same could be said (and will be said: see pt. II of this book) of numerous other historical constellations: the ideas of reformation, revolution, and nation, which take on a stable and determined structure only after undergoing a long formative period. What I am saying here is that the dominant idea of the Middle Ages (if it is possible to encompass such a complex span of time) is not the idea of Europe—far from it—but the idea of Christianity, with its various avatars. A process is nonetheless already at work with its first designations, but this will not precipitate decisively into a continental figure until the fifteenth century. (2) Furthermore, the idea of Europe does not directly impose itself either, as a direct designation for the new situation, during the Renaissance, when Europe had firmly taken shape. For all its explicit statements, the sixteenth century is only moderately European. It is during the seventeenth century that the idea imposes itself and that the name comes into common use as appropriate. Ideas take time. See Rougemont, *Idea of Europe*, pp. 51–123; Pastoureau and Schmitt, *Europe: Mémoire et emblèmes*, pp. 49–140; and Lecoq, "L'Europe, émergence d'une image" (which Laurent Ripart kindly brought to my attention).

86. See Moschus, pp. 190ff. The description takes up more than twenty verses.

87. See Herodotus, *Histories* 4.45.

88. In a sense, the cow too will come back. Europa's brother Cadmus leaves Tyre to look for his sister: "Cadmus and his companions proceeded on foot to the Delphic Oracle. When he asked where Europe might be found, the Pythoness advised him to give up his search and, instead, follow a cow and build a city wherever she should sink down for weariness.... some cowherds... sold him a cow.... This beast he drove eastward through Boeotia, never allowing her to pause until, at last, she sank down where the city of Thebes now stands, and here he erected an image of Athene" (Graves, *Greek Myths*, 58e–f, p. 195, following Pausanias, *Description of Greece*, 9.12.1–2).

89. See Brague, *Europe, la voie romaine*, pp. 30–34.

90. On the sea, see Hegel, *Philosophy of History*, pp. 92ff.

91. For example, Europe crossing over, Europe abducted. This myth is admittedly not Roman, but Rome did not invent the sea; it extended and universalized it into the principle of its space and its world. The marine element calls for some transportation at the origin, and the myth of Europe, a myth of sea- and border-crossers, is a striking example. But foundation is something else: in order to found, one has to tear the origin away from the motion of the marine element, *snatch it away from the sea*, and bury it. "An oracle had warned Hesiod to avoid the 'Nemean' area. Thus Hesiod took care to stay away from the Peloponnesian road. But he went to Oenoë, in Ozolian Lokris, and there he seduced the daughter of his host. The young woman's brothers trapped him in a place precisely called 'Nemea,' killed him, and threw his body into the sea. A pod of dolphins found him; they carried his body to the mouth of the Corinthian Gulf, at Rhion and Molykria. The Lokrians were celebrating the feast of 'Rhia,' at Molykria, when they saw the poet's body, with his marine cortege, wash ashore. They immediately sought out the murderers, found them, and threw them into the ocean. Hesiod's body was buried near Nemea, but the exact place is unknown: the people of Naupaktos are keeping it a secret so as to prevent the Orchomenians, who want to remove the poet's ashes, from doing so" (Paul Mazon, preface to Hesiod, *Théogonie*, pp. xii–xiii). Let us recall that this body is the body of a founder; see n. 83 above.

92. "Her genius was not creative but assimilative; its function was not to originate but to adapt; and not unfrequently, in the process of adaptation, to transmute. Her intellectual activities are, I think, happily described by one of the writers as those of a great 'intermediary'" (H. H. Asquith, introduction to *Legacy of Rome*, ed. Bailey, p. 2). See also Brague, *Europe, la voie romaine*, pp. 30ff.

93. "If this were all, one might be disposed to conclude that Rome had left little of her own to the modern world. . . . There is, however, one great and conspicuous exception—the legacy of Roman Law. This was the domain in which Rome showed constructive genius. She founded, developed, and systematized the jurisprudence of the world" (Asquith, introduction to *The Legacy of Rome*, ed. Bailey, p. 8). [Note that the French translation introduces "civilized" here: "la jurisprudence du monde civilisé" (*Héritage de la Grèce et de Rome*, ed. Finley and Bailey, p. 465).—Trans.] See also Brague, *Europe, la voie romaine*, pp. 30ff.

94. See Hegel quoted in this book, pt. I, §7.

95. Imperial Roman law is the becoming universal, extensive transfer, and topical generalization of this abstraction, and specifically of its Greek metaphysico-mathematical aspect.

96. *Arma, obsides, frumentum, pecuniam imperare*: such Latin phrases, referring to the procurement, respectively, of arms, hostages, corn or wheat, and money, appear in Julius Caesar, *Gallic War*.—Trans.

97. Ernout and Meillet, *Dictionnaire étymologique de la langue latine*, p. 311.

98. "The development of a common law for the empire accompanied, as it helped to promote, the development of a common citizenship. From early days, far

back in the history of the Republic, the praetors had been gradually formulating in their edict a new procedure and system of law, which should be generally applicable to cases in which others than Roman citizens were concerned. . . . Commercial reasons dictated the growth of the new jurisprudence: a law was needed for commercial cases, in which foreign traders were concerned, and which grew more and more frequent as Rome became more and more a commercial city. The *ius civile* of Rome . . . was too archaic, and too much the law of a limited agricultural community, to suit these cases; and the law which the praetors began to apply, and which was thus the foundation of the *ius gentium*, was the more modern merchant law which had come into being, and attained a general validity, in the Mediterranean area. Building on this foundation . . . the praetors formulated in their edict a system of law which had at once the simplicity . . . and the universality of application which would suit the conditions of general Mediterranean trade. This simple and universal law, thus formulated by the praetors, became connected with the conception of a law of nature" (Barker, "Conception of Europe," in *Legacy of Rome*, ed. Bailey, p. 68).

99. Thus far I have used the two terms "Christianity" and "religion" parsimoniously, because of my circumspect approach to their apparent self-evidence. One would have to produce the concept of "religion" (e.g., Christian religion) with some rigor and accept that the (Christian) religious *as such* is not contemporaneous with the events discussed here (that is, the constitution of the empire and the church). The constitution of Christianity, and thus of the "Christian religion," comes later and is something else. Overlooking this, in a way, would be like refusing to take into account the birth of aesthetics during the Enlightenment with the pretext that cathedrals and frescoes already existed during the Middle Ages. But we have to admit that refusing to think of the assembly (*ecclesia*) of the first disciples of Christ *as religion* is consonant with a certain (Protestant) theology, Karl Barth's, for example. That is too bad—or good. See pt. II, § 12 of this book.

100. See pt. III of this book.

101. At least the first part, "neither Greek nor Jew": see Gal. 3:28, Rom. 10:12, Eph. 2:14–15, Col. 3:11.

102. "There remains another branch of Literature . . . in which Rome can truly be said to have led the way: that of Letter-writing. Cicero was here the pioneer, and in his eight or nine hundred letters he has shown himself a master of all the resources of epistolary Art" (Asquith, introduction, *Legacy of Rome*, ed. Bailey, p. 3). Cicero: according to this hypothesis, the consolidation of this genre barely preceded the formation of the empire.

103. Hegel, *Philosophy of Right* [Dyde], p. 233; emphasis added and text modified to approximate more closely the German text and its French translation, which introduce the notions of legal relations and contracts. German text: "So bringt sie ferner durch diß größte Medium der Verbindung entfernte Länder in die Beziehung des Verkehrs, eines den Vertrag einführenden rechtlichen Verhältnisses" (Hegel, *Grundlinien der Philosophie des Rechtes*, p. 234). French translation

cited by the author: "ce trafic lui-même crée des rapports juridiques où s'introduit le contrat" (Hegel, *Principes de la philosophie du droit*, para. 247, pp. 252–53). Dyde's original translation is as follows: "By means of the sea, the greatest medium of communication, the desire for wealth brings distant lands into an intercourse, which leads to commercial exchange."—Trans.

104. "Heaven's high providence in vain / Has sever'd countries with the estranging main [i.e., sea—Trans.]" (Horace *Carm.* 1.3, in *The Odes and Carmen Saeculare*).

105. Hegel, *Philosophy of Right*, pp. 233ff.; emphasis added and trans. and punctuation slightly modified.

106. Apropos of this last segment, the [French] translator and commentator Robert Derathé adds the following note: "As E. Fleischmann notes (op. cit., p. 250 [i.e., Fleischmann, *La philosophie politique de Hegel*]), this is an allusion to Fichte, who writes in 'Der geschlossene Handelsstaat' [The Closed Commercial State] (bk. 3, beginning of chap. 3): 'Certain parts of the surface of the earth, together with their inhabitants, are visibly determined by nature to form whole political entities. Their entire area is kept apart from the rest of the earth by large rivers, seas, inaccessible mountains. . . . It is these hints from nature—regarding what should remain together or be separated—to which one refers when one speaks of the *natural boundaries* of realms: a consideration one should take far more seriously than one commonly does'" (Hegel, *Principes de la philosophie du droit*, p. 252n; Fichte, "Der geschlossene Handelsstaat" [The Closed Commercial State], p. 480).

107. Dr. Jean-Marc Fischer, who for years has lived and worked with the Macuna people in the Amazonian region of Colombia, has called the zone where they gather "Apaporis," after the name of a tributary of the Amazon River along which they are scattered—and this designates their meeting. "Water is in fact the uniting element, and it is the mountains which create divisions. . . . France and Spain, for example, are separated by the Pyrenees. . . . Mountains create divisions between nations, customs, and characters. *But a country is constituted by the river which flows through it, and both banks of the river properly belong to one and the same country.* Silesia is the basin of the Oder, Bohemia and Saxony are the valley of the Elbe, and Egypt is the valley of the Nile" (Hegel, *Philosophy of World History* [Nisbet], p. 159; emphasis added).

108. "Similarly, history tells us that Brittany and Britain were united for centuries under English rule, and it took many wars to sever the links between them. Sweden formerly possessed Finland, as well as Courland, Livonia, and Estonia. Norway, however, did not belong to Sweden, but had a far more cordial relationship with Denmark" (Hegel, *Philosophy of World History* [Nisbet], p. 160). To choose a random Mediterranean example, the links between Oran (Algeria) and Valence (France), or Oran and Alicante (Spain), exhibit an undeniable, centuries-long vitality, despite the religious, political, national, and thus military, barriers that have kept the south and north Mediterranean coasts apart.

109. Here is another ordinary example, picked up during a trip, which confirms Hegel's remarks: residents of Bergen (Norway) today sometimes mention their city's stronger ties until the twentieth century with London than with the Norwegian hinterland. We can see that this is not a matter of proximity. Here Hegel goes very far: "Cadiz used to have closer links with America than with Madrid" (Hegel, *Philosophy of World History* [Nisbet], p. 159).

110. Fichte, "Der geschlossene Handelsstaat" [The Closed Commercial State], p. 480; emphasis added.

111. Hegel, *Philosophy of World History* (Nisbet), p. 160.

112. "Allow me a piece of advice when working: there is always an advantage, when analyzing concepts, in starting from very concrete and simple situations and not from philosophical precedents, *or even from the problems* as such (the one, the multiple, etc.)—for example, regarding multiplicities, you have to start from, What is a *pack* (of animals, different from a single animal)? What is an *ossuary*? Or, as you have done so well, What is a *relic*? And regarding events, What is five P.M.?" (Deleuze, preface, in Martin, *Variations*, p. 8).

113. Hegel, *Philosophy of History* (Sibree), p. 95.

114. "Elle est retrouvée. / Quoi?—L'Éternité. / C'est la mer allée / Avec le soleil [It has been found again. / What?—Eternity. / It is the sea gone away / With the sun]" (Rimbaud, *Œuvres*, p. 160).

115. See Brague, *Europe, la voie romaine*, p. 9.

116. Or even other empires. The (truly fascinating) question regarding what the very idea of empire owes to orientalism remains to be discussed in depth. See Barker, "Conception of Europe," in *Legacy of Rome*, ed. Bailey. See also Jan Patočka's hypotheses, discussed in pt. III of this book.

117. See Derrida, *L'autre cap*; the famous quotation by Paul Valéry appears on p. 26. In this, Rougemont sees a topos of geographical discourse, more particularly in the eighteenth and nineteenth centuries. [See Rougemont, also quoting Valéry, in *Idea of Europe*: "'Will Europe become *what it is in reality*—that is, a little cape on the continent of Asia? . . . ' Elsewhere Valéry calls Europe 'a kind of cape of the old continent, a western appendix to Asia'" (pp. 30 and 30n26).—Trans.]

118. Hegel, *Philosophy of World History* (Nisbet), p. 196. And he goes on, "The sea provides that wholly peculiar outlet which Asiatic life lacks, the outlet which enables life to step beyond itself. It is this which has invested European political life with the principle of individual freedom." We may juxtapose to these remarks facts (or fantasies) such as: "Europe is the continent of water. . . . This restless, infinitely carved-up peninsula, is in fact the most watered place in the world: there is a kilometer of coast for every 289 square kilometers of land. Water seeps in everywhere, travels upward into broad estuaries or fjords, and surrounds coastal islands or islets. There is no distance from the sea that much exceeds a thousand kilometers, and most places are much closer (Switzerland, known as a continental country, is less than six hundred kilometers away from the ocean and three hundred from the

Adriatic Sea).... But water is not only at the periphery. Three great liquid avenues start from the 'water tower of Europe' bordered by the triangle formed by Bern, Stuttgart, and St. Moritz, and they have been (and still are) the axes of the West's traffic. In the webbing of this primary network, a system of rivers takes shape, which harmoniously distributes water everywhere, diversifies broad connecting basins, unfolds, and then meets the sea" (Voyenne, *Histoire de l'idée européenne*, p. 12).

119. And this brings about the ambiguous heritage of Rome for Europe: "the Roman Empire could not have arisen in the continent" (Hegel, *Philosophy of World History* [Nisbet], p. 196). Like Rome, Europe is constituted by its relationship with the sea. But as a continent, Rome was impossible—for Europe, of course, this is more equivocal: Europe is really a continent, but a noncontinental continent, as it were, a peninsula. (See the theme of Europe as a bigger Greece, e.g., in Rougemont, *Idea of Europe*, p. 31.)

120. As we know, this is what Marxism will thematize as its "three sources": English political economy, French socialism, and German philosophy.

121. See Balibar, "L'Europe après le communisme," p. 82.

122. See Guénoun, "Sur les (prétendues) sorties du (prétendu) communisme."

123. See Balibar, "L'Europe après le communisme."

124. As Derrida puts it; see id., *Schibboleth*, p. 96, and *Specters of Marx*.

125. As Karl Marx proposed to do with Hegelian dialectics.—Trans.

PART II: ON NATIONAL REVOLUTION

1. Whereas Muslims who preserved their religious allegiance remained after Islam lost political control elsewhere (e.g., in Aquitaine and Sicily), in Andalusia it was wiped from the map, according to Stétié, *Lumière sur lumière*. Though Stétié's argument is valid only for western Europe, and the situation in the Balkans was different, it perhaps corresponds in some respects to my characterization of the constitution of Europe as the repression [*refoulement*] of Islam. However, Islam is making a comeback, as with all repressed memories.

2. See the debate over whether Turkey belongs in Europe.

3. See Brague, *Europe, la voie romaine*, pp. 108–20.

4. The Eastern Roman Empire thus invokes Greece to reflect on its difference with Rome. (From Fichte to Heidegger, Germanity similarly claimed to be a return to Hellenicity, above and against the reference to Rome and the Latin legacy.) Nevertheless, Byzantium remains the Eastern Roman Empire: Constantinople is a Rome redone, reproduced, and doubled. See *Histoire de l'Europe*, ed. Carpentier and Lebrun, pp. 185–86, esp.: "When Constantine decided to found Constantinople, he intended to reproduce Rome on the shores of the Bosporus. Even if it was necessary to twist the map a bit to find seven hills in it, the city's organization strove to reproduce the ancient city in Latium" (p. 184).

5. On the long genesis of the European idea during the Middle Ages, see, e.g.,

Lecoq, "L'Europe, émergence d'une image." The awareness of a purely "western" singularity evidently played a large part in the constitution of what *we* call Europe, that is to say, western Europe. This related, of course, to the schism with the Eastern Orthodox Church, the existence of the Eastern Roman Empire, and the ongoing rivalry with it. But let us reiterate that this difference, no matter how important, does not seem characteristic of the idea of Europe in this process. What is worked up in it again is simply the idea of the Occident, which does not clearly delineate Europe, since the debate about what constitutes eastern Europe is endless. Its eastern limit is Europe's undecidability. As for the southern limit, there is no difficulty in determining it. One has to read the process of Europe's formation within the history of its relationship with Islam, notably in preaching and raising armies for the Crusades and being involved in them. Notwithstanding that it has often been said that this was when Europe was formed, however it was more in the nature of a gestation or genesis: Europe takes shape, no doubt, but it does not *recognize* itself as such—and does not take on this name. For Europe as a figure clearly to come to light, it will require the image (and the imaginary) of the continent, which is not drawn up until the late fifteenth century, in the double and opposite movement of the fall of Constantinople and the takeover of Granada.

6. "The essence of a thing never appears at the outset, but in the middle, in the course of its development, when its strength is assured" (Deleuze, *Movement-Image*, p. 3). Approximately during the fifteenth century because *approaching* things in their movement is an *approximation*, the capture of processes and propagating waves, and not the figural vision of fixed essences.

7. It cannot be regarded as a coincidence that the collapse of Europe's western extreme coincides with its delimitation as a continent, forcing it to formulate its difference from the New World by attempting to set a new marker. This will later influence two typologies of Europeanism: the first seeking to integrate Europe—western Europe, in essence—and (North) America into an all-encompassing Occidentalism; the second, to resituate Europe at the center of the world, between its age-old east and the newly appeared west: a Europe of the middle, central Europe. And thus the two problematic parts of Europe (western Europe, central Europe) will always correspond to two very different ideas of European specificity and will not be able simply to be two distinct neighboring regions: each carries its own supposed essence of Europe, a destinal affirmation divergent from the other. Finally (and mainly) the appearance of America *reproduces*—*exactly*—the initial gesture from which Europe came forth: torn away from a native land, carried away overseas, toward an unknown, nameless land mass across the way. In this sense, America is evidently a remade and doubled Europe, and this will not fail to have effects upon Europe's own awareness of itself during its decisive configuration as the old continent.

8. Charles V's relations with Rome are more than ambiguous: to *bring back* Germany to Rome presupposes remaking Rome, even if it means breaking it. See Chastel, *Le sac de Rome*, passim.

9. The configuration of these places is often *prescribed* by the old divisions of the empire, and the kingdoms confine themselves to the spaces of old imperial provinces. We shall come back to this in the context of the Germanic kingdom.

10. Benveniste, *Indo-European Language and Society*, pp. 311–12.

11. Clearly, the limits of the kingdom are not those of the crown lands or royal domain. However, it is the determination on the ground of the royal domain that constitutes its heart and model, which stands out increasingly in the course of history. It is the royal domain's power to extend and progressively become homogenized (through annexation and the subordination of vassals) that tends to absorb the kingdom and blend it with itself. The kingdom, which might be nothing but a coalition of seigneuries, is established and turns into a kingdom starting from its local determination, and the royal domain provides its dynamic pole, its territorial scheme, and its base. See the expression *domaine du royaume* [royal domain] in *Dictionnaire historique de la langue française*, ed. Rey, 1: 622.

12. "Rex Franciae est imperator in regno suo": see Berl, *Europe et Asie*, p. 300; Beaune, *Naissance de la nation France*, pp. 56–57 and n. 135; Krynen, *Empire du roi*.

13. In the course of these analyses, it will have become clear to the reader that the provisionally adopted concept and designation of the *theologico-political* are ill-suited, on both sides of the structure. "Theological" is not a suitable term for ecclesiality construed as the element of the common or commonality, that which comes to be assembled. Rather, it designates a discourse about gods—and this is not the targeted object here, even if one should ponder the mutual connection of these notions. And "political" is even less suitable on some levels, since this whole matter comes about as a division of the political, which splits into "sovereignty" versus "community." In certain respects, the term "political" might even better suit the church: archeologically, at least, the political is the agency of that which assembles itself. (Let us note, for example, that the first division between the "King's Two Bodies" analyzed by Ernst Kantorowicz in an English context differentiates between the "natural Body" [which is ordinary and human] and the "Body politic" of the king. Now, in this opposition, the "Body politic" relates to "the mediaeval concept of the king's *character angelicus*. The body politic of kingship appears as a likeness of the 'holy sprites and angels,' because it represents, like the angels, the Immutable within Time" [Kantorowicz, *King's Two Bodies*, p. 8]. Here, the political is thus exactly the ecclesial—the supposed theological, if you will.) If I have clung to this (double) term, it is to bring out the tension between the hypotheses formulated here and the analyses circulating nowadays, and to signal toward some fields of effectiveness that these analyses cover: the indestructible relation, since Roman times, that links questions of power and "religious" questions, in their dissociation *and* their agreement. We shall come to terms with the "religious" later on. Unfortunately, the term "ecclesio-imperial" is not a winner as far as euphony is concerned. What to do?

14. My reticence regarding this formulation is understandable, since it assumes the equivalence of the political with the field of sovereignty, which is inappropri-

ate inasmuch as anachronistic for the period in question, in which the term "political" was not used in this sense, and has the drawback of blocking any reflection about the rise and the constitution of *politics*, in the continuation of the process.

15. "The Capetians persist in preserving the original character of kingship. The coronation and the sacred character of kingship are revered . . . and the role of the royal minister approaches that of the bishop by design. Liturgical and other practices, such as the king's [therapeutic] touching of sufferers of scrofula [for this reason called "the King's evil" in England—Trans.], reinforced the importance of religious and mystical elements" (Genet, *Le monde au moyen âge*, p. 92). Or, in a wider context: "The king is anointed by the Lord . . . he should not be counted among the laymen: 'His separation from them is proper,' said a polemicist from that time. 'For anointing him with holy oil has made him partake in the priesthood'" (Bréhier, *Antiquité et moyen âge*, p. 101). But this sacerdotal charge is already present in the etymological characterization: "This dual notion is present in the important expression *regere fines, a religious act*. . . . This is the operation carried out by the *high priest* before a temple or a town is built and it consists in the delimitation on a given terrain of a *sacred plot of ground* [*l'espace consacré*]. The magical character of this operation is evident: what is involved is the delimitation of the interior and the exterior, the realm of the sacred and the realm of the profane, the national territory and foreign territory. The tracing of these limits is carried out by the person invested with the highest powers, the *rex*" (Benveniste, *Indo-European Language and Society*, pp. 311–12; emphasis added). See also Curtius, *Die französische Kultur*, p. 58. In the English example, the symmetry of functions was especially clear: the king is "pope in his realm" (Kantorowicz, *King's Two Bodies*, p. 19).

16. "'Singularizing oneself' carries away with it the actual, practical, and empirical individual, which is to say, the body. For Aristotle and then for Thomas Aquinas himself, individualism resides in materiality. Aquinas fashioned a particular concept for this, the concept of *materia signata*, that is, 'designated' or determined matter. Completely determined matter, *materia signata vel individualis*, is matter one regards with the determined dimensions of a singular body—that is to say (as the same text, *De ente et essentia*, puts it), *hoc os et haec caro*, this bone and this flesh. This determination, which is also the display, or material, physical, extended, and corporeal exposition, is what I shall call the last and ultimate transcendental trait of the singular. . . . Singular ones are not possible as pure spirits" (Jean-Luc Nancy, "Un sujet?" in *Homme et sujet*, ed. Weil, p. 101).

17. This could spark a problematization of the sacred (which I have left out as a concept until now). The sacrament would be that which the church lays or deposits (as the sign of itself) upon a person or a thing. The sacrament is an ecclesial deposit upon a body. And this *deposit of a sign* de-sign-ates an *injection, or infusion, of being*: what is injected (condensed) in a body in this way? The being of the church, of the assembly: that is to say, being-in-common. The sacrament, in depositing a

sign onto a body, is a sign of the infusion or the condensation of the common in the singular. It thus becomes understandable that the *essential* sacrament, the archsacrament, is the Eucharist. (See pt. III of this book.) From time immemorial, the common, inasmuch as it is assembled, has sought refuge outside of the world, in the beyond of another world removed from the authority of the empire. The sacrament, then, is the deposit of this commonality (which is removed from the world) onto a corporeal singularity. That is why, as many have noted, the sacred can appear in the operation of separation (of the delimitation or disjunction of the sacred and the profane). This dissociation pertains to the world and its ecclesial double, *marked upon the world*: in truth, it bears the mark of the common, which has withdrawn. The sacrament is the deposit upon the body of the sign of this (withdrawn) commonality, which thus comes back—condensed—in the body.

18. On the church and the body of Christ, see pt. III of this book.

19. Which is to say, the territory as an abstract land, defined by a *deed*, a record of ownership, competence, or scope.

20. Alain Rey's *Dictionnaire historique de la langue française* says of the term *royaume* [kingdom]: "masculine noun; first, *reialme* (ca. 1080 C.E.) then *roiaume* (ca. 1196) and *royaume* (13th cent.), is an alteration, in connection with 'royal,' of *réiame*, roiame, 'state governed by a king,' traced to the end of the 12th cent. and until the middle of the 14th cent., but probably older. This word, taken to come from the Latin *rex, regis* ('king'), in fact represents the Latin *regimen, -inis*, 'direction, government,' which gave the more academic *régime*. Old Provençal, which uses all three terms *regeme, regeime*, and *realme* for 'state governed by a king,' supports this hypothesis" (2: 1844). It is worth noting that this meaning (of the kingdom as the state), the main one in French, is unknown in Latin, which possesses equivalent terms for *roi* [king], "direction," and "government," but not the term *royaume*. This entity is post-Roman.

21. Hegel, *Philosophy of Right* (Dyde), states: "[258] The state, which is the realized substantive will, having its reality in the particular self-consciousness raised to the plane of the universal, is absolutely rational. . . . Rationality, viewed abstractly, consists in the thorough unity of universality and individuality. . . . [260] The state is the embodiment of concrete freedom. In this concrete freedom, personal individuality and its particular interests, as found in the family and civic community, have their complete development. In this concrete freedom, too, the rights of personal individuality receive adequate recognition. These interests and rights pass partly of their own accord into the interest of the universal. Partly, also, do the individuals recognize by their own knowledge and will the universal as their own substantive spirit, and work for it as their own end" (pp. 240–48). In Hegelian terms, this moment of the universal is that of the union of universality and singularity. See also Kant, "Das Staatsrecht," in *Kant's Werke* [Ak.], 6: 315 ["Rechtslehre," para. 47; in English, Kant, "Doctrine of Right," in *The Metaphysics of Morals*, trans. Mary Gregor].

22. But it is a process: the kingdom is not a completed unit, but, on the contrary, the movement of unification of multiple functions, which progressively form a web of links (the texture of their organization as a state). "The *royal domain* . . . roughly extends from the Oise River to the Loire, around the episcopal cities of Senlis, Paris, Orleans, and Sens. The Capetian ruler is Count of Paris, Dreux, and Orléans. . . . He keeps in touch with the 'royal bishoprics' (strategically, Bourges, Reims, and Langres are the most important ones). All the same, one should not picture this domain to be united and homogeneous, like a modern territory: it is a composite set of rights and powers, over which lords and vassals harshly fought" (Genet, *Le monde au moyen âge*, p. 90).

23. Notably the Gallican and Anglican churches.

24. See the French law on the separation of the churches and the state of December 9, 1905.

25. And therefore also the nobility and the clergy.

26. In French, "l'identité de l'État, c'est bien lui," echoing Louis XIV's statement, "l'État, c'est moi."—Trans.

27. Rey's *Dictionnaire historique de la langue française* says of the term *religion*: "It seems that unlike other languages, even Indo-European ones, western languages have given a specialized sense to a term distinguishing the apparatus of beliefs and rites from all other social institutions. This break and this transfer correspond to a distinct thinking about an area that had never been thought to be separated, since archaic societies do not isolate sacrality from sociality, the constitution of the social being intrinsically religious for them" (2: 1758). This dissociation of the socialized and the sacralized only takes effect when several "sacralities" are distinguished amid a common sociality, a process that obviously precedes any possible "desacralization." Or in other words, "de-sacralization" appears first as another sacrality—as religion.

28. This etymology is doubtful. See ibid. and discussion of the term in Benveniste, *Indo-European Language and Society*. In any case, the "re" is shared by the two main etymological hypotheses—*religare* and *relegere*.

29. See Benveniste, *Indo-European Language and Society*, chap. 7, "Religion and Superstition," pp. 516–28.

30. "What does *religio* mean? The question has been discussed since ancient times, and even then scholars were unable to agree. Modern scholars remain no less divided. Opinions waver between two alternatives each of which is favoured from time to time and finds new supporters" (ibid., p. 518).

31. "It seems to us that this sense, which is demonstrated by ancient usage without the slightest ambiguity, imposes as the only possible interpretation of *religio* the one given by Cicero, who attached it to *legere*" (ibid., p. 521).

32. Ibid., pp. 521–22.

33. One should perhaps attempt to think through this the other way around: every party, perhaps, is religious in some fashion. I am not proposing a bland

typology of behaviors (scissionism, sectarism, and so on), but something more radical, which would require some research about the *constitution of politics* from religious division. This is a task that goes beyond the limits of the present work.

34. "Reformation" is a rather peculiar term. If one follows Benveniste's interpretation, and "religion" signifies to "take up again a choice already made," "*retractare*," "to revise the decision which results from it," it designates exactly what is proper or essential to the religious disposition as such. Reforming implies reconstituting the supposedly initial religious choice, coming back to it and re-producing it, making it resurface in its purity at its origin and its originality: because of this, reformation, which is always a return to the (supposed) origin of the cult, breaks with its dominant form—a heterodoxy posited as a recovered orthodoxy. In this sense, one may say that all the founders of religions have been reformers, and every great religion the product of reformation gestures: by Moses, Jesus, and Muhammad, but also Gautama Buddha, Confucius, and Luther.

35. Reconquista of the peninsula—Europe, that is, which earned them the dignified designation of Catholic King and Queen (granted by Pope Alexander VI in 1496).

36. Documented in Beaune, *Naissance de la nation France*.

37. See Sieyès, *Qu'est-ce que le Tiers-État?* pp. 12–13; *What Is the Third Estate?* (Blondel), p. 60.

38. It is best, however, to avoid giving too much fetishistic credit to these archeologies. It would be dangerous as well as simplistic and simply wrong to insist on construing European divisions on the basis of an indefinite reproduction of differences in origin, that is, Germanity versus Romanity—all the more so since a closer look shows these matters to be far from simple. Let us rather say that, even if this old rift has left actual traces in the "country," and its local or social delineations, it is above all true that when the new divisions occur (and religious scission is one of them), they can summon up the old delineation as an imaginary recourse to help identify or guarantee the new break. Luther keeps invoking the old division to think up the new one. But it is a recourse, a *fixation*: the appeal to an image while aiming at an identity and ensuring it. It is not a predetermination of the new by the old.

39. See Michelet, *Renaissance et Réforme*, pp. 358ff.; "La Réforme française," ibid., pp. 419ff.; and sections of "Les guerres de religion," ibid., pp. 496–616.

40. The *Grand dictionnaire encyclopédique Larousse* states: "Signed by Henri IV at Nantes on April 13, 1598. . . . Declared 'perpetual and irrevocable,' this Edict grants Protestants the freedom of conscience in the entire kingdom and authorizes them fully and freely to practice their worship . . . in two localities of each bailiwick . . . and in the castles of lords with the power of life and death [*hauts justiciers*]; but Protestant worship remains outlawed at the court, in Paris, and within a radius of five miles around the capital, as well as in a few episcopal cities.

Protestants will have to observe Catholic holidays and pay taxes to the clergy. They will enjoy all civil rights and be admitted to colleges, universities, and hospitals, and be allowed to hold public office. Chambers . . . composed of a balance of Catholic and Protestant magistrates and established at Paris, Castres, Grenoble, and Bordeaux will deal with their judicial proceedings. [Protestants] keep the right to have their own consistories, colloquies, and synods at the provincial and national levels, and for eight years are granted about one hundred fortified places [*places de sûreté*] whose [Protestant] governors and garrisons will be paid by the king. . . . With this act of tolerance, the principle of the unity of faith, considered . . . the most solid foundation of the unity of the state, is officially abandoned. Very audacious for its time . . . the Edict of Nantes turns the French state into a Catholic and Protestant state, and its king, who is Catholic [having converted from Protestantism—D.G.], the protector of Protestant churches"(7: 7268). This is a rather strange outcome twenty-five years after the massacres. The theologico-political unity seems split along a vertical line, prolonging the unity implemented at the head (in the person of the converted king) with a kind of slit from top to bottom, slicing the trunk of the kingdom into two part(ie)s, with each religion garnering high-level dignitaries, nobles of various ranks, local magistrates, towns, assemblies, and fortified strongholds.

41. Edict of the Revocation of the Edict of Nantes, signed by Louis XIV on October 18, 1685, "which ended the legal existence of Protestantism in France (except in Alsace). . . . This edict . . . makes Protestant worship illegal, orders the demolition of [Protestant] churches, the closing of Reformed schools, compulsory Catholic baptism and marriage, [and] the expulsion of pastors who refuse to convert" (ibid., 9: 8957–58).

42. Huguenots fled to the Netherlands, England, Germany, and Switzerland (ibid.).

43. Benveniste, *Indo-European Language and Society*, p. 307.

44. In the early 1980s, in thinking about mass dissidence—for example, in Poland—the emerging concept of "society" in this sense mattered (see *La Pologne, une société en dissidence*, ed. Erard and Zygier).

45. *Dictionnaire historique de la langue française*, ed. Rey, 2: 2055.

46. All things considered, this metaphor—a push from the bottom to the top, where what comes back or returns does not necessarily reoccur at the same point, but instead resurfaces here or there—is more fitting than that of a return to the initial place. *Résurgence*: "reappearance on the surface, as a spring with a large output, of an underground body of water" (ibid., p. 1789).

47. Ibid., p. 2055.

48. See pt. IV of this book.

49. *Surrection*, "The use of the word is attested for 'the act of rising' (1507, *surrexion*). It is seemingly not used before the beginning of the twentieth century, at which time its usage becomes geological, to mean (1904) the uplift in one piece

of a zone of the terrestrial crust. Its figurative meanings are 'apparition, emergence' (about 1950)" (ibid., p. 2056).

50. Ibid., p. 1800.

51. To pursue the medical fantasy: cancer is the pathology of the repressed (reemerging).

52. See Weber, *Protestant Ethic*, esp. chap. 2.

53. The said process will encounter the effects of extension that the revolutionary sequence—let's say the French one, which is the focus here—itself produces, though this sequence is not global and worldwide in its first manifestation, but *revolutionary*, precisely—coming back to the place of what has been repressed. It nevertheless has global effects (1830, 1848, and so on), just as capitalism or Protestantism soon produce revolutionary effects (e.g., the American Revolution). This serves as evidence that the resurgence of the repressed fits rather badly within the framework that the figure of the return outlines for it (the idea of revolution). It always-already overflows it. Later on, revolution will determine the world, the world as a whole, as the only place to which it can come back. A worldwide revolution, then. But this comes later: the theme of the revolution is not yet articulated in this way in the phase in which I am trying to characterize it. On the contrary: at this point, the world and society stand as the two poles of a dual choice.

54. Alternatively: the corporeality of the kingdom is not "only" metaphorical; rather, it is its metaphoricity (its transferential quality) that constitutes the effectivity of the political as such. The transfer of this corporeality to a collective entity makes up politics, in the modern sense of the word (see pt. III of this book).

55. To describe the metaphorical logic of the murder of the king by decapitation is not to approve it. I unhesitatingly place myself in the camp of the revolutionaries but refuse to take pleasure in or justify this murder. One can try to explain a murder in terms of its circumstances or its time period—but I am denying this one any *justice*. It is time to stop subscribing to the logic of murder, *regardless of its circumstances*. Instead, let us think that in this act, the revolution was caught up in its own imaginary and figural ploy—that, in this, it manifested its entrapment by the imaginary of the return (of revenge, vengeance, debt, and capital punishment). Which is to say—in prevision—its defeat.

56. "Populus autem non omnis hominum coetus quoquo modo congregatus, sed coetus multitudinis iuris consensu et utilitatis communione congregatus" [the people is not every group of men, associated in any manner, but is the coming together of a considerable number of men who are united by a common agreement about law and rights] (Cicero, *Republic* 1.25). No doubt, one of the specificities of the *dēmos* is that it is summoned to the assembly. *Dēmos* differs from *ethnos*, for example, in that the latter word "is not solely used of men but also of animals, such as bees, whereas *dēmos* is never used in such applications" (Benveniste, *Indo-European Language and Society*, p. 372).

57. This memory persists in a certain determination of the people *inasmuch as they are the people*, which is to say, as being, substratum, and substance of the common, which "conquers" sovereignty only on this account and at this price: as subject—subject of sovereignty, sovereign-subject. See my book *L'enlèvement de la politique*.

58. *Dictionnaire historique de la langue française*, ed. Rey, 2: 1306.

59. One can also see this (and though the correlation is too blunt and calls for a sharper elaboration, it is valid in its principle) in the tracing of borders and selection of elites by the French colonial and the Russo-Soviet empires. In each case, what was involved was the local refiguration of a project of universality. One could more broadly say that *something national* as such comes up in the de-composition of empires. "Since the end of the Roman Empire, or rather since the disruption of the Empire of Charlemagne, Western Europe appears to be divided into nations. . . . Nations, understood in this way, are a new feature in history. Antiquity knew them not," Renan observes in *What Is a Nation?* (p. 63). On such "production of nations," see Dommange, "Le miroir identitaire," and Guénoun, "Sur les (prétendues) sorties du (prétendu) communisme" (this hypothesis owes much to Étienne Balibar; see esp. Balibar and Wallerstein, *Races, nations, classes*).

60. *Gens de robe* in French.—Trans.

61. Sieyès, *What Is the Third Estate?* (Blondel), p. 72; see also chap. 2.

62. *Qu'est-ce que le Tiers-État?* opens with the famous formula: "The plan of this book is fairly simple. We must ask ourselves three questions. 1. What is the Third Estate? *Everything*. 2. What has it been until now in the political order? *Nothing*. 3. What does it want to be? *Something*" (ibid., p. 51).

63. "The old aristocracy detests new nobles. . . . Thus it relegates the other nobles to the order of the Third Estate to which, obviously, they no longer belong" (ibid., p. 62).

64. Ibid., p. 57; emphasis added.

65. Ibid.

66. Ibid., p. 61. (The emphasis on the repeated word "common" is mine. Sieyès emphasizes "one."—D.G.)

67. Ibid., p. 58.

68. The story is wonderfully told in Michelet, *French Revolution*.

69. "On the 15th of June, Sieyes, with boldness and prudence, demanded that the Commons should assume the title of *Assembly of the known and acknowledged representatives of the French nation*. . . . They knew Sieyes too well not to suspect that this proposal was a step to lead to another, bolder and more decisive. . . . And indeed, on the second day of the battle, the light burst forth. Two deputies served as precursors to Sieyes. M. Legrand proposed that the Assembly should constitute itself a *General* Assembly. . . . M. Galand demanded that . . . the Assembly should constitute itself the legitimate and active Assembly *of the representatives of the French nation*. Sieyes then laid aside every obscurity and circumlocution, and

proposed the title of *National Assembly*. . . . On the following morning, at the moment of voting. . . . The different motions might be reduced to three, or rather to two:—1st. That of Sieyes—*National* Assembly. 2ndly. That of Mounier—Assembly of the Representatives of the *Major* part of the Nation, in the absence of the *Minor* part. The equivocal formula of Mirabeau ['representatives of the French people'—D.G.] was equivalent to Mounier's, as the word *people* could be taken in a limited sense, and as the *major part of the nation*. . . . With Mounier's arithmetic and unjust justness, and with Mirabeau's equivocation, the nation remained *a class*, and the fixed property—the land—constituted also *a class* in the face of the nation . . . Sieyes, being put to the vote at once, had near five hundred votes for him, and not one hundred against him. Therefore the Assembly was proclaimed *National Assembly*. . . . In presence of a multitude of four thousand deeply affected spectators, the six hundred deputies, standing in profound silence, with up-raised hands and contemplating the calm, honest countenance of their president, listened to him whilst reading the formula [of the oath—D.G.], and exclaimed: 'We swear.' A universal sentiment of respect and religion filled every heart" (Michelet, *French Revolution*, pp. 98–103).

70. "The king, still undecided, . . . was contented to command (in order to prevent the clergy from uniting with the Third Estate) that the hall be shut on the morrow (Saturday June 20th); the pretext was the preparations necessary for a royal meeting to be held on the Monday. . . . At eight o'clock, the hour appointed the night before, [Bailly, the president—D.G.] repaired to the door of the hall with a great number of deputies. Being stopped by the sentinels, he protested against the hindrance, and *declared the meeting convened*. Several young members made a show of breaking open the door; the officer commanded his soldiers to arm. . . . Behold our *new kings*, put out, kept out of doors, like unruly scholars [*écoliers* (schoolboys—Trans.)]. Behold them wandering about in the rain, among the people, on the Paris avenue. *All agree about the necessity of holding a meeting, of assembling*. Some shout, Let us go to the Place d'Armes! Others, to Marly! Another, to Paris! . . . . The deputy Guillotin made a less hazardous motion, to repair to Old Versailles, and take up their quarters in the Tennis-court [Jeu-de-Paume]—a miserable, ugly, poor, and unfurnished building, but the better on that account. [The Assembly—D.G.] remained standing all day long, having scarcely a wooden bench" (ibid., pp. 106–7). "Behold them now in the Tennis-court [Jeu-de-Paume—Trans.], assembled in spite of the king. But what are they going to do? . . . It was one of the moderate party, Mounier of Grenoble, who proposed to the Assembly the celebrated declaration: That wherever it might be forced to unite, *there was ever the National Assembly* [up to this point, emphasis added]; that *nothing could prevent it* from continuing its deliberations. And, till the completion and establishment of the constitution, it took *an oath never to separate*" (ibid., p. 108).

71. On the topic of assembling as coming-to-be-common, see Guénoun, *L'enlèvement de la politique* and "De l'assemblement," in *L'exhibition des mots*.

72. Michelet, *French Revolution*, p. 105.

73. This is clear when Sieyès writes, "I do not speak of the clergy here. In my way of thinking, the clergy is not an order but rather a profession charged with a public service. . . . From this point of view, which is the true one in my opinion, there is only one order, that of the nobility. They are truly a people apart but a false people" (Sieyès, *What Is the Third Estate?* [Hunt], p. 67).

74. Rousseau's words are recognizable here: see Rousseau, "The Social Compact," in *Social Contract*, bk. I, chap. 6; and Guénoun, *L'enlèvement de la politique*.

75. Nation: "Legal person constituted by the collection of individuals composing the state," in the definition officially adopted by the Assembly (*Dictionnaire historique de la langue française*, ed. Rey, 2: 1306).

76. In other words, what obliges the assembly to cohere around its own embodiment as a person? See, further, Guénoun, *L'enlèvement de la politique* and pt. III of this book.

77. Sieyès constructs and elaborates this concept based to a great extent on Rousseau's arguments and permeates it with precise philosophical references, even when they remain implicit. See his last chapter: "What Remains to Be Done. Development of Certain Principles" (Sieyès, *What Is the Third Estate?* [Blondel], pp. 140ff.).

78. "Declaration of the Rights of Man," The Avalon Project: Documents in Law, History and Diplomacy (Yale University), http://avalon.law.yale.edu/18th_century/rightsof.asp (accessed October 31, 2012).—Trans.

79. Ibid.: "3. The principle of all sovereignty resides essentially in the nation. No body nor individual may exercise any authority which does not proceed directly from the nation. 4. . . . the exercise of the natural rights *of each man* has no limits [*bornes*—Trans.] except those which assure *to the other members of the society* the enjoyment of the same rights" (emphasis added).

80. This scene was replayed at the trial of Nicolae and Elena Ceaucescu in Romania in 1989: the revolution declared the death sentence imposed on the Ceaucescus to be the *last one*, but it could not avoid pronouncing it and executing it. This is how the dependence builds (and expresses itself) in the relationship with the parental figure of the couple put to death. The fascination with them immediately took on the conspicuous form of an edited montage of life- and death-images, a hallucinated long shot. [The images of Libya's former ruler Mu'ammar Gadhafi following his death in 2011 are another example.—Trans.]

81. "The National Assembly declaring then that the French nation renounces the declaration of any war aimed at conquest, and that it will never use its powers against the liberty of any people" [May 22, 1790]; and then, "The National Convention decrees: . . . Art. 11. The French nation declares that it will treat as an enemy the people who, refusing liberty and equality, or renouncing them, might wish to keep, recall, or deal with the prince or the privileged castes" [December 15, 1792] (Godechot, *La pensée révolutionnaire*, pp. 120, 161).

82. Revault d'Allonnes, *D'une mort à l'autre*, p. 44.

83. This double constitution appears at the very inception of the empire. "Under Augustus, the decision is made to put down the Germans by occupying their land all the way to the Elbe River. At the end of a military campaign that lasted three years (from 12 to 19 B.C.E.), Drusus reached this river. Germany, attached to Belgium, becomes a Roman province. But . . . a plot, instigated and inspired by Arminius ('Hermann'), succeeds in routing the Roman legions in the Teutoburg Forest. The Roman defeat becomes an open wound during the reign of Augustus, and it leads to a punitive expedition that allows Germanicus to avenge this affront at Teutoburg and to announce the complete pacification of the country to Tiberius, in 17 C.E. However, the emperor does not opt for complete occupation. He makes the decision to cut Germany in two: the land on the left bank of the Rhine is integrated into the Roman world; the land farther away from the Rhine remains in the 'half-barbarian world.' . . . 'Roman Germany,' which remains faithful to Rome overall, develops along with the empire. . . . As for 'independent Germany,' the scarcity of available clues hardly makes it possible to arrive at a clear idea of its history" (Poidevin and Schirmann, *Histoire de l'Allemagne*, p. 20).

84. Benveniste, *Indo-European Language and Society*, pp. 507–8.

85. The same will apply to Italy, as is predictable in this schema. See Leopardi, *Discorso sopra lo stato presente dei costumi degl'Italiani* (Discourse on the Present State of Italian Customs), p. 18.

86. This does not rule out the dream (on the contrary, it explains it) that every kingdom has of being the empire restored. It is a dream, a fictive identity, inescapable but imaginary: in truth, the kingdom is the empire undone.

87. Poidevin and Schirmann, *Histoire de l'Allemagne*, p. 32.

88. I am borrowing the phrase "the people as such" from Balibar and Wallerstein, *Races, nations, classes*, pp. 126ff.

89. Gravier, introduction, in *Les grands écrits réformateurs*, p. 28. He adds: "The formula . . . can be found in *Inspicientes* (*die Anschauenden*), a dialogue by Hutten" (ibid.). Ulrich von Hutten (1488–1523) was a humanist knight whose writings, shortly before Luther, express the precise point of view of the "Christian Nobility of the German Nation" to whom the reformer would address his "Open Letter."

90. I use "theological" to clarify the stakes here. Strictly speaking, one should say "ecclesiological." See Dostoyevsky, *The Possessed*, pt. 2, chap. 1, §7, in which Shatov reveals his theories about the nation and religion.

91. Luther, "An Open Letter to the Christian Nobility of the German Nation Concerning the Reform of the Christian Estate," titled in German "An den christlichen Adel deutscher Nation von des christlichen Standes Besserung."

92. This passage deals with the agents and partisans of the papacy. Ibid. p. 65; emphasis added. [Henceforth, page references for Luther's "Open Letter" will appear in the body of the text.—Trans.]

93. "For as the body is one, and hath many members, and all the members of that one body, being many, are one body: so also is Christ. . . . we [are] all baptized into one body, whether we be Jews or Gentiles, whether we be bond or free. . . . For the body is not one member but many. . . . If the whole body were an eye, where were the hearing? If the whole were hearing, where were the smelling? . . . And if they were all one member, where were the body? . . . And the eye cannot say unto the hand, I have no need of thee: nor again the head to the feet, I have no need of you. . . . Now ye are the body of Christ, and members in particular" (Bible [KJV], 1 Cor. 12:12–27).

94. "But ye are a chosen generation, a royal priesthood, an holy nation, a peculiar people. . . . Which in time past were not a people, but are now the people of God" (1 Peter 2:9–10).

95. "And [Thou] hast made us unto our God kings and priests: and we shall reign on the earth" (Rev. 5:10).

96. "For as we have many members in one body, and all members have not the same office: / So we, being many, are one body in Christ, and every one members one of another" (Rom. 12:4–5).

97. See the passages of 1 Cor. and 1 Peter quoted earlier.

98. The Greek answer was fairly clear: it is the polis that assembles. Who assembles there? The *dēmos*. Now, the *dēmos* is also delimited by a place. ("*Dēmos* is a territorial and political concept, and it designates *both* a division of land and the people who inhabit it" [Benveniste, *Indo-European Language and Society*, p. 372; emphasis added].) The circumscription that the polis traces out (starting with the *dēmos* and sometimes against its previous delimitations) is the *intra muros* space of the city-state, of the city, or (as in Athens) the grouping of spaces that it determines. In truth, the *political* question about the place and the gathering—asking which came first and was at the origin and at the foundation—is irrelevant and senseless in this context. The question as such only arises from the moment when the assembly and the place become dissociated and incompatible—let us say, from the moment of the constitution of the republic and then of the empire, as the circumscription of a space whose inhabitants cannot possibly all gather. It is colonization and the movement of extensive universalization that produce what will become the national question: where do those who are assembling come from? Of which place are they natives?

99. One could say it is in the Germans' hands partly because of an error: "the pope unjustly and by violence robbed the true emperor of his Roman Empire . . . and gave it to us Germans." But, Luther adds, "I would not advise that we give it up"; "it matters not to Him where an empire comes from; it is His will that it shall be ruled" ("Open Letter," p. 156).

100. See Guénoun, *Le printemps*, pt. 3, pp. 133ff.

101. It is paradoxical that the French use the Latin name of the imperial province of Germania [as opposed to the word *Allemagne*—Trans.] to designate all that

is specifically Germanic and foreign to any Romanity. On the names of Germany, see Nancy, "Monogrammes."

102. *Grands écrits réformateurs*, Gravier introduction, pp. 30 and 50.

103. "Annates" = "The first-fruits, or entire revenue of one year, paid to the Pope by bishops and other ecclesiastics of the R.C. Church on their appointment to a see or benefice"—*Oxford English Dictionary*, s.v.

104. "Germany is no longer a state," Hegel asserts, which is admittedly a little different. He keeps repeating this strange thesis—it's a kind of leitmotiv—in "The German Constitution (1798–1802)" (e.g., pp. 6–7, 14–15). On pages 10ff., where the focus is on a (very rapid) history of Germany with respect to this question, for example, we move directly from the assertion (about Germany, in the Middle Ages, presumably) that "the nation constituted a people without being a state" (p. 10) to an analysis of the contemporary situation, characterized by an undermining of the state (pp. 11ff.), without ever coming across a time in which the state was formed as such. Hegel seems to suggest that the German state was natively formed in a defective and failing way, as a fault or default of the state: "These spheres of power were fixed with the passage of time. The parts of the universal political power became a multiplicity of exclusive property, independent of the state itself . . . every individual member of the political hierarchy . . . everything which has rights or duties in relation to the state—has acquired them for itself; and in view of this reduction of its power, the state has no other function but to confirm that it has been deprived of its power. . . . The principles of German public law should therefore not be derived from the concept of the state. . . . German constitutional law is not a science based on principles but a register of the most varied constitutional rights [Gm., *Staatsrechte* (i.e., rights of the state—Trans.)] acquired in the manner of civil law [Gm., *Privatrecht* (i.e., private law—Trans.)]" (pp. 11–12). Or later, this astounding formula: "The German political edifice is nothing other than the sum of the rights which the individual parts have extracted from the whole [state]" (p. 13), which suggests precisely that the state (the political edifice) is constituted in Germany *as lack of the state* (the sum of the rights subtracted from the state), the summation of a subtraction, a cumulative collection of what was taken away from a state that has never been effectively constituted. The sentence goes on to state that "this justice, which watches carefully to ensure that no power remains in the hands of the state, is *the essence of the constitution*" (p. 13; emphasis added).

105. See Lacoue-Labarthe and Nancy, *Mythe nazi*, pp. 28ff.

106. The town of Biberach in Swabia.

107. Wieland, "Ueber teutschen Patriotismus," pp. 5–6. [Further page references to this essay appear in the body of the text.—Trans.]

108. Hegel, "German Constitution," p. 12.

109. In parentheses, Wieland adds, "as a patriotic spirit also breathed through them [our imperial cities—Trans.], and the *constitution* as well as the circum-

stances of that time were still protecting them from the pressures of their neighbors" (Wieland, "Ueber teutschen Patriotismus," p. 7; emphasis added).

110. See Lacoue-Labarthe, *Fiction du politique*, pp. 107 and 118–22. My thinking about Germany owes a great deal to the analyses in this book and other books by Philippe Lacoue-Labarthe (in particular, *Musica ficta: Figures de Wagner*), as well as to many conversations with him, so numerous that I shall not even try to identify them by date.

111. Fichte, *Addresses to the German Nation*; e.g., pp. 59, 69.

112. Wieland underscores, ". . . who love it above everything else, and are ready to bring considerable sacrifices not only for its safeguard and protection against a common enemy but also, when the danger has passed, for its well-being, the healing of its injuries, the promotion of its acceptance, its inner flourishing, and its outer appearance" (Wieland, "Ueber teutschen Patriotismus," p. 7).

113. "Our languages are different—should our concepts differ because of that? Are *Liberté* and *Égalité* no longer the same jewels of mankind if we call them *Freiheit* and *Gleichheit* [liberty and equality—Trans.]? Since when has the difference in languages made it impossible to obey the same law? And Russia's sovereign despot—doesn't she rule over a hundred populations with different tongues? Aren't Hungarians, Bohemians, Austrians, the Brabantians, and the Milanese all speaking their own language, though they all are the subjects of the same emperor? And weren't half the inhabitants of the world once called citizens of Rome? Why would it be more difficult for free people as a community to subscribe to eternal truths, grounded in the nature of man, than it was for the slave to obey his master? . . . Away with these hypocritical, feeble pretexts. What is true remains true, in Mainz as well as Paris" (Georg Forster, "On the Relationship of the People of Mainz to the Franks"); see also Jean Jaurès, *La Révolution et l'Europe*, on Foster, pp. 198–99, and more information about this entire episode, pp.161–209. See also Guénoun, *La levée*, pp. 46ff.

114. See the annotations to the French translation of the essay (Wieland, "Du patriotisme allemand," p. 28n5).

115. It will have become clear that, in my view, there is no patriotism of this kind anywhere, no autonomous "natural" feeling expressing the autoposition of a "national reality." Patriotism is a production of feeling carried out at a determined juncture, such as the German situation mentioned here.

116. "The nation is revolutionary" (*h11*).

117. As did Napoleon himself, German political thinkers—justifiably, for the most part, at least in this matter—regarded Napoleonic imperialism as descending directly from revolutionary expansionism. (The question of *what was lost* in the transition from the Revolution to the empire is obviously distinct.) It is impossible to cite these authors, given the way in which this corpus of writings about the hostile reaction to the Revolution and the empire seems to blend with the whole history of political, philosophical, and literary romanticism. In any case, romanticism

is mixed up in this project of Germany's (counter)revolutionary (re)constitution, running along one of its (two) principal trajectories, from Hegel ("The German Constitution") to Fichte (*Addresses to the German Nation* [see also Fichte, *Werke 1808–1812*—Trans.]), E. T. A. Hoffmann (e.g., "Die Vision auf dem Schlachtfelde bei Dresden" [The Vision on the Battlefield at Dresden], in *Sämtliche Werke*, vol. 2/1, published in French in Hoffmann, *Contes retrouvés*, pp. 37ff.), Richard Wagner, and even Martin Heidegger. On the two romantic trajectories, see Guénoun, "Walter Benjamin et 'nous,'" reprinted in *L'exhibition des mots*.

118. The repercussions of the king's trial followed by his execution led to lengthy comments and debates in Germany. See Lefebvre, *La Révolution française vue par les Allemands*, chaps. 4 and 5, pp. 83ff. See also Rogozinski, "Crime inexpiable."

119. For Kant (though he was well disposed toward the revolutionary spirit, and quite a francophile in this regard), this is the "inexpiable crime": not the king's murder (other peoples had put their monarchs to death in earlier times) but his being tried in court and his execution made legal—a complete reversal of European judicial *principles*. See Rogozinski, "Crime inexpiable."

120. See esp. Frederick II, "Considérations sur l'état présent du corps politique de l'Europe" and "Essai sur les formes de gouvernement, et sur les devoirs des souverains" (1777), both in *Œuvres posthumes*, 6: 3–52, 53–88; *Anti-Machiavel*; and *De la littérature allemande* (1780), which "while proclaiming the nonexistence of a national literature (in 1780), greatly contributed to sparking a reaction with the blossoming of Weimarian literature," according to Robert Pitrou, "Frédéric II," in Grimal, *Dictionnaire des biographies*, 1: 560.

121. E.g., see Luther, "Open Letter," p. 83.

122. See Beaune, *Naissance de la nation France*; Sieyès, *What Is the Third Estate?* (Blondel), p. 60 ("Why should [the Third Estate] not repatriate to the Franconian forests all the families who wildly claim to descend from the race of the conquerors . . . ").

123. As well as educational, in the spirit of Jules Ferry, and republican.

124. De Gaulle said in a speech at the meeting of the Free French in Kingsway Hall, London, on March 1, 1941: "Il y a un pacte, vingt fois séculaire, entre la grandeur de la France et la liberté du monde" [There is a pact—it is twenty centuries old—between the greatness of France and the freedom of the world], a claim reproduced on the De Gaulle Memorial at Colombey-les-Deux-Églises. Ms. Catherine Trouillet of the Charles de Gaulle Institute kindly provided me with this information. (It is worth noting that De Gaulle places the birth of France at the same time as the Roman Empire—and Christ.)

125. See the third address in Fichte, *Addresses to the German Nation*.

126. Revolutionized *society* is an archi-nation.

127. Like Germany facing Napoleon—but Spain and Russia as well.

128. Lenin, "Three Sources," pp. 21–28. See also Balibar, *Philosophie de Marx*, p. 9.

129. Italian Fascism arose at the junction of the French postsocialism of Georges Sorel and the influence of German idealism (Giovanni Gentile), and the fact that this took place in *Rome* should be carefully considered.

130. Germany, Spain, Italy, but not England.

131. Because Europe was the world's center of gravity, as well as the place where worldhood was generated and realized.

132. Because Germany was Europe's center of gravity—the hub of its industrialization and proletarization—*and the locus of its defeat*.

133. These phenomena are named for the Portuguese dictator António de Oliveira Salazar (1889–1970); Charles de Gaulle (1890–1970); and Joseph Stalin (1879–1953).—Trans.

134. Lenin's death helps to date—or give some context to—the situation. The determining factor is that the German revolution was crushed and the European revolutionary process stopped.

135. What remains to be explained, among many other things, is the persistence of Stalinism after the fall of Nazism. See Guénoun, "Sur les (prétendues) sorties du (prétendu) communisme."

PART III: TRANSPORTS OF ORIGIN

1. See Marx, *Capital*, vol. 1, §3. Marx's famous note to the French edition is a reaction to the phrase "labor process" [*procès de travail*]: "The word '*procès*' (process) which expresses *a development considered in the totality of its real conditions* has long been a part of scientific language throughout Europe. In France it was first introduced slightly shamefacedly in its Latin form—*processus*. Then, stripped of this pedantic disguise, it slipped into books on chemistry, physics, physiology, etc., and into a few works of metaphysics. In the end it will obtain a certificate of complete naturalization. Let us note in passing that in ordinary speech the Germans, like the French, use the word *Prozess* (*procès*, process) in the legal sense [i.e., trial]." Althusser quotes Marx's note in "Marx's Relation to Hegel," p. 185.

2. Althusser defines this "theory of history we owe to Hegel as *a dialectical process of production of forms (figures)*" (Althusser, "Marx's Relation to Hegel," p. 181).

3. The French title of this chapter is "Charges."—Trans.

4. "This point is indeed a mere idea, a *focus imaginarius*" (Kant, *Critique of Pure Reason*, p. 533).

5. See pt. I, §8 of this book.

6. "The only *subject* of the process of alienation is *the process itself in its teleology*" (Althusser, "Marx's Relation to Hegel," p. 183). The emphasis is Althusser's.

7. See Jean-Luc Nancy, "Un sujet?" in *Homme et sujet*, ed. Weil, pp. 47–114.

8. "There is no subject to the process: *it is the process itself which is a subject in so far as it does not have a subject*" (Althusser, "Marx's Relation to Hegel," p. 184).

9. Deleuze has thought about this tearing away [*arrachement*] of pure becoming (and therefore of time) away from the movement (and therefore from space) as the passage from the movement-image to the time-image. See Deleuze, *Image-mouvement* and *Image-temps* (esp., e.g., *Image-temps*, pp. 7–37). On the idea of setting apart pure time, as the time of pure change, see Tarkovsky, *Sculpting in Time*.

10. See Deleuze, *Image-mouvement*, p. 37; *Movement-Image*, p. 22.

11. We can see that this diverges from the thought of transport being "eigentlich leer" (properly empty). [In German: "Der tragische transport ist nemlich eigentlich leer . . . " (for tragic transport is actually / properly empty), in Hölderlin, "Anmerkungen zum Ödipus," p. 250 ("Remarks on 'Oedipus,'" p. 101).—Trans.]

12. Though the tracing is never "pure": see Derrida, *De la grammatologie*, pp. 61–62, *Psyché*, p. 87, and *Mémoires d'aveugle*, pp. 48–49. Paola Marrati has kindly provided these precise references.

13. Indeed, in this (turned-around) sense, Europe is Roman. Rémi Brague's thesis is confirmed (see Brague, *Europe, la voie romaine*): Romanity is what makes Europe. But it does not exhaust the *directional sense* of it: there still has to be the returning, which, for its part, proceeds from an *exhaustion*, a *reversal* of the Roman movement.

14. See G. H. Stevenson, "Communications and Commerce," in *Legacy of Rome*, ed. Bailey, pp. 141–72.

15. The French title of this chapter is "De l'étant."—Trans.

16. Analogously, one could say that our "western" religions feed on themes, place-names, and various terms that originated in places of the Orient: Galilee, Babylon, Jerusalem, and so on. As for Rome, what it borrowed from Greece extends much farther than religious mythologies—to all kinds of discourses.

17. See also earlier discussion in pt. I, chap. 2, of Husserl's "Vienna Lecture." See also Derrida, *Problem of Genesis in Husserl's Philosophy*, pp. 154–57; and Gérard Granel, "L'Europe de Husserl." [Page references to the "Vienna Lecture" appear in the body of the text.—Trans.]

18. On the equation between History and European history, see Patočka, *Plato and Europe*, p. 222: "in this sense, we say that history is the history of Europe."

19. See also ibid., pp. 65ff.

20. "We speak in this connection of the natural primordial attitude, of the attitude of original natural life, of the first originally natural form of cultures, whether higher or lower, whether developing uninhibitedly or stagnating" ("Vienna Lecture," p. 281).

21. How can passion occur without interest? Without wishing to deal with this problem fully ("We shall not go into this in detail," p. 285), Husserl suggests a pathway: incipient theoretical interest is "a variant of curiosity" (ibid.). Disinterested passion springs from wonder or astonishment (Gk., *thaumazein*) and develops "as an intrusion into the course of 'serious living,' either as a result of originally

developed life-interests or as a playful looking-about [Gm., *spielerische Umschau*; Fr., *regard jeté par jeu*] *when one's quite immediate vital needs are satisfied* or when working hours are over. Curiosity (here understood not as a habitual 'vice') is also a variant, *an interest which has separated itself off from life-interests*, has let them fall" ("Vienna Lecture," p. 285; emphasis added). It is tempting to set these indications alongside Freud's discussion of curiosity in *Leonardo da Vinci*, pp. 25–28. See also *Curiosité en psychanalyse*, ed. Sztulman and Fénelon, pp. 7, 32–53, and passim (thank you to J. Ph. Schlick for this reference).

22. The triad nature-native-nation is a little less visible in German but Husserl nonetheless explicitly enunciates it within a few lines: "The individual men who reorient themselves, as men within their universal life-community (their *nation*), continue to have their *natural* interests; through no reorientation can they simply lose them; this would mean that each would cease to be what he has become from *birth* onward" ("Vienna Lecture," p. 281; emphasis added).

23. "Extrascientific culture, culture not yet touched by science, consists in tasks and accomplishments [Gm., *Aufgabe und Leistung*] of man in finitude" ("Vienna Lecture," p. 279).

24. Husserl, "Vienna Lecture" (Lauer), p. 156. [For a closer match with the original, this text quotes from two translations of the "Vienna Lecture" (see Works Cited), in imitation of the author, who uses both the Granel and Derrida and the Ricœur translations, with an eye on the German text. For the text in French, see Husserl, "La crise de l'humanité européenne et la philosophie," in *La crise des sciences européennes et la phénoménologie transcendantale*, trans. Gérard Granel and Jacques Derrida, 347–83 (Paris: Gallimard, 1976); and *La crise de l'humanité européenne et la philosophie*, trans. Paul Ricœur, bilingual ed. (Paris: Aubier-Montaigne, 1977).—Trans.] The theme of infinity runs throughout the text; see, e.g., "Vienna Lecture," pp. 276–78. ["Infinite task" is a phrase also quoted by Rodolphe Gasché in the title and throughout his book *Europe, or the Infinite Task*.—Trans.]

25. ". . . a new human epoch emerging and beginning to grow, the epoch of a humanity that from now on will and can live only in the free fashioning of its being and its historical life out of rational ideas and infinite tasks" (Husserl, "Vienna Lecture" [Lauer], p. 156). This brings to mind Ludwig Feuerbach: "The consciousness of the infinite is nothing else than the consciousness of the infinity of the consciousness; or, in the consciousness of the infinite, the conscious subject has for his object the infinity of his own nature [Gm., *Wesen*; Fr., *essence*]" (Feuerbach, *Essence of Christianity*, p. 21.). With Husserl, this consciousness of infinity occurs, in history, as *theoria*.

26. Patočka, *Plato and Europe*, pp. 77–78.

27. Philippe Lacoue-Labarthe, notes from the seminar "Littératures et philosophie mêlées" at the University of Strasbourg, March 22, 1994. Starting with this hypothesis, Lacoue-Labarthe determined the literary experience as the experience

of the return from the dead, as rising up again from the abode or the house of the dead—as the matrix of a certain determination of experience as such. A similar theme is broached in Lacoue-Labarthe, *La poésie comme expérience*, pp. 143–44.

28. "This is that singular thing about Europe: as I told you, *only in Europe* was philosophy born in this way, in the awakening of man out of tradition into the presence of the universe, only in Europe, or better said, in what was the embryo [Fr., *germe*—Trans.] of Europe—Greece" (Patočka, *Plato and Europe*, p. 88).

29. In the development that follows, I mainly refer to Patočka, *Plato and Europe* and Patočka, *Heretical Essays*. Patočka makes direct reference to Husserl's "Vienna Lecture" in *Heretical Essays*. [Further page references for these two works, respectively designated as PE and HE, can be found below and in the body of the text.—Trans.]

30. ". . . the Athenian *polis* is something that crystallizes gradually in conflicts with its neighbors as well as in the struggles of political parties. . . . Here, in very specific conflicts on a modest territory and with minimal material is born *not only the Western world and its spirit but, perhaps, world history as such*. The Western spirit and world history are bound together in their origins: it is the spirit of free meaning bestowal, it is the shaking of life as simply accepted with all its certainties and at the same time the origin of new possibilities of life *in that shaken situation, that is, of philosophy*" (HE, p. 41; emphasis added).

31. "All these myths have the same meaning: man is at the same time a creature of truth and this *truth is damnation for him*. . . . The greatness—that which made Greek philosophy what it is and that which made it the foundation of all of European life—is that from this Greek philosophy developed a *plan for life*, one that stated it is not damnation, but *human greatness*! . . . What is told to us by myth is the natural human stance. Human life is damnation, it is horror, because, as Pascal said, 'The end is always bloody, however famous the comedy may have been.' This is the *natural* human stance. . . . The Greek idea is the following: in just this situation it is shown that man has *various* possibilities on the basis of this original situation. Only then, in this situation, he has to prove himself; only then he has to show himself as a creature who really does make phenomenon, that means clarity, *truth the law of his life*" (PE, pp. 35–36; Patočka's emphasis).

32. "For Plato, because he discovered the principle of the care of the soul, *for the first time* the soul is something that even in its fate after death is something that lives from within" (PE, p. 126; emphasis added).

33. "This motive is captured in myths just in a mythical, and that means in a purely material, way" (PE, p. 53).

34. ". . . a stance of uprootedness" (HE, p. 76).

35. This is the theme virtually driving Patočka's books *Plato and Europe* and *Heretical Essays*.

36. See HE, pp. 39–40.

37. See on this topic Guénoun, "Le dénudement," in *L'exhibition des mots*.

38. "History differs from prehistoric humanity by the *shaking of accepted meaning*" (Patočka, HE, p. 62).

39. For example, "The basis of meaning, in Weischedel's terms, is problematicity; in Heidegger's terms, the concealment of what-is [i.e., beingness—Trans.] as a whole as the foundation of all openness and all uncovering" (HE, p. 77).

40. The concept of world, as it is used here, undermines its elaboration in this book (see pt. I, §3). Husserl and Patočka write "world" to designate what *theoria* is targeting, or what is revealed as phenomenon. In this they may be at risk of a confusion, or an anachronism—or both: they do not seem, properly speaking, to aim either at the *cosmos* (in its Greek sense) or specifically at the *mundus*, and it seems to me that these two notions should not be viewed as the same. It is about "beingness" ("what is") [*das Seiende* (Gm.); *l'étant* (Fr.)—Trans.] that they are speaking; about totality, or baring [*mise à nu*], or that-which-is as such. Then why this insistent, marked word? Why the "world"? See the discussion in pt. II, §22.

41. "After the catastrophe of the Greek polis, it became important that this *inheritance* remain alive, an inheritance of thinking about the state where philosophers might live, about a state of justice founded not on mere tradition, but rather on *looking-in*" [Cz., *nahléd-nutí*] (PE, p. 88). See also: "I would only like to show that in the conception of the care of the soul is encompassed something like *the ideal of the truthful life*, that is a life that, as much as [*sic*] in praxis as in its activity of thinking, always directs itself by *looking-in*" (PE, p. 107).

42. "[Vilem] Mrštík therefore speaks of 'that dreadful immobility of suicides'" (HE, p. 59).

43. Patočka emphasizes "one"; my emphasis for the remainder.—D.G.

44. ". . . how fundamental is the difference between *home* and *foreign* [Cz., *cizina*]. . . . The near world is the world of good, which is proven by a long tradition of human action in precisely tried and still repeated forms. Only within them is man capable of trust and living-at-home within existence, trust that does not disappoint. While at the same time, there is the constant threat of that which is unusual, not falling into these forms of rootedness, that which Germans call *unheimlich, das Unheimliche*, that is, what is *threatening par excellence*" (PE, p. 54).

45. "When Plato says θαῦμα ἀρχὴ τῆς σοφίας (wonder is the origin of wisdom), and Aristotle speaks of how people started to philosophize διὰ τὸ θαυμάζειν (it is owing to their wonder), out of wonder, amazement—this is what they mean. There is no amazement in myth; myth is not in wonder about anything, it knows everything beforehand" (PE, p. 59).

46. Husserl, "Vienna Lecture" (Lauer), pp. 175–76; emphasis added. The last sentence does not appear in the German editions that I consulted. But the consequential relation is clearly laid out in the development on this page and the preceding one. [German text: "Die in der Tradition konservativ Befriedigten und der philosophische Menschenkreis werden einander bekämpfen, und sicherlich wird der Kampf sich in der politischen Machtsphäre abspielen. Schon in den Anfängen

der Philosophie beginnt die *Verfolgung*" (Husserl, "Krisis des europäischen Menschentums," p. 335); my emphasis—Trans.].

47. See Patočka, PE. [E.g., "the philosophical ideal of life in truth" (PE, p. 104); "... *man could make at least the human world a world of truth and justice*. How this can be achieved is the very subject of the care of the soul" (PE, p. 36).—Trans.]

48. "This philosophical-political schema, where the philosopher does not perish ... also revolves around the problem of the soul and care for it. ... And that is the reason why ... Plato introduces this connection to political life in context of the state" (PE, p. 111).

49. "And naturally, understanding this matter means coming into conflict with ordinary perception, which understandably looks at right and justice and so on entirely differently, which looks at right and justice as a matter of utility, an external utility. ... In ordinary perception, right and justice is regard for others. ... This dual way of seeing, the common way of seeing and the way of seeing of the philosopher are inevitably in conflict" (PE, pp. 104–5).

50. "When the question [raised by Adeimantus, explicitly so in the French translation—Trans.] of law-giving comes into the new community, Socrates says that these are small details, with which he will not concern himself. We are interested not in law-giving in its entirety and in its details—it does not concern what will be, let us say, taxes, and what punishments will be meted out [Plato, *Republic* 4.425ff.], but rather that most important thing—the only one this is about—the regulation of upbringing, education, which leads the guardians from the first moment of their existence" (PE, p. 121).

51. "We could also speak of the natural world ... if we were to understand by it the world prior to the discovery of its problematic character. The nonproblematic world is one in which concealment is not experienced as such. That does not mean that such a world would not have or know secret things, the sacred, or the mysterious; on the contrary, it can be full of such things ... but it lacks the experience of the transition [Fr., *passage*], of the emergence of what-is [Fr., *l'étant*] as phenomenon out of obscurity into the openness in the course of which even that which allows what-is to become manifest shows itself and thereby and only thereby sets questions about what-is on a firm foundation" (HE, p. 12). ["What-is" translates the German term *das Seiende*. It is often translated into French as *l'étant*, and in English as "what is," "that which is," "beingness," "being," "entity," and so on (in an ontological, at times Heideggerian, context). It stands in contrast to the substantivized form of "to be" in German (*das Sein*) and French (*l'être*); in English, "to be" lacks any potential for being reasonably substantivized, except in the gerund ("being" or "Being").—Trans.]

52. "... the life of such societies is focused on the acceptance and maintenance of life ... it is rooted in the immediacy of being human, for which openness itself is not revealed or life problematic ..." (HE, p. 29).

53. On the Greek word *nomos*, which forms part of *oikonomia*, see PE, p. 104.

54. *Nahlédnutí* in Czech.—Trans.

55. I am borrowing this expression from Thomas Dommange, "Sommes-nous capables d'un monde?" See also Patočka, *Plato and Europe*: "And because of this, the soul capable of something like that must be cared for" (p. 80). And further, ". . . for all that, it must take place in something that is *capable of looking-in*. To look-in means to *see*. This means it all takes place in a being to whom the world manifests itself. The being has its own special privilege in contrast to all other worldly beings of which we are aware" (PE, p. 95).

56. "Their manifestation, however, is itself historical" [Fr., *historiale*] (HE, p. 10).

57. ". . . this conception—the problem of manifesting and manifestation—is from the very beginning the ground of all reflection of European peoples reflecting upon their situation in a peculiar guise" (PE, p. 42).

58. ". . . transcendence towards the world" (HE, p. 49).

59. "For in the Roman Empire the care of the soul assumes the form of striving for a rule of law throughout the global community" [*oikoumenē* (Gk. for community) in the French translation—Trans.] (HE, p. 83). And also, "The moment this great empire was wrecked, the primeval example [Fr., *prototype*] of all empires, it left behind a heritage—if we have states at all it is because this empire existed" (PE, p. 89).

60. Patočka asks the question explicitly, in *Plato and Europe*, and in *Heretical Essays* ("These reflections should not be understood as an idealization of the Greek *polis*" [HE, p. 41]).

61. The sudden appearance of the political principle was marked by the victory of Greece over the Asian empire—the "most powerful that had hitherto ruled over the world, the synthesis of all eastern monarchies in the form of the Persian Empire" (PE, p. 110). Thus, this "situation demonstrated the principle of *freedom* . . . to be more powerful, to be, in fact, the *most powerful* on earth" (PE, p. 82). But Rome also inherits its collapse: "Altogether we can thus say that the European heritage remains the same in the various forms in which the care for the soul is transformed in the two great historical catastrophes, that of the *polis* and that of the Roman Empire" (HE, p. 83). "The contemporary decline of the Athenian community is, as we know, represented by the fate of Socrates" (PE, p. 110).

62. "From the moment that the perishing of the *polis* had already been decided, philosophy transformed itself into what was to be its image for millenia [*sic*], transforming itself into metaphysics in Plato and Democritus" (HE, p. 65). "Metaphysics itself grows out of a particular historical situation, from the situation of the decline of the polis, the decline of Athens" (PE, p. 129).

63. On the liberation that political life represents and Arendt's interpretation of Aristotle, see HE, p. 40. And further, ". . . we could deduce the very beginning of history in the proper sense of the word. We can speak of history where life becomes free and whole, where it consciously builds room for an equally free life" (HE, pp. 40–41). "[T]he Greek world is the representative of the principle

of freedom. But of course, we have to understand this in the Greek sense of the word: this is the world of free nobles, that is people who are—as Hannah Arendt nicely phrased it—despots in their own home so they might be equals in their city. They are absolute masters of their households, but in the *city* they are *equals*" (PE, pp. 81–82).

64. "The Greek world is not united. It is organized into independent tiny city-states (πόλεις), and these have various regimes, such as democracy, such as aristocracy where only a certain group rules, such as tyranny where only one rules. And of course, tyranny *is already a retreat from this Greek principle*, it already is decline. Yet in the Greek cities, tyranny can only last for a short time. Of all the Greek cities, *Athens is the most Greek*, because it is the guarantor of freedom for every other city. That was shown in the Persian wars" (PE, p. 82; emphasis added).

65. "That, however, means life on the boundary which makes life an encounter with what there is, on the boundary of all that is where this whole remains insistent because something quite other than individual entities, interests, and realities within it inevitably emerges here" (HE, p. 39).

66. "[W]ithin this care of the soul I catch sight of the essential heritage of Europe, that is to say, what in a certain sense made European history what it is. *This does not mean that these thoughts were realized here*, it only means that they were a certain ferment, without which we cannot conceive of European reality" (PE, p. 107; emphasis added). And further, "Metaphysics itself *grows out of a particular historical situation, from the situation of the decline of the polis, the decline of Athens*. It creates a heritage that can survive in the declining polis, and survives even the decline of Hellenism, and helps so that after the decline of the Roman Empire still another formation is conceived, that is, Europe in the proper sense of the word. The surviving of the heritage is obviously also its change, but this metaphysical foundation still endures. And *surprisingly*, upon it the domain of European life is spread out, is generalized" (PE, p. 129; emphasis added).

67. Philosophy (and science to a certain extent) seems less productive during this time than during its intense beginnings—with massive exceptions, however, such as the Stoics' contribution, which provides a kind of "philosophical ideology" to the empire, by putting much work into the elaboration of the schemas of universality.

68. Let us recall that the poem was written at the exact same time as Augustus's constitution of the imperial regime.

69. The *Aeneid* has been seen as an *Odyssey* (bks. 1–6) followed by an *Iliad* (bks. 7–12), dividing it into two equal halves following the (reversed) structure of the Homeric poems.

70. Laying claim to Trojan origins did not stop with Rome: the foundation narratives of France (and Germany, too) feature them as well. See Beaune, *Naissance de la nation France*, pp. 25–74.

71. But stating this still does not explain it. Shall one say that the theoretical,

at bottom, did not come to terms with imperial domination, as domination of the world? That no matter what one may say, it may be with something other than *the world* that the theoretical is dealing, and much rather with *beingness*, the illuminating transcendence of (and toward) *that which is*; and not the world, which deals with subjection and hegemony? Domination could then capture this illumination, fix it (as an image), and transmit it—but not reproduce it.

72. See pt. I, § 5.

73. Unlike Marcel Gauchet (*Désenchantement du monde*, pp. 12ff.), I reject dependence on the past as an autonomous structure that is independent and thinkable by itself. It presupposes, it seems to me, the constitution of a temporality that seems ("intuitively") posterior to the structures of the "first religion" of which Gauchet speaks. The idea of this dependence mobilizes a temporality set apart, as an autonomous category, in which I tend to see one of *our* structures in organizing the *world*. To put it in terms of debt, as Gauchet does, I would rather seek something like being indebted to the locus, to the "there."

74. With the first ancestor, and just *like* him, the first god also arrives. The issue of what makes the gods ancestors or not is discussed later. But with arrivals, the link is clear. Thus, Herodotus, explaining that the "names of almost all the gods also came to Greece from Egypt," sees the explanation in the founders' arrival in Greece. "I will absolutely deny that the similarities between the Greek and the Egyptian versions of the [Dionysian—Trans.] rites are coincidental. . . . The most likely scenario, in my opinion, is that Melampus [introducer of the rites into Greece] learnt these Dionysian rites from Cadmus of Tyre and those who accompanied him on his journey from Phoenicia to the country now known as Boeotia" (*Histories* 2.49–50, pp. 115–16). Recall that Cadmus came to Greece to look for his abducted sister Europē (*Histories* 4.147; and on the ancestors' divine descent, see 2.143–44).

75. I obviously owe this concept to Derrida, but its proposed use here distinguishes itself from his, to a certain extent—perhaps a question of materialism.

76. As time passes, it comes back more: time goes by and the remains diminish.

77. See Rousseau, "Discours sur l'inégalité," in *Œuvres complètes*, 2: 224. On gathering points, see Rousseau, *Essai sur l'origine des langues*, p. 102. [In English, "Discourse on the Origin and Foundations of Inequality Among Men, or Second Discourse"; "Essay on the Origin of Languages," both in *The Discourses and Other Early Political Writings*].

78. See Aristotle, *Physics* 4.1–5; *Rhetoric* 1.2.1358a10–31; 2.22–26; *Topics*, passim. See also Brague, "Le lieu," in *Aristote et la question du monde*, pp. 273–322; and Thionville, *De la théorie des lieux communs dans les 'Topiques' d'Aristote*.

79. Aristotle, *Rhetoric* 1.2.22.

80. See Chantraine, *Dictionnaire étymologique de la langue grecque*, 1: 1125.

81. See Aristotle, *Rhetoric* 2.26.1403a18: "element (or topic) [topos—Trans.] is a head under which several enthymemes are included," which Moreau and Hamelin translate as follows: "Un lieu, c'est ce en quoi coïncident [*sic*] une pluralité de

raisonnements oratoires" (Moreau, *Aristote et son école*, p. 48n2; Hamelin, *Système d'Aristote*, p. 228). The Ruelle and Vanhemelryck translation is: "ce à quoi reviennent beaucoup d'enthymèmes" (Aristotle, *Rhétorique*, p. 294). [On the translation of "enthymemes" by (Fr.) "raisonnements oratoires" (oratorical reasonings), see Aristotle, *Rhetoric* 1.2.8: "I call an enthymeme a rhetorical syllogism."—Trans.]

82. Aristotle, *Physics* 4.4; emphasis added.

83. On the other hand, we know that "Aristotle declares transport / locomotion [*phora*—Trans.] to be the first movement, ranking it first in the plurality of movements" (Brague, *Aristote et la question du monde*, p. 276n2; numerous references appear here).

84. Aristotle, *Physics* 4.1. Brague comments on this passage (*Aristote et la question du monde*, pp. 274ff.).

85. Aristotle, *Physics* 4.2.

86. ". . . for not everything that is in place, but only movable body [*kinēton sōma*]" (ibid., 4.5). A passage, then, from the *proposition* to the *term*? From syntax to semantics?

87. Ibid., 4.2.

88. Ibid., 4.5.

89. Brague, *Aristote et la question du monde*, pp. 278ff.

90. "This example is *you*. Aristotle calls on the listeners of his teaching in a way so rare as to be remarkable. This procedure is not without parallel but it is unique in the *Physics*. We should therefore ask why Aristotle needs such an unusual example, all the more striking in that it interrupts the flow of the argument" (Brague, *Aristote et la question du monde*, p. 287).

91. See Nancy, *Des lieux divins*, for a problematic on this topic that is quite different.

92. *Dictionnaire historique de la langue française*, ed. Rey, 1: 1127.

93. Hegel, *Aesthetics*, 2: 638.

94. Ibid., 1: 84.

95. Ibid., pp. 85–86.

96. Ibid., p. 84; emphasis added.

97. Isa. 40:3–5 (KJV). See also Luke 3:4–6: "As it is written in the book of the words of Esaias the prophet, saying, . . . Prepare ye the way of the Lord."

98. Hegel, *Aesthetics*, 1: 84; *Ästhetik I/II*, pp. 143–45.

99. See Hegel, *Aesthetics*, 2: 638; *Vorlesungen über die Ästhetik*, 2: 276; *Esthétique* (Jankélévitch), 3: 33.

100. French text: "le but de la cohésion *et cette cohésion même*" (Hegel, *Vorlesungen über die Ästhetik*, 2: 276; my modified translation and emphasis—D.G.). German text: "dem Zweck dieses Zusammenhalts und als dieser Zusammenhalt."

101. "Die Gemeinsamkeit der Konstruktion wird zugleich der Zweck und Inhalt des Werkes selbst" (ibid.). [*Zweck* is also "purpose."—Trans.]

102. Ibid.

103. Ibid.

104. Hegel, *Aesthetics*, 2: 638; *Esthétique* (Jankélévitch), 3: 33; *Esthétique: Textes choisis*, p. 27. Emphasis added.

105. Of course this brings to mind Peter Brook's famous incipit: "I can take any empty space and call it a bare stage" (Brook, *Empty Space*, p. 9).

106. Hegel, *Ästhetik I/II*, p. 144; Hegel *Aesthetics*, 1: 84: "the lightning-flash of individuality."

107. See Aristotle, *Physics* 4.2, 4. ["Containance" is used to translate *contenance*, introduced by the author with an added element of "containment."—Trans.]

108. See Heidegger, "Der Ursprung des Kunstwerkes," in *Holzwege*, pp. 22ff (29ff. marginal pagination).

109. Hegel, *Aesthetics*, 1: 85. German text: "[Die Gemeinde (community—Trans.)] ist die geistige Reflexion [spiritual reflection—Trans.] in sich jenes sinnlichen Daseyns.... Die gediegene Einheit in sich [compact unity in itself—Trans.] des Gottes in der Skulptur zerschlägt sich [is shattered—Trans.] in die Vielheit vereinzelter Innerlichkeit [into the plurality of the inner lives of individuals—Trans.], deren Einheit keine sinnliche, sondern schlechthin ideell ist. Und so erst ist Gott selber als dieses Herüber und Hinüber [this to-and-fro—Trans.], als dieser Wechsel seiner Einheit in sich und Verwirklichung im subjektiven Wissen und dessen Besonderung, wie der Allgemeinheit und Vereinigung der Vielen, wahrhaft Geist—der Geist in seiner Gemeinde" (Hegel, *Vorlesungen über die Ästhetik*, 1: 110–11; Hegel, *Aesthetics*, 1: 85–86).

110. Hegel, *Aesthetics*, 1: 86; *Vorlesungen über die Ästhetik*, 1: 111.

111. "... it is a rule in the Divine activity to prepare no 'place' without it receiving a Divine spirit" (Ibn al-'Arabi, *Wisdom of the Prophets*, no pagination; *Sagesse des prophètes*, p. 22, and also pp. 71–72, 93, and 169).

112. "*Local gods*, identified with objects in the sky, were thought to be embodied in stones, trees and other natural things; good and evil spirits were believed to roam the world in the shape of animals.... It has been suggested ... that gods were thought of as dwelling in a sanctuary, a *haram*, a place or town set apart from tribal conflict, serving as a centre of pilgrimage" (Hourani, *History of the Arab Peoples*, p. 11; emphasis added).

113. See Exod. 13:21–22, 14:19–20.

114. See Drai, *Sortie d'Égypte*, passim.

115. See Ernst Bloch, "Exodus in the Concept of Yahweh," in *Atheism in Christianity*, pp. 71ff (German ed.: Bloch, "Exodus in der Jachwevorstellung selber, Enttheokratisierung," in *Atheismus*, pp. 115–66).

116. Ibid.

117. The clear-cut mark of what Bloch terms futurity—with the "future as open determinedness of Being" (Gm., "Mit Futurum als offener Seinsbestimmtheit")—is conveyed by the *future tense* of God's reply to Moses, "I will be who I will be" (Gm., "Ich werde sein, der ich sein werde"), unfairly translated, it seems (and thus

hellenicized; see Exod. 3:14), as "I am that I am" (Bloch, *Atheismus*, p. 85; see also Drai, *Sortie d'Égypte*, p. 22).

118. Exod. 20:2–4, from the Elohist as translated by Jean Bottéro in id., *Naissance de Dieu*, pp. 62–63; emphasis added. [Shown here is my English version of Bottéro's translation, which deviates from other versions. The King James Version is as follows: "I am the Lord thy God, which have brought thee out of the land of Egypt, out of the house of bondage. / Thou shalt have no other gods before me. / Thou shalt not make unto thee any graven image, or any likeness of any thing that is in heaven above, or that is in the earth beneath, or that is in the water under the earth: / Thou shalt not bow down thyself to them, nor serve them: for I the Lord thy God am a jealous God . . . "—Trans.]

119. Bottéro, *Naissance de Dieu*, p. 63; emphasis added.

120. Kant, *Critique of Judgment*, para. 29, p. 143. See the comment on this passage in Philippe Lacoue-Labarthe, "La vérité sublime," in Courtine et al., *Du sublime*, pp. 97–147.

121. Kant, *Critique of Judgment*, para. 29, pp. 143–44.

122. Ibid.; emphasis added.

123. Ibid.

124. Freud, *Moses and Monotheism*, pp. 111–22. [Further page references to this book, abbreviated as MM, appear parenthetically in the body of the text.—Trans.] Lacoue-Labarthe, for his part, makes a connection with Freud, *Moses of Michelangelo*. See Lacoue-Labarthe, "La vérité sublime," in Courtine et al., *Du sublime*, pp. 119–23.

125. Though this point is not unchallengeable. Let us recall its discussion by Spinoza (see Spinoza, *Theologico-Political Treatise*, chap. 3). [On the term "sublime": in German (e.g., in Kant), the sublime is *das Erhabene*, but *sublim* is also used. Freud makes reference, in this religious context, to the "heights of sublime abstraction," i.e., "zu den Höhen sublimer Abstraktion" (Freud, *Der Mann Moses*, p. 33).—Trans.]

126. In a footnote Freud explains that he uses this compound term, *Triebverzicht* [*Trieb* (drive or instinct) and *Verzicht* (renunciation)] as an abbreviation for "renouncing the satisfaction of an urge [or drive, or compulsion] derived from an instinct."—Trans.

127. The distinction between the Greek and Jewish contributions—their heterogeneity—continues to be at issue here. Nevertheless, they have in common a tendency to oppose magic and ritualism, or myth, insofar as it conveys and legitimizes rituals and magic. On this point, there are remarkable parallels between Husserl's analyses in the "Vienna Lecture" and Freud's in *Moses and Monotheism*. Cf. also Scholem, *Walter Benjamin*, p. 259: "What matters is not infinity but eliminating magic" ("Es kommt nicht auf die Unendlichkeit an, sondern auf die Ausschaltung der Magie").

128. Transcendence *toward*: we frequently take transcendence to be an autono-

mous and separate space (by erasing the moving and transitioning aspects that this term implies)—e.g., divine space as opposed to human space. But the term denotes a way onward, an elevation, an access—a passage across, temporal as well as spatial, a crossing of boundaries and barriers. One should perhaps distinguish two modes of transcendence, a *transcendence-toward*, and a *transcendence-of*. *Transcendence-of* would function as a deposit or folding-back of the movement of *transcendence-toward*: a *transcendence-toward*, too, but immobilized, reduced, spatialized in op-position—deposed transcendence.

129. "While it is not a question that Aristotle thematized, the concept of world is a question addressed to his thinking, precisely and paradoxically insofar as it is missing from it" (Brague, *Aristote et la question du monde*, p. 6).

130. Classical? Brague adds a nuance: "this absence . . . then turns out to be characteristic of Hellenism before Aristotle and after him" (ibid.).

131. Ibid. See also Plato, *Timaeus*: "Now the whole Heaven, or Cosmos, or if there is any other name which it specially prefers, by that let us call it" (28b). See also Chantraine, *Dictionnaire étymologique de la langue grecque*, 1: 570.

132. On this articulation, see Plato, *Timaeus* 17a–28b.

133. Husserl, "Vienna Lecture," p. 276; emphasis added.

134. In a very partial sense, the distinction made here can be backed up with one stage of Heidegger's analysis: "*Neither the ontic description of innerworldly beings nor the ontological interpretation of the being of these beings gets as such at the phenomenon of 'world'*" (Heidegger, *Being and Time*, p. 64). This allows the view that Greek thought, even insofar as it examines the being of what is [*l'être de l'étant*], does not aim at the worldliness of the world as such. The focus on what I have termed the transcendence of beingness or what-is is not enough to qualify a thought system as a thinking of the world. Wordliness is not the being of beingness, nor is it even the position of the being of all beingness or all that is. Heidegger adds a little later, "'Worldliness' is an ontological concept and designates the structure of a constitutive factor of being-in-the-world" (ibid.). On this score, "'World' is ontologically not a determination of *those* beings [Fr., *l'étant*—Trans.] which Dasein essentially is *not*, but rather a characteristic of Dasein itself" (ibid.). And so the world is determined by a mode, moment, or characteristic of being-in-the-world [Fr., *être-au-monde*]. In this sense, and to bring this thesis nearer to the present problematic, the worldhood of the world is situated less in the position of the being of that which is [*l'être de l'étant*], or the being of all beings [*de tous les étants*] (which the Greeks knew, of course) than in a mode of positing and constituting a determined way of grasping this being [*être*], namely, what I am designating here as the *mode of unity* of the unity of the totality of that which is or beingness. What makes up the world is the mode—moment or character—of the experience by way of which one posits the unity of the totality of the world, in accordance with a certain determination of this unity.

135. See pt. I, §3.

136. On Marcus Aurelius, see www.iep.utm.edu/marcus (accessed July 8, 2012).—Trans.

137. That the invention of the empire is thus a question of metaphor, recurrence, and, partially at least, because of the geopolitical situation, the transfer of non-Greek (e.g., Persian) models need cause us no difficulty here; this is not enough of a reason to consider the Roman empire to exemplify an immovable imperiality whose essence manifests itself in all the great despotic formations, including China and pre-Columbian monarchies of the Americas. The empire that we are dealing with here is Roman because the concept that designates it was constructed during Roman times, at the same time as the reality that it describes. It is this Latin word that we use to designate "empires." A rigorous approach demands that one consider the supposed earlier empires as nothing but possible provenances, and the later ones as derivative—and still other ones as hypothetical assimilations.

138. That is, in the conflictual space of the difference of religions.

139. Most of the early Christian apologies were personally addressed to emperors. "In the technical sense of the term, apologies were legal defense speeches, and in fact these works are legal arguments to obtain from emperors the legal recognition of the Christians' existence in an officially pagan empire. One finds in them partial reports about the Christian faith, and a few attempts to justify it to Greek philosophy," Étienne Gilson points out in *Philosophie au moyen âge*, p. 15. Justin's *First Apology* is addressed to Hadrian, and his *Second Apology* to Marcus Aurelius, as are Melito of Sardis's *Apology* and Athenagoras's *Supplication*, and so on (ibid., pp. 15–33). [See Justin Martyr, *Apologies*; Melito, *On Pascha and Fragments*; and Athenagoras, *Apologeticks*.—Trans.] There is no mystery about these addresses: even if their object seems modest and aims at allowing worship and not at converting emperors, the empire is the space where the new religion—and its framework of possible dissemination—has to be authorized, and on this score, together with Greek thought, the empire is its common locus. The emperors' conversion will be an outcome; the determining phenomenon is the spreading of Christianity and its congruence with this world. Gilson's allusion to "a few attempts to justify it to Greek philosophy" is not restrictive: it was because of their very precocious character that there were only "a few attempts." Justifying the Christian religion to Greek philosophy was an ongoing process (ibid., pp. 34–137).

140. Virgil's *Bucolics* 4 anecdotally suggest that Christianity is the religion of the "age of the empire," since it has been seen as both a prophetic announcement of the birth of Jesus and a hymn celebrating Augustus's childhood, which seems more plausible. More than the balance of divination and flattery, however, it is the interchangeability of the two interpretations that is thought-provoking.

141. Later, when Catholicity is called into question, and thus becomes an object of thought, it will be designated by this Greek name.

142. The determination of this god as god of the exit, of liberation already precedes this *henotheism*. The assertion of this god's priority, preeminence, and the "jealousy" that makes him demand exclusive worship follows.

143. I allude to the difference between contemplated space and traveled [*parcouru*] space suggested by Pierre Alféri, which Thomas Dommange comments on in "Sommes-nous capables d'un monde?"

144. The limitations were local: "most of them local gods, dating from the period when the country was divided into numerous provinces" (MM, p. 19).

145. MM, pp. 20–21; emphasis added. See also: "The new imperialism was reflected in the development of the religious ideas . . . the idea arose of a universal god Aten to whom restriction to a single country and a single people no longer applied" p. 59). "In the case of the genesis of monotheism, however, we can point to no external factor other than the one we have already mentioned—that this development was linked with the establishment of closer relations between different nations and with the building up of a great empire" (MM, p. 108).

146. However, as Freud shows, the reduction of polytheism affects theism itself: (a) starting with the religion of Aten, "everything to do with myths, magic and sorcery is excluded from it" (MM, p. 24); (b) "Nothing was to be heard any more of Osiris and his kingdom" (ibid.); and above all, this process produces a "highly spiritualized religion" (p. 46). Freud throws a very distinct light on this "spiritualization" of religion.

147. Outside of the logical genesis of the concept of empire, this probably corresponds to the factual genesis of the historical empire, the premises of imperiality having taken shape during what has been termed "Athenian imperialism," which was inherent in the constitution of Athens. See pt. I, § 3 of this book.

148. See pt. II, § 12.

149. The lag is quite slight. This is the time that focuses on a Judeo-Hellenic rapprochement, the centuries from the first to the fourth C.E., when *this intersection* constitutes itself as a primordial theological question and acquires its structure. See Gilson, *Philosophie au moyen âge*.

150. Why put "Jewish" in quotation marks? Because while the Greeks think of themselves as, and call themselves, Greeks, the "Jews" neither think nor name themselves "Jewish" plainly and evenly from the beginning to the end of the process that the biblical tales relate. Although there is a filiation and a tradition from Abraham to Daniel—and of course even to Jesus—it seems quite reductionist to gather these fifteen centuries of history under the category of one "religion," and, what is more, one that is assimilated to what we term "Judaism" today. Judaism as a religion has a point of birth and particularization that needs to be determined: Jean Bottéro, for example, places the date within the later prophetic era (see Bottéro, "Ezéchiel et la fondation du judaïsme," in *Naissance de Dieu*, pp. 145ff.). Whether or not one agrees with this dating, one should understand Judaism as a concrete historical entity, seen through its formation and its transforma-

tions, and not as a transhistorical essence running from Abraham to the disputes of the Chief Rabbinate of Paris.

151. John 3:16 (KJV). See also: ". . . and the bread that I will give is my flesh, which I will give for the life of the world" (John 6:51).

152. See pt. III, § 21.

153. See, e.g., KJV: "For God sent not his Son into the world to condemn the world; but that the world through him might be saved" (John 3:17); "[We] know that this is indeed the Christ, the Saviour of the world" (John 4:42); "I came not to judge the world, but to save the world" (John 12:47); and also, no doubt metaphorically, "As long as I am in the world, I am the light of the world" (John 9:5).

154. This is what makes the death of Christ into a new exodus, according to the schema of Easter. This death is thematized as a new exit from Egypt, which is to say setting across and away, free of the world—with Old Testament Egypt retrospectively reinterpreted as the figure of the world, as mentioned. See, e.g., John 13–17, from "Now before the feast of the passover, when Jesus knew that his hour was come that he should depart out of this world unto the Father . . . " (John 13:1), to the long prayer that follows (John 17:1–26). But also, "Moreover, brethen, I would not that ye should be ignorant, how that all our fathers were under the cloud, and all passed through the sea; / And were all baptized unto Moses in the cloud and in the sea; / And did all eat the same spiritual meat; / And did all drink the same spiritual drink: for they drank of that spiritual Rock that followed them: and that Rock was Christ" (1 Cor. 10:1–4). The Pauline accent here is quite different.

155. See Bailly, *Adieu*.

156. E.g., Hegel, *Phänomenologie des Geistes*, p. 590; Nietzsche, *Gay Science*, para. 108, p. 109.

157. The Greek word *skhēma* is translated as *figure* in the French Jerusalem Bible: "Car elle passe, la figure de ce monde." [The KJV translates it as "fashion": "For the fashion of this world passeth away."—Trans.]

158. Let us say gnostic, but not only in the narrow meaning of the term. Patočka's "Christian Platonicism," for example, is not completely devoid of this, since he energetically denies the importance of the Hebraic contribution to Christianity and therefore to Europe. See Patočka, *Plato and Europe*, pp. 128, 149ff. [See also Gasché, *Europe*, p. 238.—Trans.]

159. Matt. 26:31.

160. We can see that this branching out is also scriptural: the tale of the institution of the Eucharist appears in the Synoptic Gospels (Matt. 26:17–29, Mark 14:12–25, Luke 22:7–20), and in Paul (1 Cor. 11:23–25). However, it is absent from the story of the paschal meal in John 13:17, and it is precisely the Johannine text that forcefully develops a theology of the world. It is as if two theological interpretations of the death of God stood side by side (or opposed): the one as exit from the world, the other as bodily transfer (and these perhaps come down to two ways of understanding incarnation: coming to the world *or* incorporation). One would then

have to interpret why the one comes later than the other (in the process, probably, of the passage from the practices of the early communities to a more "worldwide" view). It remains that in the corpus constituted as an organic whole ("Christianity"), the birth functions as a coming to the world, and the death as a transfer to the bodies of the disciples.

161. One can easily see here a premise and a condition for what the West will later develop as the transcendence of individuality.

162. Luther, *Ausgewählte Werke*, 2: 137. ["Denn Christus sagt: 'Wo zwei miteinander eins sind auf Erden, da bin ich in ihrer Mitte." Here Luther modifies his own translation, which had been, "Denn wo zween oder drey versamlet sind *in meinem Namen / Da bin ich mitten unter inen*" (Where two or three are gathered *in my name*, there I am among them) (Matt. 18:20, in Luther Bible [1545]); my emphasis.—Trans.]

163. See Guénoun, *L'enlèvement de la politique*.

164. Not in inmost interiority—in privacy and secrecy, and *on this score* supposed to be outside of the world—but precisely *between and among* you, Ernst Bloch protests: "Jesus hat nie behauptet: 'Das Reich Gottes ist in euch,' die Stelle (Luk. 17,21) lautet vielmehr richtig übersetzt: 'Das Reich Gottes ist mitten unter euch [Gk., *entos umōn*]'" (Jesus never asserted, 'The kingdom of God is within you'; instead, rightly translated, this passage [Luke 17:21] says, 'The kingdom of God is in the very middle among you'") (Bloch, *Atheismus*, p. 125). But doubt is no longer permissible after the Eucharist: it is in you, within each of you, within the body of each of you.

165. Why only the baptized? We should stop at this, of course, and determine the significance of this separation, which provisionally limits the ability of the Reformation to extend "democratically."

166. We can see in this a Protestant precedent for the *generality* of Rousseau's will, which resists any *particularity* (any appropriation by a *part* of the common) in exercising one's will.

167. Paul's indications are quite numerous. They do not, as far as we know, establish any explicit and direct link with Eucharistic sharing, but formulate the unity of Christians (or men; or men and women) as the unity of the body of Christ, either on the model of a functional cohesiveness, or in accordance with the schema of the gathering. "For as we have many members in one body, and all members have not the same office: / So we, being many, are one body in Christ, and every one members one of another" (Rom. 12:4–5). See also 1 Cor. 12:12–28, esp. 27–28; and also, for a somewhat different aspect, 1 Cor. 6:15; or Eph. 1:22, 2:14–16, 3:6 ("the Gentiles should be fellow heirs, and of the same body, and partakers of his promise in Christ by the gospel"), 4:4, 4:12–16 (esp. "for the perfecting of the saints, *for the edifying of the body of Christ*: / till we all come in the unity of the faith"; emphasis added), 5:23–30; and Col, 1:18–24, 2:17–19, and 3:15 ("also ye are called in one body").

168. During one of the sessions of Jean-Luc Nancy's seminar "Geophilosophy of Europe," Université Marc Bloch, Strasbourg, fall and winter 1991–92.

169. Nancy's remark was brief and allusive. This explanation is my own.

170. See Stétié, *Lumière sur lumière*, p. 49.

171. See Dagorn, *Geste d'Ismaël*, p. 162n42, and Delcambre, *Mahomet*, p. 22.

172. We may assume that "the abrogating verses in Sūrat an-Najm exalt the Kaʿbah at the expense of the other shrines. It is worth remembering in this connexion [sic] that with the growth of Muḥammad's power, these shrines were all destroyed," William Montgomery Watt writes (*Muhammad at Mecca*, p. 104).

173. Hourani, *History of the Arab Peoples*, p. 17.

174. Watt, *Muhammad at Mecca*, pp. 96, 158–61.

175. The original controversy, of course, and not the other one (not, i.e., Salman Rushdie's novel of that title, even if the violent response evoked by Rushdie's book can doubtless be understood in connection with the ambiguity of the original story). See Watt, *Muhammad at Mecca*, pp. 104–9, and Benslama, *Fiction troublante*, passim.

176. See Watt, *Muhammad at Mecca*, pp. 33ff., 39, 158–61. For a simplified discussion of this, see Delcambre, *Mahomet*, pp. 32, 40, and 42.

177. Hourani, *History of the Arab Peoples*, p.7; Watt, *Muhammad at Mecca*, pp. 1–23.

178. Receding nomadic lifestyles (sedentarization), but also *urbanization*, nonagricultural sedentarization, based on new commercial and financial practices, offer some hints. Watt insists on this aspect of the situation in Mecca: "The Qu'rān appeared not in the atmosphere of the desert, but in that of high finance" (Watt, *Muhammad at Mecca*, p. 3). What is involved is a changing flow (from nomadic traffic to financial exchanges) as much as the passage from mobility to fixity or the other way around.

179. See Hourani, *History of the Arab Peoples*, p.7; Watt, *Muhammad at Mecca*, pp. 1–23.

180. See Hourani, ibid.; Watt, ibid.

181. See Koran, surah 30 (The Romans), 2–9: "The Romans are vanquished, / In a near land, and they, after being vanquished, shall overcome, / Within a few years. Allah's is the command before and after; and on that day the believers shall rejoice, / . . . but most people do not know. / . . . Have they not travelled in the earth and seen how was the end of those before them? They were stronger than these in prowess, and dug up the earth, and built on it in greater abundance than these have built on it, and there came to them their apostles with clear arguments; so it was beseeming for Allah that He should deal with them unjustly, but they dealt unjustly with their own souls."

182. Ibid.: "Then evil was the end of those who did evil, because they rejected the communications of Allah and used to mock them." See the whole text of surah 30.

183. See Rodinson, *Mahomet*, chaps. 1 and 2, pp. 21–59.

288   *Notes to Part III*

184. The term *débilité* is from Berl, *Europe et Asie*, p. 53.
185. Ibid., p. 54.
186. Koran (Berque), p. 674.
187. Koran, surah 87 (The Most High), 18–19. There are numerous other mentions, of course, as shown for example in the index to Berque's translation of the Koran (or in any other similar compilation), with its multiple entries linked to Old or New Testament figures (Abraham, Jacob, Isaac, Solomon, Gabriel, Jesus, Mary, and so forth). A traditional tale reports that Muhammad's (older) wife, after one of his "mystical" crises, sought advice from a cousin. "His name was Waraqa ibn Nawfal and he was a scholar with a wide knowledge of the scriptures, both Jewish and Christian. . . . He said, 'This is the *nāmūs* that was revealed to Moses'" (Rodinson, *Muhammad*, p. 73). [According to Rodinson, *nāmūs* "was the Greek word *nomos*, meaning Law" (ibid.).—Trans.]

188. The way in which Judaism developed and spread during this era defines and inscribes it within the structures of the Roman world. The Jewish Diaspora was [in this sense] Roman. And, from this point of view, even if the Judaism that Muhammad encountered was doubtless quite peripheral, it was not isolated, or separable, from what Judaism had become, during more than five centuries, as a component of the Roman *world*.

189. In this context, let us note the idea, echoed by Bernard Lewis, that *the very concept of religion* might be linked to the emergence of Islam: "Indeed, it has been argued with perhaps some exaggeration that the notion of religion as a class or category, of which Judaism, Christianity, and Islam are individual examples, originated only with the advent of Islam and the ability of Muslims to perceive and recognize two distinct predecessors to their own form of religious revelation and polity. No such awareness can be found among earlier Christians or Jews nor among any of the other cults of the ancient world. For a Muslim, the advent of Muḥammad and the revelation of the Qur'ān marks the last in a series of similar events through which God's purpose was revealed to mankind. There had been a number of prophets whom God had sent on a mission to mankind as bearers of a revealed book. Muḥammad was the seal of the prophets and the Qur'ān the final and perfect revelation. All that was of value in earlier revelations was contained in it. What was not contained in it was due to the corruption or distortion of earlier revealed texts" (Lewis, *Muslim Discovery of Europe*, p. 64). And Lewis adds: "The principle of separateness and coexistence is usually justified by citing Sura 109. 'Say: O Unbelievers! I shall not worship what you worship. You do not worship what I worship. . . . *To you, your religion. To me, my religion.*' This was a new notion, without antecedents in either Christian or Jewish belief and practice" (ibid., p. 65; emphasis added). This view is clearly very close to what I have suggested about the religious as inscribing division, as well as a bond between that which has been divided. See pt. II, §12 of this book.

190. One of the canonical episodes of the Prophet's biography reports a trip

during his adolescence to Syria, in Byzantine territory. See Watt, *Muhammad at Mecca*, pp. 33ff., and Delcambre, *Mahomet*, pp. 32–33.

191. "The usual account is that on one day shortly after his return to Medina from al-Ḥudaybiyah Muḥammad sent out six messengers with letters for the Najash-ī or Negus of Abyssinia, for the governor of Bostra (Buṣrā) to hand on to the Byzantine emperor, for the Persian emperor (perhaps sent by way of the Yemen), for the Muqawqis or ruler of Egypt" (Watt, *Muhammad at Medina*, p. 41). According to the same traditional accounts, which Watt does not accept as credible on this issue, what these messages contained was a kind of summons addressed to the rulers: "he conceived of Islam as a universal religion and summoned the Byzantine and Persian emperors and other lesser potentates to accept it" (ibid.; see also p. 44).

192. However, the relation to Abrahamic genealogy is ambiguous.

193. This phase cannot be dated with exactitude: its movement is a component of the entire constitution of Islam, from the first conflicts with Meccans, the struggles and the decision to leave, to most of the stay at Medina. It will not be absent either (at least not completely) from the following time period. Let us say that it is a dominant trend in the first phase, before a kind of reversal, which I shall try to show. Regarding this first phase, I essentially follow Rodinson, *Muhammad*.

194. Ibid., p. 159.

195. See also Watt, "These scanty details are sufficient to show that Muḥammad's interest in the tribes on the route to Syria was not simply a matter of chance. These tribes were either Christian or had some acquaintance with Christianity, and because of this may have been more attracted to Islam than to the pagans farther south" (*Muhammad at Medina*, p. 45). And further, "the road north had a prominent place in Muḥammad's strategic thinking" (p. 105).

196. See ibid., pp. 13ff.

197. Koran, surah 2 (The Cow), 140–44. See also Rodinson, *Muhammad*, pp. 215ff.

198. French translations of this passage in the Koran are: "Ainsi vous constituons-Nous communauté médiane" (Berque); "une Communauté éloignée des extrêmes" (Masson); "une nation intermédiaire" (Kazimirski).

199. It may be Arabism as such that is born in this way. It seems that the signifier "Arab" in the meaning of "national" is absent from testimonies predating the Koran. See Watt, *Muhammad at Medina*, p. 143.

200. In French, $h18$ is: "L'Islam (se) retourne vers le lieu."

201. See Watt, *Muhammad at Medina*, p. 69.

202. I owe my knowledge of these details linked to Muhammad's family genealogy, as well as the meanings of the Zamzam Well and the recourse to the genealogy of Ishmael, to Fethi Benslama, *Nuit brisée*, pp. 208–18; "L'enfant et le lieu," pp. 56–58.

203. See Dagorn, *Geste d'Ismaël*, passim, esp. chap. 4, pp. 127–66.

204. The link between the two genealogies is not only one of ancestry: like

all Arabs, Muhammad does descend from Ishmael, but his personal connection is more of a doubling: in a way, the story of Muhammad *restarts* the story of Ishmael, repeats the same near-death and the same act of saving him. Moreover, Muhammad's ancestor (his grandfather) *discovers* the ancestry, unearths the origin, and reveals the source.

205. Gen. 21:17 (KJV). See also Dagorn, *Geste d'Ismaël*, passim.

206. Still, it is noteworthy that the stone and the spring are adjacent. Even if each seems to convey an ontological primariness of the place (as plenitude by way of the stone, and as re-origination or re-sourcing by way of the spring), each nonetheless carries distinct values: the place as a being-there [*être-là*] that is compact and homogeneous within itself, on the one hand; and the place as gift, rushing, and extroversion of being, on the other—thus a split, after all, which dualizes this absolutely first unity as if by a double absoluteness and primariness.

207. One of the most contentious theological vices is *shirk*, or associationism, that is, giving God associates, and thus betraying, altering, or affecting his uniqueness, and both Christianity (because of the Trinity) and philosophy (because of the theory of secondary causes) are guilty of it. See Gardet, *Hommes de l'Islam*, p. 206 and n. 10.

208. Islam involves neither an original sin nor a historical incarnation: it lacks the division that makes the fall, or redemption, ontologically possible. That is why it only knows one language (as the language of revelation), and one space.

209. See Rodinson, *Fascination de l'Islam*, pp. 35–53, and passim.

210. We often hear that the specificity of Europe is based on the break with the empire and Eastern Orthodox Christianity. This is true, but let us recall that this separation is indefinitely produced as ambiguous and never clear-cut. Strictly, the split with the east can only posit a west. The Byzantine schism traces out the opposition between western Europe and eastern Europe in our geography. But that distinction, as the words themselves clearly put it, does not posit any European specificity: since there are *two Europes* opposed in it, and therefore, if you will, two parts of Europe, which presuppose a common concept of Europe. Of course, eastern Europe is in a sense also an outside of Europe. Patočka repeats this insistently—Europe amounts to its westernness, in a very deep sense (see Patočka, HE). But in my view, this shows that it is only in its ambiguity that this oriental difference is constitutive of Europe, whereas Islam and the retreat before it posit Europe as such, as the figure of a *withdrawn world* [*monde replié*].

PART IV: NO RETURNS

1. My reflections here on the common, being-common, and being-in-common were made possible by writings by Jean-Luc Nancy, especially *La communauté désœuvrée* (*The Inoperative Community*) and "La Comparution / The Compearance," although the proposed hypotheses often differ from his.

2. On the determination of the common as being [*être*], see pt. IV, §27.

3. In French: "du peuple manque" (see Deleuze, *Time-Image*, p. 220).

4. As in the saying, "J'étais au bal, y avait du populaire" (I was at the dance, there were lots of folks—Trans.).

5. See Kant, *Critique of Pure Reason*, p. 392; Wittgenstein, *Tractatus Logico-Philosophicus* (Ogden), p. 31.

6. Hypotheses such as "one has to think the real in its regional differences, as multiple, partial, without homogeneous totalization," etc., are obviously unifying propositions—ideas involving the world.

7. See Braudel, *Civilisation matérielle*, vol. 3: *Le temps du monde*, and id., *Dynamique du capitalisme*, pp. 82 ff.

8. See Lenin, "Imperialism as a Special Stage of Capitalism," in *Imperialism, the Highest Stage of Capitalism*, pp. 265ff.

9. I am not looking here into the validity of Lenin's descriptions (made in 1916, in the middle of the "imperialist war").

10. This analysis of worldwide globalization opens with very famous words: "A spectre is haunting Europe" (Marx and Engels, *Manifesto of the Communist Party* [henceforward cited as *Manifesto*], p. 14).

11. "From the serfs of the Middle Ages sprang the chartered burghers of the earliest towns. From these burgesses the first elements of the bourgeoisie were developed" (Marx and Engels, *Manifesto*, p. 15).

12. Marx and Engels, *Manifesto*, p. 15. I am indebted to Thomas Dommange for rereading this passage and the next one from this perspective. These pages owe a great deal to suggestions he made.

13. Immanuel Wallerstein insists on this worldwide dimension from the start of what he terms "historical capitalism": "In the real world of historical capitalism, almost all commodity chains of any importance have traversed these state frontiers. This is not a recent innovation. It has been true from the very beginning of historical capitalism" (Wallerstein, *Historical Capitalism*, p. 31). He locates these origins precisely "in late-fifteenth-century Europe" (p. 19). More particularly, he forcefully asserts: "The modern state was never a completely autonomous political entity. The states developed and were shaped as integral parts of an interstate system" (pp. 56–57), which seems to agree with my hypothesis that states constituted themselves from fragments of the preceding Roman empire and not from their own internal logic. To my way of thinking, it is this native interinvolvement that transforms into the states' later interdependence—and perdures because (global) structural dependence does not stop at the fall of the empire. Wallerstein analyzes this worldwide globality not with the concept of imperialism but by reworking that of "world-economy" or "capitalist world-economy" (pp. 19ff.), sometimes construed as "world-system" (pp. 19, 39), and even "European world-economy" (p. 19). It is a matter of accounting for the fact that "the historical development of capitalism has involved the thrust towards the commodification of everything" (p. 16). And this

does not necessarily imply that the category "empire" is abandoned: Wallerstein has recourse to the notion of "world-empire" ("the dynamic of the concentration of military power led to recurrent thrusts to transform the interstate system into a world-empire" [p. 57])—which after all is not far removed from the canonical definition of imperialism. Most interesting in these analyses (it seems to me) is the fact that worldwide globalization is not considered according to the common view that sees it as de-localization (the loss of local singularity for the benefit of a single, homogeneous, and undetermined worldwide space). On the contrary, "world-economy" proceeds as localization or relocalization (p. 36), by way of a "hierarchization of space" (p. 30), and notably the "polarization between the core" (defined as the winners in unequal capitalist exchanges) and "peripheral zones" (p. 30, defined conceptually as the zone of the losers in this exchange). It is not the opposite; it is not the position that implies a win or a loss, but the fact that one is globally winning or losing that defines a zone as central or peripheral (pp. 31–32). Capitalism produces its geography (pp. 38ff.), and the space of the world is not smooth. A cynical geography, to be sure, but not in-different.

14. See above, pt. I, §3.

15. Whether this grasping should legitimately be called "experience" is a question that we shall have to ask ourselves.

16. Without claiming to remake a history of art or a systematic aesthetics, let me formulate two remarks: (1) I am taking *theater* here to be the paradigmatic art form in the epoch or age of the assembly. But we could articulate the concept of it together with that of architecture or sculpture, at least as arts that preceded *image capture*. Neither architecture nor sculpture is essentially grappling with images as such; they are not arts of frontality, and the audience has no need to stand *in front*, but rather inside or around—and these are determinations that correspond to modes of assembling. From the Charioteer of Delphi to the Laocoön statue, we know that one of the evolutions most easily noticed is precisely the passage from a sculpture made to be seen from more than one side, which convenes its viewers *around* it, to a sculpture wanting to be seen from the front—frontalized—and thus arguably *a sculpture from the age of painting* (see Schefold, *Art of Classical Greece*, p. 22). (2) At the other pole, it seems that we have little to gain (and much to lose) from thinking of video as an extension of cinema. It is altogether different. To reflect upon this question in a useful way, one has to start by analyzing the *process of constituting an audience* before a television or video monitor, and understand what relation it establishes with what is offered to one's view and hearing—because of the spectators' mode of assembling, their behavior during ongoing programming, screens of various sizes, *audiovisual* articulation, and finally (especially?) the effects induced or produced by the simultaneity of *live* shows. In this sense, any general rhapsodizing about "screens"—the whole downscaled "screenology" ubiquitous in magazines and some seminars—most often displays (through pointless assimilations, as in references to the "civilization of images," and so on) an abysmal *lack of*

thinking. Of course, video comes from the world's factory of images (but also *and perhaps even more so* from radio); however, it comes from it with procedures that one has to analyze carefully simply to avoid missing what is new—something that *goes out* of the world in order perhaps to invite us to think its exit.

17. See Fried, *Absorption and Theatricality*, passim; and Eisenstein, "Du cinéma en relief," in *Le mouvement de l'art*, pp. 97–158.

18. See Guénoun, *L'exhibition des mots*, pp. 12–19.

19. Heidegger, "Die Zeit des Weltbildes," in *Holzwege*, pp. 75–113 (marginal pagination [henceforth in parentheses following the page number—Trans.], pp. 69–104); in French, "L'époque des conceptions du monde," in *Chemins qui ne mènent nulle part*, pp. 99–146. The form of the title in French is obviously surprising. Let us skip over the translation of *Zeit* by *époque*, having to do with the "epoch," no doubt, since the translation (like *Zeit und Sein* [Time and Being]) is from 1962. The translation of *Bild* [image] by *conception* is more astonishing, all the more so since the text analyzes the relation of *Bild* with vision and seeing. But, ultimately, what is most questionable is this substitution of the plural *les conceptions* for the singular of *des Weltbildes*, a substitution that the translators themselves point out (p. 453n) in all honesty. Here the most peculiar and revelatory operation is at work: what the translation resists is admitting that the image of the world as such (and not such or such an image, even unified under the concept of their plurality) marks the "epoch" [Fr., *époque*] or defines the new age [Gm., *Neuzeit*]. Many thanks to Paola Marrati for her suggestion that I reread this text carefully.

20. Heidegger, *Holzwege*, p. 89 (82); *Chemins qui ne mènent nulle part*, p. 117. [The translation of passages from *Holzwege* (henceforth HW) are mine.—Trans.]

21. "Here, 'world' is naming beingness as a whole" (ibid.).

22. "To represent [Gm., *vorstellen*] here means to say: to set up [Gm., *stellen*] before oneself something one has taken from oneself [Gm., *von sich her*], and to secure what is set up [Gm., *das Gestellte*] as such a thing. . . . Being is no longer what has been present here, but rather that which only representation will have set up opposite us, the ob-ject [Gm., *Gegen-ständige*]" (HW, p. 108 [100]; *Chemins qui ne mènent nulle part*, pp. 140–41). [Further page references to Heidegger, *Holzwege* are mostly given in the body of the text.—Trans.]

23. I would like to suggest the phrase *image-monde* [in French] for *Weltbild*, since this sentence is built on their opposition—in the sense in which Deleuze differentiates movement-image or time-image from images *of* movement or time.

24. "But in every place where [*wo*] beingness does *not* become interpreted in this sense, the world cannot shift into the picture, and there can be no world image" (HW, p. 90 [83]). The translation [both into French and into English—Trans.] here includes the rather heavy term "become" to bring out *wird* [from *werden*, "to become"; used as an auxiliary verb to form the passive—Trans.] in the original [Heidegger's sentence is: "Überall dort, aber, wo das Seiende *nicht* in diesem Sinne ausgelegt wird."].

25. See HW, p. 100 [92], addendum (*Zusatz*) 5; and *Being and Time*, paras. 11–24.

26. I am thinking here of the concept *obraznost*, which Sergei Eisenstein formed—as François Albéra tells us—from the Russian word *obraz*, image. Albéra translates it as *imagicité* ["imaginicity" in literature about Eisenstein—Trans.], a term that suggests the intermediary term "imagic," which is not necessary and does not (as I understand it) come up in Russian. *Imagéité* (imageness) is made from "image," or, if we need an adjective, from *imagé* (imaged or pictured). See François Albéra, introduction, in Eisenstein, *Cinématisme, peinture et cinéma*, p. 10.

27. This (wide) periodization of the "modern" matches exactly Hegel's periodization of the "romantic," which is also very extensive—and relies perhaps on an implicit reminder of what is *Roman* in the word *romantic*. See Lacoue-Labarthe and Nancy, *L'absolu littéraire*, pp. 11–13. Definition of "modern": "1361, Oresme, from Vulgar Latin *modernus* (6th century, Cassiodorus), from *modo*, recently" (Dauzat et al., *Nouveau dictionnaire étymologique et historique*; alphabetically arranged, s.v. *moderne*). Cassiodorus: "Latin statesman and writer (490–580). Praetorian prefect; historiographer for Theodoric the Great; mediator between the Roman and barbarian worlds; in 540, he retired to the monastery at Vivarium [in Calabria], which he had founded and where he introduced the custom of copying manuscripts. In his main work, *Institutiones divinarum et saecularium litterarum*, which served as a guide for medieval culture, he gathered important religious and secular knowledge" (*Grand dictionnaire encyclopédique Larousse*, 2: 1847).

28. It may be the general structure of the *imago mundi* that "modern art" tackles, *starting from the image* and in the age of the image, in contemplating the displacement of this mode of pictoriality, challenging or de-constructing it. Modern art: that which, from Manet to Kandinsky (and around and beyond them), seeks to *make* images say, Let's break the image, let's get out of it—enough with images already. An image at the limits of the image, an image wishing to push the boundaries of any image, of all that can be pictured, or *imagined*; a program of pressuring the imaginary, summoning the imaginary to the extreme outer borders of its unimaginable limits—by all means, then, an art of the sublime.

29. "The time period [Gm., *Zeitalter*] that is determined through this event . . . sets itself up on its own as the new one [Gm., *das neue*]. Being new pertains to the world that has become image" (HW, p. 92 [85]).

30. "With Descartes, the completion of Western metaphysics begins. But since such a completion is only possible again as metaphysics, modern thinking has its own prominence" (HW, p. 99 [91]).

31. "However, one should not interpret [machine technology], wrongly, as a simple practical application [Gm., *Anwendung*] of modern mathematical science [Gm., *mathematische Naturwissenschaft*]. Machine technology is itself an autonomous transformation of praxis in such a way that it then requires the use [Gm., *Verwendung*] of mathematical science" (HW, p. 75 [69]).

32. I.e., "Hellenicity" (p. 94 [86]); "beginning of Greek thinking" (p. 105 [97–98]); "to Greek appreciation" (p. 91 [84]); "the Greeks" (p. 94 [87]); "Man in the Greeks' basic relationship to beingness" (p. 105 [97]).—Trans.

33. German text: "Das Seiende ist das Aufgehende und Sichöffnende, was als das Anwesende über den Menschen als den Anwesenden kommt" (HW, p. 90 [83]).—Trans.

34. Let us recall Patočka's gesture—his gesture, precisely, because what is at stake here is rather different—when he writes, "From the moment that the perishing of the *polis* had already been decided, philosophy transformed itself into what was to be its image for millenia [*sic*], transforming itself into metaphysics" (Patočka, HE, p. 65). And further, "[in the European heritage] the care for the soul is transformed in the two great historical catastrophes, that of the *polis* and that of the Roman Empire" (ibid.).

35. Heidegger, HW, pp. 100–101 [93]; emphasis added. One might boldly translate *Zusammenstand* [substantive related to *zusammenstellen*—Trans.] into French as *con-tenance* ["con-tainance"], or *continence*, in the "continental" sense that I have been using here. *Continent*, "masculine noun, borrowed (1532) from the Latin *continens*, adjectival present participle of *continere* (see *contenir*): to hold together" (*Dictionnaire historique de la langue française*, ed. Rey, 1: 486).

36. "Machine technology to this day remains the most visible offshoot of the essence [Gm., *Wesen*] of modern technics, which is identical with the essence of modern metaphysics" (HW, p. 75 [69]).

37. And this is shown by Italy's singular place in the process of the Renaissance, as well as, in the Italian peninsula, by the decisive significance of unearthing the remnants of Rome, a kind of trauma brought on by the display of this buried world—still there. See Chastel and Klein, *L'âge de l'humanisme*, pp. 95–100 (esp. pp. 99–100); and Du Bellay, *Antiquities of Rome*, passim.

38. On the avatar of the idea of empire and the (positive) idea of "spiritual imperialism," see Fernando Pessoa, "Sébastianisme et le cinquième empire" [Portuguese title: "Sebastiano e o Quinto Imperio."—Trans.], in id., *Chemin du serpent*, pp. 295ff.

39. Descartes, *Discourse on Method*, p. 35. "Masters," in any case. And on determination "to change my desires rather than the order of the world," see ibid., p. 14.

40. This military vocabulary also appears elsewhere: "The fundamental process of modern times is the conquest [Gm., *Eroberung*] of the world by the image" (HW, p. 94 [87]). What is dominated is also the very thing that resists (see pt. III, §2). It is not as if a benevolent harmony had preestablished the predisposition of the dominated ones to resist, and that in this way everything that is subjected might have an affinity for resistance. No. The concept of domination is simply understood here as that which exerts itself over that which resists—without which there is nothing at all to dominate. That which is dominating subjects that which is dominated inasmuch as this domination is not a given, being the

stakes of a struggle or a confrontation. "Domination" means imposition, forcing, and ultimately violence toward beings. Domination is not superiority; it is mastery, overlordship, sovereignty, or suzerainty over things or beings—*Herrschaft*, indeed. And so, the concept of domination calls for the idea—the physical or energetic idea, as it were—of a resistance that has been opposed, subjected, and (temporarily, at least) overcome. The mastery bears upon that which (slave or subject) has been enslaved or subjected. In saying this, one is thus indicating, provisionally—in view of a completely different development or program from the one in this book—that if the world is *what is subjected to the empire*, it is also necessarily *that which is resisting it. The world resists* imperiality. In a sense, there is a constitutive necessity for the world to enter into a relationship of resistance with the empire (with imperialism, caesarism, or the Reich). Should one rely on this and expect its victory to project a liberated future? That is the question, and it is political. Or should one fear that this resistance of the world might be too closely associated with the domination it opposes, too caught up in its economy and its game—and choose instead to move to another terrain?

41. Marx, *Capital*, p. 41 and elsewhere. [Spellings of Marx's terms in German here follow Marx, *Das Kapital* (1883)—Trans.]

42. Wallerstein, *Historical Capitalism*, p. 16.

43. Debord, *Société du spectacle*, p. 24.

44. "In the same way the exchange values of commodities must be capable of being expressed in terms of something common to them all, of which thing they represent a greater or less [*sic*] quantity. / This common 'something' [Gm., *dieß Gemeinsame*] cannot be either a geometrical, a chemical, or any other natural property of commodities" (Marx, *Capital*, p. 27; Marx, *Das Kapital* [1883], p. 69). [Quotations are from Marx, *Capital*, unless this English edition from 1887 diverges much from the German text of 1883 or the French text quoted by the author. When it does, I have used and translated the relevant passages in Marx, *Das Kapital* (1883). The author's main source is Marx, *Le capital* (trans. Lefebvre et al.).—Trans.]

45. And also, "the exchange of commodities is evidently an act characterised by a total abstraction [Gm., *Abstraktion*] from use value" (Marx, *Capital*, p. 27). [Further page references to Marx, *Capital*, mostly appear in the body of the text.—Trans.]

46. See Rodrigo, "Marx et la phénoménologie," pp. 94–95.

47. See Pierre Macherey, "À propos du processus d'exposition du *Capital*," in Althusser et al., *Lire Le Capital*, 1: 234ff.

48. Marx, *Das Kapital* (1883), p. 64.

49. Ibid., p. 82, gives the phrase "Träger von Werth" in quotation marks. In Marx, *Le capital*, p. 53, Roy translates it as *porte-valeur*. Rancière, "Concept de critique," p. 136, writes *Wertträger*. [The standard English translation (see, e.g., Marx, *Capital*, p. 35) is "depository of value."—Trans.]

Notes to Part IV   297

50. Marx, *Das Kapital* (1883), p. 101. [German text: "Das Geheimnißvolle der Waarenform besteht also einfach darin, daß sie den Menschen die gesellschaftlichen Charaktere ihrer eignen Arbeit als gegenständliche Charaktere der Arbeitsprodukte selbst, als gesellschaftliche Natureigenschaften dieser Dinge zurückspiegelt . . ."—Trans.]

51. See Rodrigo, "Marx et la phénoménologie," p. 95; and Rancière, "Concept de critique," p. 135.

52. Marx, *Capital*, p. 47; *Das Kapital* (1883), p. 101.

53. Marx, *Das Kapital* (1883), p. 110 (my emphasis; the interpolation is Marx's). Toward the end of the pages about fetishism, Marx is seized with the curious desire *to make commodities speak*. "Could commodities themselves speak, they would say: Our use value may be a thing that interests men. It is no part of us as objects [Gm., *Er kömmt uns nicht als Dingen zu*]. What, however, does belong to us as objects [i.e., as things; Gm., *Was uns aber dinglich zukömmt*—Trans.], is our value" (Marx, *Capital*, pp. 51–52). Strange prosopopeia. Indeed, Marx notes that use value is a human fact—unarguably, since it takes human beings to have an "interest" in use; and, furthermore, exchange and use are opposed (as he has repeatedly said), and therefore, from this strange point of view of the commodities (the point of view of exchange: "What, however, does belong to us as objects [things—Trans.], is our value. *Our natural intercourse as commodities proves it*" [p. 52; emphasis added]), the difference from use thus appears as the difference from the human. And this makes the commodity—expressing itself as such—posit itself as nonhuman, and *therefore as a thing*. Commodities speak as things; *commodities are formulated and shaped as things*. This is the trap into which the economist falls when, speaking from the bottom of the soul of the commodities [Gm., *aus der Waarenseele heraus*], he believes that he is discovering that what belongs [Gm., *zukömmt*] to the "commodities as objects [as things—Trans.] is [their] value" (ibid.).

54. As in the colloquial expression "to be fixated on something" (to fetishize something).

55. Balibar, *Philosophie de Marx*, p. 66.

56. Marx, *Capital*, p. 47; emphasis added.

57. Marx speaks here of the "mystical character of commodities," and of "the mystical veil" of the "life-process of society" (Marx, *Capital*, pp. 46, 51).

58. Balibar, *Philosophie de Marx*, p. 66.

59. Objectality linked to "object choice" (e.g., of partial objects), of which fetishism could be a specific example. Jacques Lacan speaks of "a finality that allows itself to be instinctual, in the sense that it is based on the image of the maturation of an ineffable object, the Object with a capital O that governs the phase of objectality (to be distinguished, significantly, from objectivity by virtue of its affective substance)" (Lacan, "The Direction of the Treatment and the Principles of its Power," in *Écrits* [trans. Sheridan], p. 269).

60. It is in the sense of "being a reflection" and not "to reflect" that the commodity mirrors or reflects the image—as a reflection, not as a mirror. One could not argue that the commodity is the mirror, the real thing that sends an image back to an observer. The commodity is this image itself, this reflection—what Balibar, in a psychological sense, terms "this representation." In the opposite hypothesis, the commodity, *qua* commodity, would have to be a material reality that is the mirror and send back the image; and Marx does precisely indicate, in the development of his optical comparison, that "the existence of the things *qua* commodities, and the value relation between the products of labour which stamps them as commodities, *have absolutely no connection with their physical properties and with the material relations arising therefrom*. There is a definite social relation between men, that assumes, in their eyes, *the fantastic form* of a relation between things" (Marx, *Capital*, p. 47; emphasis added). The commodity is not a material object that "sends back" an image; it "reflects" in the way our words reflect our thoughts. The commodity is the reflection itself, not the reflecting surface.

61. Marx, *Capital*, p. 47. See also n. 60 above on the commodity as reflection.

62. See Rancière, "Concept de critique," p. 137, as well as the rest of the passage, pp. 133–38.

63. Marx, *Capital*, p. 46. In this context, Rancière calls upon a great quotation from Marx: "This *inversion* (*Verkehrung*) by which the sensibly-concrete counts only as the form of appearance of the abstractly general and not, on the contrary, the abstractly general as property of the concrete, characterises the expression of value. At the same time, it makes understanding it difficult. If I say: Roman Law and German Law are both laws, that is obvious. But if I say: Law (Das Recht), this abstraction (Abstraktum) *realises itself* in Roman Law and in German Law, in these concrete laws, the interconnection [is] becoming mystical" (cited in Rancière, "Concept de critique," pp. 137–38). [Marx's text is from Marx, "The Value-Form," para. 3, no pagination. The word "is" has been added.—Trans.] And Rancière adds, "The process that here characterizes the mode of existence of value is the one that characterized the operation of Hegelian speculation for Marx in his youth, as he illustrated it in *Die Heilige Familie* [*The Holy Family*—Trans.] with the dialectics of abstract fruit realized in concrete pears and almonds. . . . Reality is speculative" (ibid., p. 138).

64. See Heidegger, "Der Ursprung des Kunstwerkes" (The Origin of the Work of Art), in HW, pp. 1–74.

65. See Rancière, "Concept de critique," pp. 189–98.

66. See Iacono, *Fétichisme*, who reminds us that "the word 'fetish' comes from the Portuguese *feitiço*, which in turn comes from the Latin *facticius*, meaning 'artificial'" (p. 5).

67. Marx, *Capital*, p. 27. The word "Erscheinungsform" is in quotation marks in the 1989 German edition (i.e., Marx, *Das Kapital* [1883]). Rancière's translation is *forme d'apparition* (on pp. 131, 139, 145, and others); he also cites Jules Molitor

whose translation of the phrase is *forme de manifestation* (on pp. 128, 147–48, 161; see Rancière, "Concept de critique").

68. See Marx, *Das Kapital* (1883), p. 70.

69. Marx, *Capital*, p. 28. See Rodrigo, "Marx et la phénoménologie," pp. 94–100.

70. Marx, *Capital*, p. 28. The price is not the same as the value. See Marx, *Capital*, pp. 66ff.

71. Marx, *Capital*, p. 28, has "embodied": "human labour in the abstract has been embodied or materialized in it." See also *Das Kapital* (1883), pp. 70ff.—Trans.

72. Marx, *Capital*, p. 28. This is one of the first occurrences in the text of the term "world of commodities" (*Waarenwelt*).

73. See pt. IV, § 25.

74. Balibar, *Philosophie de Marx*, p. 65.

75. *Waarenwelt* is the spelling used in Marx, *Das Kapital* (1883). The current spelling is *Warenwelt*.—Trans.

76. One additional remark: the analysis that we have followed here in Marx has a kind of echo or analogy at one point of Heidegger's analysis. In the sixth addendum (*Zusatz*) to his essay "Die Zeit des Weltbildes" [The Time of the World Image], Heidegger analyzes two developments of the essence of the image (*Wesen des Bildes*) as expressing the modern interpretation of beingness (Gm., *Auslegung des Seienden* [HW, pp. 100–101 [93]). The first is domination [Gm., *Herrschaft*] of the system (see pt. IV, § 25 of this book). Then Heidegger adds, "For the modern interpretation of beingness, the representation of value [Gm., *die Vorstellung des Wertes*] is as essential as the system" (ibid.). Obviously, the value whose concept appears at this point is not determined as a merchant value. However, articulation of the becoming-image with the formation of values follows, which cannot but attract our attention from the present perspective. The image–value articulation, it should be noted, is related to a deprivation or loss of being (Gm., *des Seins verlustig*), which never appears as such in Marx (even if a fair number of his interpreters have wanted to detect it there, for a variety of reasons). The loss (Gm., *Verlust*) of being comes up at the exact point where Marx summons up *abstraction*: at the point of letting go of thingness and suspending it, a kind of *epochē* of the use-value, and therefore of the thing. This (arguably essential) difference noted, Heidegger's analysis nonetheless leads to observing how one "measures [Gm., *bemißt*] ... beingness in accordance with values, and makes the values themselves into the goal of all one's doings, comings and goings [Gm., *Tuns und Treibens*]" (HW, p. 101 [93–94]). He adds, "This is only one step away from making the values themselves into objects" (ibid.). Values made into objects: let us admit that we are not far removed from a theory of value-objectivity (Gm., *Wertgegenständlichkeit*). This movement here pertains to the world's becoming-image: "Value is the objectivization of one's needful aims in representatively settling oneself in the world as image" (HW, pp. 101–2 [94]). (The difference between Heidegger and Marx also

has to be seen in regard to their respective positioning of the concept of representation. See Rancière, "Concept de critique"; Althusser et al., *Lire Le Capital*, 2: 170. But this becoming-image is a loss. With Marx, it is an abstraction (see Macherey, "À propos du processus d'exposition du *Capital*," in Althusser et al., *Lire Le Capital*, 1: 248).

77. See pt. II of this book.

78. Europe is not Rome's only daughter: Islam, with its claims to planetary unification—like capitalism, and against it in certain respects—is another. This unification, then—in this mode, which I have characterized as monotheistic, and thus monotopical—is a kind of alternative, a fundamentalist alternative, if you will, as is capitalist fundamentalism itself. But one cannot be sure that future becomings (history and stories) are going to be willing to restrict themselves to this face-to-face framework.

79. Debord's *Société du spectacle* was first published in 1967.

80. See Guénoun, *L'exhibition des mots*, p. 30.

81. It is not surprising that Heidegger would subscribe to a counterrevolutionary program, conveying as such something of the revolutionary idea and will.

82. Debord, *Société du spectacle*, p. 25. The entire second section, "La marchandise comme spectacle" (The Commodity as Spectacle), deals with this analysis. In the quoted sentence, the expressions (notably *ne . . . plus* in French) point toward the schema of loss noted earlier, which is very present in these pages, even explicitly: Debord speaks of "loss of quality" (in the quantitative becoming of things, p. 22). In any case, Debord's *Société du spectacle* summarily articulates most of the themes covered in my argument: fetishism (p. 21), worldwide globalization (p. 22), visualization (p. 25), effectivity of illusions (p. 28), abstraction (p. 49). The text—allusively but clearly—invokes the same texts by Marx. These themes had undoubtedly been explored at considerable depth earlier by others, e.g., in Althusser et al., *Lire Le Capital*. Debord would no doubt have objected strongly to a comparison with *Lire Le Capital*, however, given that it dates from 1965, and the analyses of the *specular commodity* developed in it were masked by more controversial concerns at the time. But in retrospect, there is patently a thematic convergence.

83. Or desired as a possession. Images, as we know, efficiently play with desire—the desire to possess something.

84. If word assonances and the play between their signs were to be automatically validated, one would evidently have to make the connection, here, in French, between *l'avoir* ("the to have" or "having") and *là-voir* ("the to see" or "that which there is to see"). But setting these terms side by side, while quite welcome for obvious *conceptual* reasons (pulling together acquisition and image, as in *taking pictures* [*prise de vue*]), remains gratuitous from a lexical vantage point. "Having being" [*l'avoir l'étant*] is more important: being [*l'étant*] *as* having [*avoir*]; having [*l'avoir*] as assignation of beingness [*l'étance*], and thus as beingness itself [*l'étance-même*]; being and having [*l'étant et l'avoir*] conjoined or merged.

85. The two are not unrelated, as we have just seen with respect to the image and the commodity. This was Debord's clairvoyance.

86. In some respects, one could imagine a different underneath: the underneath of repression [*refoulement*], of active burial—in the present, so to speak—underneath as a function of the present, because what one buries there is that which one wishes to neutralize or conceal. A *production of underneath* is imaginable, in the objective sense of a complement, because it is indeed imaginable that here and there the common that one wishes to distance from the world is constituted there as being underneath. But it is always an "as."

87. The feeling is clear (though the development of this thesis would require quite a different ["ontological"] ambition than the one displayed here) that this statement (the common is the becoming of being) implies another latent one, impatiently asking to be unfurled: that the common is the being of being [*le commun est l'être de l'être*]. For the becoming of being is what makes being into that which is coming on—being, not as a state (a being), but as *the act* "*to be*," the *coming of* "*to be*," and the *process of* "*to be*"—as the *verb* "to be," the verbality and processuality of being, not the substantivity, substantiality (nominality) of being; that which raises "to be" into being, its becoming-being—and thus the common. To bring the question of the common into close proximity with the ontological difference: this is the demon that lurks in these very lines; for instance, a little earlier, when we suggested that being proper (the property of being) is at bottom a modality of having—an essentialization or an identifying return of possession—and that *common being*, therefore, stands out on the background of what I have proposed we think of as *being having* [*l'étant l'avoir*]. On being as being in common, see Nancy, *Communauté désœuvrée*, pp. 201ff.

88. The word "sense" is here used in a meaning close to that elaborated by Jean-Luc Nancy, even if his use of it is set up very differently—particularly with regard to the world. See Nancy, *Sens du monde*, passim.

89. This renewed attention to genesis I owe to Paola Marrati. See Marrati, *Genesis and Trace*, and Derrida, *Problem of Genesis in Husserl's Philosophy*.

90. As far as the Persian Empire is concerned, this is evidently questionable. Universal history would not be what it is without its relationship with Persia. We can see this clearly, from Herodotus to Hegel.

91. Ancient societies, seen and characterized from a historical position that is ours: a teleological concept, if you will, but in which the *telos* is simply our present history—not as the finality of a determined future to-come [*à-venir*] but as the acknowledgment of a history that has taken place.

92. Surely, "history" itself is a determined production, a discursive type and body born and developed in certain places and at certain dates—a historic formation. It is probable that there are societies that have known no such thing. But to recognize this historicity of history itself does not in any way mean conceding anything to a supposed immobility of "empires."

93. Like a fly or midge [*moucheron*] "caught in a cobweb"; see *Petit Robert* s.v. *moucheron*.

94. See pt. I, §8.

95. When an empire says, "I am immobile," one should not take it at its word—it is untrue. The proof for this is that they die. A certain fiction regarding the nonhistoricity of empires, or societies, gives credit to their imaginary designs.

96. In this context, the complex workings of "we" in philosophical exposition should be analyzed. There is the customary "we" that avoids the "I" (why?). But also Kant's "we," for example, in his description of a common experience: "In all judgments through which we state that something is beautiful, we let no one have a different opinion" (Kant, *Kritik der Urteilskraft*, para. 22, p. 239). And further, the assertive "we," such as Nietzsche's in "Wir guten Europäer" (We good Europeans) (see Nietzsche, preface, and elsewhere, in *Jenseits von Gut und Böse* [*Beyond Good and Evil*]).

97. Plural because it is dual; duality opens up *this* nonclosure of the one. See Badiou, "Qu'est-ce que l'amour?" (What Is Love?), in id., *Conditions*, pp. 256ff.

98. "For this reason, social analysis can learn incomparably more from individual experience than Hegel conceded. . . . In the hundred and fifty years since Hegel's conception was formed, some of the force of protest has reverted to the individual . . . part of the social force of liberation may have temporarily withdrawn to the individual sphere" (Adorno, Dedication, in *Minima Moralia*, pp. 17–18; see also para. 97, pp. 148ff.).

99. See *Petit Littré*, s.v., *transport*: "Violent movement of passion that puts one beside oneself. 'For him I feel transports of hatred' (Corneille)" (p. 2304). And see, e.g., Rousseau, *Essay on the Origin of Languages*, in *Discourses and Other Early Political Writings*, p. 268; and Derrida, *De la grammatologie*, pp. 269–72.

100. See Gunkel, "Le transport musical de Jean-Jacques Rousseau."

101. "How do we let ourselves be moved to pity? By transporting ourselves outside ourselves" (Rousseau, *Essay on the Origin of Languages*, in *Discourses and Other Early Political Writings*, pp. 267–68; cited by Derrida, *De la grammatologie*, p. 272n). Or more clearly still, "In effect, how can we let ourselves be stirred by pity unless we go beyond ourselves [*en nous transportant hors de nous*] and identify ourselves with the suffering animal? By leaving, so to speak, our own nature and taking his?" (Rousseau, *Emile*, bk. IV, no pagination; Derrida, ibid.).

102. In Rousseau, the imagination has something to do with the development of human commerce, language, and exchanges. For example, "The imagination which causes so many ravages among us, never speaks to the heart of savages" (Rousseau, *Discourse on Inequality*, pt. I, no pagination; in French, *Œuvres complètes*, 2: 225). It is no doubt because certain dispositions or faculties seem "quite out of reach for savage man, for want of any communication with his fellows, which is to say, for want of the instrument used in this communication and the needs that make it necessary" (Rousseau, *Œuvres complètes*, 2: 250). It is not that

he is lacking imagination, which is a natural faculty; imagination does not "speak" to him [or her], according to Rousseau.

103. A symptomatic script often present in Rousseau, even more so than the one of imaginary transport. See Gouhier, "Expansion et resserrement selon Rousseau," in *Les méditations métaphysiques de Jean-Jacques Rousseau*, pp. 107–17.

104. Political transport should be mentioned: *insurrectional transport*, for example—passionate, at times aesthetic, in great part ethical—as in transports (a "rush") of solidarity.

105. Rousseau, *Œuvres complètes*, vol. 1, passim, e.g., pp. 381–83. [In English, see Rousseau, *Rousseau, Judge of Jean-Jacques*. The term *amour-propre* is mostly used nowadays to designate one's pride, as in *amour-propre blessé*, "hurt pride."—Trans.]

106. Platonic love does not aim at the existing other but, through him or her, at an ideal. "Thou shalt love thy neighbour *as thyself*" is the commandment in the Old Testament (Lev. 19:18), and, without wishing to reduce the significance of this, it is, precisely, *as thyself*. "Love your enemies," Christ says in Matt. 5:43–46; there is no merit in loving one's friends.

107. It should still be noted that at the very point where this self-sufficiency of individuals extremely and radically attempts to experience or express itself, it exceeds itself absolutely. Auto(bio)graphical undertakings bear witness to this. With Augustine, this opens up *as a confession*: the self narrates itself because of a divine call, which posits and shapes it. With the moderns, the telling loses this foundation in divine exteriority, instead experiencing and stating itself as a defect, the self stealing away from itself (Montaigne), or expanding itself to the dimensions of the absolute collective—madness of the self, often played out in an identification with Christ. See Rousseau, *Rousseau, Judge of Jean-Jacques*; Nietzsche, *Ecce homo*. The position of the self as an essence drives to madness—mad about the common, mad about the divine. (The reference here is to the seminar *Écriture de soi* [Self-Writing] held at the University Marc Bloch in Strasbourg in 1993–94, organized by Yves Delègue, Camille Dumoulié, Denis Guénoun, Philippe Lacoue-Labarthe, and Jean-Luc Nancy, with the participation of Jérôme Thélot and Jean-Christophe Bailly.)

108. "The *contents* of the dream of happiness, however, are linked with what could be termed the *unhappiness* of man: in that the beginning of our existence in the care of others who are accepting us most closely approaches total satisfaction, a total satisfaction that encompasses all sides and dimensions of the human essence, leaving none aside. This happiness of total acceptance, which is so fully satisfied that it cannot even let any wish emerge, turns out to be the other side of the fundamental unconcealment and exposure of one's own being, which is its fundamental sensibility [Gm., *Grundbefindlichkeit*]; and in this is based the deep wish, in intoxicated self-oblivion, to rid oneself of this fundamental burden, thanks to the acceptance of our whole being on the part of another who sets off and keeps up this intoxicated desire, and this, he or she will only do when he or she finds the same

desire safely kept in our own acceptance of it. For this fundamental reason, Eros is the only way of overcoming our worldly burden [Gm., *Weltlast*] that is equal [Gm., *ebenbürtig*] to one's fundamental sensibility, and the other has therefore turned into the underwriter and center of one's own happiness and life meaning. It is not an insidious aggression of the other's freedom, nor a will to incorporate him or her, nor the achievement of freedom denied, nor an abuse of the other for one's own purpose; rather, it is an attempt to be carried by carrying, to give happiness by taking it, and in this blending and exchanging of happiness, to transform the burden into fulfillment" (Patočka, "Réflexion sur l'Europe," pp. 204–5; "Die Selbstbesinnung Europas" [Europe's Self-Reflection]). [My translation, from the typescript of the original text, which Patočka wrote in German, kindly provided by Erika Abrams, Jan Patočka's renowned translator and editor.—Trans.]

109. See Heidegger, "The Problem of the Finitude in Man and the Metaphysics of *Dasein*," in id., *Kant and the Problem of Metaphysics*, pp. 226ff.

110. What passes across death and punctures it? Spirit? Perhaps. But this is rather Derrida's proposition: beneath the syntagma *la vie la mort* [*life death*], the schema of passing across death—and life. A revenant, a specter. For me, things fall in place differently. *It is life that is passing.* Or to say it in my way, it is *matter*, in a certain sense. Matter as bearer-of-life: that which travels across death (my death, death of my self). Matter goes across finitude, poking a hole in it. Within a thinking of finitude, materialism does not fit (behave) so well.

111. Feuerbach, *Essence of Christianity*, p. 20. [Translation modified. Emphasis in German text.—Trans.]

112. "The animal can exercise no generic function [Gm., *Gattungsfunktion*] without another individual external to itself" (ibid., p. 20 [translation modified—Trans.]).

113. Ibid., p. 22.

114. Marx reads this page (published in 1841) and reorganizes it in his problematic known as that of the "young Marx," and thus under the authority of the schema of alienation, as an infinite degradation of the man-woman relationship as well as the relationship of man to himself. See Marx, "Private Property and Communism."

115. Feuerbach, *Essence of Christianity*, p. 206; emphasis added [slightly modified—Trans.]. See also Michel Henry's aggressive commentary, in Henry, *Marx*, vol. 1: *Une philosophie de la réalité*, pp. 92–102, and esp. p. 98.

116. Even if it is also that—the I is nothing else except a projected image. See Lacan, *Écrits*, pp. 93ff.

117. Rousseau, *Essay on the Origin of Languages*, in *Discourses and Other Early Political Writings*, p. 268. He goes on, "Think how much acquired knowledge this transport presupposes!" (ibid.). See also Derrida, *De la grammatologie*, pp. 269–72.

118. See *Dictionnaire historique de la langue française*, ed. Rey, 1: 762, s.v. *expérience*.

119. The reference here is to the thought of Philippe Lacoue-Labarthe, particularly in *La poésie comme expérience*, passim, and pp. 30–31 on the etymology of "experience."

120. On the etymology of *Europē*, see Rougemont, *Idea of Europe* ("The Etymologies," pp. 25–30); "Eurôpé . . . a woman with large eyes, a lovely way of looking, a beautiful face" (p. 28).

121. This interpretation of the myth converges with Massimo Cacciari's while being its opposite. For him, in the west, Europe carries on with its own "[sun] setting" (It., *tramonto*) nature—the horizon of its own vanishing. His hypothesis (or one might say his orientation) is thus closely related to mine. A closer reading, however, shows that his analyses seem to invite Europe *to set and lie down*, or eclipse itself, through a kind of hatred (It., *odio*), fight (It., *lotta*), or war (It., *guerra*) carried out *against* (It., *contro*, *versus*) oneself. (Hence the positive reference to the *sobs* of the princess, found in Horace's "Ode to Galatea"—see Rougemont, *Idea of Europe*, pp. 14–15.) Here, on the other hand, what is involved is letting go, and a kind of faithfulness, which is another thing. See Cacciari, *Geofilosofia dell'Europa*, pp. 157–59.

122. See Spinoza, *Theological-Political Treatise*, chap. 3 ("On the Vocation of the Hebrews, and Whether the Prophetic Gift Was Peculiar to Them").

Works Cited

Adorno, Theodor. *Minima Moralia: Reflections on a Damaged Life*. Trans. E. F. N. Jephcott. London: Verso, 2005.
Aeschylus. *Fragments*. Trans. Alan H. Sommerstein. *Works*. Vol. 3. Cambridge, Mass.: Harvard University Press, 2008.
———. *Persians*. Trans. Herbert Weir Smyth. www.perseus.tufts.edu/hopper/text?doc=Perseus:text:1999.01.0012. Accessed September 7, 2012.
———. *Prometheus Bound*. Trans. Herbert Weir Smyth. www.perseus.tufts.edu/hopper/text?doc=Perseus:text:1999.01.0010. Accessed September 7, 2012.
Althusser, Louis. *Écrits philosophiques et politiques*. Vol. 1. Paris: Stock-Imec, 1994.
———. *Lenin and Philosophy and Other Essays*. Trans. Ben Brewster. New York: Monthly Review Press, 1971.
———. "Marx's Relation to Hegel." In id., *Politics and History: Montesquieu, Rousseau, Hegel, and Marx*, trans. Ben Brewster, 163–86. London: New Left Books, 1972.
———. "Sur le rapport de Marx à Hegel." In *Hegel et la pensée moderne*, ed. Jacques d'Hondt, 85–111. Paris: Presses universitaires de France, 1970.
Althusser, Louis, Pierre Macherey, Jacques Rancière, et al. *Lire Le Capital*. 2 vols. Paris: Maspéro, 1965.
Aristotle. *Physics*. Trans. R. P. Hardie and R. K. Gaye. http://classics.mit.edu/Aristotle/physics.html. Accessed September 7, 2012.
———. *Politics: Books VII and VIII*. Trans. Richard Kraut. Oxford: Clarendon Press, 1997.
———. *Rhetoric*. Trans. John Henry Freese. www.perseus.tufts.edu/hopper/text?doc=Perseus:text:1999.01.0060. Accessed September 7, 2012.
———. *Rhétorique*. Trans. Charles-Émile Ruelle and Patricia Vanhemelryck. Paris: Livre de Poche, 1991.
———. *Topics*. Trans. W. A. Pickard-Cambridge. http://classics.mit.edu/Aristotle/topics.html. Accessed September 7, 2012.
Athenagoras. *The Apologeticks of the Learned Athenian Philosopher Athenagoras*. Trans. and ed. David Humphreys. London: G. James and R. Smith, 1714.

Badiou, Alain. *Conditions*. Paris: Seuil, 1992.
Bailey, Cyril, ed. *The Legacy of Rome*. Oxford: Clarendon Press, 1924. French translations of the essays in this book can be found in *L'héritage de la Grèce et de Rome*, ed. Finley and Bailey.
Bailly, Anatole. *Dictionnaire grec-français*. Paris: Hachette, 1950. Cited as Bailly dictionary.
Bailly, Jean-Christophe. *Adieu: Essai sur la mort des dieux*. La Tour d'Aigues, France: Éditions de l'Aube, 1993.
Balibar, Étienne. "L'Europe après le communisme." *Les temps modernes* 547 (February 1992): 56–89.
———. *La philosophie de Marx*. Paris: La Découverte, 1993.
———. "Quelles frontières de l'Europe?" In *Penser l'Europe à ses frontières*. La Tour d'Aigues, France: Éditions de l'Aube, 1993.
Balibar, Étienne, and Immanuel Wallerstein. *Races, nations, classes: Les identités ambigües*. Paris: La Découverte, 1988.
Barker, Ernest. "The Conception of Europe." In *The Legacy of Rome*, ed. Cyril Bailey, 45–89. Oxford: Clarendon Press, 1924.
Beaune, Colette. *Naissance de la nation France*. Paris: Gallimard, 1993.
Benslama, Fethi. "L'enfant et le lieu." [*Cahiers*] *Intersignes* 3 (Fall 1991): 51–68.
———. *Une fiction troublante: De l'origine en partage*. La Tour d'Aigues, France: Éditions de l'Aube, 1994.
———. *La nuit brisée: Muhammad et l'énonciation islamique*. Paris: Ramsay, 1988.
Benveniste, Émile. *Indo-European Language and Society*. Trans. Elizabeth Palmer. Coral Gables, Fla.: University of Miami Press, 1973. Translation of *Le vocabulaire des institutions indo-européennes*.
———. *Le vocabulaire des institutions indo-européennes*. 2 vols. Paris: Minuit, 1969.
Bergson, Henri. *Matière et mémoire*. 7th ed. Paris: Presses universitaires de France–Quadrige, 1990.
———. *Matter and Memory*. Trans. N. M. Paul and W. S. Palmer. New York: Zone Books, 1991.
Berl, Emmanuel. *Europe et Asie*. Paris: Gallimard, 1969.
Bloch, Ernst. *Atheism in Christianity: The Religion of the Exodus and the Kingdom*. Trans. J. T. Swann. London: Verso, 2009.
———. *Atheismus im Christentum: Zur Religion des Exodus und des Reichs*. Frankfurt am Main: Suhrkamp, 1968.
Bottéro, Jean. *Naissance de Dieu*. Paris: Gallimard, 1992.
Bourgeois, Bernard. "La philosophie allemande de l'Europe (de Kant à Hegel)." *Philosophie politique* 1 (1991): 83–104.
Brague, Rémi. *Aristote et la question du monde*. Paris: Presses universitaires de France, 1988.

———. *Eccentric Culture: A Theory of Western Civilization.* Trans. Samuel Lester. South Bend, Ind.: St. Augustine's Press, 2002. Translation of *Europe, la voie romaine*.

———. *Europe, la voie romaine.* 2d ed. Paris: Critérion, 1993.

Braudel, Fernand. *Civilisation matérielle, économie et capitalisme: XVe–XVIIIe siècle.* 3 vols.: 1. *Les structures du quotidien*; 2. *Les jeux de l'échange*; 3. *Le temps du monde.* Paris: Colin, 1979.

———. *La dynamique du capitalisme.* Paris: Flammarion, 1988.

———. *The Perspective of the World.* Trans. Siân Reynolds. London: Collins, 1984. Translation of *Le temps du monde*.

Bréhier, Émile. *Histoire de la philosophie.* Vol. 1: *Antiquité et moyen âge.* Paris: Presses universitaires de France, 1991.

Brook, Peter. *The Empty Space.* New York: Simon & Schuster, 1996.

Cacciari, Massimo. *Geofilosofia dell'Europa.* Milan: Adelphi, 1994.

Carpentier, Jean, and François Lebrun, eds. *Histoire de l'Europe.* Paris: Points-Seuil, 1992.

Chantraine, Pierre. *Dictionnaire étymologique de la langue grecque.* 4 vols. 1968. Paris: Klincksieck, 1990.

Chastel, André. *Le sac de Rome: Du premier maniérisme à l'art de la Contre-Réforme.* Paris: Gallimard, 1989.

Chastel, André, and Robert Klein. *L'Europe de la Renaissance. L'âge de l'humanisme.* Paris: Éditions des Deux-mondes, 1963.

Cicero. *On the Commonwealth.* Trans. George Holland Sabine and Stanley Barney Smith. Indianapolis: Bobbs-Merrill, 1960. Cited as Cicero, *Republic*.

Commynes, Philippe de. *Mémoires.* Paris: Rollin, 1747.

Corneille, Pierre. *The Cid; Cinna; The Theatrical Illusion.* Trans. John Cairncross. Harmondsworth, UK: Penguin Books, 1975.

Courtine, Jean-François, Michel Deguy, Éliane Escoubas, Philippe Lacoue-Labarthe, et al. *Du sublime.* Paris: Belin, 1988.

Curtius, Ernst Robert. *The Civilization of France: An Introduction.* Trans. Olive Wyon. New York: Macmillan, 1932.

———. *Die französische Kultur: Eine Einführung.* 2d ed. Munich: Francke, 1975.

Dagorn, René. *La geste d'Ismaël: D'après l'onomastique et la tradition arabes.* Geneva: Droz, 1981.

Dauzat, Albert, Henri Mitterand, and Jean Dubois. *Nouveau dictionnaire étymologique et historique.* 2d ed. Paris: Larousse, 1971.

Debord, Guy. *La société du spectacle.* 1967. Paris: Gallimard, 1992.

———. *The Society of the Spectacle.* Trans. Donald Nicholson-Smith. New York: Zone Books, 1994.

Delcambre, Anne-Marie. *Mahomet, la parole d'Allah.* Paris: Gallimard, 1987.

Deleuze, Gilles. *Cinema 1: The Movement-Image*. Trans. Hugh Tomlinson and Barbara Habberjam. London: Continuum, 2004. Cited as *Movement-Image*.

———. *Cinema 2: The Time-Image*. Trans. Hugh Tomlinson and Robert Galeta. Minneapolis: University of Minnesota Press, 1989. Cited as *Time-Image*.

———. *L'image-mouvement*. Paris: Minuit, 1983.

———. *L'image-temps*. Paris: Minuit, 1985.

Deleuze, Gilles, and Félix Guattari. *Qu'est-ce que la philosophie?* Paris: Minuit, 1991.

———. *What Is Philosophy?* Trans. Hugh Tomlinson and Graham Burchell. New York: Columbia University Press, 1996.

Derrida, Jacques. *L'autre cap*. Paris: Minuit, 1991.

———. *De la grammatologie*. Paris: Minuit, 1967.

———. "D'où vient l'Europe?" In *Penser l'Europe à ses frontières*. La Tour-d'Aigues, France: Éditions de l'Aube, 1993.

———. *Mémoires d'aveugle: L'auto-portrait et autres ruines*. Paris: Réunion des musées nationaux, 1990.

———. *Memoirs of the Blind: The Self-Portrait and Other Ruins*. Trans. Pascale-Anne Brault and Michael Naas. Chicago: University of Chicago Press, 1993.

———. *Of Grammatology*. Trans. Gayatri Spivak. Baltimore: Johns Hopkins University Press, 1976.

———. *The Other Heading: Reflections on Today's Europe*. Trans. Pascale-Anne Brault and Michael B. Naas. Bloomington: Indiana University Press, 1992.

———. *Le problème de la genèse dans la philosophie de Husserl*. Paris: Presses universitaires de France, 1990.

———. *The Problem of Genesis in Husserl's Philosophy*. Trans. Marian Hobson. Chicago: University of Chicago Press, 2003.

———. *Psyché: Inventions de l'autre*. Paris: Galilée, 1987.

———. *Psyche: Inventions of the Other*. Trans. Peggy Kamuf et al. Stanford, Calif.: Stanford University Press, 2007.

———. *Schibboleth: Pour Paul Celan*. Paris: Galilée, 2003.

———. *Specters of Marx: The State of the Debt, the Work of Mourning, and the New International*. Trans. Peggy Kamuf. New York: Routledge, 1994.

———. *Spectres de Marx: L'état de la dette, le travail du deuil et la nouvelle Internationale*. Paris: Galilée, 1993.

Descartes, René. *Discourse on Method and Meditations on First Philosophy*. Trans. Donald A. Cress. 4th ed. Indianapolis: Hackett, 1998.

Dionysius of Halicarnassus. *The Roman Antiquities of Dionysius of Halicarnassus*. Trans. Earnest Cary and Edward Spelman. 7 vols. Cambridge, Mass.: Harvard University Press, 1937–50.

Dommange, Thomas. "Le miroir identitaire." *Lignes* 18 (January 1993): 137–49.

———. "Sommes-nous capables d'un monde?" Diplôme d'Études Appliquées thesis, Université Marc Bloch, Strasbourg, 1993.
Dostoyevsky, Fyodor. *The Possessed*. Trans. Constance Garnett. New York: Macmillan, 1948.
Drai, Raphaël. *La sortie d'Égypte: L'invention de la liberté*. Paris: Fayard, 1986.
Du Bellay, Joachim. *The Antiquities of Rome*. Trans. Richard Helgerson. In id., *The Regrets; with, The Antiquities of Rome, Three Latin Elegies and the Defense and Enrichment of the French Language*, ed. Richard Helgerson, 247–79. Bilingual ed. Philadelphia: University of Pennsyvania Press, 2006.
Dubois, Pierre. *Recovery of the Holy Land*. Trans. Walther I. Brandt. New York: Columbia University Press, 1956.
Eisenstein, Sergei. *Cinématisme: Peinture et cinéma*. Trans. [from Russian to French] Anne Zouboff. Brussels: Complexe, 1980.
———. *Le mouvement de l'art*. Trans. [from Russian to French] B. Epstein. Ed. François Albéra and Naum Kleiman. Paris: Cerf, 1986.
Erard, Zoé, and Georges M. Zygier, eds. *La Pologne, une société en dissidence*. Paris: Maspéro, 1978. Includes texts from the Workers' Defense Committee [K.O.R.], Leszek Kołakowski, Adam Michnik, Jacek Kuron, et al.
Ernout, Alfred, and Antoine Meillet. *Dictionnaire étymologique de la langue latine*. 4th ed. Paris: Klincksieck, 1985.
Euripides. *Andromache*. Trans. David Kovacs. http://www.perseus.tufts.edu/hopper/text?doc=Perseus:text:1999.01.0090. Accessed September 7, 2012.
———. *Fragments*. Trans. and ed. Christopher Collard and Martin Cropp. In *Fragments: Oedipus–Chrysippus, Other Fragments*. Cambridge, Mass.: Harvard University Press, 2009.
———. *Hecuba*. Trans. E. P. Coleridge. www.perseus.tufts.edu/hopper/text?doc=Perseus:text:1999.01.0098. Accessed September 3, 2012.
———. *Ion*. Trans. Robert Potter. *The Complete Greek Drama*. Ed. Whitney J. Oates and Eugene O'Neill. Vol. 1. New York: Random House, 1938. www.perseus.tufts.edu/hopper/text?doc=Perseus:text:1999.01.0110. Accessed September 7, 2012.
Feuerbach, Ludwig. *The Essence of Christianity*. Trans. Marian Evans (George Eliot). New York: Calvin Blanchard, 1855. http://babel.hathitrust.org/cgi/pt?seq=9&id=nyp.33433067406193&view=image&q1=inner+life&start=1&size=100&page=root&orient=0. Accessed September 7, 2012.
———. *Das Wesen des Christentums*. www.zeno.org/Philosophie/M/Feuerbach,+Ludwig/Das+Wesen+des+Christentums. Accessed September 7, 2012.
Fichte, Johann Gottlieb. *Addresses to the German Nation*. Trans. R. F. Jones and G. H. Turnbull. Chicago: Open Court, 1922–23.

———. "Der geschlossene Handelsstaat: Ein philosophischer Entwurf als Anhang zur Rechtslehre und Probe einer künftig zu liefernden Politik." In id., *Sämtliche Werke*, ed. J. H. Fichte, 3:387–513. Berlin: Veit, 1845.

———. *Werke 1801–1812*. Ed. Reinhard Lauth et al. Stuttgart: Frommann-Holzboog, 2005.

Finley, Moses, and Cyril Bailey, eds. *L'héritage de la Grèce et de Rome*. Trans. Geneviève Ladjadj-Koenig. Paris: Laffont, 1992.

Fleischmann, Eugène. *La philosophie politique de Hegel: Sous forme d'un commentaire des "Fondements de la philosophie du droit."* Paris: Plon, 1964.

Forster, Georg. "On the Relationship of the People of Mainz to the Franks" ["Über das Verhältnis der Mainzer gegen die Franken"]. Speech delivered to the Society of the Friends of the People in Mainz, November 15, 1792. http://germanhistorydocs.ghi-dc.org/sub_document_s.cfm?document_id=3574. Accessed September 7, 2012.

Frederick II, king of Prussia ["Publié par Mr. de Voltaire"]. *Anti-Machiavel ou Essai de critique sur le Prince de Machiavel*. The Hague: P. Paupie, 1740. New ed. Amsterdam: La Caze, 1741. http://gallica.bnf.fr/ark:/12148/bpt6k940196/f4.image. Accessed July 12, 2012.

———. *De la littérature allemande*. 2d ed. Berlin: Geiger, 1902.

———. *Œuvres posthumes*. 2d ed. Berlin: Voss & Decker, 1788.

Freud, Sigmund. *Leonardo da Vinci and a Memory of His Childhood*. Trans. Alan Tyson. London: Routledge, 1999.

———. *Der Mann Moses und die monotheistische Religion: Drei Abhandlungen*. Amsterdam: Allert de Lange, 1939.

———. *Moses and Monotheism: Three Essays*. Trans. James Strachey et al. In *The Standard Edition of the Complete Psychological Works of Sigmund Freud*, 23: 3–137. London, Hogarth Press, 1964. Cited as MM.

———. *The Moses of Michelangelo*. Trans. James Strachey et al. In *The Standard Edition of the Complete Psychological Works of Sigmund Freud*, 13: 211–38. London, Hogarth Press, 1914.

Fried, Michael. *Absorption and Theatricality: Painting and Beholder in the Age of Diderot*. Berkeley: University of California Press, 1980.

Fukuyama, Francis. *The End of History and the Last Man*. New York: Free Press, 1992.

Gardet, Louis. *Les hommes de l'Islam: Approche des mentalités*. Paris: Hachette, 1977.

Gasché, Rodolphe. *Europe, or the Infinite Task: A Study of a Philosophical Concept*. Stanford, Calif.: Stanford University Press, 2009.

Gauchet, Marcel. *Le désenchantement du monde: Une histoire politique de la religion*. Paris: Gallimard, 1985.

Genet, Jean-Philippe. *Le monde au moyen âge: Espaces, pouvoirs, civilisations*. Paris: Hachette, 1991.
Gilson, Étienne. *La philosophie au moyen âge: Des origines patristiques à la fin du XIVe siècle*. Paris: Payot, 1986.
Godechot, Jacques. *La pensée révolutionnaire en France et en Europe, 1780–1799*. Paris: Colin, 1969.
Gouhier, Henri. *Les méditations métaphysiques de Jean-Jacques Rousseau*. Paris: Vrin, 1970.
Grand dictionnaire encyclopédique Larousse. 10 vols. Paris: Larousse, 1984.
Les grands écrits réformateurs. Trans. and ed. Maurice Gravier. Paris: Flammarion, 1992.
Granel, Gérard. "L'Europe de Husserl." In id., *Écrits logiques et politiques*, 37–58. Paris: Galilée, 1990.
Graves, Robert. *The Greek Myths*. London: Penguin Books, 1992.
Greenberg, Mitchell. *Canonical States, Canonical Stages: Oedipus, Othering, and Seventeenth-Century Drama*. Minneapolis: University of Minnesota Press, 1994.
Grimal, Pierre, ed. *Dictionnaire des biographies*. 2 vols. Paris: Presses universitaires de France, 1958.
Guénoun, Denis. *L'enlèvement de la politique: Une hypothèse sur le rapport de Kant à Rousseau*. Belfort, France: Éditions Circé, 2002.
———. *L'exhibition des mots et autres idées du théâtre et de la philosophie*. 2d ed. Belfort, France: Éditions Circé, 1998.
———. *La levée: Théâtre*. Reims, France: Le Grand Nuage de Magellan, 1989.
———. *Le printemps*. Arles, France: Actes Sud, 1985.
———. *Un Sémite*. Belfort, France: Éditions Circé, 2002.
———. *A Semite*. Trans. Ann and Bill Smock. New York: Columbia University Press, 2013.
———. "Sur les (prétendues) sorties du (prétendu) communisme en Europe." *Lignes* 18 (January 1993): 126–36.
———. "Transferts d'un corps enlevé." Ph.D. thesis, Université Marc Bloch, Strasbourg, 1994.
Gunkel, M. "Le transport musical de Jean-Jacques Rousseau." M.A. thesis, Université Marc Bloch, Strasbourg, 1993.
Hamelin, Octave. *Le système d'Aristote*. Paris: Vrin, 1985.
Hegel, Georg Wilhelm Friedrich. *Aesthetics: Lectures on Fine Art*. Trans. T. M. Knox. 2 vols. Oxford: Clarendon Press, 1975.
———. *Ästhetik I/II*. Stuttgart: Reclam, 1989.
———. *Esthétique: Textes choisis*. Ed. Claude Khodoss. Paris: Presses universitaires de France, 1990.

———. "The German Constitution (1798–1802)." Trans. H. B. Nisbet. In id., *Political Writings*, ed. Laurence Dickey and H. B. Nisbet, 6–101. Cambridge: Cambridge University Press, 1999. German title of the essay: "Kritik der Verfassung Deutschlands."

———. *Grundlinien der Philosophie des Rechts*. Berlin: Nicolaische Buchhandlung, 1821.

———. *Introduction à l'esthétique*. Trans. Samuel Jankélévitch. Paris: Flammarion, 1979. Cited as *Esthétique* (Jankélévitch).

———. "Kritik der Verfassung Deutschlands." http://germanhistorydocs.ghi-dc.org/docpage.cfm?docpage_id=3968. Accessed September 7, 2012.

———. *Lectures on the Philosophy of History*. Trans. [from the 3rd German ed.] John Sibree. London: H. G. Bohn, 1861. Cited as Hegel, *Philosophy of History* (Sibree).

———. *Lectures on the Philosophy of World History: An Introduction*. Trans. Hugh Barr Nisbet. Cambridge: Cambridge University Press, 1981. Cited as *Philosophy of World History* (Nisbet).

———. *Phänomenologie des Geistes*. Ed. Johann Schulze. Berlin: Duncker & Humblot, 1832.

———. *Philosophy of Right*. Trans. Samuel Walter Dyde. London: Bell and Sons, 1896. Cited as Hegel, *Philosophy of Right* (Dyde).

———. *Principes de la philosophie du droit*. Trans. Robert Derathé. Paris: Vrin, 1989.

———. *La raison dans l'histoire: Introduction à la philosophie de l'histoire*. Trans. K. Papaoiannou. Paris: Plon, 1965. Translation of Hegel, *Die Vernunft in der Geschichte*, ed. J. Hoffmeister.

———. *Die Vernunft in der Geschichte*. Ed. Johannes Hoffmeister. Hamburg: F. Meiner, 1955.

———. *Vorlesungen über die Ästhetik*. Ed. Heinrich Gustav Hotho. 2 vols. Berlin: Duncker & Humblot, 1835–37.

Heidegger, Martin. *Being and Time*. Trans. Joan Stambaugh. Rev. Dennis J. Schmidt. Albany: State University of New York Press, 2010.

———. *Chemins qui ne mènent nulle part*. Trans. Wolfgang Brokmeier and François Fédier. Paris: Gallimard, 1986. Translation of Heidegger, *Holzwege*.

———. *Holzwege*. Frankfurt am Main: Vittorio Klostermann, 1977. Gesamtausgabe. Vol. 5. http://scribd.com/doc/63815050/Heidegger-GA-05-Holzwege. Accessed September 7, 2012. Cited as HW.

———. *Kant and the Problem of Metaphysics*. Trans. James S. Churchill. Bloomington: Indiana University Press, 1965. http://scribd.com/doc/57824460/Kant-and-the-Problem-of-Metaphysics-by-Martin-Heidegger. Accessed September 7, 2012.

———. *Kant und das Problem der Metaphysik*. 6th ed. Frankfurt am Main: Klostermann, 1998.

———. *Sein und Zeit*. 19th ed. Tübingen: Niemeyer, 2006.

———. *Zollikoner Seminare*. Frankfurt am Main: Klostermann, 1987.

Henry, Michel. *Marx*. 2 vols. Paris: Gallimard, 1976.

Herodotus. *The Histories*. Trans. Robin Waterfield. Oxford: Oxford University Press, 1998.

Herodotus and Thucydides. *Œuvres complètes*. Trans. A. Barguet and D. Roussel. Pléiade ed. Paris: Gallimard, 1964.

Hesiod. *Théogonie. Les travaux et les jours. Le bouclier*. Trans. and ed. Paul Mazon. 1928. Paris: Les Belles Lettres, 1986.

———. *Theogony. Works and Days. Shield*. 2d ed. Trans. Apostolos N. Athanassakis. Baltimore: Johns Hopkins University Press, 2004.

Hoffmann, E. T. A. *Contes retrouvés*. Trans. [German to French] Albert Béguin and M. Laval. Paris: Phébus. 1983.

———. "Die Vision auf dem Schlachtfelde bei Dresden." In id., *Sämtliche Werke* [in 6 vols.], 2/1: 479–82. Frankfurt am Main: Suhrkamp, 1993.

Hölderlin, Friedrich. "Anmerkungen zum Ödipus." In id., *Sämtliche Werke: Frankfurter Ausgabe*, ed. Dietrich E. Sattler, 16: 249–58. Basel: Stroemfeld; Frankfurt: Roter Stern, 1988.

———. "Remarks on 'Oedipus.'" In id., *Essays and Letters on Theory*, trans. Thomas Pfau, 101–8. Albany: State University of New York Press, 1988.

Homer. *The Homeric Hymns*. Trans. Apostolos Athanassakis. Baltimore: Johns Hopkins University Press, 1976.

Horace. *Odes*. Trans. John Conington. www.perseus.tufts.edu/hopper/text?doc=Perseus:text:1999.02.0025. Accessed September 7, 2012.

Hourani, Albert Habib. *A History of the Arab Peoples*. 2nd ed. Cambridge, Mass.: Harvard University Press, 2002.

Husserl, Edmund. "Die Krisis des europäischen Menschentums und die Philosophie." In id., *Die Krisis des europäischen Menschentums und die transzendentale Philosophie: Eine Einleitung in die phänomenologische Philosophie*, ed. W. Biemel, 314–48. Husserliana 6. The Hague: Nijhoff, 1954. German text of the "Vienna Lecture."

———. *On the Phenomenology of the Consciousness of Internal Time (1893–1917)*. Trans. John Barnett Brough. Dordrecht: Kluwer, 1991.

———. "Philosophy and the Crisis of European Man." In id., *Phenomenology and the Crisis of Philosophy*, trans. Quentin Lauer, 149–92. New York: Harper & Row, 1965. Cited as "Vienna Lecture" (Lauer).

———. "The Vienna Lecture: Philosophy and the Crisis of European Humanity." In id., *The Crisis of European Sciences and Transcendental Phenomenology:*

An Introduction to Phenomenological Philosophy, trans. David Carr, 269–300. Evanston, Ill.: Northwestern University Press, 1970. Cited as "Vienna Lecture."

Iacono, Alfonso M. *Le fétichisme: Histoire d'un concept*. Paris: Presses universitaires de France, 1992.

Ibn al-'Arabi. *La sagesse des prophètes*. Trans. [into French] Titus Burckhardt. Paris: Albin Michel, 1974.

———. *The Wisdom of the Prophets: Twelve Chapters of the Fusus al-Hikam*. Trans. [from *La sagesse des prophètes*] Angela Culme-Seymour. Aldsworth, UK: Beshara Publications, 1975. www.besharapublications.org.uk/pages/wisdom.html#_edn11. Accessed September 7, 2012.

Jaurès, Jean. *Histoire socialiste de la Révolution française*. Vol. 4: *La Révolution et l'Europe*. 1923. Paris: Éditions sociales, 1989.

Julius Caesar. *Gallic War*. www.perseus.tufts.edu/hopper/text?doc=Perseus:text:1999.02.0001. Accessed September 7, 2012.

Justin Martyr, Saint. *Justin, Philosopher and Martyr: Apologies*. Ed. Denis Minns and Paul Parvis. New York: Oxford University Press, 2009.

Kant, Immanuel. *The Critique of Judgement*. Trans. J. H. Bernard. 2d ed. London: Macmillan, 1914. Web edition by Steve Thomas. http://ebooks.adelaide.edu.au/k/kant/immanuel/k16ju/complete.html. Accessed September 7, 2012. Cited as *Critique of Judgment*.

———. *Critique of Pure Reason*. Trans. Norman Kemp Smith. London: Macmillan, 1929. Web edition originally prepared by Stephen Palmquist. www.hkbu.edu.hk/ppp/cpr/toc.html. Accessed September 7, 2012.

———. *Idée d'une histoire universelle au point de vue cosmopolitique*. Trans. [from German to French] J.-M. Muglioni. Paris: Bordas, 1988. Cited as *Idée*.

———. "Idee zu einer allgemeinen Geschichte in weltbürgerlicher Absicht." *Berlinische Monatschrift* 4 (November 1784): 385–411. http://books.google.de/books?id=4W43AAAAMAAJ&printsec=frontcover&hl=de#v=onepage&q&f=false. Accessed September 7, 2012. Cited as *Idee*.

———. *Kant's gesammelte Schriften*. Vol. 15: *Anthropologie*. Vol. 2. Berlin: Walter de Gruyter, 1969. Cited as Ak. 15/2.

———. *Kant's Werke*. Vol. 6. Berlin: Reimer, 1907. Cited as Ak. 6.

———. *Kritik der Urteilskraft. Kants gesammelte Schriften*. Vol. 5. Berlin: Walter de Gruyter, 1971.

———. *The Metaphysics of Morals*. Trans. Mary Gregor. Cambridge: Cambridge University Press, 1991.

———. "The Natural Principle of the Political Order Considered in Connection with the Idea of a Universal Cosmopolitical History." In *Kant's Principles of Politics, Including His Essay on Perpetual Peace: A Contribution to Political Science*. Trans. William Hastie. Edinburgh: Clark, 1891. http://oll.libertyfund.org

/?option=com_staticxt&staticfile=show.php%3Ftitle=358&chapter=56078&layout=html&Itemid=27. Accessed September 7, 2012. Translation from the German "Idee zu einer allgemeinen Geschichte in weltbürgerlicher Absicht." Cited as UH.
Kantorowicz, Ernst H. *The King's Two Bodies: A Study in Mediaeval Political Theology*. 1957. 7th ed. Princeton: Princeton University Press, 1997.
Koran. *Le Coran: Essai de traduction*. Trans. [into French] and ed. Jacques Berque. Paris: Éditions Sindbad, 1990. Cited as Koran (Berque).
———. *Le Coran*. Trans. [into French] Albin de Biberstein-Kazimirski. Ed. Mohammed Arkoun. Paris: Flammarion, 1991. Cited as Koran (Kazimirski).
———. *Le Coran*. Trans. [into French] Denise Masson. Pléiade ed. Paris: Gallimard, 1991. Cited as Koran (Masson).
———. *The Holy Qu'ran*. Trans. M. H. Shakir. Tahrike Tarsile Qu'ran, Inc. 1983. http://quod.lib.umich.edu/k/koran/. Accessed September 7, 2012.
Krynen, Jacques. *L'empire du roi: Idées et croyances politiques en France, XIIIe–XVe siècles*. Paris: Gallimard, 1993.
Lacan, Jacques. *Écrits*. Paris: Seuil, 1966.
———. *Écrits: A Selection*. Trans. Alan Sheridan. London: Routledge, 2001.
Lacoue-Labarthe, Philippe. *La fiction du politique: Heidegger, l'art et la politique*. Paris: Bourgois, 1987.
———. *Heidegger, Art and Politics: The Fiction of the Political*. Trans. Chris Turner. Oxford: Blackwell, 1990.
———. *Musica ficta: Figures de Wagner*. Paris: Bourgois, 1991.
———. *Musica ficta: Figures of Wagner*. Trans. Felicia McCarren. Stanford, Calif.: Stanford University Press, 1994.
———. *La poésie comme expérience*. Paris: Bourgois, 1986.
Lacoue-Labarthe, Philippe, and Jean-Luc Nancy. *L'absolu littéraire: Théorie de la littérature du romantisme allemand*. Paris: Seuil, 1978.
———. *The Literary Absolute: The Theory of Literature in German Romanticism*. Trans. Philip Barnard and Cheryl Lester. Albany: State University of New York Press, 1988.
———. *Le mythe nazi*. La Tour d'Aigues, France: Éditions de l'Aube, 1991.
———. "The Nazi Myth." Trans. Brian Holmes. *Critical Inquiry* 16, no. 2 (Winter 1990): 291–312.
Lecoq, Danielle. "L'Europe, émergence d'une image: VIIe–XVIe siècles." In *L'Europe et la Bible*, ed. Mireille Mentré and Bernard Dompnier, 23–44. Clermont-Ferrand: Bibliothèque municipale et interuniversitaire, 1992.
Lefebvre, Joël. *La Révolution française vue par les Allemands*. Lyon: Presses universitaires de Lyon, 1987.

Lenin, Vladimir, Ilyich. *Imperialism, the Highest Stage of Capitalism.* In id., *Selected Works*, 1: 667–766. Moscow: Progress Publishers, 1963. www.marxists.org/archive/lenin/works/1916/imp-hsc/ch07.htm. Accessed September 7, 2012.

———. "The Three Sources and Three Component Parts of Marxism." Trans. George Hanna. In id., *Collected Works*, 19: 21–28. Moscow: Progress Publishers, 1977. www.marxists.org/archive/lenin/works/1913/mar/x01.htm. Accessed September 7, 2012.

Leopardi, Giacomo. *Discorso sopra lo stato presente dei costumi degl'italiani.* Rome: L'Unità, 1993.

———. *Discours sur l'état actuel des moeurs des Italiens.* Trans. [Italian to French] Michel Orcel. Paris: Allia, 1993.

Lewis, Bernard. *The Muslim Discovery of Europe.* New York: Norton, 2001.

Liddell, Henry George, and Robert Scott. *A Greek-English Lexicon.* Ed. Henry Stuart Jones et al. Oxford: Clarendon Press, 1996. Cited as Liddell and Scott's *Greek-English Lexicon*.

Luther, Martin. "À la noblesse chrétienne de la nation allemande." In *Les grands écrits réformateurs*, trans. and ed. Maurice Gravier, 103–99. Paris: Flammarion, 1992. German title: "An den christlichen Adel deutscher Nation von des christlichen Standes Besserung."

———. *Ausgewählte Werke.* Ed. Hans Heinrich Borcherdt. Vol. 2. 3rd ed. Munich: C. Kaiser, 1953.

———. "An Open Letter to the Christian Nobility of the German Nation Concerning the Reform of the Christian Estate: 1520." Trans. Charles M. Jacobs in *Works of Martin Luther*, 2: 55–164. Philadelphia: A. J. Holman, 1915. German title: "An den christlichen Adel deutscher Nation von des christlichen Standes Besserung." Cited as "Open Letter to the Christian Nobility" or "Open Letter."

Marrati, Paola. *La genèse et la trace: Derrida lecteur de Husserl et Heidegger.* Dordrecht: Kluwer, 1998.

———. *Genesis and Trace: Derrida Reading Husserl and Heidegger.* Trans. Simon Sparks. Stanford, Calif.: Stanford University Press, 2005.

Martin, Jean-Clet. *Variations: La philosophie de Gilles Deleuze.* Paris: Payot, 1993.

Marx, Karl. *Capital: A Critique of Political Economy.* Vol. 1. Trans. Samuel Moore and Edward Aveling. Ed. Friedrich Engels. Moscow: Progress Publishers, 1887. www.marxists.org/archive/marx/works/1867-c1/index.htm. Accessed September 7, 2012. Cited as *Capital*.

———. *Le capital: Livre I.* Trans. J.-P. Lefebvre et al. Paris: Presses universitaires de France, 1983.

———. *Le capital: Livre I.* Trans. Jules Molitor. Paris: Allia, 1998.

———. *Le capital: Livre I, sections 1 à 4*. Trans. Joseph Roy. Paris: Flammarion, 2008.

———. *Das Kapital: Kritik der politischen Ökonomie: Erster Band, Hamburg 1883*. In id. and Friedrich Engels, *Gesamtausgabe*, II/8. Berlin: Dietz, 1989. Cited as Marx, *Das Kapital* (1883).

———. "Private Property and Communism." *Economic & Philosophic Manuscripts of 1844*. Third Manuscript. Trans. Martin Mulligan. www.marxists.org/archive/marx/works/1844/manuscripts/comm.htm. Accessed September 7, 2012.

———. "The Value-Form." Appendix to the 1867 German ed. of *Capital*; the appendix was originally titled "Wertform." Trans. Mike Roth and Wal Suchting. www.marxists.org/archive/marx/works/1867-c1/appendix.htm. Accessed September 7, 2012.

Marx, Karl, and Friedrich Engels. *Die heilige Familie, oder Kritik der kritischen Kritik: Gegen Bruno Bauer und Consorten*. Frankfurt am Main: Literarische Anstalt, 1845.

———. *Manifesto of the Communist Party*. Trans. Samuel Moore and Friedrich Engels. In id., *Selected Works*, 1: 98–137. Moscow: Progress Publishers, 1969. www.marxists.org/archive/marx/works/1848/communist-manifesto. Accessed September 7, 2012.

Melito, Saint, bishop of Sardis. *On Pascha and Fragments*. Trans. and ed. Stuart George Hall. Oxford: Clarendon Press, 1979.

Michelet, Jules. *Historical View of the French Revolution: From Its Earliest Indications to the Flight of the King in 1791*. Trans. C. Cocks. London: H. G. Bohn, 1860. Cited as *French Revolution*.

———. *Renaissance et Réforme: Histoire de France au XVIe siècle*. 1855. Paris: R. Laffont, 1982.

Moreau, Joseph. *Aristote et son école*. Paris: Presses universitaires de France, 1985.

[Moschus of Syracuse]. *Bucoliques grecs*. Vol. 2: *Pseudo-Théocrite. Moschos. Bion. Divers*. Trans. and ed. Philippe-Ernest Legrand. Paris: Belles Lettres, 1953.

———. *Theocritus, Bion and Moschus*. Trans. Andrew Lang. London: Macmillan, 1924. Cited as Moschus.

Nancy, Jean-Luc. *La communauté désœuvrée*. 2d ed. Paris: Bourgois, 1990.

———. "La Comparution/The Compearance: From the Existence of 'Communism' to the Community of 'Existence.'" Trans. Tracy B. Strong. *Political Theory* 20, no. 3 (August 1992): 371–98.

———. *The Gravity of Thought*. Trans. François Raffoul and Gregory Recco. Atlantic Highlands, N.J.: Humanities Press, 1997.

———. *The Inoperative Community*. Trans. Peter Connor et al. Minneapolis: University of Minnesota Press, 1982. Translation of *La communauté désœuvrée*.

———. *Des lieux divins*. Mauvezin, France: Trans-Europ-Repress, 1987.

———. "Monogrammes XII: Allemagne, Deutschland, Germany." *Futur Antérieur* 17 (March 1993): 71–74.

———. *L'oubli de la philosophie*. Paris: Galilée, 1986.

———. *Le sens du monde*. Paris: Galilée, 1993.

———. *The Sense of the World*. Trans. Jeffrey S. Libbrett. Minneapolis: University of Minnesota Press, 1997.

Nancy, Jean-Luc, and Jean-Christophe Bailly. *La comparution*. 2d ed. Paris: Bourgois, 2007.

Nietzsche, Friedrich. *Beyond Good and Evil*. Trans. Ian Johnston. http://ebooks.adelaide.edu.au/n/nietzsche/friedrich/n67b. Accessed September 7, 2012.

———. *Ecce homo: Wie man wird, was man ist*. Nietzsche Source. Digital Critical Edition. Ed. Giorgio Colli and Mazzino Montinari. www.nietzschesource.org/texts/eKGWB/EH. Accessed September 7, 2012.

———. *The Gay Science*. Trans. Josefine Nauckhoff. Ed. Bernard Williams. New York: Cambridge University Press, 2001.

———. *Jenseits von Gut und Böse*. Leipzig: Naumann, 1886. www.nietzschesource.org/texts/eKGWB/JGB. Accessed September 7, 2012.

Ovid. *Metamorphoses: A New Translation, Contexts, Criticism*. Trans. and ed. Charles Martin. New York: Norton, 2010.

Pastoureau, Michael, and Jean-Claude Schmitt. *Europe: Mémoire et emblèmes*. Paris: Éditions de l'Épargne, 1990.

Patočka, Jan. *Heretical Essays in the Philosophy of History*. Trans. Erazim Kohák. Chicago: Open Court, 1996. Cited as Patočka, HE.

———. *Plato and Europe*. Trans. Petr Lom. Stanford, Calif.: Stanford University Press, 2002. Cited as Patočka, PE.

———. "Réflexion sur l'Europe." *Liberté et sacrifice: Écrits politiques*. Trans. [from Czech and German to French] Erika Abrams. Grenoble, France: J. Millon, 1990.

Pausanias. *Description of Greece*. Trans. W. H. S. Jones and H. A. Ormerod. www.perseus.tufts.edu/hopper/text?doc=Perseus:text:1999.01.0160. Accessed September 7, 2012.

Penser l'Europe à ses frontières. La Tour d'Aigues, France: Éditions de l'Aube, 1993. Proceedings of the meeting "Geophilosophy of Europe" held in Strasbourg under the auspices of the Carrefour des littératures européennes, November 7–10, 1992.

Pessoa, Fernando. *Le chemin du serpent: Essais et pensées*. Trans. [from Portuguese to French] Michel Chandeigne, Françoise Laye, and Jean-François Viégas. Paris: Bourgois, 1991.

[*Petit Littré*] *Dictionnaire de la langue française*. Paris: Gallimard-Hachette, 1959. Cited as *Petit Littré*.

[*Petit Robert*] *Le Nouveau Petit Robert: Dictionnaire alphabétique et analogique de la langue française*. Paris: Le Robert, 2012. Cited also in earlier editions, as *Petit Robert*.

Pindar. *Fragments*. Trans. William H. Race. *Nemean Odes. Isthmian Odes. Fragments*. Cambridge, Mass.: Harvard University Press, 1997.

———. *Nemean* 4. In id., *Odes*. Trans. Diane Arnson Svarlien. www.perseus.tufts.edu/hopper/text?doc=Perseus%3Atext%3A1999.01.0162%3Abook%3DN.%3Apoem%3D4. Accessed September 7, 2012.

Plato. *Minos*. Trans. W. R. M. Lamb. www.perseus.tufts.edu/hopper/text?doc=Perseus%3Atext%3A1999.01.0180%3Atext%3DMinos. Accessed September 7, 2012.

———. *Minos*. Trans. [into French] Joseph Souilhé. In id., *Œuvres complètes*. Vol. 13, Part 2: *Dialogues suspects*. Paris: Les Belles Lettres, 1930.

Plato. *The Republic*. 2 vols. Trans. Paul Shorey. www.perseus.tufts.edu/hopper/text?doc=Perseus:text:1999.01.0168. Accessed September 7, 2012.

———. *Timaeus*. Trans. W. R. M. Lamb. http://www.perseus.tufts.edu/hopper/text?doc=Plat.+Tim.+&fromdoc=Perseus%3Atext%3A1999.01.0180. Accessed September 7, 2012.

Poidevin, Raymond, and Sylvain Schirmann. *Histoire de l'Allemagne*. Paris: Hatier, 1992.

Rancière, Jacques. "Le concept de critique et la critique de l'économie politique des *Manuscrits de 1844* au *Capital*." In Althusser et al., *Lire Le Capital*, 1: 93–210. Paris: Maspéro, 1965.

———. "The Concept of 'Critique' and the 'Critique of Political Economy' (from the *Manuscripts of 1844* to *Capital*." Trans. Ben Brewster. In *Ideology, Method and Marx: Essays from Economy and Society*, ed. Ali Rattansi, 74–180. London: Routledge, 1989.

Renan, Ernest. *Poetry of the Celtic Races: And Other Studies*. Trans. William G. Hutchison. London: Scott, 1896.

Revault d'Allonnes, Myriam. *D'une mort à l'autre: Précipices de la Révolution*. Paris: Seuil, 1989.

Rey, Alain, ed. *Dictionnaire historique de la langue française*. 2 vols. Paris: Robert, 1993.

Rimbaud, Arthur. *Œuvres*. Paris: Garnier, 1960.

Rodinson, Maxime. *La fascination de l'Islam, suivi de Le seigneur bourguignon et l'esclave sarrasin*. Paris: Presses-Pocket, 1993.

———. *Mahomet*. Paris: Seuil, 1975.

———. *Muhammad*. Trans. Anne Carter. London: I. B. Tauris, 2002.

Rodrigo, Pierre. "Marx et la phénoménologie: Besoin, richesse et forme-valeur." *Les études philosophiques* 1 (January–March 1992): 85–100.

Rogozinski, Jacob. "Un crime inexpiable (Kant et le régicide)." *Rue Descartes* 4 (April 1992): 99–120.

Rougemont, Denis de. *The Idea of Europe.* Trans. Norbert Guterman. New York: Macmillan, 1966.

———. *Vingt-huit siècles d'Europe: La conscience européenne à travers les textes, d'Hésiode à nos jours.* Paris: Payot, 1961.

Rousseau, Jean-Jacques. *A Discourse Upon the Origin and the Foundation of the Inequality Among Mankind.* http://etext.lib.virginia.edu/toc/modeng/public/RouMank.html. Accessed September 7, 2012. Cited as *Discourse on Inequality*.

———. *The Discourses and Other Early Political Writings.* Trans. and ed. Victor Gourevitch. Cambridge: Cambridge University Press, 1997.

———. *Du contrat social.* Ed. Bertrand de Jouvenel. Paris: Livre de Poche-Pluriel, 1978.

———. *Emile.* www.ilt.columbia.edu/publications/emile.html. Accessed September 7, 2012.

———. *Essai sur l'origine des langues.* Ed. Jean Starobinski. Paris: Gallimard-Folio, 1990.

———. *Œuvres complètes.* Ed. Michel Launay. 3 vols. Paris: Seuil, 1971.

———. *Rousseau, Judge of Jean-Jacques, Dialogues.* Trans. Judith R. Bush, Christopher Kelly, and Roger D. Masters. In *The Collected Writings of Rousseau.* Vol. 1. Hanover, N.H.: University Press of New England, 1990.

———. *The Social Contract or Principles of Political Right.* Trans. G. D. H. Cole. New York: Dutton, 1913. Cited as *Social Contract*.

Schefold, Karl. *The Art of Classical Greece.* Trans. J. R. Foster. New York: Crown, 1966.

Scholem, Gershom. *Walter Benjamin: Die Geschichte einer Freundschaft.* Frankfurt am Main: Suhrkamp, 1975.

Shakespeare, William. *Twelfth Night, or What You Will.* New York: Palgrave, 2001.

Sieyès, Emmanuel Joseph. *Qu'est-ce que le Tiers-État?* 1789. Paris: Pagnerre, 1839. http://books.google.de/books?id=ogJBAAAAcAAJ&dq=sieyes+qu'est-ce+que+le+tiers-etat&source=gbs_navlinks_s. Accessed September 7, 2012.

———. *What Is the Third Estate?* Trans. M. Blondel. New York: Praeger, 1964. Cited as *What Is the Third Estate?* (Blondel).

———. *What Is the Third Estate?* Trans. Lynn Hunt. In *The French Revolution and Human Rights.* New York: St. Martin's Press, 1996. Cited as *What Is the Third Estate?* (Hunt).

Sophocles. *Fragments.* Trans. Hugh Lloyd-Jones. Cambridge, Mass.: Harvard University Press, 1994.

Spinoza, Baruch. *Theologico-Political Treatise.* Trans. Michael Silverthorne and Jonathan Israel. Ed. Jonathan Israel. Cambridge: Cambridge University Press, 2007.

Stétié, Salah. *Lumière sur lumière, ou, l'Islam créateur*. Le Revest-les-Eaux, France: Cahiers de l'Égaré, 1992.
Sztulman, Henri, and Jacques Fénelon, eds. *La curiosité en psychanalyse*. Toulouse: Privat, 1981.
Tarkovsky, Andrei. *Le temps scellé: De l'"Enfance d'Ivan" au "Sacrifice."* Trans. Anne Kichilov and Charles H. de Brantes. Paris: L'Étoile/*Cahiers du cinéma*, 1989. Translation of *Die versiegelte Zeit*.
———. *Sculpting in Time: The Great Russian Filmmaker Discusses His Art*. Trans. Kitty Hunter-Blair. Austin: University of Texas Press, 1987. Translation of *Die versiegelte Zeit*.
———. *Die versiegelte Zeit*. Trans. [Russian to German] Olga Surkova. Munich: Ullstein, 1986.
Thionville, Eugène. *De la théorie des lieux communs dans les "Topiques" d'Aristote: Et des principales modifications qu'elle a subies jusqu'à nos jours*. Paris: Vrin, 1983.
Thucydides. *History of the Peloponnesian War*. Trans. Richard Crawley. London: Dent, 1910.
Thucydides and Herodotus. *Œuvres complètes*. Trans. A. Barguet and D. Roussel. Pléiade ed. Paris: Gallimard, 1964.
Valéry, Paul. "The Crisis of the Mind." In id., *Collected Works*, ed. Jackson Matthews, vol. 10, *History and Criticism*, trans. Denise Folliot and Jackson Matthews, 23–36. New York: Bollingen Foundation and Pantheon Books, 1962.
Virgil. *Aeneid*. Trans. John Dryden. www.perseus.tufts.edu/hopper/text?doc=Perseus:text:1999.02.0052. Accessed September 7, 2012.
Voyenne, Bernard. *Histoire de l'idée européenne*. Paris: Payot, 1964.
Wallerstein, Immanuel. *Historical Capitalism*. 1983. London: Verso, 2003.
Watt, William Montgomery. *Mahomet*. Trans. François Dourveil, Solange-Marie Guillemin, and François Vaudou. Paris: Payot, 1989. Includes *Mahomet à La Mecque* (1958) and *Mahomet à Médine* (1959).
———. *Muhammad at Mecca*. Oxford: Clarendon Press, 1960.
———. *Muhammad at Medina*. Oxford: Clarendon Press, 1962.
Weber, Max. *The Protestant Ethic and the Spirit of Capitalism with Other Writings on the Rise of the West*. Trans. Stephen Kalberg. 4th ed. New York: Oxford University Press, 2009.
Weil, Dominique, ed. *Homme et sujet: La subjectivité en question dans les sciences humaines*. Paris: Harmattan, 1993.
Wieland, Christoph Martin. "Du patriotisme allemand." In *Philosophie et politique en Allemagne (XVIIIe–XXe siècles)*. Trans. [German to French] J.-C. Merle et al. *Les cahiers de Fontenay* 58–59 (June 1990): 13–28. German title: "Ueber teutschen Patriotismus."

———. "Ueber teutschen Patriotismus: Betrachtungen, Fragen und Zweifel" (On German Patriotism: Observations, Questions, and Doubts). *Der Neue Teutsche Merkur* 2 (May 1793): 3–21. Cited as "Ueber teutschen Patriotismus."

Wittgenstein, Ludwig. *Tractatus Logico-Philosophicus*. Ed. Kevin C. Klement. http://people.umass.edu/klement/tlp/index.html. Accessed September 7, 2012. Cited as *Tractatus Logico-Philosophicus* (Klement).

———. *Tractatus Logico-Philosophicus*. Trans. Charles K. Ogden. London: Routledge, 1990. Cited as *Tractatus Logico-Philosophicus* (Ogden).

Cultural Memory in the Present

Maria Boletsi, *Barbarism and Its Discontents*

Sigrid Weigel, *Walter Benjamin: Images, the Creaturely, and the Holy*

Roberto Esposito, *Living Thought: The Origins and Actuality of Italian Philosophy*

Henri Atlan, *The Sparks of Randomness, Volume 2: The Atheism of Scripture*

Rüdiger Campe, *The Game of Probability: Literature and Calculation from Pascal to Kleist*

Niklas Luhmann, *A Systems Theory of Religion*

Jean-Luc Marion, *In the Self's Place: The Approach of Saint Augustine*

Rodolphe Gasché, *Georges Bataille: Phenomenology and Phantasmatology*

Niklas Luhmann, *Theory of Society, Volume 1*

Alessia Ricciardi, *After* La Dolce Vita*: A Cultural Prehistory of Berlusconi's Italy*

Daniel Innerarity, *The Future and Its Enemies: In Defense of Political Hope*

Patricia Pisters, *The Neuro-Image: A Deleuzian Film-Philosophy of Digital Screen Culture*

François-David Sebbah, *Testing the Limit: Derrida, Henry, Levinas, and the Phenomenological Tradition*

Erik Peterson, *Theological Tractates*, edited by Michael J. Hollerich

Feisal G. Mohamed, *Milton and the Post-Secular Present: Ethics, Politics, Terrorism*

Pierre Hadot, *The Present Alone Is Our Happiness, Second Edition: Conversations with Jeannie Carlier and Arnold I. Davidson*

Yasco Horsman, *Theaters of Justice: Judging, Staging, and Working Through in Arendt, Brecht, and Delbo*

Jacques Derrida, *Parages*, edited by John P. Leavey

Henri Atlan, *The Sparks of Randomness, Volume 1: Spermatic Knowledge*

Rebecca Comay, *Mourning Sickness: Hegel and the French Revolution*

Djelal Kadir, *Memos from the Besieged City: Lifelines for Cultural Sustainability*

Stanley Cavell, *Little Did I Know: Excerpts from Memory*

Jeffrey Mehlman, *Adventures in the French Trade: Fragments Toward a Life*
Jacob Rogozinski, *The Ego and the Flesh: An Introduction to Egoanalysis*
Marcel Hénaff, *The Price of Truth: Gift, Money, and Philosophy*
Paul Patton, *Deleuzian Concepts: Philosophy, Colonialization, Politics*
Michael Fagenblat, *A Covenant of Creatures: Levinas's Philosophy of Judaism*
Stefanos Geroulanos, *An Atheism that Is Not Humanist Emerges in French Thought*
Andrew Herscher, *Violence Taking Place: The Architecture of the Kosovo Conflict*
Hans-Jörg Rheinberger, *On Historicizing Epistemology: An Essay*
Jacob Taubes, *From Cult to Culture*, edited by Charlotte Fonrobert and Amir Engel
Peter Hitchcock, *The Long Space: Transnationalism and Postcolonial Form*
Lambert Wiesing, *Artificial Presence: Philosophical Studies in Image Theory*
Jacob Taubes, *Occidental Eschatology*
Freddie Rokem, *Philosophers and Thespians: Thinking Performance*
Roberto Esposito, *Communitas: The Origin and Destiny of Community*
Vilashini Cooppan, *Worlds Within: National Narratives and Global Connections in Postcolonial Writing*
Josef Früchtl, *The Impertinent Self: A Heroic History of Modernity*
Frank Ankersmit, Ewa Domanska, and Hans Kellner, eds., *Re-Figuring Hayden White*
Michael Rothberg, *Multidirectional Memory: Remembering the Holocaust in the Age of Decolonization*
Jean-François Lyotard, *Enthusiasm: The Kantian Critique of History*
Ernst van Alphen, Mieke Bal, and Carel Smith, eds., *The Rhetoric of Sincerity*
Stéphane Mosès, *The Angel of History: Rosenzweig, Benjamin, Scholem*
Pierre Hadot, *The Present Alone Is Our Happiness: Conversations with Jeannie Carlier and Arnold I. Davidson*
Alexandre Lefebvre, *The Image of the Law: Deleuze, Bergson, Spinoza*
Samira Haj, *Reconfiguring Islamic Tradition: Reform, Rationality, and Modernity*
Diane Perpich, *The Ethics of Emmanuel Levinas*
Marcel Detienne, *Comparing the Incomparable*
François Delaporte, *Anatomy of the Passions*
René Girard, *Mimesis and Theory: Essays on Literature and Criticism, 1959-2005*
Richard Baxstrom, *Houses in Motion: The Experience of Place and the Problem of Belief in Urban Malaysia*

Jennifer L. Culbert, *Dead Certainty: The Death Penalty and the Problem of Judgment*

Samantha Frost, *Lessons from a Materialist Thinker: Hobbesian Reflections on Ethics and Politics*

Regina Mara Schwartz, *Sacramental Poetics at the Dawn of Secularism: When God Left the World*

Gil Anidjar, *Semites: Race, Religion, Literature*

Ranjana Khanna, *Algeria Cuts: Women and Representation, 1830 to the Present*

Esther Peeren, *Intersubjectivities and Popular Culture: Bakhtin and Beyond*

Eyal Peretz, *Becoming Visionary: Brian De Palma's Cinematic Education of the Senses*

Diana Sorensen, *A Turbulent Decade Remembered: Scenes from the Latin American Sixties*

Hubert Damisch, *A Childhood Memory by Piero della Francesca*

José van Dijck, *Mediated Memories in the Digital Age*

Dana Hollander, *Exemplarity and Chosenness: Rosenzweig and Derrida on the Nation of Philosophy*

Asja Szafraniec, *Beckett, Derrida, and the Event of Literature*

Sara Guyer, *Romanticism After Auschwitz*

Alison Ross, *The Aesthetic Paths of Philosophy: Presentation in Kant, Heidegger, Lacoue-Labarthe, and Nancy*

Gerhard Richter, *Thought-Images: Frankfurt School Writers' Reflections from Damaged Life*

Bella Brodzki, *Can These Bones Live? Translation, Survival, and Cultural Memory*

Rodolphe Gasché, *The Honor of Thinking: Critique, Theory, Philosophy*

Brigitte Peucker, *The Material Image: Art and the Real in Film*

Natalie Melas, *All the Difference in the World: Postcoloniality and the Ends of Comparison*

Jonathan Culler, *The Literary in Theory*

Michael G. Levine, *The Belated Witness: Literature, Testimony, and the Question of Holocaust Survival*

Jennifer A. Jordan, *Structures of Memory: Understanding German Change in Berlin and Beyond*

Christoph Menke, *Reflections of Equality*

Marlène Zarader, *The Unthought Debt: Heidegger and the Hebraic Heritage*

Jan Assmann, *Religion and Cultural Memory: Ten Studies*

David Scott and Charles Hirschkind, *Powers of the Secular Modern: Talal Asad and His Interlocutors*

Gyanendra Pandey, *Routine Violence: Nations, Fragments, Histories*

James Siegel, *Naming the Witch*

J. M. Bernstein, *Against Voluptuous Bodies: Late Modernism and the Meaning of Painting*

Theodore W. Jennings, Jr., *Reading Derrida / Thinking Paul: On Justice*

Richard Rorty and Eduardo Mendieta, *Take Care of Freedom and Truth Will Take Care of Itself: Interviews with Richard Rorty*

Jacques Derrida, *Paper Machine*

Renaud Barbaras, *Desire and Distance: Introduction to a Phenomenology of Perception*

Jill Bennett, *Empathic Vision: Affect, Trauma, and Contemporary Art*

Ban Wang, *Illuminations from the Past: Trauma, Memory, and History in Modern China*

James Phillips, *Heidegger's* Volk: *Between National Socialism and Poetry*

Frank Ankersmit, *Sublime Historical Experience*

István Rév, *Retroactive Justice: Prehistory of Post-Communism*

Paola Marrati, *Genesis and Trace: Derrida Reading Husserl and Heidegger*

Krzysztof Ziarek, *The Force of Art*

Marie-José Mondzain, *Image, Icon, Economy: The Byzantine Origins of the Contemporary Imaginary*

Cecilia Sjöholm, *The Antigone Complex: Ethics and the Invention of Feminine Desire*

Jacques Derrida and Elisabeth Roudinesco, *For What Tomorrow . . . : A Dialogue*

Elisabeth Weber, *Questioning Judaism: Interviews by Elisabeth Weber*

Jacques Derrida and Catherine Malabou, *Counterpath: Traveling with Jacques Derrida*

Martin Seel, *Aesthetics of Appearing*

Nanette Salomon, *Shifting Priorities: Gender and Genre in Seventeenth-Century Dutch Painting*

Jacob Taubes, *The Political Theology of Paul*

Jean-Luc Marion, *The Crossing of the Visible*

Eric Michaud, *The Cult of Art in Nazi Germany*

Anne Freadman, *The Machinery of Talk: Charles Peirce and the Sign Hypothesis*

Stanley Cavell, *Emerson's Transcendental Etudes*

Stuart McLean, *The Event and Its Terrors: Ireland, Famine, Modernity*

Beate Rössler, ed., *Privacies: Philosophical Evaluations*

Bernard Faure, *Double Exposure: Cutting Across Buddhist and Western Discourses*

Alessia Ricciardi, *The Ends of Mourning: Psychoanalysis, Literature, Film*

Alain Badiou, *Saint Paul: The Foundation of Universalism*

Gil Anidjar, *The Jew, the Arab: A History of the Enemy*

Jonathan Culler and Kevin Lamb, eds., *Just Being Difficult? Academic Writing in the Public Arena*

Jean-Luc Nancy, *A Finite Thinking*, edited by Simon Sparks

Theodor W. Adorno, *Can One Live after Auschwitz? A Philosophical Reader*, edited by Rolf Tiedemann

Patricia Pisters, *The Matrix of Visual Culture: Working with Deleuze in Film Theory*

Andreas Huyssen, *Present Pasts: Urban Palimpsests and the Politics of Memory*

Talal Asad, *Formations of the Secular: Christianity, Islam, Modernity*

Dorothea von Mücke, *The Rise of the Fantastic Tale*

Marc Redfield, *The Politics of Aesthetics: Nationalism, Gender, Romanticism*

Emmanuel Levinas, *On Escape*

Dan Zahavi, *Husserl's Phenomenology*

Rodolphe Gasché, *The Idea of Form: Rethinking Kant's Aesthetics*

Michael Naas, *Taking on the Tradition: Jacques Derrida and the Legacies of Deconstruction*

Herlinde Pauer-Studer, ed., *Constructions of Practical Reason: Interviews on Moral and Political Philosophy*

Jean-Luc Marion, *Being Given That: Toward a Phenomenology of Givenness*

Theodor W. Adorno and Max Horkheimer, *Dialectic of Enlightenment*

Ian Balfour, *The Rhetoric of Romantic Prophecy*

Martin Stokhof, *World and Life as One: Ethics and Ontology in Wittgenstein's Early Thought*

Gianni Vattimo, *Nietzsche: An Introduction*

Jacques Derrida, *Negotiations: Interventions and Interviews, 1971-1998*, ed. Elizabeth Rottenberg

Brett Levinson, *The Ends of Literature: The Latin American "Boom" in the Neoliberal Marketplace*

Timothy J. Reiss, *Against Autonomy: Cultural Instruments, Mutualities, and the Fictive Imagination*

Hent de Vries and Samuel Weber, eds., *Religion and Media*

Niklas Luhmann, *Theories of Distinction: Re-Describing the Descriptions of Modernity*, ed. and introd. William Rasch

Johannes Fabian, *Anthropology with an Attitude: Critical Essays*

Michel Henry, *I Am the Truth: Toward a Philosophy of Christianity*

Gil Anidjar, *"Our Place in Al-Andalus": Kabbalah, Philosophy, Literature in Arab-Jewish Letters*

Hélène Cixous and Jacques Derrida, *Veils*

F. R. Ankersmit, *Historical Representation*

F. R. Ankersmit, *Political Representation*

Elissa Marder, *Dead Time: Temporal Disorders in the Wake of Modernity (Baudelaire and Flaubert)*

Reinhart Koselleck, *The Practice of Conceptual History: Timing History, Spacing Concepts*

Niklas Luhmann, *The Reality of the Mass Media*

Hubert Damisch, *A Theory of /Cloud/: Toward a History of Painting*

Jean-Luc Nancy, *The Speculative Remark: (One of Hegel's bon mots)*

Jean-François Lyotard, *Soundproof Room: Malraux's Anti-Aesthetics*

Jan Patočka, *Plato and Europe*

Hubert Damisch, *Skyline: The Narcissistic City*

Isabel Hoving, *In Praise of New Travelers: Reading Caribbean Migrant Women Writers*

Richard Rand, ed., *Futures: Of Jacques Derrida*

William Rasch, *Niklas Luhmann's Modernity: The Paradoxes of Differentiation*

Jacques Derrida and Anne Dufourmantelle, *Of Hospitality*

Jean-François Lyotard, *The Confession of Augustine*

Kaja Silverman, *World Spectators*

Samuel Weber, *Institution and Interpretation: Expanded Edition*

Jeffrey S. Librett, *The Rhetoric of Cultural Dialogue: Jews and Germans in the Epoch of Emancipation*

Ulrich Baer, *Remnants of Song: Trauma and the Experience of Modernity in Charles Baudelaire and Paul Celan*

Samuel C. Wheeler III, *Deconstruction as Analytic Philosophy*

David S. Ferris, *Silent Urns: Romanticism, Hellenism, Modernity*

Rodolphe Gasché, *Of Minimal Things: Studies on the Notion of Relation*

Sarah Winter, *Freud and the Institution of Psychoanalytic Knowledge*

Samuel Weber, *The Legend of Freud: Expanded Edition*

Aris Fioretos, ed., *The Solid Letter: Readings of Friedrich Hölderlin*

J. Hillis Miller / Manuel Asensi, *Black Holes / J. Hillis Miller; or, Boustrophedonic Reading*

Miryam Sas, *Fault Lines: Cultural Memory and Japanese Surrealism*

Peter Schwenger, *Fantasm and Fiction: On Textual Envisioning*

Didier Maleuvre, *Museum Memories: History, Technology, Art*

Jacques Derrida, *Monolingualism of the Other; or, The Prosthesis of Origin*

Andrew Baruch Wachtel, *Making a Nation, Breaking a Nation: Literature and Cultural Politics in Yugoslavia*

Niklas Luhmann, *Love as Passion: The Codification of Intimacy*

Mieke Bal, ed., *The Practice of Cultural Analysis: Exposing Interdisciplinary Interpretation*

Jacques Derrida and Gianni Vattimo, eds., *Religion*

The authorized representative in the EU for product safety and compliance is:
Mare Nostrum Group
B.V Doelen 72
4831 GR Breda
The Netherlands

www.ingramcontent.com/pod-product-compliance
Lightning Source LLC
Chambersburg PA
CBHW030323240426
43673CB00040B/1259